UNSETTLED AMERICANS

UNSETTLED AMERICANS

Metropolitan Context and Civic Leadership for Immigrant Integration

Edited by John Mollenkopf and Manuel Pastor

CORNELL UNIVERSITY PRESS   ITHACA AND LONDON

First published 2016 by Cornell University Press
First printing, Cornell Paperbacks, 2016
Printed in the United States of America

Library of Congress Cataloging-in-Publication Data

Names: Mollenkopf, John H., 1946– editor. | Pastor, Manuel, 1956– editor.
Title: Unsettled Americans : metropolitan context and civic leadership for
    immigrant integration / edited by John Mollenkopf and Manuel Pastor.
Description: Ithaca ; London : Cornell University Press, 2016. | ©2016 |
    Includes bibliographical references and index.
Identifiers: LCCN 2015038568 | ISBN 9781501702662 (cloth : alk. paper) |
    ISBN 9781501702679 (pbk. : alk. paper)
Subjects: LCSH: United States—Emigration and immigration—Social aspects.
    Immigrants—United States—Social conditions. | Social integration—United
    States. | Urban policy—United States.
Classification: LCC JV6475 .U54 2016 | DDC 305.9/069120973—dc23
LC record available at http://lccn.loc.gov/2015038568

Cornell University Press strives to use environmentally responsible suppliers and materials to the fullest extent possible in the publishing of its books. Such materials include vegetable-based, low-VOC inks and acid-free papers that are recycled, totally chlorine-free, or partly composed of nonwood fibers. For further information, visit our website at www.cornellpress.cornell.edu.

Cloth printing   10 9 8 7 6 5 4 3 2 1
Paperback printing   10 9 8 7 6 5 4 3 2 1

Contents

Acknowledgments

Some important journeys begin by chance.

This book project was nurtured by the Building Resilient Regions (BRR) network sponsored by the John D. and Catherine T. MacArthur Foundation and led by our friend and colleague Margaret Weir of UC Berkeley. The seed was planted as the BRR data working group, led by Manuel Pastor, assembled a database that we could use to select case study comparisons for the project as a whole. It was impossible not to see the disparate economic trajectories of American regions or the profound demographic impact that immigration was having on them. Armed with this data, the BRR members decided to explore four key metropolitan challenges: persistent economic decline; rapid growth, often on the suburban fringe; the shifting geography of poverty; and responses to fast-growing immigrant populations.

The two editors have long been steeped in the literature on the new regionalism, metropolitan equity, and race relations. All the topics on the BRR agenda appealed to us: figuring out how to rekindle growth, address sprawl, or tackle economic distress in inner-ring suburbs. But the challenge of immigrant integration holds a special meaning for us. We have written frequently on this topic, developed research centers charged with exploring it, and actively engaged with immigrant-supporting activities. Little did we know that this dynamic topic would become even more volatile as we studied it: over the course of this project, immigration politics whipsawed from the restrictionist wave in Arizona and the South to the welcoming attitudes in California and the Midwest, from the brink of reform in 2013 to its utter collapse and dissolution into executive actions in 2014 and 2015. Our team was certainly trying to focus on a moving target.

It became increasingly clear to us, however, that the significant variation in metropolitan receptivity to immigrants revealed not only what helped or hindered immigrants from finding their place, but was a primary dimension of regional collaboration. If regional actors are at each other's throats about their new neighbors, they are also not likely to find consensus on how best to achieve economic growth or reduce poverty. Struggling over strangers, in short, works against regional resilience.

We must thank a lot of people for helping us reach that insight. Most important are our coauthors, all of whom agreed to develop a (more or less) common theoretical framework, case study protocol, and approach to writing. Els de

Graauw, Juan De Lara, Jaime Dominguez, Diana R. Gordon, Michael Jones-Correa, Paul G. Lewis, Doris Marie Provine, Rachel Rosner, and Jennifer Tran proved to be thoughtful and dedicated collaborators—and they also join us in thanking the informants in the metropolitan regions they visited for sharing their insights.

We also need to thank our research staff members for their exemplary help. On the quantitative side, Justin Scoggins and Jennifer Tran of the USC Center for the Study of Immigrant Integration (CSII) helped assemble and then perfect the BRR database used in this volume, while Mirabai Auer, Alejandro Sanchez-Lopez, and Vanessa Carter, all of CSII, used and supplemented that data to create the tables, charts, and maps in this volume. Steven Romalewski and Joseph Pereira of the CUNY Graduate Center's Center for Urban Research also assisted in the initial development of the database and other quantitative exercises along the way.

On the qualitative side, CUNY's Marta Pichardo Medina provided early assistance for the New York case study, while Robert Chlala and Stephanie Canizales of CSII helped update several of the case studies and edit the manuscript. Heddy Nam and Vanessa Carter did manuscript copyediting and assembly, with Vanessa playing her usual amazing role as chief writing supervisor for both the first and second drafts of the full manuscript. Completion would not have been possible without the organizing talents of CSII program manager Rhonda Ortiz, who reminded us that task lists and deadlines were our friends. And, finally, thank you to the rest of the staff and student researchers of USC CSII, whose flexibility and teamwork made it possible to move this book through to publication.

We benefited greatly from our years of discussions with members of the BRR network. They helped us test early ideas and shared their wisdom. Our program officers at MacArthur, Erika Poethig (now at the Urban Institute), and then vice president for U.S. programs (and now president) Julia Stasch provided guidance and direction as well as financial support. Margaret Weir, the brilliant leader of the BRR network, provided intellectual advice and held us to account—and we needed both as we tried to steer our research team. All the other members of that network informed our thinking, with special nods of appreciation to Bill Barnes, Katherine Foster, Bill Lester, Amy Liu, Sarah Reckow, and Todd Swanstrom.

Many colleagues outside the BRR network gave us valuable feedback; they included Shannon Gleeson, Pierrette Hondagneu-Sotelo, Dowell Myers, Mai Nguyen, Karthick Ramakrishnan, Audrey Singer, Roberto Suro, Jody Agius Vallejo, Monica Varsanyi, and William Vega, as well as two anonymous reviewers for this press. Thank you to the James Irvine Foundation for providing supplemental funding to support a meeting in December 2013 to solicit important feedback on the manuscript. Special thanks are due to Joshua Hoyt, executive director of the National Partnership for New Americans, who gave an extensive critique of the manuscript at that meeting in December 2013, reassuring us that we were on the right track *and* reminding us of how central the agency of immigrants themselves has been in shaping their contexts of reception. We knew this, having worked with so many advocates for immigrant integration in our respective metropolitan areas. But in an analytic world that often focuses on institutions, organizations, and acronyms, he reminded us that this arena is also full of activists, indeed movement leaders, who include not only immigrant advocates but business, labor, religious, and civic figures who refuse to let fear and separation divide their regions. This volume seeks to understand what factors and strategies lead some regional climates to welcome immigrants and others to resist them—but we have enough of what BRR researcher Sarah Reckow once called "normative gumption" to hope that this work is not just good social science, but an admonition for all of us to work toward a more receptive approach.

After all, many important journeys begin without clear final destinations. Those who have come to America have made a choice, but they have also been driven by weak economies, civil wars, and political persecution, all of which were the luck of the draw in place of birth. The progress one makes on the journey reflects not just the determination of the travelers but also help from those who extended their hands along the way. We thank all those that helped us on this voyage of research and writing and hope that the result contributes to a more welcoming America.

John Mollenkopf, New York
Manuel Pastor, Los Angeles

UNSETTLED AMERICANS

THE ETHNIC MOSAIC

Immigrant Integration at the Metropolitan Scale

John Mollenkopf and Manuel Pastor

In April 2010, the Arizona legislature passed a law (SB 1070) requiring local law enforcement and public agency officials to determine the immigration status of an individual when they had "reasonable suspicion" that the individual might be an undocumented immigrant. A maelstrom of national debate ensued, with advocates of the legislation arguing that the state was right to protect itself against a surge of "illegals," while opponents suggested that Arizona would soon fall into racial profiling and scare away hardworking legal immigrant residents.

What happened in Phoenix didn't stay in Phoenix: state and local political leaders in Alabama, Georgia, and elsewhere worked to pass legislation aimed at what some called "enforcement through attrition"—the notion that local authorities should enforce their own interpretation of immigration law in such a way as to make life so difficult for undocumented residents that they would leave the country on their own. These actions both reflect and drive public opinion, which, especially within the Republican voting base (Pew Research Center 2014), disapproves of granting benefits to illegal immigrants. As tempers heated between those supporting more restrictive policies and those supporting less restrictive policies, the only thing on which both sides seemed to agree was that local authorities were justified in taking a long-established federal responsibility into their own hands (Gulasekaram and Ramakrishnan 2012).

The local action in recent years has not been confined to those who are hostile to immigrants, legal or not. The country's largest protest against SB 1070 took place on May 1, 2010, in Los Angeles—and the city's mayor and its Catholic archbishop welcomed the protesters at the end of their march. In New Haven,

Connecticut, far from chasing away the undocumented, city authorities developed a new approach by granting municipal ID cards to undocumented residents and other city residents. San Francisco has adopted a series of measures to raise pay and increase benefits for immigrant workers, as well as adopting a municipal ID card. New York City has just followed suit.

Meanwhile, immigrant advocates in the state of Illinois have persuaded state and city leaders to promote "immigrant integration," including the development of new immigrant services and a campaign to encourage naturalization. And in late 2010, Utah, one of the nation's most conservative states, adopted the so-called Utah Compact, an agreement between business, civic, religious, and immigrant leaders to conduct a civil conversation about immigration, devise local strategies to further immigrant economic and social advancement, and "oppose policies that unnecessarily separate families"—a clear dig at the enforcement-happy approach of Arizona and its southern copycats.[1]

In 2013 in California, the state passed a slate of immigrant integration bills. They ranged from reinstituting driver's licenses for undocumented Californians to the Trust Act—slowing deportations and protecting families—to two further measures to prevent retaliation against immigrant workers. All these bills came twenty years after the state had initially chosen immigrant exclusion through Proposition 187, a measure aimed at denying all public benefits, including education, to undocumented immigrants. Other 2013 bills made advances in the areas of workers' rights and employment, health and human services, and language access and education (California Immigrant Policy Center 2013).

The geographic (and temporal) diversity in attitudes toward immigrants underscores a key point: while the federal government has the formal responsibility for determining how many immigrants come into the country and for preventing those who lack permission from entering, it falls to local and regional jurisdictions to frame the living experience of immigrants. In this context, local and regional coalitions of civil leaders set the political tone for whether localities welcome new immigrant populations or resist their presence (Rodríguez 2014).

This geographic diversity in "warmth of welcome" has been particularly pronounced since the mid-2000s, mostly because the ongoing stalemate over revising federal immigration law prompted states and localities to take matters into their own hands, with local political "entrepreneurs" on both sides being influenced by movements and countermovements in the national debate (Varsanyi 2010; Gulasekaram and Ramakrishnan 2015). But even if the federal government eventually reconsiders and actually does change national immigration policy—something made more likely by the increasing number of Asian and Latino voters who overwhelmingly rejected anti-immigrant rhetoric in the 2012 elections (Pastor et al. 2014)—local jurisdictions will play a central and crucial role in determining how reforms gets implemented and what it will mean for the daily lives of immigrants and their neighbors.

A second key aspect of the situation is that immigrant populations have been growing rapidly outside the core urban areas with long traditions of receiving immigrants. Not only has this taken place in the new receiving areas of the South, but it is also occurring in full force in the suburbs (Singer 2008; Wilson and Svajlenka 2014). As a result, immigration policy should likely be thought of not just in terms of controlling borders but also in terms of local policies that either welcome immigrants and promote their welfare or attempt to take enforcement into local hands. Paying closer analytical attention to this "spatial turn"—that is, to the geographic variation of the warmth of immigrant reception—is also consistent with a larger shift in sociology, economics, and political science toward understanding how spatial arrangements and contexts play an important part in explaining broader outcomes. An important development in this regard has been a renewed focus on regionalism, particularly on how the national economy is constituted by metropolitan regions with coherent economies but fragmented governance. The need for action at a regional scale poses the challenge of constructing—or facing the consequences of failing to construct—metropolitan coalitions to address the challenges of regional growth (Benner and Pastor 2012; Brookings Institution 2010; Dreier, Mollenkopf, and Swanstrom 2001).

This book focuses on how metropolitan regions are responding politically to the challenge of integrating new immigrant communities. By immigrant integration, we simply mean the extent to which new immigrant communities are making economic, social, and civic progress, and closing gaps with the native-born mainstream. While a great deal of research has been done on this broad question, the research reported here is distinctive in two respects. First, we are interested in how different kinds of localities react *politically* to the challenge of integrating immigrants: How do local political and civic and community leaders respond? How do they seek to frame the question of the rise of new immigrant communities? What policy responses do they propose and adopt? How do immigrants themselves seek to shape the narrative and the policy package? Second, we explore the *metropolitan* dimension of this dynamic. We wish not only to understand the political responses in the central cities where immigrants have traditionally been concentrated, but also in their new suburban concentrations. And we want to know the extent to which central city and suburban actors influence each other, either informally or through regional alliances or institutions. What shapes central city responses? Do suburban responses differ? Does the longer central city history and legacy of immigrant-serving activities spill over into the suburbs—or not? And what role do counties and states play?

These two foci stem from our belief that the rate of progress for immigrants and their children is not just a function of their own human or social capital, but also reflects the contours of their locations and how they interact with the native-born (Kasinitz, Mollenkopf, and Waters 2004). We believe these place-based variations will have long-term consequences. We recognize that current snapshots of immigrants' progress do not capture their longer-term trajectories. What looks like a poor immigrant community today may be a launching pad for success for later generations. Careful cohort work has shown that most immigrants make progress across generations, something that focusing on recent arrivals often obscures (Myers 2008). However, the warmth of welcome can help determine whether a first location is a stepping-stone or a sinkhole.

While metro areas matter for migrants, migrants also matter for metro areas. International migration is a key factor reshaping metropolitan America. Like many large forces of transformation, it can produce benefits—immigrants add to the labor force, contribute taxes, and start new businesses. However, cities, regions, and states have some good reasons to worry when the immigrant influx is large and fast and/or consists mainly of low-income and poorly educated individuals, particularly those without authorization. These conditions can produce significant fiscal costs for local jurisdictions called upon to provide face-to-face services (such as law enforcement, primary education, or health services) to new and different groups who may not speak English and who are unfamiliar with local standards and programs. Clearly, it is expensive to promote intergenerational upward mobility by providing primary, secondary, and higher education, nearly all of which is paid for by states and localities.

Immigration policy thus has a fundamental asymmetry: the federal government determines how many and what type of immigrants to admit, but local governments mount the programs that integrate them. At present, the federal government provides little direct aid to assist local governments in doing so. In the aggregate, immigrants seem to have a net positive impact on metropolitan economies. Economists are finding mounting evidence that immigrants have a neutral to complementary impact on the existing native-born workforce (Card 2005; Ottaviano and Peri 2012; Peri 2006)—and even those who more staunchly stood on the side of substitutionary effects have softened (Aydemir and Borjas 2010; Borjas, Grogger, and Hanson 2009, 2012). Immigrants may also have more of a disposition to entrepreneurship, another boon for local economic activity (Vallejo 2013). Immigrant communities also lean toward environmentally friendly mass transit, with housing and work patterns that encourage more sustainable development, a concern of increasing importance to America's metro areas (Kersten et al. 2012).

It is also the case that that immigration correlates strongly with metropolitan economic growth (think Houston versus Cleveland). Of course, this relationship is partly circular: immigrants move toward economic opportunity, and, indeed, they can often find such opportunity even amid decline (Fiscal Policy Institute 2009; Waldinger 1999). But there are causal arrows as well: our econometric work on nearly two hundred U.S. metropolitan regions shows that regions with a larger immigrant share at the beginning of a time period subsequently have greater growth, even when we hold constant such factors as the presence of manufacturing or the initial unemployment rate (Benner and Pastor 2012, 48). And the popular literature is now filling with examples of small declining mill towns that have been helped to rebound by new immigration.

Although the rise of new immigrant communities may revitalize neighborhoods, boost real estate values, and bolster the workforce in residential construction, landscaping, and related activities, new immigrants, who tend to have lower incomes and larger families than the native-born population, can impose some real fiscal challenges for the local governments that need to provide them with education and social services. Some research suggests that rapid recent immigration can also disconcert the majority group's sense of cultural integrity and erode social solidarity (Putnam 2007). But this is not an automatic outcome. Others find that neighborhood disadvantage (for example, the lack of housing or jobs and a deteriorating physical environment) matters more for local solidarity than diversity per se; such disadvantage undermines local confidence in future work and prospects and disrupts collective identity and sense of community belonging (Fieldhouse and Cutts 2010; Forrest and Kearns 1999; Twigg, Taylor, and Mohan 2010). And other research shows that public policy can mediate the effects of diversity: countries with institutional initiatives aimed at immigrant integration and economic equity see little to no declines in social cohesion (Kesler and Bloemraad 2010). We believe that, on balance, deliberate actions to encourage receptivity to demographic change can also produce positive gains for regions and for America.

Others agree. Some regions have tried to use public policy to shift the balance toward positive responses, turning the rising immigrant presence to their advantage, diminishing its negative effects, containing conflicts generated by the arrival of new migrants, and promoting educational and labor market advances by immigrants and their children. In a fully proactive region, central city and suburban parts of the region may engage in informal or formal collaborations. In most regions, however, the urban core responds with positive measures, but suburban jurisdictions are much less welcoming and regional collaboration is limited, particularly around issues of immigrant integration. Quite a few unwelcoming regions react negatively across the board to the new immigration, resulting in political squabbles that may damage regional prospects in other arenas (for example, by projecting a retrograde image that makes the region less attractive to talented and generally tolerant skilled workers).

This book seeks to better understand the forces, actors, and strategies shaping regional responses to the challenge of immigrant integration and to draw lessons about how to promote more coherently positive responses. As indicated, we believe that encouraging positive regional responses to new immigrants will generate a long-term payoff in economic growth, political cooperation, and greater eventual social cohesion. We understand that some do not share this opinion—that they are "unsettled" by those who are now settling in America—and this book is not primarily about trying to convince them. Rather, we start from the premise that immigrant integration is useful for metro regions and work to understand the conditions under which it does or does not happen.

About the Volume

Scholars who have examined the question of why local political actors respond positively or negatively to rapid recent immigration in the United States and Western Europe have often focused on individual attitudes (which, when aggregated, presumably drive the actions of local politicians) and in how those individual responses are shaped by local political opportunity structures and other contextual factors, including the tenor of national politics (Hochschild and Mollenkopf 2009; Hopkins 2010; Ramakrishnan and Wong 2010). Others have focused on how the introduction of new immigrant minority communities alters the dynamics of political competition among native-born racial and ethnic groups in different settings (Mollenkopf 2013). This clearly differs depending on whether the city has had a history of white-black conflict and competition or has been more fluid (with significant presence, for example, of native-born Latinos).

Inevitably, we must place the political meaning of the rise of new immigrant minority groups in the context of the history of the civil rights movement in the given locale. This takes on a different valence in the South, where the region's white majority is composed largely of white Protestants, as compared to the North, where a region's white majority has much more Catholic or Jewish immigrant ancestry. Finally, we must distinguish between what goes on at the level of official policy and day-to-day practices by front-line public workers. Some scholars have suggested that even when the larger political atmosphere is heated, workers in public agencies may practice receptivity by flying "under the radar" to assist immigrants, especially the undocumented, in ways that local public opinion might not accept were these practices to become visible (Jones-Correa 2008a; Marrow 2009).

The rapid rise in immigration since 1980 certainly predisposes some members of the local native-born population toward opportunistic anti-immigrant responses; lacking past experience with immigrants, many places in the South or even the suburban parts of traditional receiving regions lack the institutional flexibility or responsiveness to forge positive measures. In these settings, local political entrepreneurs—that is, those seeking to make political gains and build political careers—may wish to mobilize anti-immigrant sentiment as a way to shift the political balance in their favor, with considerable anecdotal evidence suggesting that conservative grassroots activists and Republican political strategists believe that taking anti-immigrant positions favoring national and local enforcement can stir up their base for electoral campaigns. (Of course, pro-immigrant political entrepreneurs in settings favorable to them also try to mobilize sentiment to support their positions.)

The rapidity and recency of immigration do not, by themselves, preordain an unfavorable outcome for immigrants. Silicon Valley, for example, has a particularly high share of foreign-born, and it has given a quite positive reception to both high- and low-skilled immigrants, belying an iron link between scale and speed of change on the one hand and local politics on the other. In any case, we know that having a long history of large immigrant populations, Democratic elected officials, and a dense network of immigrant-serving social service and immigrant advocacy organizations all seem to work in favor of warmer receptions (de Graauw, Gleeson, and Bloemraad 2013). Certainly, the mix between unskilled workers and highly educated professionals influences the response, partly because it affects how easy it is to negatively "racialize" immigrants.

In short, the authors of this volume try to go beyond a simple focus on the scale of new immigrant arrivals and look at how the different parts of that stream interact with the local political structure and each other. We explore these relationships in seven metropolitan areas, comparing responses to the rise of new immigrant communities both *across* older and newer receiving destinations and *within* each of them—looking both at the central cities where immigrants initially concentrate but also the suburban and exurban areas where they are increasingly finding homes. We measure positive urban and regional receptivity primarily through the adoption of new programs to promote immigrant integration, the redesign of existing programs to take account of new immigrant client groups, the enforcement approach taken by local governments toward undocumented immigrants, and the degree of cooperation between local governments, nonprofit service delivery organizations, and immigrant advocacy groups. We measure negative receptivity in terms of the presence of anti-immigrant mobilization, the adoption of strong enforcement measures, and the failure to provide necessary basic services like translation in everyday transactions with local government.

Key Themes

Three themes emerge from our work. The first is that negative responses are more likely to flourish when there is greater "demographic distance" between the newly arriving immigrant groups and the native-born populations. At one end of the spectrum are situations where largely low-skilled, often undocumented immigrant populations from Mexico and Central America arrive in areas with white Protestant majorities, as in the case of Phoenix. Such receiving contexts, almost by definition, have little past experience with integrating earlier immigrant groups. On the other end of the spectrum, highly heterogeneous immigrant populations, including well-educated along with low-skilled members, may arrive in contexts of reception in which the native-born populations are also highly heterogeneous, as in New York, Chicago, or Los Angeles. Of particular interest are southern cases, where "demographic distance" must be measured not only against native whites, but against African Americans (for perceptive analyses of Atlanta, Nashville, and small-town North Carolina see Marrow 2009 and Winders 2013). The presence of great demographic distance inclines many old-timers to perceive newcomers to be outside the mainstream and likely to generate more demands for service than they contribute to the local tax base. Conversely, regions respond more positively when they have already "mainstreamed" earlier waves of immigrants who coincidently became a constituency base (that is, voters).

A second theme emerging from our case studies is that while demographic characteristics certainly shape the terrain on which political reactions take place, local actors have latitude, and adopt strategies that reflect not just demographics but also the political cultures, structures, and dynamics of the receiving regions. Our examples highlight the importance of several particular characteristics of the receiving contexts. One is the presence of conservative populist political entrepreneurs, usually but not always in the Republican Party, who see political benefits from adopting strong enforcement measures against undocumented immigrants and negatively stereotyping or racializing immigrants more generally; they can, of course, sometimes be countered by pro-immigrant political entrepreneurs, but such contexts require some underlying mobilization of immigrant communities and their allies, most likely in places with an already long-settled immigrant population. Conservative anti-immigrant populists mainly tap into anxieties among native whites that their dominant positions may be at risk, but may also highlight labor market and residential competition between immigrants and native-born minority groups. This echoes findings by Ramakrishnan and colleagues (Gulasekaram and Ramakrishnan 2012, 2015; Ramakrishnan and Wong 2010) that Republican political orientations are one of the strongest predictors of the proposal and adoption of anti-immigrant legislation at the local level. On the other hand, the presence of pro-immigrant political forces, whether labor unions, immigrant-serving nonprofits, or the Democratic Party, may temper this tendency. In particular, our cases highlight an aspect not generally considered in the literature: that regional business leadership groups can play a positive role. If such leaders believe that promoting a sense of welcome is good for the regional business climate, they can be a counterweight to anti-immigrant political entrepreneurs.

Finally, all the cases highlight the differences between the central city settings in which immigrants formerly concentrated and the suburban settings in which they are now increasingly locating. While immigrants are still moving to big cities, the center of gravity of immigrant settlement is rapidly shifting outward. And suburban contexts of reception are quite different: the density of residential concentrations is much lower; the development of institutions serving immigrant communities is just beginning, if such institutions are present at all; suburban political jurisdictions have far less governmental capacity (often by choice); and suburban schools have less experience with ethnic and racial and linguistic diversity. Reactions have often been quite negative in these locales; Vicino, for example, in *Suburban Crossroads* (2013), dissects the cases of Carpentersville, Illinois; Farmer's Branch, Texas; and Hazelton, Pennsylvania.

And it is not just the preexisting character of suburbs; immigrant communities in suburban settings have a different character from those in central cities. Drawing on Zelinsky and Lee, Brettell (2008, 165) has stressed the non-clustered style of place making (or "heterolocalism") by Indian immigrants outside Dallas, with commercial enterprises like supermarkets and event spaces becoming nodes for interaction among widely spread-out families. Arguably, the suburban settings reinforce all the other barriers to civic mobilization among immigrants, like recency of arrival and lack of political knowledge.

Our cases also highlight the difficulties that immigrant advocacy organizations based in the traditional central city receiving areas have in beginning to operate on a regional basis. None of our study areas show what could be called a fully integrated regional or metropolitan response, although the San José area (which is encompassed by a single county, Santa Clara County) has so many municipalities with large immigrant populations that county government has become a significant pro-immigrant actor. Immigrant advocates in Chicago have also projected their influence into the suburbs by getting the State of Illinois to take a number of positive steps. The conclusion returns to some of the ways in which stronger and more favorable metropolitan responses can be developed.

Which Regions?

This book grows out of the "Building Resilient Regions" (BRR) research network that was funded by the John D. and Catherine T. MacArthur Foundation and guided by our colleague Margaret Weir at the University of California, Berkeley. As part of this larger research network, we coordinated our list of cases with the regions being studied by other working groups looking at economic decline, rapid growth, the suburbanization of poverty, and transportation and environmental challenges. Collectively, the network agreed to focus on twenty metropolitan areas. From those, we initially chose six to study immigrant integration: three longtime recipients of immigrants (New York, Chicago, and Los Angeles), and three more recent destinations (Charlotte, Phoenix, and San José). We eventually distinguished and selected a seventh metro area, the so-called Inland Empire of Southern California (Riverside and San Bernardino Counties), because it constituted a new receiving metropolis juxtaposed beside another large and traditional receiving area (Los Angeles).

New York and Los Angeles are obvious choices because they are the two biggest traditional gateways (with Singer [2008] classifying the former as "continuous" and the latter as "post World War II"). These metropolitan areas have a highly diverse set of new and "mature" immigrant communities (with three in ten immigrants in the United States living in one or the other, along with slightly more of their children). They provide a matched pair with complicated mixes of immigrants and natives but also with core cities with well-developed infrastructures for immigrant organizing, advocacy, and service that sometimes work outside the central cities but may also not fully stretch across the entire metropolitan area. Both have recently been the subject of major studies on the trajectories of second-generation youth (Kasinitz et al. 2008; Kasinitz, Mollenkopf, and Waters 2004; Telles and Ortiz 2008). Finally, immigrants are moving straight into the suburbs of both regions, blurring the historical patterns of initial arrival in the central city followed by spillover into adjacent suburbs, and allowing us to examine variation in response *within* metropolitan areas.

We chose Chicago to round out our trio of traditional receiving areas and San José as an exemplary new receiving area. Both have large and diverse immigrant populations, and both have done more than many areas to adopt successful immigrant integration policies. Chicago has experienced migration from Mexico and Eastern Europe, which has spread away from the central city over the last decade. San José, the biggest city in Silicon Valley, is a relatively new immigrant destination that has attracted Asian immigrants to its sprawling primary city and northern suburbs (some of which are now cities in their own right), as well as Mexican immigrants to its southern and eastern agricultural areas.[2] Both regions also have nationally notable immigrant integration programs; learning why and how these programs evolved can provide a better understanding of what explains positive responses, as well as useful policy lessons for the future.

The two new destinations of Charlotte and Phoenix have offered welcomes that contrast with each other as well as with that of San José. While not without tensions and gaps in service delivery, Charlotte has been relatively welcoming, or at least not overtly hostile, partly because its business and civic leadership wants to present the city as a model for North Carolina and the "New South." Phoenix has offered a decidedly cooler reception, with its county sheriff, Joe Arpaio, serving as a celebrated example of a local law enforcement official taking up the enforcement of immigration law—although the central city itself has not shared the anti-immigrant impulse to the same extent as the county and the state. The Inland Empire, as mentioned, sits beside, but at some distance from, a traditional gateway, Los Angeles, but its immigrant presence is much newer than that in LA, and the rapid recent increase of its immigrant population dramatically changed local political dynamics. (In this respect, it is an interesting comparison with the east end of Long Island, discussed in the New York chapter.) These cases illustrate how the absence of an institutional infrastructure for immigrant integration magnifies the challenges for achieving such integration, but also how the presence of other civic infrastructures can provide a scaffold for integration, if the relevant actors make a different set of political calculations.

How the Analysis Was Done

While we try to synthesize and draw broad lessons from the whole body of work presented here, this is, in fact, an edited collection. However, it differs from most edited volumes because we have crafted it as a single enterprise, not just a set of loosely related chapters. The two coeditors convened a team of researchers who developed a shared analytical and research framework and met periodically through the research process to share results, refine the framework, and think through policy implications. The researchers conducted historical background research and interviewed a mix of regional actors with a standard interview protocol and a common set of questions. Els de Graauw, John Mollenkopf, and Diana Gordon covered New York, with initial research assistance from Martha Pichardo, while Jaime Dominguez examined Chicago, Michael Jones-Correa studied Charlotte, Paul Lewis and Doris Marie Provine covered Phoenix, and Manuel Pastor, Rachel Rosner, Jennifer Tran, and Juan De Lara (in various combinations) examined Los Angeles, San José, and the Inland Empire.

All the researchers joined in developing common interview protocols, provided the whole team with field notes, and participated in debriefings. In synthesizing the case studies, the editors went back to the researchers with questions, did supplemental research, and sought feedback from the group about whether our preliminary conclusions reflected their field experiences. Some of our conclusions are more speculative than others. These are, after all, just seven cases, albeit complemented by our broader research experience in other settings. We try to indicate clearly which hypotheses we think are better tested and confirmed in the data and which need further research.

In the end, of course, each author is responsible for her or his own contribution—and the reader will notice analytic differences (as well as varied writing styles). But as the coeditors, we have sought to synthesize our colleagues' discoveries in our introductory and summary chapters—and as so often happens in such projects, we have long ago forgotten where our ideas end and their (usually better) ideas begin. We thus take full responsibility for whatever shortcomings might be found here and only modest credit for whatever nuggets of wisdom readers may take away.

A Road Map to the Book

The next chapter offers a brief history of immigration trends in the United States and how the various flows have intersected with the question of regional receptivity, making its spatial variation an important topic of research. We then present a detailed profile of the cases using historical and recently released U.S. Census data. We detail the nature of immigrant flows to the central cities and suburbs of the seven metropolitan regions and contrast them with the native-stock populations. The chapter highlights the importance of the specific mixes of immigrants and native-born populations in particular contexts of reception—especially in terms of continuity of flows, socioeconomic status, national origin, and likely undocumented status—and the political implications of the resulting "demographic distance" between the new immigrants and the native-born populations. We also highlight differences between central cities and inner and outer suburbs in all the cases.

The chapter specifically points to the importance of the presence or absence of relatively higher-income and more-educated immigrants, the size composition of different immigrant groups, the share of undocumented immigrants, the social position of immigrants compared with native-born minority groups, and the presence or absence of an immigrant heritage among native-born whites. We argue that these general factors set up the conditions under which the native-born mainstream might or might not "racialize" immigrants or consider them to be a distinctly separate population. The spatial distribution of immigrants within metropolitan areas may influence native responses as well. But to truly understand the variations in the patterns of political responses to immigrants, one must get to the institutional structures, political cultures, and political opportunity structures within and between the various metro regions.

The following chapters shift from this qualitative analysis to specific examples, with the first three taking up more traditional gateways and the next four the newer locations. Chapter 3 opens the set of chapters on traditional immigrant gateways. In this first section, Els de Graauw, Diana Gordon, and John Mollenkopf examine the case of New York, with a comparison between the welcoming actions of the city government and conflicts and hostilities in an outer suburb. They suggest that the variation between central city and suburb demonstrates several key lessons: the importance of a heritage of celebrating immigration to setting a regional tone; the importance of a sizable immigrant vote within a strong party system at the mayoral level; and the importance of interaction between, on the one hand, suburban political figures who as part of their political strategy see gains in excluding immigrants, and, on the other, advocates who have promoted pro-immigrant measures. We also consider the role of Mayors Michael Bloomberg and Bill de Blasio locally and nationally and suggest that while Bloomberg's contribution to national immigrant integration efforts was perhaps idiosyncratic, it highlights the importance of business leadership that we also find in other cases.

In chapter 4, Jaime Dominguez also takes up immigrant integration in the context of a strong political machine, persistent black-white cleavages, and intense neighborhood identification and competition in Chicago. These factors created an opening for white Democratic mayors to include Latino immigrants in their voting base as white ethnic voting declined, a strategy that did not prevent an insurgent Latino candidate from challenging the mayor in 2015. More broadly, Dominguez suggests that the presence of Eastern European immigrants has diminished the appetite of greater Chicago's native-born white population to "racialize" the immigrant integration debate. He points to variation between different suburbs and also underscores the importance of immigrant-oriented social services at the county and state level won by immigrant social justice organizations; he argues that some suburbs have been more welcoming because immigrant advocacy groups followed a conscious strategy to influence suburban policies. City-based immigrant activists achieved this broader influence through positive actions taken by state government. Finally, he considers whether the presence of regionalist efforts "spill over" to a more positive frame around immigrant integration.

In chapter 5, Manuel Pastor, Juan De Lara, and Rachel Rosner consider the city and county of Los Angeles, a place where immigrant communities have built their power through social movements that are now reshaping the regional political landscape. They find that, through their participation in broader multi-issue, multiethnic coalitions oriented toward leadership development, community organizing, and pragmatic policy change, these actors have helped press policy makers and secured wins for immigrant communities in policy arenas from labor to education. While Los Angeles may appear to have less-visible institutions for immigrant integration than do other regions, these social movements have increased the political penalties for anti-immigrant rhetoric and actions by integrating with the region's movement for progressive change. The authors also examine a different sort of suburb from those considered in several other cases, one where half the residents are immigrants and where they and their allies have taken hold of the reins of local government. However, the authors conclude that even with the work social movements have done both to shape direct policy and to build longer-term political power, these groups must spend considerable effort securing the implementation of policy. As such, much work remains to institutionalize immigrant integration in the region, and cementing durable changes may require stronger participation from business and philanthropic partners.

In chapter 6, Juan De Lara looks at California's San Bernardino and Riverside Counties, also known as the "Inland Empire" and once a white Republican outpost. African Americans and Latino immigrants and nonimmigrants have transformed the Inland Empire by moving there for cheaper housing. The sudden changes, and the political mismatch between the prevailing leadership and the new demographics, have produced a wave of anti-immigrant activism. De Lara draws parallels to the Phoenix case in terms of rapidity of change, demographic difference between old and young, and fragmentation and weakness of the business community, as well as the absence of political mobilization among the new immigrants. Added to the mix: as the housing market collapsed after 2007, many new residents were stuck in the Inland Empire without employment, with a tenuous grip on housing, and without the social service infrastructure of more traditional receiving locations. This contrast with Los Angeles allows us to examine variation within one of the most far-flung metropolitan areas in the United States.

Michael Jones-Correa's study of Charlotte, North Carolina, which makes up chapter 7, considers another kind of new destination. The case points both to the advantages and limits of business leadership. He argues that Charlotte has long had a business elite concerned about the city's role as a national financial center in the New South. Under their influence, Charlotte took a leadership role on school desegregation, downtown development, and regional economic strategies. This served to constrain anti-immigrant politics as Latino immigrant communities grew rapidly within the city and county. Nonetheless, the ground shifted as a former Charlotte mayor became an anti-immigrant governor, playing to a conservative Republican legislature, and some local anti-immigrant political figures picked up this lead. The example points to the lack of services in newer destinations, including suburbs, but also how elite opinion can constrain many conservative populist impulses.

The opposite is true of Phoenix. In chapter 8, Doris Marie Provine and Paul Lewis explore a place made famous in the immigration field by an energetic county sheriff who has cracked down on undocumented immigrants. However much this served his political career, the authors argue, his actions also respond to the sentiments of a native majority made uneasy by the rapid growth of immigrant communities, a significant presence of unauthorized immigrants, and their overwhelmingly Mexican national origin. These conditions have enabled Sheriff Arpaio, among others, to inflame the situation. At the same time, the larger political response has been enabled by a long-standing metropolitan fragmentation and lack of regional business leadership.

The San José / Silicon Valley metropolitan area is dissected by Manuel Pastor, Rachel Rosner, and Jennifer Tran in chapter 9. It is a hopeful case—and so good for offering the last word. The authors note that the immigrant population here has grown even more rapidly than in any other case in the book, but the region nonetheless offers a welcoming atmosphere and has taken important public and philanthropic steps to spur immigrant integration. The authors argue that the diversity in skills and national origins of the immigrant population helps to "deracialize" the issue; moreover, the valley's business elites rely on high-skilled immigrants, yielding positive attitudinal spillovers to less-skilled immigrants. The high degree of regional business collaboration in the Silicon Valley on promoting technology industries reliant on high-skilled immigrants has led business to be a local force for immigrant integration and a national force for comprehensive immigration reform.

In the concluding chapter, the editors cull the central themes from the cases, reexamine the factors that drive positive and negative responses to the new immigration, and seek to unpack the political dynamics by which they play out. We also highlight the metropolitan spatial dimension of these dynamics. We then examine the implications for research and practice. On the practice side, we suggest some new federal policies that would speed immigrant integration, promote receptivity, and defuse tensions. We go beyond our cases by highlighting some "best practices" developed around the country, noting which ones work, why, and where. Finally, we highlight what we believe to be the most important remaining research questions and explain how building on the case study method used here could help answer them.

We hope that the reader will close this book with three thoughts in mind. The first is simply to understand that the metropolitan dimension is an important part of the immigrant integration challenge. This topic is beginning to receive more attention partly because, as the data presented in the next chapter highlight, immigration has been moving to the suburbs. Research and practice both need to operate on a metropolitan and regional scale. We trust that the ways in which we have used a regionalist lens and a comparative case study and mixed-methods approach will contribute to that development. Second, we hope reading this volume will underscore for the reader that immigrants have experienced a great range of different receptions within and across metropolitan regions and that our work has identified some of the main demographic structures and political dynamics that help to predict the challenges any region will face.

Finally, we have also highlighted the ways in which metropolitan leaders, particularly from the business community, but also from civic organizations, labor unions, and social movements, play an important yet often overlooked role in shaping regional reactions to immigrants. Civic and political leaders may rally public opinion to recognize new immigrant communities and support public policies and programs that mitigate the service challenges they pose, thus making the most of immigrant potentials. On the other hand, civic and political leaders may rally public opposition to immigration, fostering harsher enforcement toward unauthorized immigrants and chilling the reception of new immigrants in ways that underutilize or even reject their talents. In short, structural elements may shape the field of action, but in the end public will and political courage have great influence on the outcomes. Both will be needed if the nation is to do a better job at integrating immigrants and building resilient regions.

2

THE CASES IN CONTEXT

Data and Destinies in Seven Metropolitan Areas

Manuel Pastor and John Mollenkopf

Why does receptivity toward immigrants differ so much within and across regions? While this question is central to the entire volume, we must start by acknowledging that explaining local variation is only part of the overall answer. Local responses are highly sensitive to the tenor of national debate about immigration and the ways in which national political actors seek to frame or politicize, or even racialize, the issue. For example, high-impact national events such as the September 11, 2001, attacks on the World Trade Center and Pentagon make public opinion substantially more volatile and alter the dynamics in local contexts of reception, for example for Muslim immigrants. This can lead to problems of interpretation: it is hard to disentangle whether the fraught local politics around newer immigrants stems from their specific local circumstances or because they arrived at a particularly heated time in the national immigration debate.

Nevertheless, we believe the variation in the valence or tone of immigrant reception at the metropolitan level is largely explained by how local demographic changes interact with local political dynamics. Our case studies and the concluding chapter will carefully examine when and how local political actors may work against local and national trends by taking pro-immigrant positions, either because they are responding to the actual or potential influence of an immigrant (or immigrant-sympathetic) voting bloc, or because it may serve other interests, such as fostering a perception that a region is more tolerant and therefore more attractive to new businesses. They also explore when and how, as in Phoenix and Charlotte, local political actors—in this case two county sheriffs—can mobilize sentiment against "illegal immigrants." In either event, our case studies seek to trace out the ways in which key actors, whether regional business elites, civic and nonprofit organizations, the labor movement, or immigrant advocates, have sought to foster a receptive or welcoming environment. Local business elites can be particularly influential on this score. We note, for example, that Silicon Valley firms have taken a pro-immigrant stance, both locally and nationally; that business leaders supported the Utah Compact; and that the metropolitan Phoenix business community was ultimately able to persuade the Arizona legislature not to adopt further anti-immigrant measures.

Grassroots immigrant activism and the growth of nonprofit immigrant-serving and advocacy organizations have also made important differences in the settings studied here, particularly the central cities. Immigrant communities themselves are beginning to organize politically as their members begin to engage local public officials and run for office—and as they and their children join the active electorate in increasing numbers. As immigrant populations have grown, many longtime community-based organizations have taken up their cause, and many new pro-immigrant organizations have been created. Local philanthropies have helped to broaden this base, and in some places the Catholic Church and local trade unions have also bolstered these efforts. Particularly interesting are "Welcoming America" organizations that seek to build bridges between the majority populations with little or no immigrant heritage in their immediate backgrounds and newly arriving immigrant communities. Such organizations usually operate in the urban core, although there are some exceptions. In a few instances, such as the Illinois Coalition for Immigrant and Refugee Rights, such advocacy organizations have been able to leverage change at the state level, which affected not only the central cities but also their surrounding areas. Indeed, national linkages between the major immigrant rights organizations based in Chicago, New York, Boston, San Francisco, and Los Angeles have provided valuable support for national efforts at policy reform.

This volume therefore undertakes an in-depth exploration of contrasting cases in order to understand the metropolitan variation in responses to the larger challenge of the rapid growth of immigrant populations over the last forty years, which has come as a shock to many places unaccustomed to immigration. This chapter details the basic data trends for each case study region. We start by reviewing recent immigration to the United States, highlighting when, why, and where the share of foreign-born grew after the mid-1960s and particularly after 1980. For the early part of this period, immigration was relatively uncontroversial and generally headed to traditional areas. By the 1990s, however, the sheer volume of new arrivals and their intersection with new strategies of border enforcement led different types of immigrants to new places, creating a new spatial matrix for immigrant reception. Audrey

Singer (2004) offers a helpful and influential typology for this new immigrant geography.

We provide the basic demographic characteristics for each case examined in this volume. We look first at the size and composition of the foreign-born population, as well as their recency of arrival and specific locations within the metropolitan area. We then highlight such key characteristics as the share that is undocumented, income and educational levels, the speed at which immigrants are acquiring English, and their presence in the active presidential electorate. We conclude by suggesting some ways in which these larger demographic patterns are likely to shape the field of action in each case study.

Immigration and Reception

The contemporary wave of immigration can be traced to the Hart-Celler Act of 1965. Prior to this measure, restrictionist laws passed in 1924 and 1927 capped overall immigration and limited admissions from particular countries by imposing quotas based on the presence of their immigrants as of 1890. In practice, this favored immigrants from Western Europe and restricted immigration overall, and, combined with the impact of the Depression and World War II, contributed to the steady decline until the mid-1960s of the foreign-born share of the American population (figure 2.1). While native white Protestants looked down on the ethno-religious heritages of the Central and Southern European immigrants of the 1880–1920 period, the service of their young adult children in World War II and their upward mobility afterward dramatically reduced differences between immigrant ethnic groups and native-born whites and swelled the number of second- and third-generation Americans. This process, along with postwar economic support for suburbanization, enabled the children of the previous great wave of immigration to assimilate and achieve a norm of "whiteness" (Alba and Nee 1997; Singer 2010; and Katznelson 2005).

Hart-Celler raised the overall limits on immigration and ended country quotas in favor of a first-come, first-serve system for distributing a global pool of visas (Keely 1971; Zolberg 2009).[1] Along with a shift to promoting family reunification (and not counting arriving family members under the quota system), this launched a new dynamic in the overall flow of immigrants and their geographic origins. As a result, immigrants hailed increasingly from the Caribbean, Latin America, and East and South Asia, and the ethnic character of the foreign-born shifted from nearly three-quarters non-Hispanic white in 1970 (the first year for which we have reliable data on Hispanics) to more than 80 percent nonwhite in 2010–2012 (figure 2.2).[2]

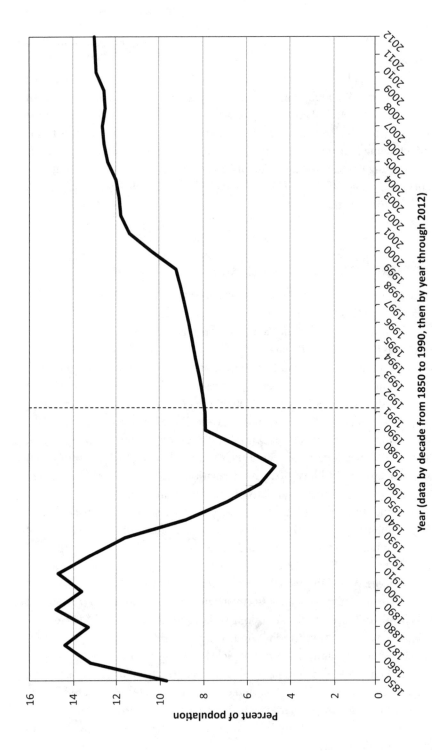

FIGURE 2.1. Percent of U.S. population foreign-born, 1850–2012

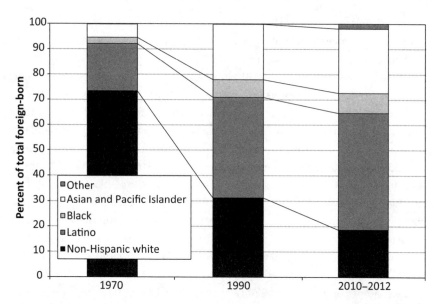

FIGURE 2.2. Changing racial composition of foreign-born in the United States, 1970–2012

While the Hart-Celler reform shifted the ethnic composition of America's immigrant population, that process was reinforced by the Immigration Reform and Control Act (IRCA) of 1986. IRCA provided amnesty to nearly three million undocumented residents, mostly from Mexico, and this in turn led many of those newly legalized residents to seek to bring family members to the United States. It also bolstered the trajectories of their native-born children, the new second generation. These legal residents also provided a social context of support for new unauthorized arrivals, and the combination of this attraction, economic and social crises in Mexico and Central America, and a relative lack of workplace enforcement led to a swelling of the undocumented population: by 2010, estimates of the unauthorized population ranged from 11.2 to 11.5 million, with more than 80 percent of the group hailing from Latin America (Hoefer and Rytina 2012; Passel and Cohn 2011).

Partly because of the sheer scale of arrivals, the geography of immigrant settlement also changed markedly. In an earlier era, new immigrants and their attendant negative (and positive) impacts were concentrated primarily in the large central cities that have traditionally served as the main receptors for immigrants—places like New York, Miami, Chicago, Los Angeles, and San Francisco. The long history of immigration to these cities helped them to develop a wide range of institutional mechanisms to ease the newcomers' arrival and transition. However, since the mid-1990s, immigration has shifted away from these traditional destinations toward entirely new metropolitan areas, such as Charlotte and Phoenix.

This is not simply a question of older locations filling up and inducing immigrants to look elsewhere. Since 1990, efforts to reinforce border controls at major gateways from Mexico, especially Tijuana–San Diego and El Paso, led Mexican and Central American immigrants to enter through Arizona and also to move toward nontraditional metropolitan areas and rural areas with more demand for unskilled labor than existed in Southern California (Light 2006; Massey 2008, 333–35). As a result, Mexican migrants made Georgia, North Carolina, Arizona, and Nevada into major destinations alongside California, Texas, and Illinois (Zúñiga and Hernández-León 2006). California is an exemplar of the trend: though it was home to 35 percent of the nation's immigrants in the late 1980s, it attracted only 19 percent of new arrivals from 2004 to 2007 (Bohn 2009).

Immigrant destinations have also shifted *within* metropolitan regions. The traditional view, best expressed by sociologist Douglas Massey, equated upward socioeconomic mobility with outward residential mobility: as immigrants gained an economic foothold, they would pull themselves out of economically disadvantaged inner-city neighborhoods and head to the suburbs (Massey 1985). Although this narrative fit traditional gateways like New York and Chicago, and seemed to capture overall trends for many decades, new analyses have challenged this notion of spatial assimilation (Iceland and Scopilliti 2008). On the one hand, existing patterns of racial and class segregation constrained nonwhite immigrants to live side by side with blacks (Blackwell, Kwoh, and Pastor 2010; Clark and Blue 2004). Meanwhile, wealthier immigrants established new suburban enclaves (Zhou 1999), and relatively poor immigrants moved along with native-born poor to inner-ring suburbs being abandoned by the native lower middle class (Kneebone and Berube 2014); a good example of the latter pattern is Maywood in Los Angeles, a case to which we return later. This means that some places *within* metropolitan areas were experiencing an immigrant presence for the first time, and many were ill-equipped for the consequences. (Exurban areas, another place with little infrastructure to support new immigrants, were in need of low-skilled service workers, and some newcomers moved accordingly [Marcelli 2004]).

In appraising these trends, Audrey Singer (2008) has developed a new typology of receiving areas.[3] She suggests that "spatial assimilation by movement to the suburbs" only fits "continual gateways" like New York and Chicago, where the foreign-born share has historically exceeded the national average and where the built environment (a crowded central city adjoined by clearly distinct suburbs) suits the process (Singer 2004). In many metropolitan areas that grew rapidly after World War II, the foreign-born percentage did not exceed the national average until after 1950. While these sprawling regions—places like Los Angeles and Miami—are also considered traditional gateways (albeit of more recent vintage), the usual socioeconomic distinctions between city and suburb are less sharp, and many immigrants in these metropolitan areas have headed directly for the suburbs (Orfield 2002; Pastor 2001). Finally, Singer (2004) also identifies newly emerging immigrant-receiving regions in which the traditionally low foreign-born share of the population has surged rapidly after 1980; as with the postwar cities that more recently arrived at their designation as traditional gateways, immigrants in these emerging areas have often "leapfrogged" directly into suburbs (see also Pastor 2012).

A Quantitative Overview of the Cases

How do these trends and new realities show up in the cases examined in this book? To look at this, we draw on data assembled for the BRR network that contains economic, civic, social, housing, geographic, and demographic measures for several decades for all 934 Core-Based Statistical Areas (CBSAs) in the United States. CBSA boundaries have been made consistent to compare measures across the 1970, 1980, 1990, and 2000 Censuses and recent versions of the American Community Survey (ACS). Unfortunately, the Census and ACS standard tables do not always detail key outcomes by nativity, so we tabulated most measures concerning immigrants using the Public Use Microdata Samples (which contain individual observations and so can be tabulated in novel ways) for various years.

The Demographics of the Foreign-Born

Figure 2.3 begins the quantitative background analysis by showing the relative sizes of the overall and foreign-born populations of our seven metropolitan areas, with the order arranged by the size of the metro population. As can be seen, Los Angeles and New York have much larger shares of immigrants as well as much larger populations overall. Though Chicago is a traditional gateway with a large immigrant population, the share of its population that is foreign-born is much smaller than in San José and even smaller than in the Inland Empire (Riverside–San Bernardino). Phoenix and Charlotte both have smaller overall populations, and Phoenix has a larger foreign-born share than Charlotte, perhaps suggesting one reason why the politics have been more heated in the former than the latter.

The seven regions have distinct immigrant patterns in terms of the growth of the immigrant population over time. Figure 2.4 compares the traditional metropolitan areas (New York, Chicago, and Los Angeles) with the emerging

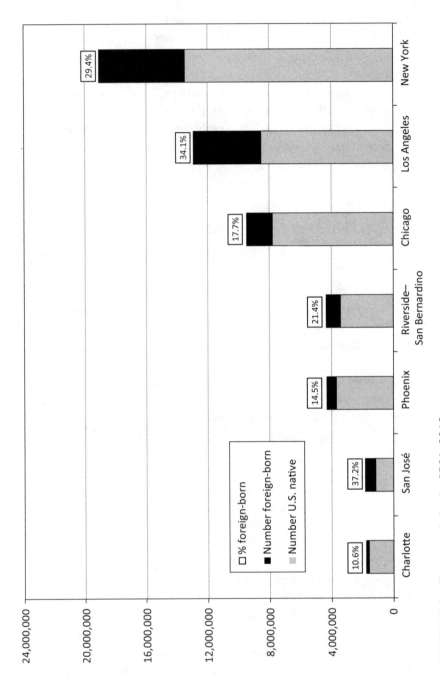

FIGURE 2.3. Total population by CBSA, 2012

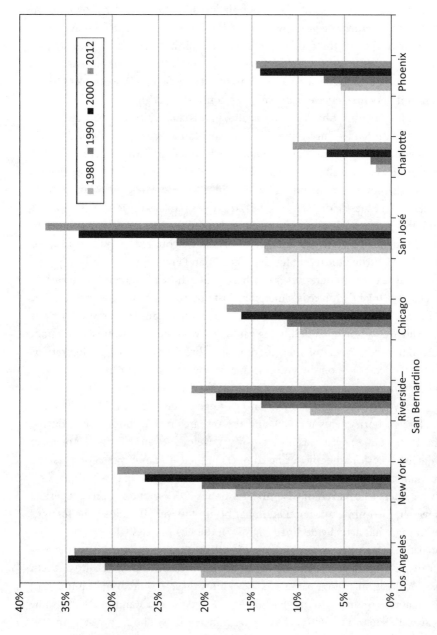

FIGURE 2.4. Percent foreign-born population by CBSA, 1980–2012

ones (Charlotte, Phoenix, Inland Empire, and San José). To facilitate contrast, we change the ordering of the regions in this and subsequent figures from that used in figure 2.3—which was by population size—to an order moving from traditional to emerging gateways (with one nuance described below). As noted, we think of the first three as large and long-established immigrant gateways; we think of the next two as highly diverse and successfully integrating gateways, albeit with more recently arrived immigrants in one (San José); we think of Charlotte and Phoenix as newer gateways with contrasting degrees of receptivity.

The Inland Empire has a somewhat ambiguous characterization. Singer (2004) labels the Riverside–San Bernardino metropolitan area as a post–World War II immigrant gateway, meaning a location in which the foreign-born are a new but increasing presence after the 1940s. This would seem to make it a more mature gateway, although the Inland Empire had nearly the lowest share of immigrants in 1980 of all the regions she classifies this way, as well as the lowest share at the end (that is, 2000). On the other hand, its share of the foreign-born continued to rise through 2011, even as that measure fell in its neighbor metropolitan area, Los Angeles. Moreover, the recent history of the Inland Empire, particularly its political conflicts over immigration, is much more like those of emerging locations. In a sense, the Inland Empire is "emerging," just not from the tiny base that could be observed in Charlotte or Phoenix in 1980. However, because it contrasts with Los Angeles, we will call it an "adjoining gateway." We chose it to contrast immigrant integration across one of the geographically broadest regional configurations in the United States on the grounds that it may have been receiving "spillover" immigration and hence spillovers in terms of policy and political conflicts.

In any case, the figure shows that Los Angeles and New York had the highest foreign-born shares in 1980, and those shares rose in both locales during the 1990s. Los Angeles was affected by a wave of incoming Central American migrants, most frequently fleeing conflicts in their home countries or pursuing economic opportunities, as well as family members migrating to join other family members who had attained legal status under IRCA. In the most recent period, however, the immigrant population has begun to level off; indeed, the foreign-born share has actually declined slightly in the Los Angeles CBSA (Core-Based Statistical Area, or metro area), something that runs contrary to the usual popular image of immigrants continuing to stream into Los Angeles. Comparatively, New York's immigration pattern has been more diverse. Moreover, its immigrant population continues to grow, while Myers, Pitkin, and Ramirez (2009) show that California's population has become increasingly "homegrown"—that is, more likely to be born in California than to have migrated from abroad or other states—although a significant portion of that California-born population is the children of immigrants.

Chicago shows a similar tapering in growth, although its immigrant share is lower than in the two other big gateways. San José has shown the most rapid share increases for the foreign-born; and while this also seems to be leveling off to some degree, San José notably had a higher share of the foreign-born in 2012 than either Los Angeles or New York.[4] Charlotte and Phoenix both had few immigrants in the 1980s and 1990s but high growth during the 1990s—the Latino population grew 394 percent in Charlotte over that period—though the final immigrant share in both locales was still well below all the other four regions. The Inland Empire shows very steady growth throughout; unlike Phoenix, which has flattened out in recent years, perhaps as a result of the political and social atmosphere, the Riverside–San Bernardino metro area saw a steady uptick and it is now far more immigrant than Chicago, despite having started from a smaller initial share of immigrants.

Table 2.1 breaks out the foreign-born population by recency of arrival, with the top line indicating the overall share of immigrants in the population and the next four lines indicating the composition of those immigrants in terms of year of arrival. New York, Los Angeles, and the Inland Empire have the lowest shares of recent arrivals among their foreign-born, reflecting their status as more mature destinations. Chicago and San José have the same share of the foreign-born that arrived since 2000 as do New York or Los Angeles, with all of these much higher than Los Angeles or the Riverside–San Bernardino metro region. Note, however, that immigrants make up a higher share of the overall population in San José than in Chicago, making the former city's comparatively graceful acceptance of immigrants of special interest. Charlotte and Phoenix have the highest shares of recent arrivals, with Charlotte's immigrant population even more recent than that of Phoenix—although Phoenix's overall share of immigrants in the population is five percentage points higher.

The sources of recent immigrants, indicated in the lower panel of table 2.1, may also influence the politics of reception. For the Los Angeles metropolitan area (which includes Orange County as well as LA County), less than a third of recent arrivals are of Mexican origin, something that might surprise readers whose views have been formed by popular images rather than data realities. That is followed by other Latin Americans (including the major Central American groups) and then a series of Asian groups. In New York, non-Mexican Latin Americans make up the largest share of the recent flow, with Dominicans being most prevalent among a diversity of other national origin groups; while we stick here with the "all other Latino" for consistency with the other metro regions, if we had separated out Dominicans, they would be a larger share of the recently arrived foreign-born than the fast-rising Mexican-origin population, and only slightly smaller as a share than the group from the West Indies. Next in the New

TABLE 2.1 Selected statistics on immigrants in seven CBSAs, 2010–2012

	MAJOR ESTABLISHED IMMIGRANT GATEWAYS			HIGHLY DIVERSE AND SUCCESSFULLY INTEGRATING GATEWAYS		NEW GATEWAYS WITH CONTRASTING RECEPTION	
	LOS ANGELES	NEW YORK	RIVERSIDE–SAN BERNARDINO	CHICAGO	SAN JOSÉ	CHARLOTTE	PHOENIX
Recency of Migration (2010–12)							
Percent of population foreign-born	34%	29%	22%	18%	37%	10%	14%
of that:							
Entered 2000 or later	27%	34%	23%	32%	35%	48%	34%
Entered 1990–1999	26%	27%	26%	31%	29%	31%	30%
Entered 1980–1989	25%	19%	26%	16%	20%	12%	19%
Entered before 1980	22%	20%	25%	21%	16%	10%	17%
Nativity of immigrants who entered 2000 or later (2010–12)							
1st largest group	Mexican 30%	All other Latino 28%	Mexican 47%	Mexican 35%	Asian Indian 35%	Mexican 28%	Mexican 41%
2nd	All other Latino 17%	West Indian 10%	All other Latino 14%	Eastern European 15%	Mexican 19%	All other Latino 24%	All other Latino 11%
3rd	Chinese 8%	Asian Indian 8%	Filipino 7%	Asian Indian 10%	Chinese 12%	Asian Indian 11%	Western European 7%
4th	Filipino 7%	Chinese 8%	Chinese 4%	All other Latino 7%	Vietnamese 7%	African 8%	Asian Indian 7%
5th	Korean 6%	Mexican 7%	Asian Indian 3%	Chinese 5%	Filipino 5%	Western European 5%	African 4%

Note: Author's calculations from a pooled sample of the 2010–2012 ACS. Other Latinos includes immigrants from all other Latin American countries but excludes those from the West Indies. In Phoenix and Riverside–San Bernardino the share of recent immigrants with unknown ancestry was ranked near the top but is not included here.

York list are Asian Indians and Chinese (with Eastern Europeans not far behind but not sizable enough to make the top-five list).

Mexicans are an even larger share of recent arrivals in Chicago than in Los Angeles, but their share of the overall population is about half that of Los Angeles, simply because immigrants in general make up a smaller share of Chicago's population. Chicago's second-largest group of recent immigrants is Eastern European, a fact that may deter the "racialization" of immigration by reminding current residents that they are descendants of populations that assimilated in the past. In San José, Mexican immigrants are slightly under a quarter of all recent arrivals, with Asian populations—particularly from India, China, and Vietnam—making up the next largest groups. This creates another sort of barrier to racialization. Indeed, in the San José context, the word "immigrant" conjures up not only lower-skilled Mexican laborers, but also higher-income and highly educated Asian immigrants (Jiménez 2009). Of course, it is important to acknowledge that many Asian immigrants are also poorly educated and not faring well, particularly those from Southeast Asia, including the Vietnamese that constitute the fourth-largest immigrant group in the San José metro region—but here we are talking about the way that immigrant diversity colors perceptions, and certainly the image of the highly skilled Asian engineer or entrepreneur has an impact.

In Charlotte, just under 30 percent of the region's recent immigrants are Mexican, followed by a group of Latin Americans of diverse national origins, then Asian Indians and Africans. Meanwhile, 41 percent of the immigrants who arrived in Phoenix in the year 2000 or after are of Mexican origin, a proportion much higher than in every other locale except for the Inland Empire. As can be seen in the table, the share for this adjoining gateway (Riverside–San Bernardino) is about half, suggesting a rather monolithic presence. In both Phoenix and the Inland Empire, this vast preponderance of Mexicans, many undocumented (particularly in Phoenix), has made racialization of immigrants especially easy.

It is challenging to estimate the undocumented share of immigrants in these metropolitan areas. After all, those without legal status are seeking not to be noticed, let alone counted. However, a series of researchers have tried to do this, and table 2.2 provides CBSA estimates based on county-level estimates from the Migration Policy Institute (which were released in late 2015 and are based on 2013 estimates using a 2009–2013 pooled version of the American Community Survey).[5] To get to the CBSAs, we summarized all available county data. Not all the underlying counties had a large enough sample to be reliable, and so the totals may be somewhat understated. However, it is reasonable to put undocumented populations at over 140,000 in San José, nearly 300,000 in the Inland Empire, about 400,000 in Chicago, more than 850,000 in the New York CBSA (which includes

TABLE 2.2   Estimated unauthorized immigrant population for select CBSAs, 2013

CBSA	ESTIMATE
Los Angeles	1,336,000
New York	866,000
Riverside–San Bernardino	296,000
Chicago	405,000
San José	142,000
Charlotte	55,000
Phoenix	190,000

Source: Migration Policy Institute, *Unauthorized Immigrant Population Profiles*, http://www.migrationpolicy.org/programs/us-immigration-policy-program-data-hub/unauthorized-immigrant-population-profiles

part of New Jersey), and well over 1.3 million in the Los Angeles metro area (which also includes Orange County). The Phoenix metro area is estimated to have nearly 200,000 undocumented immigrants—a population that has attracted so much negative attention in that state. The Charlotte metro area has a relatively small number of undocumented immigrants (although we are missing the smaller, neighboring, rural counties, since our estimate is just for Mecklenburg County).

Cities and Suburbs

How have these trends played out within these metropolitan areas? We begin by breaking out the foreign-born share in every metropolitan area's cities and suburbs from 1980 to 2012. First, a word on what constitutes "cities" and suburbs is in order. In previous decades, the Census broke down metropolitan populations between central cities and the rest of a metropolitan area; in the mid-2000s, however, the Census began distinguishing metro area (or Core-Based Statistical Area) populations between those in "principal cities" and those in suburbs (again, the rest of the metro area). However, the Census now includes many older suburbs among the principal cities. In the Los Angeles metropolitan area, for example, the twenty-five principal cities include Compton, Pomona, and Newport Beach—places few observers would consider the central cities (or most important drivers) in the region and would more likely think of as suburban appendages to Los Angeles or Anaheim.

Because of this, researchers at the Brookings Institution have adopted a complicated set of rules to determine a region's "primary" cities that involve determining whether a city is in the CBSA name, whether it is the largest in the metro area, and then making room, if necessary, for two additional cities with populations of at least 100,000 (Brookings Institution 2010). We follow a similar procedure with the BRR database and designate "prime" cities—or, for ease in the table below, simply "cities"—as the first principal city listed in the CBSA name for the top-50 CBSAs (in terms of population), along with any other principal city in the CBSA with a population greater than 150,000 or with greater than 80 percent of the top city's population, and, for CBSAs ranked 51st to 192nd, any other principal city with a population greater than 100,000 or with greater than 80 percent of the population of the top city in the CBSA. Our "prime cities" are thus restricted to the most important central cities in each region.

For each of our case study areas, the prime cities are as follows: for New York, they are New York City and Newark (recall that the New York CBSA includes parts of New Jersey); for the Los Angeles metro, the prime cities are Los Angeles, Long Beach, Glendale, Santa Ana, and Anaheim; for Chicago, the prime city is Chicago; for the San José metro area, it is San José; for Charlotte, Charlotte; for Phoenix, there are four prime cities: Phoenix, Mesa, Scottsdale, and Tempe; and for the Inland Empire, the prime cities are Riverside, San Bernardino, and Ontario.

As can be seen in figure 2.5, the foreign-born shares have increased steadily in both Los Angeles's prime cities and its suburbs. However, it is striking that the foreign-born share declined in the cities between 2000 and 2012, while it increased slightly in the suburbs. This is due to the rise of relatively well-off immigrant suburbs such as Monterey Park and the movement of immigrants into older inner-ring suburbs, such as the industrial suburbs along the Alameda Corridor known as the Hub Cities, including Huntington Park, Bell, Bell Gardens, and South Gate (Pamuk 2004, 20; Pastor 2012).

As shown in figure 2.5, the prime cities in the New York metropolitan area have long had large shares of immigrants, while the suburbs have not. But the growth in the suburbs has been sharp. We can see a pattern similar to that of Los Angeles: the share of the foreign-born more or less stabilized in the cities between 2000 and 2012, even as it continued to grow in the suburbs. The gap between the share that is foreign-born in city and suburb is lower in Chicago than in the other two traditional gateways, but the suburbs have also seen a sharp rise even as the share of foreign-born has fallen in the cities.

San José is a fascinating case: while the growth in the share of the foreign-born was higher in the city of San José than in the suburbs in the 1980s, since then, the growth has been faster in the adjoining suburbs than in the central city. The pattern in the Inland Empire resembles that in San José: the growth in the suburbs is more or less keeping pace with the growth in the share in the prime cities. Recall, however, that this is a disproportionately Mexican-origin population, suggesting that there could be more racialization, particularly as this newer population hits suburban locations less accustomed to an immigrant presence.

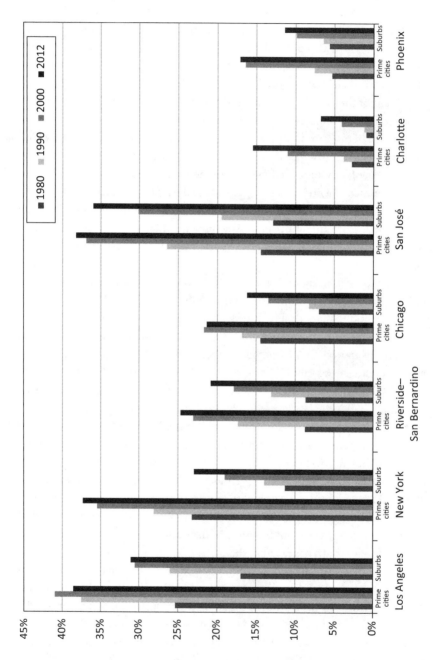

FIGURE 2.5. Percent of foreign-born population living in prime cities/suburbs, by CBSA, 1980–2012

Meanwhile, in the Charlotte metro area, the city shows much significant growth in the 1990s, but the pace picks up in the suburbs in the 2000s. The Phoenix metro area shows a sharp rise in the cities in the 1990s, with the suburbs lagging behind. However, both Charlotte and Phoenix also show immigrant movement directly to the suburbs, again suggesting a reason for "growing pains" in dealing with a new population. (These patterns are also shown in maps available in each case study showing foreign-born shares in 1980 and 2008–2012. For both the starting and endpoints, we map the data into the 2000 Census tracts, using data available from Geolytics.)

These figures make two things quite apparent. The first is simply that the size of the immigrant population has increased in all the metropolitan regions. More significant, the foreign-born have spread out from the central cities within the various metropolitan regions. The data breakdown of figure 2.5 shows that immigrants have spread into new suburban locations that may lack the civic and social-service infrastructure to deal with such change. This is one reason why each of our case studies considers not just how rapid recent immigration has affected central cities, but also how regional patterns have played out between suburbs versus prime cities, and whether immigrant organizing and service provision in the cities are linked with those activities in the suburbs.

Socioeconomic Characteristics of Immigrant Populations

Turning back to the metro areas as a whole, we now consider the variation in immigrant incomes between metropolitan areas. Figure 2.6 compares median household incomes for U.S.-born whites, U.S.-born blacks, U.S.-born and immigrant Latinos, and U.S.-born and immigrant Asians. In general, U.S.-born blacks have the lowest incomes, while U.S.-born whites and Asians have the highest, although U.S.-born blacks, U.S.-born Latinos (mostly Puerto Rican in this case), and immigrant Latinos all have equally low incomes in New York. In Los Angeles, U.S.-born Latinos fare better than blacks, while immigrant Latinos do about as well as U.S.-born blacks. Immigrant Latinos outpace U.S.-born blacks in Chicago but fare worse in Phoenix and in the Inland Empire. Immigrant Asians fare worse than native-born Asians in Los Angeles and New York, but do better in newer receiving areas, Charlotte and Phoenix. Asians, however, are small shares of the population in Charlotte and Phoenix and largest as a share in San José—where their income exceeds that of U.S.-born whites.

From the point of view of the individual case studies, we can consider these income patterns to be not only outcomes of immigrant integration—to the extent that an area is more welcoming, one would expect the economic data to be better—but also measures of the contours of reception. This is partly because the current

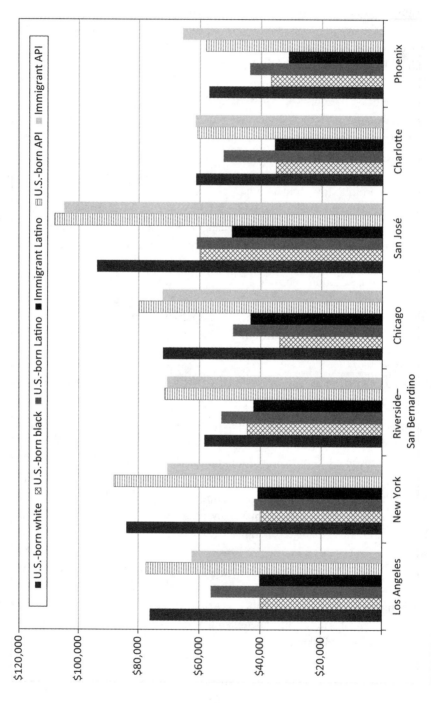

FIGURE 2.6. Median household income by CBSA, 2010–2012

snapshot says little about the trajectory over time—a low income now may simply indicate the recency of arrival—but it is also partly because higher incomes can shape the perception of immigrants and their relative contribution to the economy. In San José, where Asian immigrants have high incomes, this seems to have facilitated a positive image of and reaction to "immigrants" that rubs off on all other immigrants, including those from Latin America, even those who are less skilled and even those who are undocumented. In Phoenix, where immigrant Latinos are bringing up the bottom of income distribution, this may result in a sense of low contribution, including concerns about fiscal burdens (which may or may not be backed up by the facts).

Another factor that may better illustrate immigrant progress is English acquisition. Figure 2.7 indicates English-language ability by year of arrival for the foreign-born in each metropolitan area. Note that English acquisition is the flattest for the first two decades in San José, suggesting that the area's high share of foreign-born may be slowing the initial acquisition of English. Charlotte is the stellar performer, perhaps reflecting that older immigrants were less populous and hence in a "sink or swim" situation. Los Angeles has consistently lower numbers than Chicago or New York, but the slopes are quite similar; interestingly, the Inland Empire has a gradient similar to that of adjoining Los Angeles, something that may create cultural dislocations in this more suburban metro. Phoenix is squarely in the middle, with plenty of English proficiency as time in country increases. The problem, of course, is that Phoenix is frontloaded with recent immigrants, creating what Dowell Myers calls a "Peter Pan" fallacy—the notion that the population will never "grow up" (Myers 2008) and a profound sense that the incoming population does not want to (and probably can't) integrate.

The educational attainment of the immigrant population is also a key measure of integration. Figure 2.8 shows educational attainment for the native-born and immigrants (above the age of twenty-five and therefore likely to be available for the labor force). As might be expected, immigrants have less education than the native-born, with the interesting exception of San José, where immigrants are both slightly more likely to be college educated *and* to lack a high school diploma. The Inland Empire—followed closely by Phoenix—has the least-educated immigrants, who show a particularly large gap, compared with natives, in the share failing to complete high school. We would expect that where immigrants are more educated, they will be more likely to be perceived as economic contributors and assets to the region, hence promoting receptivity and mollifying tensions.

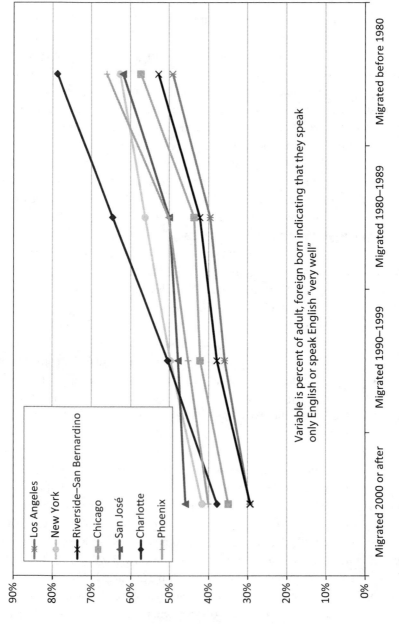

FIGURE 2.7. English-language skills by date of arrival in the United States by CBSA, 2010–2012

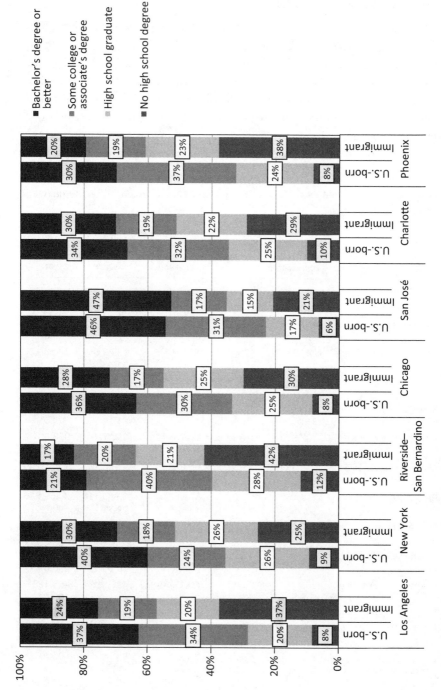

FIGURE 2.8. Educational attainment of U.S.-born and immigrant population twenty-five years and older, by CBSA, 2010–2012

Politics and Civic Engagement

Of course, receptivity also depends on whether or not immigrants themselves have a weighty voice in the political process: we expect a larger share of immigrant voters (or a more engaged set of immigrant political actors) to temper the political heat. Table 2.3 examines the votes cast by immigrants, the children of immigrants, and native-stock citizens in the November 2012 presidential election. (The term "2.5 generation" refers to native-born voters who have only one immigrant parent, while second-generation voters have two immigrant parents.) This table breaks up the regions into principal cities and suburbs rather than

TABLE 2.3 Votes cast in 2012 election by metro area, principal city vs. remainder, and immigrant status

	IMMIGRANT GENERATION STATUS				
	FOREIGN-BORN	SECOND GENERATION	2.5 GENERATION	NATIVE STOCK	TOTAL
Los Angeles principal cities	582,847 22.9%	421,366 16.6%	199,575 7.9%	1,336,681 52.6%	2,540,469 100.0%
Remainder of LA CBSA	454,652 22.8%	264,998 13.3%	122,215 6.1%	1,152,719 57.8%	1,994,584 100.0%
New York principal cities	937,508 29.9%	423,200 13.5%	144,865 4.6%	1,629,554 52.0%	3,135,127 100.0%
Remainder of NY CBSA	618,647 14.5%	395,480 9.3%	325,646 7.6%	2,932,019 68.6%	4,271,792 100.0%
Riverside–San Bernardino principal cities	28,116 8.9%	40,439 12.8%	22,678 7.2%	224,813 71.1%	316,046 100.0%
Remainder of Riverside–San Bernardino CBSA	102,605 10.7%	107,405 11.2%	84,263 8.7%	668,789 69.4%	963,062 100.0%
Chicago principal cities	113,344 8.4%	85,087 6.3%	52,556 3.9%	1,100,742 81.4%	1,351,729 100.0%
Remainder of Chicago CBSA	249,158 10.1%	152,253 6.2%	98,915 4.0%	1,969,310 79.7%	2,469,636 100.0%
San José principal cities	137,213 32.6%	19,547 4.6%	52,746 12.5%	211,890 50.3%	421,396 100.0%
Remainder of San José CBSA	33,632 10.4%	47,506 14.7%	15,935 4.9%	226,215 70.0%	323,288 100.0%
Charlotte principal cities	30,726 6.4%	2,688 .6%	10,107 2.1%	439,615 91.0%	483,136 100.0%
Remainder of Charlotte CBSA	— 0.0%	3,693 .9%	8,372 2.0%	414,481 97.2%	426,546 100.0%
Phoenix principal cities	52,278 6.0%	40,161 4.6%	45,546 5.2%	738,174 84.3%	876,159 100.0%
Remainder of Phoenix CBSA	19,110 2.9%	25,070 3.8%	32,140 4.9%	577,042 88.3%	653,362 100.0%

Source: November 2012 Current Population Survey

prime cities and suburbs, owing to sample size considerations. Immigrants and their children make up substantial shares of the active electorate not only in the principal cities of Los Angeles, New York, and San José, but also a surprisingly large share of these cities' surrounding suburbs. On the other hand, native-stock voters make up the predominant share of the voters in Chicago, Phoenix, and Charlotte, regardless of city or suburb. And in the Inland Empire, there is virtually no difference between the nativity of the voting-age population in the principal cities and the rest of the surrounding counties.

While not depicted in the table, it is interesting to note that in Los Angeles, the Inland Empire, and San José, naturalized citizens actually vote at higher rates than the U.S.-born second generation. This makes some sense: if someone went through the considerable process to become a citizen (Pastor et al. 2013; Pastor and Scoggins 2012), he or she might be more inclined to exercise that citizenship; moreover, the naturalized population is also older, a factor associated with voting. Large shares of voters and high voting rates can change the calculus for political "entrepreneurs" seeking to make electoral mileage from tensions around new populations: it makes more political sense for a politician to be pro-immigrant in Los Angeles or New York than in Phoenix or Charlotte. But this does not explain political behavior in a mechanical fashion: the share of native-born voters is similar and high in Charlotte, Phoenix, and even Chicago, but the reception of immigrants in those regions has been markedly different. Immigrants make up an even larger share of the electorate in Los Angeles than in New York, but, as we will see, actual implementation of pro-immigrant policy in Los Angeles has been more limited until recent years. This is precisely why we need detailed case studies that can capture this variation.

One other aspect of politics has to do with generational disconnect. Charlotte brings up the bottom in terms of how many of those under eighteen years old have at least one immigrant parent, with only 20 percent, while Chicago and Phoenix have 33 percent and 31 percent, respectively, and the New York metropolitan area has 44 percent (as does Riverside–San Bernardino). Around 60 percent of the young people in Los Angeles and San José have at least one immigrant parent. If one is thinking about the future of a metro region, investment in those young people—and their parents—is key to economic success.

The racial distinction between generations may overshadow that sense of a common future: as William Frey has argued, older voters may not have much sympathy for young people who are quite unlike them, creating what he calls a "cultural generation gap" (Frey 2010). This is an idea also labeled a "demographic divergence" by Pastor and Reed (2005), who also suggest that wider ethnic gaps by age can result in lower levels of infrastructure spending for the future. Frey takes a similar position, noting that this sort of generation gap can mean that "setting public priorities and fostering social cohesion . . . may take on added challenges" (Frey 2010, 85). Given that immigration has been driving demographic change in recent years—and the fact that an immigrant/nonimmigrant gap between generations is of little analytical use because the vast bulk of children of immigrants are U.S.-born—we think that calculating the "racial generation gap" is likely the best way to get at the degree of social fragmentation that might result from waves of immigrants.

Figure 2.9 looks at our various CBSAs with an in-depth calculation of the racial and ethnic composition of the older and younger populations; figure 2.10 simplifies by comparing the difference by region in a measure of the "generation gap"—the difference between the percent white of those sixty-five years and above and the percent white of those below the age of eighteen. What can be seen is that this racial gap is the biggest in the fractious Phoenix metropolitan area, followed closely by the Inland Empire, another place where there has been a jockeying for power and position as well as substantial tensions between established and newcomer populations.

While voting is one form of civic engagement, immigrants can also engage in other political and civic activities, including lobbying, petitioning, protesting, contacting public officials, joining campaigns, doing community work, and participating in labor unions, churches, nonprofit organizations, and voluntary associations (Marrow 2005; Ramakrishnan 2005). Certainly the surrounding environment influences the extent to which they do so. Janelle Wong (2006) suggests that Asian and Latino immigrants feel as though the political parties have no real interest or engagement with immigrant communities, and Louis DeSipio (2011) echoes a common view when he suggests that immigrants have lower levels of civic engagement because they often lack access to the necessary resources, including time and money, to participate in the many forms of politics in the United States. Ramakrishnan and Viramontes (2006) qualify this view, however, by suggesting that the lack of information resulting from social isolation and linguistic barriers may instead turn immigrants toward community-based work via labor organizations, advocacy and social service organizations, religious institutions, and the like, thus practicing political engagement in ways that are not captured by traditional analyses that stress voting.

The data support this notion: while immigrants may have lower levels of electoral participation, they have equal and sometimes higher levels of civic engagement in other arenas. For instance, a national survey of Mexican Americans found that U.S.- and foreign-born respondents, including noncitizens and citizens, were just as likely to participate in non-electoral civic activities, such as attending events, volunteering, or donating money to political causes (Barreto and Muñoz 2003). Local institutions, like schools and unions, are particularly

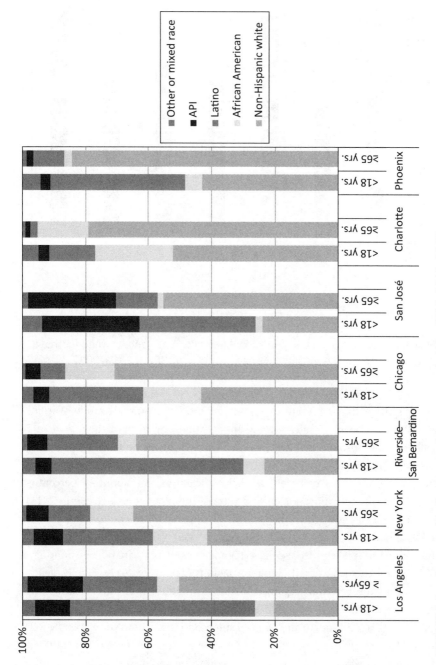

FIGURE 2.9. Demographic divergence of the young and old by CBSA, 2010–2012

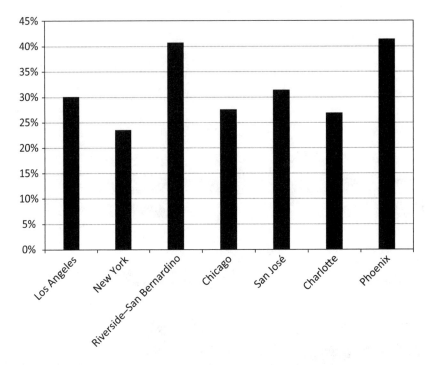

FIGURE 2.10. "Generation gap": the difference in percentage white for those sixty-five or above and those below age eighteen, by CBSA, 2010–2012

active settings for immigrant civic engagement. For example, a study of immigrant families from El Salvador and India found one-third of them were civically engaged through cultural organizations—a higher proportion than those involved in political activities (Jensen 2008). Similarly, about 35 percent of Latino parents are members of parent-teacher associations, and about 17 percent of Latino immigrants in major cities are trade union members (DeSipio 2011). These forms of engagement may be interlinked: a study of Latino workers in an LA janitors' union found that immigrant workers who participate in a social-movement union tend to also have higher rates of participation in nonunion civic activities, such as their children's schools (Terriquez 2011). Finally, demographic proximity to well-organized native-born minority groups can also influence patterns of immigrant civic engagement. Kasinitz et al. (2008) found, for example, that West Indian and Dominican second-generation young people were more highly mobilized than those of Chinese or Russian ancestry, even though the latter tended to have higher levels of education and income.

Figures 2.11 and 2.12 use data from the 2008 Civic Engagement Supplement of the Current Population Survey (CPS) to show a few measures of political

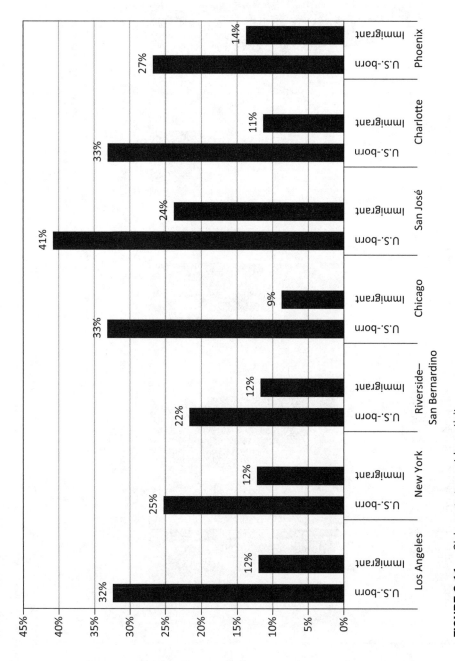

FIGURE 2.11. Civic engagement by nativity

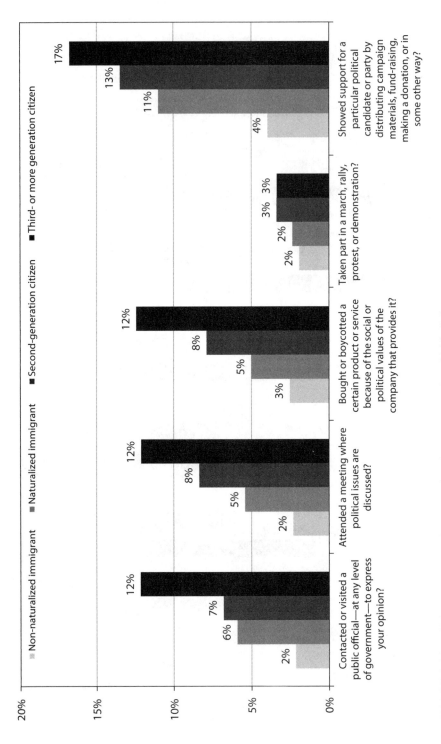

FIGURE 2.12. Civic engagement by type by immigrant generation, 2008. U.S.

Source: Current Population Survey, 2008.

Note: Sample size for some data points is below 100 but above 50.

engagement beyond voting; although there are more recent versions of this CPS supplement, the 2008 version asked more questions and covered more forms of political engagement that in subsequent years.[6] Figure 2.11 offers an aggregate measure, by BRR region, of how politically engaged in nonvoting activities were immigrants and the U.S.-born—they are counted as engaged if they did at least one of the following: visited a public official, attended a meeting where political issues were discussed, participated in a boycott because of social or political values, took part in a protest or demonstration, or actively supported a candidate.

We must be careful about interpreting these results, because the sample sizes are small, particularly in Charlotte and Phoenix. Still, across all regions, the U.S.-born are far more engaged than immigrants, with the disparity being the largest in places with long histories of migration. The gap is also quite large in areas that have been heralded as new locations for immigrant activism; note the large gap, for example, in Los Angeles (where the raw sample is large enough to provide us some confidence in these estimates). On the other hand, New York and San José both have smaller relative gaps in the level of political engagement (other than voting) and also, as we will see, have more favorable public policies. Surprisingly, immigrants in Phoenix report a higher level of engagement than in other locations. But this could be a function of a relatively small sample size (and hence less precision in the estimates) and even if true may be a reaction to anti-immigrant politics in that locale.

Figure 2.12 is a more detailed look at types of civic engagement by immigrant generation across the whole United States. The tables are broken by generation because all members of the second generation have the right to vote (as they are U.S.-born) but also because civic engagement behavior can differ. Stepick, Stepick, and Labissiere (2008), like Ramakrishnan, suggest that while prejudice and discrimination tend to make immigrant youth feel isolated from mainstream electoral politics, they may also serve as a catalyst for other forms of civic participation. For instance, immigrant and nonimmigrant youth surveyed at a state college were likely to be similarly civically engaged, but the immigrant youth often preferred to serve in ways directly impacting immigrant communities, such as multilingual tutoring and antidiscrimination campaigns (Stepick, Stepick, and Labissiere 2008). Similarly, a survey of 126 undocumented Mexican high school and college students found that the vast majority (90 percent) were civically engaged in providing a social service, activism, tutoring, or functionary work (Perez et al. 2010). Of course, there are more direct mechanisms: young undocumented and allied activists, through organizations like the national Immigrant Youth Alliance and various DREAMer campaigns, have been active in struggles to reform immigration policy and practice (Nicholls 2013).

In any case, with the exception of those participating in marches and protest (the fourth category), rates of civic engagement generally increase steeply if immigrants are naturalized and as one compares the different generations. Of course, this need not be a static outcome. While civic engagement has been correlated with socioeconomic status, education, connection to political resources on arrival, and conditions and position in the sending country, factors like English-language fluency—something that public policy affects—can also have a big impact (for example, see F. C. Garcia 1997; Jones-Correa 1998; Lopez and Elrod 2006; Lopez, Kirby, and Sagoff 2005; Portes and Rumbaut 2001; Ramakrishnan 2004; Tam Cho 1999; Verba, Schlozman, and Brady 1995). In our detailed case studies, we look at whether public authorities and civic leaders are seeking to encourage involvement by immigrants—and also how immigrants themselves are organizing to make sure that their voices are heard.

Setting Up the Cases

This chapter has provided a broad demographic overview of the cases. While the complex data rarely tell a straightforward story or add up to a simple categorization, a few patterns stand out, with implications for analyzing the regional variation in receptivity in the case studies that follow.

Los Angeles, for example, had a massive inflow of immigrants in the 1980s, with change now slowing in the city but continuing in the suburbs. Mexicans are a declining presence in the region's immigrant population, but the extraordinary number of undocumented residents reflects the legacy of the earlier wave, including from Central America. This seems like a recipe for a sort of gradual acceptance of the immigrant presence—and we characterize Los Angeles as deeply impacted by immigrant social movements but underperforming in terms of policy change. This underperformance squares with the notion of a lagged response, including the lower levels of more formal political engagement suggested by the data presented earlier.

New York has a high share of foreign-born and for several decades; if readers check back to table 2.1, they can see that the gradient from long-established to recently arrived is steeper—that is, less settled—than in Los Angeles. The growing presence of immigrants in the suburbs is also pronounced in New York. The data suggest that the immigrant community is quite diverse in origin, which, when combined with the long legacy of immigration, may work against the racialization of immigrants, although perhaps not in the suburbs. Indeed, we characterize the New York region as being strongly welcoming, with important gaps in its suburbs; we connect the central city's extraordinary receptivity to the strong immigrant presence in the urban voting public but also to the city's long history as an entry point for the foreign-born.

Chicago also has a long history of migration, with its gradient from long-term to more recent immigrants similar to that of New York. However, the foreign-born share is much lower than in New York or LA, and, like Los Angeles, the share of the foreign-born is declining in the central city while rising in the suburbs. Both the low share and the relative diversity of the immigrant community—note that the second-largest group of recent arrivals hails from Eastern Europe—also helps deter the racialization of immigration, creating favorable ground for the progress that Chicago and Illinois have made in instituting programs for "New Americans." As we will see, however, immigrant incorporation needs to be understood in the context of traditional ethnic and Democratic machine politics of Cook County and its environs. Nevertheless, the shift to the suburbs suggests that this is where we may expect conflict to emerge, as in so many other cases.

The San José metro region has experienced dramatic increases in the share of the foreign-born but has not experienced the clashes of, say, Phoenix, or even Charlotte. Once again, the diversity of the immigrants, as well as their economic and education success, may help to explain this. Yet civic leadership and public policy have also played important roles. San José elites have issued strongly pro-immigrant statements—something that cannot be said of Phoenix. Certainly, the conditions in metro Phoenix are challenging: recent arrivals are largely Mexican in origin, a large number are undocumented, and Phoenix has the largest racial generation gap of our cases (although the Inland Empire is not far behind). Charlotte is the least immigrant of our case study metro areas and certainly one where we might well expect the arrival of new and different populations to create discomfort and tension. As our case study reveals, however, Charlotte initially offered a relatively warm reception, partly in keeping with the area's reputation as part of a tolerant "New South." When it became politically beneficial for some key elected officials to turn in a less pro-immigrant direction, they shifted; this suggests that we need to consider particular historical factors, like the rise of the Tea Party in North Carolina politics, to truly understand the region. Similarly, recent immigrants to the Inland Empire are mostly Mexican and, when you add in other Latinos, the most Latin American as well. We might expect this to provide more fertile grounds for the negative racialization of the immigrant community—and the Inland Empire does have the second-largest racial generation gap of our various cases. While the fractious politics of the Riverside metro area may reflect this, it is also curious that there has not been much spillover in immigrant reception or Latino political empowerment from the adjacent LA region.

In short, the data take us only partway toward understanding the terrain. Recency and demographic contrasts, along with differences in education and income, create the potential for negative stereotyping of immigrants and perceiving them as a deficit rather than a contributor. The presence of undocumented immigrants and the geographic distribution of immigrants within metropolitan areas may influence native responses as well.

But to fully understand *why* natives might be more likely in some regions to welcome immigrants and help them advance their fortunes, we must get beneath the macro trends reviewed here and closely examine the institutions and attitudes in each region. We do this next, turning from the voice of the editors to the voices of our multiple contributors. We hope the readers find that the multiplicity of these voices brings nuance not cacophony, as the contributors have worked hard together to develop a shared path toward data collection and analysis. In the concluding chapter, we come back to the task of synthesizing the cases, drawing out their implications for policy and reflecting on the need for further research. We turn first to New York, with its iconic Statue of Liberty and Ellis Island.

3

TEEMING SHORES

Immigrant Reception in the Fragmented Metropolis of New York

Els de Graauw, Diana R. Gordon,
and John Mollenkopf

The metropolitan region centered on New York City is one of the oldest and has long been the largest metro area in the United States. Given its strategic position—built around a great natural harbor connected by waterways with the U.S. hinterland and by ocean to the rest of the world—New York City early on acquired pivotal economic functions that benefited the region and indeed the nation. By the end of the nineteenth century, the city was by far the biggest capital market, banking center, corporate headquarters location, professional services provider, port, and manufacturing and wholesaling district in North America, as well as a leading center of culture, the arts, media, and consumption. Public investments—including a mass transit and regional rail system, the regional bridge, tunnel, and highway system, three major airports, and a telecommunications and information technology infrastructure—helped drive the region's growth through the twentieth century. Being the first and largest in many economic fields enabled New York City to prosper throughout the twentieth century and into the twenty-first century, even in the face of deindustrialization, globalization, racial transition, and suburbanization.

From the outset, the metropolitan region's vibrant and growing economy attracted large numbers of immigrants. Founded by the Dutch, the city was committed from the beginning to fostering commerce between strangers. Its port was the primary gateway for the great nineteenth-century waves of migrants, initially from Ireland and Germany, and later from Central, East, and Southern Europe (Reimers 2005). Every immigrant group that entered the United States through this port deposited a sizable community in New York City and its environs, even if most ultimately moved on. These groups provided the brawn to build its buildings, the skills to operate its trades, and the cultural capital to carry out its professions. As they gradually transitioned from being immigrants to American ethnics, immigrant groups wove the fabric of the region's neighborhoods, subcultures, and political dynamics. The sequential layering and occupational specialization of these groups gave the region its iconic ethnic flavors, whether it be the Irish policeman, the Jewish teacher, the West Indian subway motorman, or the African American social worker. Almost every New Yorker—or Long Islander, Westchester suburbanite, or New Jerseyan—has a family story about ancestors coming from somewhere else, making their way upward in the regional economy, and moving to a better neighborhood. Of course many individual and family struggles underlie this generally positive outcome.

This chapter examines how the contemporary process of immigrant reception is playing out across the region, contrasting New York City at the core with Long Island's Suffolk County on the eastern edge of the region. Of course the experience of reception varies tremendously within the metro area, and we do not claim that Suffolk County represents the full span of outcomes in the region's peripheral areas. But it does illustrate some key points about the region. Though Suffolk County has many ties to the city, and newcomer populations face integration challenges in both places, we find no evidence of a coordinated regional response to immigrant integration, though some immigrant-serving organizations do cross city and county lines in their work. The region's political and geographical fragmentation makes regional action on immigrant integration difficult, as do the different histories of migration to New York City and Suffolk County and their contrasting responses to immigration-generated diversity. Furthermore, in both New York City and Suffolk County, government officials have few incentives and community advocates few resources to address immigrant integration issues on a regional basis. This means that immigrant integration discussions and initiatives are localized affairs, even as the potential for regional coordination is growing.

In what follows, we first briefly describe the demographic composition of the New York City metro region, then turn to the political dynamics in immigrant and minority representation in New York City and Suffolk County. We next discuss grassroots advocacy campaigns aimed at promoting immigrant rights in both places, focusing on language access and immigrants' interactions with law enforcement officials. Our goal is to highlight factors that facilitate or hinder these advocacy efforts, both at the local and regional levels. Our analysis draws on data from forty-four interviews with local government officials and community advocates in New York City and Suffolk County between 2009 and 2014. We also draw from Census statistics, newspaper reports, documentary evidence from community-based organizations, and government and policy reports. We conclude that while immigrant advocacy groups have pushed decision makers in New York City to adopt positive policy responses to the large-scale immigration of recent decades, advocacy groups are only now countering the hostility that has characterized Suffolk County. Moreover, although suburban immigrant advocates have drawn some expertise from their central city colleagues, no regional framework or cooperation has emerged to deal with immigrant integration issues on a metropolitan scale.

Demographic Composition

Today, the twenty-five-county New York City metro region—defined by the Office of Management and Budget as the "New York–Newark–Jersey City, NY-NJ-PA Metropolitan Statistical Area" (MSA)—includes the five counties (boroughs) of New York City, the two counties of Long Island (including Suffolk), and eighteen other surrounding counties located in southeastern New York state, northern New Jersey, and eastern Pennsylvania. According to 2012 American Community Survey data, the region embraces 19.9 million residents, 5.9 million of whom are foreign-born. Of the MSA's 17.7 million residents ages five and over, 6.5 million speak a language other than English at home. The five largest ancestry groups are Italian (2.9 million), Irish (2.2 million), German (1.5 million), Puerto Rican (1.2 million), and Polish (0.9 million). West Indians (860,000) far outnumber those of English ancestry (670,000). Chinese (600,000) and Indians (510,000) also constitute large groups. Overall, 4.3 million MSA residents are Hispanic, and 3.1 million are non-Hispanic black, while just 9.7 million (51.4 percent) are non-Hispanic white.

New York City, with 8.3 million residents, including 3.1 million foreign-born (American Community Survey 2012b), is the only large old industrial city in the Northeast that managed to pull out of a demographic and economic downward spiral that began after 1950 and to exceed its then population peak (of 7.9 million). Having recovered from a net population loss of almost 600,000 between 1970 and 1980, the city grew by 1.2 million by 2012, driven largely by international migration. As in the nineteenth century, New York City has attracted more immigrants than any other city in the United States in the late twentieth and twenty-first centuries, having drawn twice as many as Los Angeles, the nation's second-largest city. As a result, New York City continues to be one of the nation's most important crucibles of immigrant integration.

As in other old immigrant gateways, the region's foreign-born have gradually spread out from initial settlement zones in the central city. Figures 3.1 and 3.2

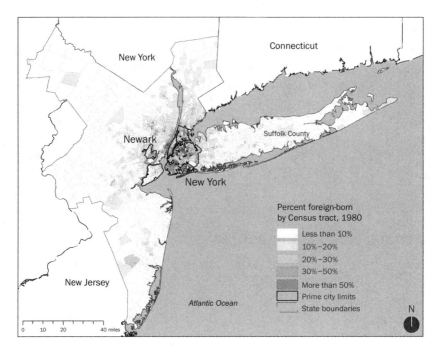

FIGURE 3.1. Percent foreign-born by Census tract, 1980, New York City

Source: 1980 Decennial Census, Census TIGER/Line, and ESRI.

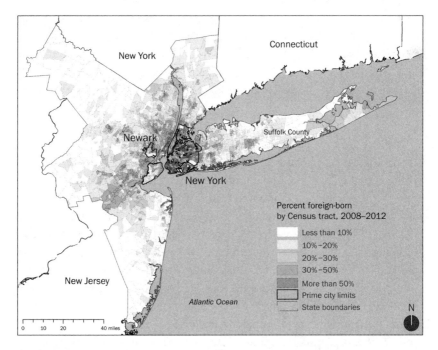

FIGURE 3.2. Percent foreign-born by Census tract, 2008–2012, New York City

Source: 2008–2012 American Community Survey (Ruggles at al. 2011), Census TIGER/Line, and ESRI.

show the pervasive spread of the foreign-born communities from their more urban concentration in 1980 to their much more widespread distribution today. The 2.9 million immigrants living in the area outside the city reside in all parts of the region, with 284,000 living in suburban Nassau County and 215,000 in exurban Suffolk County (American Community Survey 2012c). Foreign-born residents of New Jersey cluster in the inner counties around New York City, with 259,000 in Hudson County and 137,000 in Passaic County. Some of this outward movement represents suburbanization of groups that initially settled nearer the core, but many immigrants have also moved directly to the suburbs.

Given its long and continuous exposure to immigration, we will look first at the urban core, which accounts for 60 percent of the region's foreign-born, to understand the dynamics of immigrant reception in the region. Each of the "newer destinations" around that core features an interesting and distinct mix of immigrants and native-born residents. For example, 41 percent of the one hundred thousand residents of Edison, New Jersey, are foreign-born. They include a large Indian immigrant population (American Community Survey 2012c), and a Korean American served as the city's mayor between 2006 and 2010. If "ethnoburbs" (Li 1998) interested us most, Edison would be a good case against which to compare New York City in our examination of regional dynamics in immigrant integration.

We chose Suffolk County as our "new destination" because it is both connected with and distant from New York City. Part suburban sprawl, part rural outpost, and part chic summer resort (the Hamptons), it represents an outer boundary to the outward migration of the native-born and immigrants alike. Developed much later than suburban Queens or the inner Nassau County suburbs, Suffolk more closely resembles new immigrant destinations in other parts of the United States than it does most of the inner parts of the New York City metro region. Its population grew 500 percent in the second half of the twentieth century, appealing to post–World War II arrivals as an alternative (or, for part-time residents, as a complement) to New York City. Quiet, green, and affordable, Suffolk County seemed a haven of white exurbia. Until the mid-1990s, the ten towns of the county and the county's villages and hamlets were mostly non-Hispanic white and residentially segregated. Some residents commuted to New York City—and some, including police officers and firefighters, still do—but most worked in local enterprises, ranging from high tech (for example, Brookhaven National Laboratories, the State University at Stony Brook, Computer Associates Technologies, and GE Aviation Systems) to local services.

As it developed, Suffolk County attracted many kinds of immigrants. Most notably, newcomers have included low-skilled Mexicans and other Latin Americans who found jobs in construction, agriculture (including viticulture), landscaping, restaurants, and the hospitality industry. By 2000, some communities had attracted substantial numbers of racial and ethnic minorities, and minorities had become majorities in a handful of them by 2010. Riverhead (the county seat) now has a substantial immigrant Latino population; Brentwood's population of about 61,000 is now more than 60 percent Hispanic; and the university community of Stony Brook is more than 50 percent Asian. One out of six of Suffolk County's 1.5 million residents is currently foreign-born (American Community Survey 2012a). During the 1990s, the number of whites in Suffolk County declined slightly, and the number of blacks grew by 9 percent, while Asians increased by 46 percent and Hispanics by a staggering 65 percent (Suffolk County 2011). As these population trends will likely continue into the foreseeable future, questions of immigrant integration are bound to become even more salient in Suffolk County.

New York City and Suffolk County offer many sharp contrasts beyond that of city versus exurb. The city has a highly centralized and partisan political system where the mayor sets the agenda on many issues. Suffolk has an eighteen-member county legislature and a county executive who oversee certain basic services, but it also contains many towns, villages, and hamlets, as well as school and other special districts, each with its own issues. While Suffolk County has gradually become more Democratic in its partisan balance, its history is predominantly Republican. New York City, in contrast, has long been a Democratic-majority city. Furthermore, homeowner and taxpayer issues are always near the surface in Suffolk County, while tenant and social-spending issues are more common in New York City.

Suffolk County has few direct physical or political links with New York City. Certainly, the Long Island Expressway (LIE) and the Long Island Rail Road (LIRR) connect the periphery to the core. However, rail service to the eastern end of Long Island is well known for its uncertainty and slowness, while the LIE is famous for weekend traffic jams (especially during the summer). City residents and Suffolkites, furthermore, have notably different mentalities. Many Suffolk residents moved there to get away, or be away, from the city, and Suffolk County prides itself on its autonomy and Long Island assets (Suffolk County 2011). New Yorkers, in turn, think about Suffolk mainly as a weekend or vacation destination, particularly in terms of its ocean beaches. New York City also advertises itself as a well-connected global city, hosting the United Nations headquarters, 115 consulates, and more Fortune 500 companies than any other U.S. city (NYC Mayor's Office of International Affairs 2015).

Political Dynamics and Immigrant-Minority Electoral Representation

New York City

New York City comprises five separate counties or boroughs but has been consolidated in one strong-mayor governmental system since 1898. It currently has a fifty-one-member city council and also elects largely ceremonial borough presidents from each borough. The city also has a citywide comptroller, who oversees the city's finances and contracts and manages its pension funds, and a public advocate, a relatively powerless office designed to monitor and goad other city officials. The city also makes up all or part of thirteen congressional districts, twenty-six state senate districts, and sixty-five state assembly seats. In 2014, Democrats held the vast majority of these seats; Republicans held only three city council seats, one state senate seat (although three New York City Democratic senators were then voting with the Republicans), and three state assembly seats. Each county has its own party organization, and the Bronx, Queens, and Brooklyn Democratic county organizations have a strong hold on local elections. The Manhattan Democratic organization, in contrast, is relatively weak, while Staten Island is a predominantly Republican borough.

The struggle for minority empowerment in these offices and bodies has a long and tangled history (Mollenkopf 2003), but over time black and Latino representation on the city council has come to match those groups' shares of the city's voting-age citizens. Blacks, for example, make up 24 percent of voting-age citizens and hold 26 percent of seats; Latinos make up 24 percent of the potential electorate and hold 22 percent of seats. Asians are the most underrepresented group, with 11 percent of the potential voters, but only 4 percent of the seats. Overall, whites are slightly overrepresented, with 40 percent of the potential voters but 49 percent of the seats. An African American with some West Indian ancestry, William C. Thompson, served as city comptroller between 2001 and 2009, and he was succeeded by John Liu, the first Chinese American citywide elected official. Until the elevation of Melissa Mark-Viverito, a Puerto Rican, in 2014, all the speakers of the city council, who determine much of the legislative agenda, have been non-Hispanic whites. The city has had one black mayor (David Dinkins, 1989–1993). As of yet, no Asian or Latino has succeeded in capturing the city's top elective post, but they have been candidates in recent polarized mayoral elections.

Within this context, immigrant-origin candidates have gradually won election to the city council, which was enlarged and redistricted in 1991 to promote better minority representation. In that year, the first Dominican and West Indian candidates won office in Washington Heights (in Manhattan) and Flatbush (in Brooklyn), districts where their groups are concentrated. By 2014, that number had grown to five persons of Dominican background (including one immigrant), one Mexican American, one Haitian immigrant, and two immigrants from Hong Kong. They serve alongside twelve African Americans and five Puerto Ricans, so members of native-born and immigrant minority groups now hold a slight majority (twenty-six out of fifty-one) of the council seats.

While population change has gradually percolated up through the political system, many of the immigrant and native-born minority candidates have achieved office through a fairly top-down process. When generational and ethnic group succession threatens to take place, the county Democratic organizations often work hard to control which candidate from the rising group will get elected. And even when an insurgent wins, they take steps to bring him or her into the fold. These candidates often end up winning multiple-candidate primaries with a relatively small number of votes. John Liu, the former Chinese American city comptroller, was first elected to the council with Queens County Democratic organizational support.

This process is not always smooth. The first Dominican council member, Guillermo Linares, got his start through community-based organizing around education issues in northern Manhattan. He subsequently became part of the Democratic political establishment and served as the first commissioner of immigrant affairs under Mayor Michael Bloomberg. The first West Indian council member, Una Clarke, was also an outsider who became an insider. Upon her retirement, her daughter Yvette Clarke succeeded her on the council and then won a contested primary election for the U.S. Congress against the son of the African American incumbent, who was stepping down. She, too, became an influential figure in the politics of Central Brooklyn. Such gains reflect the fact that immigrants represent about 30 percent of New York City's general election voters and their children another 18 percent.

Suffolk County

Demographic changes notwithstanding, immigrant and minority political representation has not noticeably increased in Suffolk County in the last decade. One Latina sits on the eighteen-member county legislature (and several more on town councils), along with two African Americans. All eight state senators with districts in Suffolk County are white males, and Phil Ramos—a Puerto Rican born in the Bronx—is the only minority who represents one of the county's twelve state assembly districts. Ramos, a Democrat, was first elected in 2000 (and continues to serve in 2016) after redistricting created Assembly District 6 as a minority-majority district. He also filed and won a federal voting rights lawsuit to create a Latino majority District 9 in the Suffolk County Legislature in 2004. This district was initially represented by another Puerto Rican, Ricardo Montano, but he was defeated in 2013 by Monica Martinez, a young Latina political newcomer who assailed him for "absentee leadership" and occasionally siding with Republicans on issues (Brand 2013).

Suffolk County's jurisdictional fragmentation means that political issues are diverse and political power is highly decentralized. Supervisors in Suffolk County's ten towns focus more on environmental and agricultural problems than on social issues. The first concerns of most county legislators are generally taxes and economic growth, while water quality takes priority for East End politicians at all levels. Few politicians who represent the county have made immigration central in their policy agendas. But Steve Bellone, the county executive elected in 2013, has supported local efforts to improve the lives of Suffolk County's immigrants, in sharp contrast to his anti-immigrant predecessor Steve Levy. Bellone's staff has been responsive to the concerns of immigrant advocates, and he supported Monica Martinez's successful challenge to the sole incumbent Hispanic county legislator on the basis that the incumbent had insufficient commitment to his Hispanic constituents.

All three of the county's U.S. representatives are white males. They are positioned differently on immigration issues, as on other matters, and do not present a united front. Steve Israel, a liberal Democrat whose district lies mostly in Nassau County, supports comprehensive immigration reform at the national level, though he is minimally involved in local immigration issues. For six terms, Democrat Tim Bishop represented the eastern half of Suffolk County. For most of this period, Bishop supported construction of the fence along the U.S.-Mexico border, but more recently he voted against harsh immigration policies and for the DREAM Act. Overall, immigration reform was not at the top of his agenda, perhaps because the Tea Party targeted him in the 2010 and 2012 elections. The increase in Hispanic voters in Bishop's district may have helped him politically in 2012 when an anti-immigrant candidate challenged him, but it did not prevent him from losing to Republican Lee Zeldin in the Republican surge in 2014. The third congressman from Long Island, Republican Peter King, represents an area redistricted in 2011 to include many more Hispanic voters; he nonetheless often takes an anti-immigrant stance.

Despite the creation of minority-majority districts, minority voter mobilization has been low in Suffolk County, with neither Latinos nor African Americans showing high levels of turnout. Changes, however, are likely on the horizon. Among other things, a growing infrastructure of immigrant rights organizations and community groups is seeking to organize Latinos and other minorities and engage them in local civic and political affairs (Cortés 2011). Also, many children of immigrants—especially Latinos—are reaching voting age (Fiscal Policy Institute 2011). In November 2012, according to the Voting and Registration Supplement of the Current Population Survey, only 2.7 percent of the general election voters were foreign-born, but 21.6 percent more had one or two foreign-born parents. As immigrants and minorities have come to make up more of its electorate, Suffolk County has gradually become more Democratic. As public attitudes and political initiatives become more responsive to the problems of this population, these new voters may feel more energized and welcome to participate in the local political process.

Grassroots Advocacy to Promote Immigrant Rights

New York City

In the minds of many, New York City remains the quintessential immigrant gateway, with a reputation for being friendly toward newcomers. However, community advocates and most city officials who spoke with us felt strongly that the city council and mayor would not have adopted immigrant integration policies in recent years without aggressive and persistent advocacy from community-based organizations. Its long immigration history has endowed New York City with a rich infrastructure of immigrant-serving organizations, and they are strong advocates for immigrant communities. An online directory of the Mayor's Office of Immigrant Affairs lists 241 active organizations. Many religious institutions and unions also embrace immigrants' material well-being and participatory rights as a major goal. Taken together, these civil society organizations have the organizational muscle to rally support among city officials for initiatives that advance immigrant integration.

In a city as large and diverse as New York, it is complicated for these groups to build the coalitions necessary for influencing public policy on immigrant integration issues. Geographically, the city has five boroughs, fifty-nine community districts, and hundreds of neighborhoods. Demographically, its 8.3 million residents and 3.1 million foreign-born individuals hail from a wide range of nationalities and ethno-racial and socioeconomic backgrounds (American Community Survey 2012b). Politically, the city has fifty-one council members, five borough presidents, and three independently elected citywide officials, as well as over one hundred city agencies, a large number of boards and commissions, and other points of public access. The political environment is thus predisposed toward fragmentation of constituent interests and political power bases, although the strong mayor and city council speaker become focal points for constituents' actions.

Most immigrant organizations are neighborhood based, cater to particular immigrant nationality or language groups, and focus on specific service areas or policy issues. To be able to influence city politics, they work on finding common ground and articulating common agendas across immigrant groups, functional service areas, and geographies. Collaborations are also necessary because immigrant organizations can shape city policies and practices only by pooling their staff skills, membership bases, and other organizational resources.

Some collaborations have been institutionalized. The best-known is the New York Immigration Coalition (NYIC), a citywide advocacy coalition with a staff of twenty-four and nearly two hundred member organizations. It "promotes immigrants' full civic participation, fosters their leadership, and provides a unified voice and a vehicle for collective action for New York's diverse immigrant communities" (NYIC 2015). Established in 1987, the NYIC often has a seat at the policy-making table, and all our informants—including those in Suffolk County—readily identified the NYIC as a major advocacy force in the city. At the same time, not all immigrant communities in New York City participate equally in the NYIC. West Indian and West African immigrants, for example, are not well represented on its staff or among its members.

Other collaborations have occurred in a more ad hoc fashion, when organizations mobilized around particular advocacy campaigns. Issues such as language access, immigrant labor rights, housing, health care, voting rights for noncitizens, municipal ID cards, state driver's licenses, deferred action for undocumented youth, and policing and immigration enforcement have brought together immigrant organizations from across the city and involved local power brokers like the New York Civil Liberties Union and SEIU Locals 1199 (health care workers) and 32BJ (building service workers) and UNITE-HERE Local 100. This kind of coalition building is hard work, however, and several community advocates commented on ongoing tensions between immigrant organizations over turf issues as well as between smaller grassroots organizations and the larger NYIC coalition.

Many community advocates feel fortunate to work in a city where policy makers have no discernible ideological or moral reservations about immigrant rights. "It's hard for government officials to take an anti-immigrant stance in this city," a New Sanctuary Coalition staff member commented. An Immigrant Defense Project organizer added that "compared to a place like Arizona, at least city officials say they're pro-immigrant. . . . We have an audience that will listen, and we have the space to be more proactive on these issues." Finally, a Sikh Coalition employee reflected that "in New York City, conversations with city officials about immigrant rights tend to be more frank, more open, and more honest . . . and it helps that we have community advocates like [former city council speaker] Christine Quinn who have ascended to positions of power."

Indeed, it is difficult to find any statements from city officials that publicly denounce immigrants, and no local organizations push opposition to immigration. However, many advocates observed that budgetary difficulties have caused city officials to be more fiscally prudent and more wary about adopting and implementing new immigrant integration initiatives that have price tags. The size of city government, which employs about 250,000 people, also creates bureaucratic hurdles in implementing and institutionalizing integration initiatives. In sum, community advocates are less preoccupied with winning city officials' ideological and moral commitment and more focused on the daunting task of fighting the policy inertia inherent in a government the size of New York City's.

Two recent grassroots immigrant rights campaigns are illustrative. One addressed an "inclusive" issue, the second a more "exclusionary" one. The campaign to require city agencies (and certain private businesses) to create and meet standards for translation and interpretation services was a win for grassroots advocacy. The campaign to stop city officials from collaborating with federal immigration officials succeeded only recently under the de Blasio administration. Both campaigns, which are ongoing, highlight factors that facilitate and hinder community advocacy to promote immigrant rights. They also reveal that community advocates have few resources and city officials few incentives to address immigrant integration on a regional basis.

THE CAMPAIGN TO MAKE CITY GOVERNMENT MULTILINGUAL

According to Ofelia García (2002, 3), New York City has long been and continues to be "the most multilingual city in the world," making it seem as if English has been eclipsed as the vernacular. Today, many New Yorkers do lack proficiency in English: three-quarters of the city's foreign-born (ages five and over) speak a language other than English at home, and half do not speak English "very well" (American Community Survey 2012b). Lack of English proficiency creates an important barrier to educational and employment opportunities and hampers immigrants' access to public services and participation in civic and political life (Bean and Stevens 2003a; López and Estrada 2007). Because this issue affects so many different kinds of immigrants in so many areas of their lives, most immigrant-serving organizations have taken steps to strengthen immigrants' language rights, particularly with regard to accessing public services (de Graauw 2015).

In 2003, Local Law 73 created the first mandate for language access in New York City. It requires the Human Resources Administration (HRA)—the city agency that administers food stamps, Medicaid, and welfare—to provide free interpretation services regardless of the language spoken and translate application forms and key notices into Arabic, Chinese, Haitian Creole, Korean, Russian, and Spanish. Local Law 73 also created language access reporting requirements for three other safety net agencies: the Administration for Children's Services, the Department of Homeless Services, and the Department of Health and Mental Hygiene. Local Law 73 resulted from a five-year campaign mounted by a coalition of community-based organizations including the NYIC and Make the Road by Walking (now Make the Road New York, or MRNY), a grassroots organization of low-income Latinos and African Americans based mostly in Brooklyn and Queens. At the height of the campaign, over 120 more groups signed on, including SEIU Locals 32BJ and 1199, UNITE-HERE Local 6, and AFSME DC37.

As part of its campaign, the coalition targeted federal administrative and judicial officials as well as local legislators. In 1997, MRNY began documenting language discrimination at city welfare offices and, along with the NYIC, filed a civil rights complaint with the Office for Civil Rights in the U.S. Department of Health and Human Services, which found the city (and the state) to be in violation of federal civil rights legislation. In 2001, MRNY, the Puerto Rican Legal Defense and Education Fund, and the New York Legal Assistance Group won settlement of a federal class-action lawsuit, *Ramirez v. Giuliani*, about the city's (and the state's) failure to provide interpreter services and translated documents for nearly 470,000 limited-English-speaking food stamp applicants and recipients in the city. Finally, the coalition engaged in grassroots organizing that included a thousand-person march over the Brooklyn Bridge, testimonies at public hearings in city hall, and advocacy with local media to report on the issue. The resulting public attention influenced the city council to adopt Local Law 73 in 2003.

The campaign's success is explained in large part by its ability to cast language access as an anti-discrimination and civil rights issue, not an immigrant rights issue. Advocacy organizations relied on civil rights regulations to put a legal squeeze on city officials to improve access to public services for limited-English speakers. This strategy works in New York City, one community advocate commented, because "[city officials] don't want to be perceived as not doing enough to stop discrimination." Another advocate explained that the campaign's backers opted for the civil rights frame because they did not want "to polarize the issue" at a time when the debate about federal welfare reform portrayed immigrants as undeserving of government-funded services, and "Mayor Giuliani's big thing was to lower the city's welfare rolls."

The 2001 terrorist attacks on the World Trade Center and the ensuing fiscal crisis made the city council hesitant to fund language assistance services benefiting the foreign-born. The Equal Access Coalition, however, continued to mobilize around the issue and used the Immigrant Workers Freedom Ride, which culminated in New York City in October 2003, to get the attention of political candidates interested in winning Latino and other immigrant votes in the upcoming council elections. "We didn't let [candidates] speak to this crowd of nearly one hundred thousand people in Queens if they didn't first endorse the bill," said a staff member with the New York Civic Participation Project, the local organization that coordinated the New York activities for the Freedom Rides. In the end, forty-six council members supported the legislation. When Mayor Bloomberg signed the bill in December 2003, he gave his supporting speech in Spanish.

At its enactment in 2003, Local Law 73 was perhaps the strongest such legislation in the nation. It really only affected HRA, however, and it did not take long before community advocates expanded their attention to enhancing language access to other city agencies. Mini-coalitions of community-based organizations separately targeted the Department of Housing Preservation and Development, the New York City Police Department, and the Administration for Children's Services, urging city council leadership to introduce more extensive language access legislation that would cover these and other city agencies.

To head off potentially expensive and constraining legislation, the Bloomberg administration approached community advocates with the idea of an executive order setting citywide language access standards. According to one advocate, "the Mayor's Office of Immigrant Affairs was very involved," but "community organizations were not given the opportunity to comment on the order before it was published. . . . There was little room for input." But when Mayor Bloomberg signed Executive Order 120 in 2008, community organizations saw it as a big victory resulting from a decade of advocacy. This order directs all city agencies interacting with the public to provide direct services in at least the top six non-English languages spoken in the city (Spanish, Chinese, Russian, Korean, Italian, and French Creole). Since 2008, community organizations have also pressured the city council to enact Intro. 859-A (2009)—which requires chain pharmacies in the city to provide interpretation and written translation of vital documents to limited-English-proficient individuals—and Governor Andrew Cuomo to sign Executive Order 26 (2011), which requires twenty state agencies to provide translation of key documents into six non-English languages and interpretation services for all languages.

Since community organizations in New York City first took up the language access issue in 1997, their relations with city officials have often been contentious. Many advocates lament the fact that city officials have not been more open to working collaboratively with them, compelling them to use tactics such as litigation, street protests, and media shaming to get results. In commenting on the campaign for Local Law 73, one advocate said that "council members don't care about this issue unless their constituents are literally banging down their doors." Another added, "You have to be aggressive, and you need to apply constant pressure. You have to say, 'This has to happen now, and if not, we'll bother the shit out of you, lambaste you in the press, etc.' At times, you have to be nasty, otherwise [city officials] won't act."

Even ten years later, community organizations are still advocating in a contentious manner around the implementation of Local Law 73. "I'm not one of those lawyers that think litigation is the answer to everything," a Legal Services NYC staff member commented, "but we've tried to collaborate with HRA, and they're at the level where they denied the accuracy of our data that clearly shows they've failed to comply with Local Law 73." In 2009, Legal Services NYC filed a lawsuit, *Boureima et al. v. NYC HRA et al.*, against HRA on behalf of six limited-English clients who experienced discriminatory treatment while attempting to receive benefits. Legal Services NYC lost the suit on summary judgment in January 2014 and again on appeal in May 2015. Other community-based organizations are now similarly using litigation to pressure the New York City Police Department and the Board of Elections to abide by existing federal, state, and local language access laws.

Language access is a notably local affair. While advocates have engaged in some state-level advocacy, neither they nor city officials have thought about language access on a regional scale. A staff member with the Mayor's Office of Immigrant Affairs noted that they had participated only in some "best practice" meetings with the Long Island Rail Road. "Our work is [restricted] to the City of New York, so only the five boroughs," she commented. Officials of the Mayor's Office of Operations (the agency responsible for monitoring the implementation of Executive Order 120), the Administration of Children's Services, and the Department of Education also agreed that their work did not venture outside city limits.

For community-based groups, the absence of a regional perspective has more to do with the geography of their membership, limited organizational resources, and the different political cultures of New York City and Suffolk County. "We want our members to decide what issues we work on, and our members are residents of the city, not the suburbs," one explained. Another added, "Suffolk [County] is just so different. . . . It would be much more difficult for us to do that kind of language advocacy there; they're anti-immigrant." Another advocate similarly commented that "Suffolk [County] also has language access issues, especially now that their immigrant population is growing. . . . But we don't have the resources to advocate there as well, plus that's a very different political scene for us."

THE CAMPAIGN TO GET ICE OUT OF RIKERS

In addition to advocating for immigrant-friendly city policies, community organizations have mobilized against local enforcement policies and practices they see as detrimental to immigrants. In recent years, they have mounted advocacy campaigns targeting the New York City Police Department (NYPD) and the Department of Correction (DOC). The NYPD's "stop and frisk" practice, which increased sharply after 2003 in the city's less affluent black and Latino neighborhoods, has raised the ire of community advocates, as has excluding turban-wearing Sikhs from the police force and the NYPD's exempting itself from the city's "don't ask, don't tell" policy. Community advocates have also campaigned to stop the NYPD and DOC from sharing information, under the Criminal Alien and Secure Communities programs, with federal immigration officials, who then detain and deport undocumented immigrants.

A small coalition of immigrant rights organizations, law schools, and public defender offices mounted the "Get ICE Out of Rikers" campaign in 2008. For a long time, U.S. Immigration and Customs Enforcement (ICE) has stationed officers at Rikers Island, the city's main jail complex, which houses fourteen thousand inmates. Like other state and federal law enforcement agencies, ICE has real-time access to the DOC's intake records, which include information on inmates' country of birth. ICE uses these records to initiate investigations and place immigration detainers on individuals it believes are eligible for deportation. Many immigrants receiving these detainers are not accused of serious crimes, have not been proven guilty, and/or have no previous criminal record. When the city drops charges, as is common, the DOC releases such individuals, but ICE typically places them directly in detention and puts them through deportation proceedings. Between 2008 and 2010, ICE detained over seven thousand immigrant New Yorkers each year, 91 percent of whom were deported (NYU School of Law, Immigrant Defense Project, and Families for Freedom 2012). Community advocates have argued that ICE's stepped-up enforcement activities have turned the city's criminal justice system into a pipeline to immigration detention and deportation, in the process breaking apart many families and immigrant neighborhoods.

Since the "Get ICE Out of Rikers" campaign was launched, community organizations have urged the DOC to stop sharing information with ICE and to stop honoring ICE detainers. City officials did not meet these demands but did institute several changes in response to community advocacy pressure. For example, the DOC has allowed immigrant rights organizations to hold "know your rights" workshops at Rikers and required ICE agents to wear uniforms and properly identify themselves with inmates. Also, after intense negotiations with the city council, Mayor Bloomberg—who long defended the city's cooperation with federal immigration officials—ultimately gave his support to three pieces of legislation in 2011 and 2013 that limit the DOC's collaboration with ICE. Despite these policy changes, the DOC still granted 73 percent of all ICE detainer requests between October 2012 and September 2013 and transferred over three thousand people to federal immigration officials (Ruiz 2014).

More recently, following the 2014 decision in *Galarza v. Szalczyk et al.*, in which the U.S. Court of Appeals for the Third Circuit ruled that states and localities are not mandated to detain people based on ICE detainer requests, community advocates have renewed their advocacy to end all collaboration between city agencies and ICE, now under the slogan of creating an "ICE-Free NYC." Their advocacy brought about more substantial policy change when Mayor de Blasio and city council Speaker Mark-Viverito began supporting a more progressive agenda. In October 2014, community advocates pushed an overwhelming majority of city council members to pass legislation (Intros. 486-A and 487A) to stop the NYPD and DOC from honoring ICE detainers, except for individuals convicted of violent or serious felonies. This legislation, a notable victory for immigrant rights supporters, further limits the circumstances in which city officials can cooperate with federal immigration officials. Around the same time, advocates pushed the city council to approve the use of municipal ID cards to make life easier for the city's estimated five hundred thousand undocumented immigrants. The IDNYC program was launched in January 2015, with overwhelming demand and long lines for the card at libraries and other enrollment centers. By late September, the city had issued about 540,000 municipal ID cards (Fermino 2015).

Several factors long impeded community organizations from changing policy at Rikers Island. First, the city's policy makers and even some community groups long avoided the topic of ICE collaborations with the DOC. Mayor Bloomberg had no interest in the issue until late into his third term, and he did not let his criminal justice coordinator talk with advocates about the DOC-ICE collaborations. Similarly, the city council was late and reluctant to address the collaboration between ICE and DOC. "We're dealing with immigrants who have run-ins with the criminal justice system," commented an advocate with the Immigrant Defense Project. "They cannot easily be categorized as your good, hardworking immigrants. . . . It's a much tougher political sell [for council members]." Even some community groups found the issue complicated. "The last thing [advocates] want to talk about is immigrants they can't label as pure and hardworking," explained the same advocate. "It's such a value-driven system, and when you have an immigrant with serious convictions, what do you do then? . . . If you can't find a way to talk about these issues effectively, then how are you going to bring about change?" The difficulty of framing the topic in a way that enabled policy makers to speak up in defense of immigrants had hindered community advocacy.

Second, prior to the launch of the Secure Communities program in New York City in 2012, there was no specific city policy for community advocates to target. DOC-ICE collaborations had been going on since the 1990s but were never codified. Former DOC commissioner Martin Horn could not say exactly when they started, but they predated the terrorist attacks of 2001 and have been more routinized since then: "[The collaboration] unfolded sort of willy-nilly; it just grew by itself." A 2008 Freedom of Information Act request by community advocates also turned up empty-handed. "It would be better if there was something concrete, like a policy," a New Sanctuary Coalition activist commented, "because then we could fight it. But there is . . . nothing, just a long-established practice." Community advocates had the difficult task of fighting an informal bureaucratic practice that escaped the attention of the mayor and city council for a long time.

Community organizations also face the difficulty that the DOC simply does not see the issue the way advocates do. Advocates argue that the DOC facilitates the work of ICE, but the DOC maintains that it treats ICE the same as any other law enforcement agency seeking access to DOC data. "I can't as a correction commissioner pick and choose among law enforcement agencies," former DOC commissioner Horn explained. "Either I allow law enforcement agencies access to [DOC intake records], which essentially is public information, or I don't." He added that ICE's presence on Rikers Island was not controversial in the wake of 9/11. Advocates, however, have criticized the DOC for whistling to the tune of federal immigration officials, especially since the Obama administration started focusing the criminal justice system on identifying undocumented immigrants. Horn commented, though, that ICE's increased reliance on DOC data was at the initiative of ICE, not the DOC, but that the practice has now attracted attention.

Overall, there has been little regional dynamism to immigrant detention and deportation issues. Since the closing of the Varick Street Detention Center, a federal facility, in February 2010, ICE has sent many immigrant detainees to federal facilities in New Jersey. This has made community advocates more aware of how federal immigration enforcement initiatives are affecting the larger region. Some community organizations, including the Immigrant Defense Project, have subsequently developed relations with New Jersey groups, including the American Friends Service Committee, to discuss ideas for forging a common front against implementing the Secure Communities program. At the same time, resource constraints deter community organizations from building regional collaborations. Given that federal immigration enforcement affects all the cities and suburbs around New York City, the potential for regional activity remains.

Suffolk County

New York City activists view Suffolk County as generally anti-immigrant and a difficult place to organize, which was certainly accurate until the late 2000s. The Suffolk County Legislature often took cues from the county executive, neglecting immigrant needs and even failing to note violence against working-class Hispanic newcomers from Mexico and Central America. Although a coalition of immigrant supporters had formed and met regularly, it had little influence in the large, geographically fragmented area of Suffolk County and its Republican political culture. But much has changed in the past few years: public attitudes and political initiatives have become more responsive to the problems of immigrants, and local activists are building a movement with activities bent on demonstrating the political power of the Latino community.

STEVE LEVY AND THE HIGH TIDE OF ANTI-IMMIGRANT SENTIMENT

Much of the earlier anti-immigrant venom can be attributed to the previous county executive, Steve Levy. A former assemblyman, Levy was elected to office in 2003 as a Democrat,[1] on a promise of initiating strict enforcement efforts against undocumented immigrants. He attracted national attention for his rants against immigrants and their supporters, whom he publicly described as "communist," "anarchist," and "lunatic fringe" (Southern Poverty Law Center 2009, 20–21). The police also contributed to the poisonous atmosphere by failing to respond to the harassment and physical attacks on immigrants, often instigated by anti-immigrant organizations, which started in 1999. The eighteen-member county legislature—with a majority of Republicans and only two Latinos, both from the heavily minority communities of Brentwood and Central Islip—was hostile to Hispanic workers, and it proposed ordinances that fed anti-immigrant sentiment. Finally, a murderous beating in the town of Shirley landed the two perpetrators in prison for long terms and led the federal Department of Justice's Community Relations Service to intervene. Over the next few years, day laborers were victimized at a rate of more than one hundred times that of the Northeast region overall, in the affluent Hamptons as well as in working-class towns to the west on Long Island (Federal Bureau of Investigation 2004). Not surprisingly, the Southern Poverty Law Center titled its 2009 report on anti-immigrant violence in Suffolk County "Climate of Fear" and referred to Levy as "the enabler" of the widespread nativist mood (Southern Poverty Law Center 2009).

The events triggering that 2009 report also spurred a turnaround in public sentiments on immigration issues and the development of immigrant advocacy. In November 2008, a group of boys who called themselves the "Caucasian

Crew" fatally stabbed Marcelo Lucero, a thirty-seven-year-old Ecuadoran immigrant, in what turned out to be the latest instance of a regular game of "beaner-hopping," or harassing and attacking Latino men presumed to be immigrants. The attack galvanized the county. The Long Island Immigrant Alliance (LIIA), the only coalition of immigrant-serving organizations in Suffolk County at the time, held press conferences, organized a two-thousand-person vigil at the murder site, and demanded that the county legislature take action against hate crimes. Within a week after the murder, immigrant organizations developed Long Island Wins, a public relations and communications campaign to be waged through its website and blogs. Responding to many complaints, the Civil Rights Division of the U.S. Department of Justice opened an investigation of police discrimination against Latinos and indifference to crimes committed against them (DOJ-CRD 2011).

In this volatile context, supporters of immigrant rights had a hard time figuring out how to bring about inclusive change. The LIIA had brought together both small immigrant organizations and larger organizations such as SEIU Local 1199, Catholic Charities, Jobs with Justice, the New York Civil Liberties Union (NYCLU), and the local branch of the American Jewish Committee. Such organizational diversity was necessary to secure a hearing before the county legislature and other political leaders, especially since it was still dangerous to be publicly pro-immigrant in Suffolk County. As a member of an immigrant organization explained in 2009, acting in support of immigrants "out here . . . it is like being called terrorists." Levy was tremendously popular, according to two Latino county legislators who spoke to us, and he was reelected in 2007 with 96 percent of the vote. He used his popularity to help elect many local legislators and exert influence over county government to stop funding several small immigrant-serving organizations. For fear of biting the hand that fed them, those organizations chose not to be vocally or visibly involved in the immigrant rights work of the coalition. They had to work within what the director of the Suffolk County chapter of the NYCLU described as "a top-down perpetuation of hate and intolerance."

For the time being, activists had only the media platform of Long Island Wins and the newly formed Hate Crimes Task Force sponsored by DuWayne Gregory, an African American member of the county legislature. The legislature did pass Resolution 164–2010 to support the appointment of a hate crimes coordinator in the county Crime Victims Center. Community activists, however, could not advocate the inclusive initiatives supported by their counterparts in New York City. Their numbers were small, they were constantly on the defensive, and only the two minority legislators and local labor unions joined them in opposing bills targeting day laborers.

NEW POLITICAL LEADERSHIP AND OPPORTUNITIES
FOR INCLUSIVE CHANGE

After 2009, however, the mood shifted, and several important developments in 2011 offered new opportunities. In March, Levy announced that he would not run for a third term as county executive following an investigation by the Suffolk district attorney into his campaign fund-raising activities (*Newsday* 2011). The town supervisor of Babylon, Democrat Steve Bellone, was the likely successor. Endorsed by Governor Andrew Cuomo and Long Island's daily newspaper, *Newsday*, Bellone won the November election with 57 percent of the vote. His initial message was a conventional promise of efficiency and help for beleaguered taxpayers, but everyone knew that he would have to put immigration issues on his policy agenda. Bellone had already sent a powerful message at a candidate debate a week earlier in Central Islip, a largely minority and immigrant community. Hundreds of people turned out for what *Newsday* called a "historic" and "essential" meeting where residents were able to ask questions about the most immediate problems of their neighborhoods, including gangs, unemployment, farmworker visas, and anti-Muslim acts. "I hope we've started something here," Bellone reflected optimistically (Brown 2011).

The year 2011 also ushered in new organizational resources for immigrant rights advocacy. Local immigrant rights activists were energized by the statewide language access policy (Executive Order 26) signed by Governor Cuomo in 2011. Now, they believed, it was Suffolk's turn. "If the state can do it," one local organizer commented, "so can we." In November 2012, Bellone issued a countywide Language Access Policy (Executive Order 10–2012), making Suffolk the first suburban county in the country with an order that mandates interpretation and translation for six non-English languages (Spanish, Portuguese, Haitian Creole, Polish, Italian, and Chinese) in all county services. Noting that 20 percent of Suffolk residents ages five and over spoke a language other than English at home, and half of those struggled with spoken and written English, the order copied many of the provisions of the state Executive Order 26 but gave greater detail, including the prohibition of online translation tools. Given Suffolk's anti-immigrant past, a key aspect of the order was to prohibit county officials from inquiring into the immigration status of persons using county language services.

Neither the election debate nor the language access policy would have occurred without the growing strength of the local advocacy community. Although LIIA had provided an important initial organizing arena for a diverse group of immigrant supporters, it did not constitute what one community organizer calls the "advocacy infrastructure" necessary to make sustainable inroads into an environment so hostile to immigrants. That, however, is changing. Make the Road New York (MRNY), the fourteen-thousand-member immigrant organization that has been so important in the policy battles in New York City, opened an office in Brentwood in 2011. At this Long Island office, activists provide services such as English-language classes and meet regularly to develop and pursue strategies for policy change. The Long Island Civic Engagement Table (LICET)—a nonprofit organization led by MRNY, New York Communities for Change, the LIIA, and the Central American Refugee Center—seeks to transform the culture of civic engagement on Long Island by developing grassroots participation and leadership in immigrant and low-income communities of color. The Hagedorn Foundation, a Long Island–based foundation whose program priorities include immigrant assistance services and civic engagement, has simultaneously provided crucial support to finance the growth of this emerging advocacy infrastructure.

The newly organized immigrant rights groups that have advocated for better language access have drawn not only from policy advances at the state level, but also from local resources, as a community advocate at the Empire Justice Center described to us in an interview in April 2014:

> We saw disparities in the treatment of Spanish-speaking people by county agencies and delays in the provision of social services, because no one was available to communicate with them. Police were unable to prepare proper incident reports, housing complaints were not properly recorded, and health department communications were poor—the problem carried over into all areas. Our [Long Island Advocates] Coalition included domestic violence service providers, people who work with the disabled, and others. We started by identifying problems—collecting stories, making site visits to programs, recording problems. And we met with the Department of Social Services, the county police department, and the courts, especially the Family Court. We got them to agree on improvements—signage, hiring bilingual workers, more training for staff.

Also, the groups now captured the attention and support of County Executive Bellone, who instituted the symbolic "Welcoming Week" two years in a row and endorsed the work of the county's Office of Minority Affairs. In 2012, Bellone also appointed Luis Valenzuela—executive director of the LIIA and previously anathema to Suffolk County politicians—to a seat on the county's Human Rights Commission. After the legislature confirmed the appointment unanimously, the headline of a *Newsday* article read, "Clearly, Bellone Is No Levy on Immigration" (Brand 2012).

Implementation of the county language access policy is ongoing as of 2015. "There's lots of change, but still lots of work needed to get support for new policies," said the LICET coordinator. The advocate at the Empire Justice Center added that in working with county agencies on developing their language access plans, she finds some more accepting than others. "Some say, 'They should just speak English.'" Her group is not above a little manipulation, though. "Our approach is to say, 'Wouldn't you like to be a shining model?'" She mentioned a good working relationship with the Suffolk County Police Department, which recently entered into a settlement with the U.S. Department of Justice after a federal investigation found patterns of police discrimination that included lack of language access and cultural diversity on the staff. "They have to comply with the DOJ order and also with the county, so their incentive to cooperate is great." The police have become more proactive as a result by installing phones in sector cars, so police officers can communicate with Language Line, the company that has contracted with the county to provide translation by phone if no one is available to translate in person.

Language access is not the only integration issue highlighted by Suffolk County immigrant rights organizations. The campaigns of MRNY and the LICET have also included comprehensive immigration reform and passage of a state and federal DREAM Act, though neither has yet borne fruit. At a 2014 community forum sponsored by the LICET, more than half the forty audience members left cell phone messages with Representative Peter King, Suffolk County's only Republican congressional representative, urging him to sign a discharge petition to bring the Senate's comprehensive immigration reform bill to the House floor. At earlier meetings with leaders of Suffolk County's advocacy community, King—formerly an immigration hard-liner—had promised to urge House Speaker John Boehner to take action on immigration reform and provide most undocumented immigrants with a path to citizenship. He wrote Boehner on April 23, 2014. In late 2014, the activists succeeded in getting both the sheriff and the county legislature to agree not to honor ICE detainers unless immigrant defendants are charged with serious felonies.

King's change of perspective cannot be attributed solely to immigrant rights advocates. His district was redrawn in 2012 to take in a much larger proportion of Democrats and minority voters. While only 6 percent of voters in his old district were Latinos, they made up 18 percent of the total in his new district (Brune 2012). The coordinator of the LICET commented that advocacy organizations have changed the way they engage with King and his staff, which has opened new doors for dialogue. "Instead of beating up on him," he said, "we have been meeting with him in good faith and going in with responsible leaders like the Irish lobby for immigration reform, the union, educators. . . . It's constructive engagement." That engagement, however, may not go very far. After President Obama announced administrative initiatives to defer deportation and provide work visas for additional selected undocumented immigrants in November 2014, King told

Politico that the president had exceeded his executive authority and that his new initiatives amounted to "mass amnesty."

Nevertheless, as some politicians have toned down the rhetoric and activists have relied less on confrontational tactics, more dialogue and engagement on immigrant integration issues have emerged in Suffolk County. Bellone and his staff are respectful of the advocates and willing to meet with them regularly. Relations with county legislators have also markedly improved in the last few years. "I make sure to call John Kennedy [the Republican minority leader] every time there is an issue to come before the legislature," commented the director of the Suffolk County chapter of the NYCLU. "He is somewhat conservative, but good at considering the opposite view. I can talk to him for an hour on the phone, even if he is voting the other way." It is still a problem, though, that the county legislature has so few minority legislators. Two Latinos (Vivian Viloria-Fisher and Ricardo Montano) with long tenures on the county legislature moved on in recent years, both making unsuccessful bids for higher office. In early 2014, Monica Martinez (a young Latina school administer representing Brentwood), William Spencer (an African American otolaryngologist representing Huntington), and DuWayne Gregory (an African American currently serving as the legislature's presiding officer) are the only three minorities in the eighteen-member county legislature. All three are Democrats.

Despite the recent move toward inclusion, Suffolk County advocacy organizations have engaged in little regional work on immigrant integration issues. Suffolk County's immigrant rights activists, according to the LICET coordinator, are "having the same conversations as in New York City ten years ago." This does not mean, however, that they want to take cues from their more advanced city counterparts or that they want to collaborate with them. Suffolk County activists feel fortunate to have easy access to the expertise of city-based lawyers and others who can help with technical problems, yet underscored that the advocacy agendas and styles are different in the two places. Some local activists also resent the idea—expressed by some New Yorkers—that city tactics should also work in Suffolk. On this point, the director of the Suffolk County chapter of the NYCLU commented that "it's important for Long Island that it's building its own progressive movement." Suffolk activists understand, however, that New York City is in a vanguard position, and they gladly learn what the city has done, as long as they need not try to duplicate it in their own communities. One organizer with MRNY commented that she would like Suffolk organizations to join forces with New York City activists on state and federal issues, while working to maintain local autonomy to effect change locally.

The logistics of organizing are more difficult in Suffolk County than in New York City. It is not an exaggeration to say that on Long Island—and particularly in Suffolk County—geography is destiny. The size of the county and the lack of public transportation make it difficult for grassroots organizations and their members to come together to plan actions and develop advocacy agendas. It is challenging, for example, to get Latino workers from Wyandanch to attend a hearing in the county seat of Riverhead, more than forty miles away, when they have no car or are not legally permitted to drive. It is similarly difficult to organize DREAM students or to do outreach to expand the universe of recipients of the federal Deferred Action for Childhood Arrivals program.

Overall, the changed mood in Suffolk County—which one advocate described as "a discursive shift"—has made immigrant rights activists more optimistic about future policy changes. Community advocates referenced a 2013 poll that suggests that 80 percent of Long Island voters now "somewhat" or "strongly" favor immigration reform with a path to citizenship for most undocumented immigrants (Harstad Strategic Research 2013). They also spoke proudly of the recently enacted language access policy, while adding that they will continue to work on its successful implementation. They expect to organize more DREAM-ers, and they are gearing up to help eligible undocumented immigrants to apply for temporary deportation relief and work permits under the administrative initiatives announced by President Obama in November 2014. The activists think they can bring about these policy changes, pointing to the solidarity and unity among local organizations. "On Long Island, advocates work together really well," the director of the Suffolk County chapter of the NYCLU commented. "It's a growing community with no turf wars; we know whom to go to for specific issues, and we have no time to be petty. For now, that's something we should take advantage of."

No Regional Response to Immigrant Integration

Suffolk County's turn away from an anti-immigrant and nativist orientation is a case in point of how immigrants have received a relatively warm welcome across the New York City metro region. In New York City itself, the large immigrant electorate, the favorable public opinion toward immigrants, and many immigrant-origin elected officials have enabled immigrant rights advocates to make substantial strides on the issues that concern them. Suffolk County, in turn, has transformed from a place brimming with hatred toward undocumented Latino immigrants, where local public officials benefited from mobilizing anti-immigrant sentiment, to a place where immigrant rights organizations have started to develop a basic infrastructure to advocate for inclusive policies with local officials who are more willing to engage with the county's rapidly diversifying population. But even though New York City and Suffolk County now both recognize and respond to the policy needs of their immigrant residents, we cannot detect any regional coherence in the development, enactment, or execution of immigrant integration initiatives.

The absence of such a regional response reflects how different New York City and Suffolk County are as immigrant destinations. New York City has a long history of immigration and considerable experience with addressing immigrant issues in an inclusive manner. The city has a well-developed infrastructure of immigrant-serving organizations, its city council includes a significant number of immigrant-origin legislators, and immigrant voters are already flexing their power in local elections. Suffolk County, by contrast, is a new immigrant destination and relatively new to questions of immigrant diversity. There is an emerging yet comparatively thin infrastructure of immigrant-serving organizations, the county legislature has few immigrant-origin legislators, and immigrant voters have yet to be incorporated into the electoral process. As a result, each place addresses immigrant issues in a different way. The more experienced immigrant rights organizations in New York City can afford to be more aggressive in their advocacy with local, state, and federal officials, while those in Suffolk County use a more congenial and collaborative advocacy style. These and other differences make it difficult for the region to come together and develop a common response to shared immigrant integration challenges; and advocates in Suffolk County cherish their autonomy and want to develop their own solutions that are fitting with local circumstances.

The absence of a regional response also has an institutional cause and can partly be explained by the fragmented nature of politics in the region as a whole. The New York City metro region is a huge, complex, and diverse region that—in the classic phrase of Robert C. Wood (1961)—spans "1,400 governments" across twenty-five counties in four states. No inclusive regional council of governments or any other administrative structure comprehends this vast expanse. The few entities that do operate across jurisdictional lines are highly focused on specific functions, without social policy mandates that could include immigrant integration. The bi-state Port Authority of New York and New Jersey—which operates the region's major airports, the Hudson River tunnels and bridges, the PATH transit line, the port itself, and various real estate operations—is one such example. Another is the Metropolitan Transportation Authority, a New York State-City agency that operates the New York City transit system and the regional commuter rail systems. Finally, the federally mandated regional transportation planning body, the New York Metropolitan Transportation Commission, mainly has regional efficiency goals rather than regional equity goals that might include immigrant integration.

In addition to this institutional "silence," no other voices have articulated a regional response to immigrant integration. In its regional plan, *A Region at Risk* (Yaro and Hiss 1996), the Regional Plan Association (RPA) highlighted equity issues but framed them in terms of transportation and housing equity, as well as access to jobs, not immigrant integration. Despite New York's long tradition of regionalist thinking—whether through the RPA, the urban planning programs at its leading universities, or the region's various think tanks— no comprehensive analysis of regional immigrant integration challenges has been undertaken.

Even civil society actors focused on immigrant integration do not try to tackle the issue on a regional scale. The philanthropies in the region that invest in immigrant integration do so mainly on a national, not regional scale. Only the relatively small Hagedorn Foundation on Long Island has made immigrant civic engagement in the region a funding priority. With the exception of Make the Road New York—which now has offices in New York City and Brentwood, Long Island—immigrant rights organizations do not have a regional outlook or network. The New York Immigration Coalition and the Long Island Immigrant Alliance communicate with each other and similar organizations in other states, including the New Jersey Immigration Policy Network, but they do not advocate on a regional scale. Localized membership demands, scarcity of organizational resources, and the region's vast geographical scale make regional advocacy around immigrant integration challenging. Similarly, the New York City metro region has among the highest union densities anywhere in the country (and many unions include immigrant members), but they too are divided into geographic jurisdictional areas that impede common campaigns. Finally, other potential institutional proponents of immigrant integration, such as the Catholic Church, with its dioceses and archdioceses, are similarly divided.

Given that the New York City metro region counts more residents than any but the biggest European nations, but has no regional government to call its own, it is perhaps not surprising that its response to the challenges of continued immigration has lacked regional coherence. Public choice theorists might think that this is good, allowing myriad localities to develop their own responses to their own immigrant integration problems. And indeed, no one response will solve all the problems. At the same time, the region's core and periphery could clearly benefit from working more closely on immigrant integration issues, sharing issue expertise, advocacy strategies, and organizational resources. This will be especially true when federal immigration reform is enacted. In that scenario, many hundreds of thousands of undocumented immigrants in the region will be able to pursue a path to citizenship, and they will need assistance in further incorporating into the economic and civic life of the region.

4

MACHINE MATTERS

The Politics of Immigrant Integration in the Chicago Metro Area

Jaime Dominguez

Most public officials in Chicago and the surrounding metro area actively support immigrant integration in the belief that immigrants reinvigorate aging communities and contribute to their economies. Currently, immigrants and their native-born children make up almost a third of the region's population. Public opinion among native-born residents in suburban areas with less experience of immigration is decidedly more ambivalent (Krysan, Hall, and Washington 2010). As a result, some local governments in the region have responded less positively toward the rapid growth of the foreign-born. They have adopted measures to relegate immigrants to the periphery of civic life. In these places, local officials believe that providing education and other public services to immigrants puts a strain on their budget, and a few have even implemented rigid and hostile policies akin to those in Arizona. However, they do so in a context in which the State of Illinois and the City of Chicago have played a particularly strong role in framing a pro-immigrant response.

As the third-largest city in America and one that was originally built on the symbiosis between immigration and industrialization, it is not surprising that immigrants are once more reshaping the resident population of the Chicago metro area, including such suburban localities as Waukegan, Cicero, Carpentersville, Melrose Park, and Elgin. While substantial numbers of Poles, Indians, Chinese, and Filipinos have moved to the region, Mexican immigrants are by far the largest group. Indeed, they helped the City of Chicago to make its first population gain in almost fifty years in 2000. While Chicago has a long-standing Puerto Rican population, the great majority of Latinos in greater Chicago are of

Mexican origin. The fourfold Latino population increase between 1970 and 2000 also helped make Chicago an overwhelmingly minority-majority city (Dominguez 2007; Puente 2010; Paral 2011). Many observers consider the Mexican community, which accounts for 14 percent of the region's labor force, to be a robust economic catalyst (Beal 2007; O'Connor 2007). More than half of the growth in owner-occupied homes has occurred in this community, with household incomes in excess of $20 billion (Ready and Brown-Gort 2005).

As discussed in chapter 2, and shown in figures 4.1 and 4.2, the central city of Chicago and even more its suburbs have experienced significant growth in immigrant populations since 1980, though not at the same pace as LA or New York or San José. This may reflect the larger demographic trajectories of metropolitan Chicago, as the city lost population between 2000 and 2010 and the metro area grew relatively slowly. Today, 16.6 percent of the region's 9.6 million residents are foreign-born, and another 15.2 percent are the children of an immigrant (March 2013 Current Population Survey). Almost two-fifths of these first- and second-generation immigrants are of Mexican origin, with those of Polish, Indian, and Chinese origin, the next-biggest immigrant-origin groups, lagging far behind.

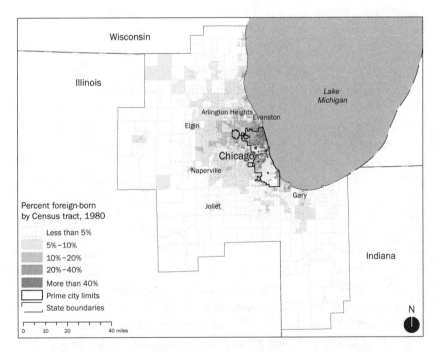

FIGURE 4.1. Percent foreign-born by Census tract, 1980, Chicago, IL

Source: 1980 Decennial Census, Census TIGER/Line, and ESRI.

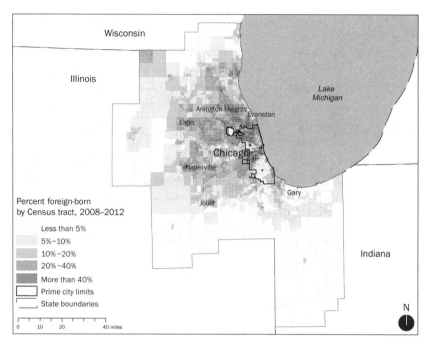

FIGURE 4.2.   Percent foreign-born by Census tract, 2008–2012, Chicago, IL

Source: 2008–2012 American Community Survey (Ruggles et al. 2011), Census TIGER/Line, and ESRI.

This chapter examines the political implications of and policy responses to the rapid growth of the Latino immigrant population first in the City of Chicago and then in some of its suburbs. Their arrival has challenged legislators and government institutions to be more responsive to the political claims of this burgeoning young population (Andrade 2010; Mendoza 2010; Munoz 2009; C. Soto 2010). In the context of the decline in the native non-Hispanic white and black populations, they have gradually become a larger share of the city's voting-age citizens (now accounting for 17 percent, compared to 26 percent for blacks and just under 50 percent for whites). Under these electoral conditions, the city's still-dominant white elected officials (though from a group in demographic decline) find it in their interest to extend greater symbolic and substantive representation to Latinos. These new circumstances have given elected leaders representing immigrant communities greater confidence about making political demands on both blacks and whites in the Cook County Democratic Party establishment and the Chicago political machine (Funes 2010; J. Garcia 2009; Nunez 2010; Yimer 2010).

The incorporation of the last great wave of Eastern European immigrants over the twentieth century has influenced Chicago's present governing practices in many ways, helping to "deracialize" the context of reception for Latino immigration. As such, immigrants of Latino origin in the larger metro area have benefited from not being boxed into a black-white racial paradigm. Indeed, they have been a swing constituency between the two. This has been important for political advancement and coalition building, because it created political spaces for immigrant-oriented social service and social justice organizations and immigrant-origin elected officials to pursue their favored policies in a politically strategic manner without being negatively racialized (Arango 2010; Kabba 2010; Munoz 2009). Since the early 1990s, Latino immigrants have benefited from former mayor Richard M. Daley's efforts to recruit, mobilize, and incorporate them into his governing coalition. The resulting Latino visibility in his administration gave pro-immigrant advocates entry points into policy formation. Today, Mayor Rahm Emanuel is following a similar strategy by, for instance, having established an office to deal with immigrant rights issues, the Office of New Americans.

The presence of a significant Latino elected leadership arising from the city's large and long-settled Puerto Rican population has also helped to foster a positive political context. In fact, some of the city and state's most ardent and prominent advocates for immigrant rights, fairer political representation, and greater political incorporation, like Congressman Luis Gutiérrez, are of Puerto Rican, not Mexican, origin. As non-Mexicans advocating on behalf of the undocumented, these politicians avoid the stigma of being seen as too politically biased toward the rapidly growing Mexican immigrant community. These Puerto Rican legislators feel they have room to speak boldly on matters relating to the region's largely Mexican immigrant population. Besides Gutiérrez, they include former city treasurer and the first Latina elected citywide, Miriam Santos, former state senator and first Latino city clerk Miguel Del Valle, and former Cook County commissioner and current alderman Roberto Maldonado.

Immigrants and the Machine

The Cook County Democratic political machine's long history of integrating immigrants has helped lead the city and county into being a place that welcomes new immigrants. Historically, political power in Chicago has been centralized in the hands of the Democratic Party and its party chairman. As in other machine-controlled cities, the longevity of party bosses and their governing apparatus has depended on successfully recruiting and retaining support from immigrant communities. Since the founding of the Chicago Democratic machine in 1931, electoral support from immigrants has allowed mayors Anton Cermak, Ed Kelly, Richard J. Daley, and his son Richard M. Daley to maintain control over the polity. In return, the party hierarchy has channeled material benefits through the precinct and ward organizations in such a way as to maintain loyalty from its white ethnic and working-class immigrant constituents (Dahl 1961). This relationship continues today; the only difference is that Latino immigrants, primarily of Mexican origin, are gradually replacing Chicago's white ethnics.

Descendants of white European immigrant voters provided the foundation of Chicago's Democratic machine for most of the twentieth century. The Irish emerged as the first ethnic power brokers, but the influx of new groups like the Poles, Italians, and Jews forced the machine to adapt, target, recruit, and incorporate them into the power apparatus over time (Trounstine 2008). Today, the Democratic organization sees Latinos as the newest potential constituency for the machine.

The city government's structure helps the machine to stay connected with immigrant communities. With the nation's second-largest city council, at fifty members, Chicago is divided into relatively small wards (districts) of about fifty thousand residents each, reflecting the geographical composition of the city. This electoral arrangement translates demography into politics fairly rapidly (with the obvious lags for naturalization, political learning, and displacing earlier generations). Ward-level political life is organized around group-based representation and is sensitive to new groups, including African Americans in the postwar era (Pinderhughes 1997). The white elected officials within the machine have relied heavily on winning political loyalty from Latino and other immigrants and using their influence to offset that of the black constituencies of the machine. While most black elected officials are loyal members of the machine, the biggest single challenge to it came from that community with the election of the city's first African American mayor, Harold Washington, in 1983. The desire to avert future challenges of this type, in turn, has given the machine its newer ethnic and class character (Simpson 2001; Trounstine 2008).

The Role of Latinos in the Formation of the Daley Political Coalition

This underlying dynamic led Mayor Richard M. Daley to focus on winning the electoral and governing support of Latinos as a key to his governing coalition after 1989. As a result, Daley was at the forefront of making greater Chicago a receptive place for new immigrants, whom he welcomed as a partner in Chicago's governing institutions (Dominguez 2007).

Richard M. Daley's mayoral victory provided both long-resident Latinos and Latino immigrants with an opportunity to chart a new path of political empowerment. In the face of a previous history of tension and competition between white ethnics and African Americans, Twenty-Sixth Ward alderman Luis Gutiér-rez's decision to support Daley, though Gutiérrez had first come to office as an opponent of the machine and an ally of Mayor Washington, would redefine Chi-cago's political landscape. (Gutiérrez now serves in Congress and is a major pro-ponent of comprehensive immigration reform at the federal level.) This critical decision marked a major break from the previous black-Latino coalition assem-bled by the Washington campaign and resulted in Daley elevating Puerto Ricans and Mexicans in his emerging electoral and governing coalitions. In return for loyalty from Latino voters, the new Daley-Latino political alliance showed sen-sitivity to immigrant interests and sped the emergence of new Latino political elites (Dominguez 2007).

Daley captured 52.4 percent of the Latino vote in 1989. Having subsequently shown support for items on the Latino agenda, Daley increased this support level to 87.3 percent in his last campaign in 2007. In return, the machine provided symbolic and material support for Latino elected leaders, immigrant-serving nonprofits, and the Mexican American electorate.

Daley's electoral alliance with Latinos was central to the durability and strength of the machine's political influence under his watch. By 2000, its base rested on a large turnout and high loyalty among white voters, support from a small percentage of black voters, and strong majorities from the growing Latino electorate. Daley cemented this arrangement by recruiting Latinos to top posi-tions within his administration, signing an executive order originally supported by Harold Washington to ban local law enforcement officials from identifying undocumented immigrants and reporting them to the Immigration and Natu-ralization Service, and, in 2005, appointing Twenty-Fifth Ward alderman Danny Solis to president pro tempore of the city council. No Latino had ever held such a prestigious post in city government. Daley was also a strong advocate of advanc-ing Latino political representation in the redistricting process during the 1990s and 2000s.

Given the influence of the Cook County Democratic organization at all levels of city, county, and state government and the robust advocacy from immigrant-serving organizations, government at all levels has adopted a number of pro-immigrant positions. Mayor Daley was an outspoken critic against such measures as Section 287(g) of the Immigration and Nationality Act, and his former police chief, Jody Weis, also strongly opposed the program, which granted immigration enforcement powers to local police officers. Daley, Weis, and the majority of the city council held that lending support to such measures would have threatened their efforts to create a better civic climate, such as the adoption of commu-nity policing measures in immigrant-heavy neighborhoods. Cook County also declared itself a sanctuary county, meaning that local government would not enter into formal arrangements with federal law enforcement on immigration matters.

In 2004, the City of Chicago also approved a resolution authorizing government agencies and financial institutions to accept the *matricula consular* as an official form of identification for the undocumented. Immigrant-rights supporters and some elected officials viewed this ID card, issued by the Mexican consulate, as an opportunity for the undocumented to engage with local government agencies. In the words of Congresswoman Jan Schakowsky, "the ID cards not only bolster communities' economic prosperity but they also deter crimes and predatory schemes against immigrants who might otherwise be carrying around a lot of cash or are reluctant to report crimes to local police."[1] Such pro-immigrant integration sentiment extended into the suburbs and beyond: Evanston joined other Chicago suburbs, including Oak Park, as well as the city of Rockford and Kankakee County, in approving a similar resolution supporting their use.

At the state level, members of the Illinois Latino Legislative Caucus initiated a bill (HB 0060) in 2003 to provide greater educational access to undocumented college students. It would classify individuals who are not citizens or permanent residents of the United States as Illinois residents if they graduated from a high school in the state, among other conditions, so that they could qualify for in-state tuition. Two vocal supporters of the legislation were State Representative Cynthia Soto (Fourth District) and State Senator Iris Y. Martinez (Twentieth District). Asked about the significance of this piece of legislation in a joint interview, both agreed that "this measure was the right thing to do because these young immigrants are not going anywhere and they are very loyal to this country and state, this is the only place they know." During the immigrant marches in March 2006, the two representatives walked hand in hand with the ICIRR and other immigrant-serving organizations. In August 2011 the state legislature finally enacted an Illinois DREAM Act (SB 2185), and Governor Pat Quinn signed it.

The Hispanic Democratic Organization

During his tenure as mayor, Daley sought to institutionalize Latino voter support by building up immigrant-oriented organizations. One of the most powerful was the Hispanic Democratic Organization (HDO). Since its inception in the late 1990s, the HDO has been instrumental in elevating the political visibility of Latinos, especially Mexican Americans. The HDO showed how a solid machine-like apparatus could build political power by helping to elect more Latinos to citywide and statewide offices and supporting Daley-backed candidates.

Though the HDO has no official connection to the mayor, he did give his blessing to its activities. The HDO quickly became an influential electoral force in

Chicago's Latino-majority wards and legislative districts, channeling the political demands of Latinos and helping Daley to fulfill functions that had once been an alderman's domain. This had a profound and debilitating effect on the ability of Latino alderman to maintain control over the daily political operations of the ward. This loss of this control would eventually help to seal their political fate.

As the HDO grew in power, enhancing Latino influence, it had the consequence of diminishing Latino political independence. The HDO's activities ranged from fielding political volunteers on Election Day for Daley-preferred candidates, to raising campaign funds, to slating and endorsing candidates to run against aldermen opposing the mayor. HDO membership was usually rewarded by access to city jobs and political appointments (Cohen, Mota, and Martin 2002). Daley's influence over redistricting further increased his ability to successfully manage the organizational, political, and leadership operations in Latino-majority wards.

Immigrant Advocacy and Service Organizations

Given the strong ward and neighborhood orientation of Chicago's political system, most immigrant-serving agencies, nonprofits, and other social service organizations operated with the idea that they should serve people residing within the demarcated wards and neighborhoods. This was reinforced by their ties to the ward political apparatus, especially the alderman and ward committeemen (Moore 2010; J. Soto 2010; White 2010). The strength of these connections often determined the applicants' success in procuring grants that allowed them to serve their constituencies (Munoz 2009; Nunez 2010; White 2010; E. Wong 2010).

At the same time, such organizations also rely on building partnerships with city agencies and larger, higher-capacity nonprofits that work on a broader scale on such issues as affordable housing, job training, and elder care (White 2010). Two key organizations of this type are the Illinois Coalition for Immigrant and Refugee Rights (ICIRR) and the United Neighborhood Organization (UNO), which have also received support from the Chicago political establishment. Historically, such Chicago-based institutions did not extend their activities to neighboring places like Elgin, Waukegan, and Carpentersville; but as these suburban areas also became new immigrant destination, the Chicago-based institutions have begun to share resources, expertise, and knowledge to help their neighbors cope with emerging challenges. As we will see at greater length below, something of a two-tier context is thus emerging among immigrant-serving organizations.

Neighborhood Networks

Given the turf-minded mentality of the alderman and ward committeemen who control the distribution of city services, most immigrant-oriented organizations exhibit a high degree of loyalty to residents of the neighborhood and serve them first. This sometimes leads immigrant-serving nonprofits to collaborate on matters relating to child and elderly care, citizenship initiatives, and health care services. (As already mentioned, the only exceptions to this phenomenon are the ICIRR and UNO, which have established citywide and regional capacities in serving metro Chicago's immigrant communities. They are discussed below.)

Several examples of cross-ward collaboration can be found in the Twenty-Fifth Ward on the lower west side of the city. Although considered a Latino-majority ward, it also contains the city's largest Chinese American community. As a result of this ethnic overlap, the ward alderman has encouraged the local immigrant-serving nonprofits to share resources. For example, the Chinese American Service League (CASL), the largest nonprofit serving Chicago's Chinese community, has developed close relationships with neighboring organizations in the heavily Mexican Pilsen neighborhood to address political representation, affordable housing, political and civic education, and preventive health care.

Esther Wong, executive director of CASL, explains that "in our mission to serve immigrants, it is vital that we, as an ethnic community, engage with Latino immigrants and draw on the experience and expertise of long-standing organizations such as the Resurrection Project, Eighteenth Street Development Corporation, and Pilsen Neighbors." She adds that "because the issues of our immigrants are in a lot of ways similar to those in Pilsen, drawing on the expertise of these nonprofits can in the long run help reduce costs and increase service delivery." Carlos Arango, executive director of Casa Aztlan in Pilsen, also embraces the idea of cooperation across ethnic groups. For him, "issues such as school crowding that directly affect my immigrant constituency cannot be seen only through the Latino lens, but also through other immigrant groups, like our friends in neighboring Chinatown."

More frequently, however, groups stick to their own immigrant clienteles. Abel Núñez, associate director of Centro Romero, observes that "as a primarily Latino-immigrant-serving organization, we feel we can be most effective in working with the Spanish-speaking population as opposed to say, the African immigrant community." And "the fact that we have the resources to carry out our citizenship and bilingual and workforce training programs makes it imperative that we engage with our Latino immigrant clientele first." Similarly, Lhakpa Tsering of the Vietnamese Association of Illinois notes that "thanks to our funding and our successful programming, we are able to directly assist our population in the areas of literacy services, after-school programming for youth, computer training and employment . . . outside of grant funding; we are fortunate as an organization that we do not have to seek outside help on these matters, we enjoy having ownership over our services."

For small organizations lacking the capacity to initiate and sustain programming, partnering with larger organizations is a necessity. For example, the United African Organizations (UAO) and the Ethiopian Community Association (ECA), which serve African immigrant communities, have lacked scale, capacity, and budget and tend to rely for help on such venerable organizations as the Chicago Urban League and the Rainbow PUSH Coalition, as well as the Pan African Association. Alle Kabba, executive director of the UAO, observes that "unfortunately, we sometimes do not have the expertise or resources to effectively support our constituency. Also, unlike organizations that are anchored in, say, the Latino and Asian immigrant communities, we don't necessarily have a cohesive African immigrant community; we are spread out everywhere and as result have to pursue of strategy of building partnerships."

Culture and Language

Culture and language also limit the degree to which different immigrant-serving organizations cooperate. Because immigrant communities are clustered in ethnic enclaves and share cultural norms, values, and traditions, immigrant-serving organizations can find it difficult to engage multiple immigrant groups. In many ways, "we know our immigrants best" is their philosophy for delivering social and health services. As executive director Charles Fredrick Daas of the Cambodian Association of Illinois (CAI) notes, "For us, connecting with people in their own language and culture is the first step in establishing trust, because without that, we will have difficulty in effectively delivering services to our clientele." The CAI believes it must conduct its outreach and programmatic efforts in accordance with Cambodian customs and norms.

In the northeast Rogers Park neighborhood, the city's most ethnically diverse immigrant neighborhood, organizations such as Centro Romero, the Cambodian Association of Illinois, the Vietnamese Association of Illinois, and the Refugee and Immigrant Service Community directly serve their constituencies, with little cooperation among them. While all of them strive to solidify healthy working relationships with their targeted population, this deters them from collaborating with one another.

Citizenship initiatives are another example of how immigrant-serving organizations work exclusively with ethnic-specific groups. Almost every organization has its own strategy for approaching the citizenship test. The Cambodian

Association of Illinois, Casa Aztlan, the Ethiopian Association of Chicago, and the Polish American Association all house programs and recruit workers who are familiar with their culture and proficient in the specific immigrant population's native tongue (J. Soto 2010; Tsering 2010).

When cross-group collaboration does occur, such as with Asian Human Services (AHS), it typically remains within a pan-ethnic framework. Located in the Chinatown neighborhood, the AHS works with nonprofits serving Asian immigrant communities regardless of language and dialect, providing language services in many Asian languages. The goal is to ease the cultural transition of each group and to bring a sense of cultural comfort among the different Asian groups in Chinatown as well as other parts in the city. Another prominent organization facilitating intra-group coalitions is the Asian American Institute, which focuses primarily on political representation, voting, and redistricting (Lin 2009).

ICIRR and UNO as Regional Sources of Organizational Capacity

Whereas ward political dynamics, neighborhood networks, and cultural norms foster targeted outreach and service delivery in ethnic-specific neighborhoods, their limited institutional and organizational capacity has created a need for larger, citywide collaborative efforts. Two metro-level umbrella organizations that provide support to a wide range of member organizations representing different immigrant groups and sustain regional immigrant integration initiatives are the Illinois Coalition for Immigrant and Refugee Rights (ICIRR) and the United Neighborhood Organization (UNO).

The ICIRR has been at the forefront of immigrant intergroup coalition building on a broader scale and helping a wide variety of smaller immigrant-serving organizations. For example, along with CONFEMEX (a confederation of Mexican hometown associations), the ICIRR planned and organized the Chicago marches to coincide with the national immigrant marches on March 10 and May 1, 2006. ICIRR has fostered many local immigrant initiatives in the metro areas, working with over 140 institutions. Under former executive director Joshua Hoyt, the ICIRR has undertaken voter registration, 2010 Census training, and the organization of local marches in support of DREAM Act legislation on September 25, 2010, teaming up with the Council of American-Islamic Relations (CAIR-Chicago) and the United African Organization. The ICIRR's ability to bridge metro Chicago's diverse immigrant communities has been critical in opening up dialogue and in building bridges between the area's different organizations. It has also exerted influence on the policies of the State of Illinois, not just the City of Chicago—not only in the enactment of the Illinois DREAM Act, but also in the creation of a Governor's Office of New Americans and a policy task force that brings twenty-five state agencies together to focus on immigrant services (Illinois 2013). In 2011, the state declined to participate further in the Secure Communities program.

The Immigrant Family Resource Program is one of the ICIRR's most important efforts. It seeks to reduce the barriers that low-income immigrant families and other limited-English-speaking persons in Illinois face when seeking public benefits and services (nutritional, medical, housing, psychological, child care, employment). In addition to in-house programming, the project funds local organizations to (1) provide information and referral services to immigrant families who need quick information and referrals about benefits and other services; (2) undertake case management services to immigrant families who need long-term assistance accessing and maintaining benefits and services; (3) provide accurate interpretation and/or translation services for immigrants who, because of language barriers, have difficulty communicating with the Illinois Department of Human Services and other agencies offering supportive services.

The United Neighborhood Organization has also been highly visible on matters of immigrant integration and empowerment. UNO began in 1984 as a grassroots empowerment organization founded by Twenty-Fifth Ward alderman Danny Solis. As a community organizer in the city's largest Mexican community, Solis was concerned about the poor socioeconomic and educational condition of Chicago's growing yet still politically invisible Latino immigrant population. From the outset, UNO sought access to government resources to build up the Latino immigrant community. An immediate goal was to bring community groups, nonprofits, block clubs, and churches together to challenge the status quo and advocate for Latino immigrants. UNO's focus was on improving education, promoting citizenship, and cultivating political leadership.

By the early 1990s, UNO had begun to evolve into more than a grassroots organization. UNO viewed the successful redistricting battles in the late 1980s and the political incorporation efforts of the Harold Washington administration as opportunities to gain leverage in the political process. Its support of Richard M. Daley's election as mayor in 1989 transformed UNO. With Daley's appointment of Solis as Twenty-Fifth Ward alderman in 1996, UNO established itself as a formidable organization with close ties to the mayor and the county machine. Contracts from public agencies like the city's Department of Planning and Development and Department of Housing and the state's Department of Public Health and Department of Commerce and Economic Opportunity have helped UNO succeed in serving its communities and lifting its members into public service.

Unlike the ICIRR, UNO is more interested in using its capacity to drive policy closely aligned with its model of immigrant empowerment. For example, while most organizations serving immigrants in Chicago support bilingual measures that facilitate integration, UNO has taken a different approach, especially when it comes to the schooling of immigrant children. In 2008, as part of Mayor Daley's Renaissance 2010 initiative to build more cutting-edge schools, UNO was rewarded with $98 million in state grants (the largest for any nonprofit in Illinois) to build and operate charter schools in immigrant-serving areas.

Even though many of its clients are not proficient in English, UNO is against bilingual education and does not believe dual-language programs facilitate social and political integration. As Juan Rangel, former CEO of UNO, states, "We are about empowering our community, and the way to best integrate the children and their immigrant parents is by instructing them in English only." While this attitude may not be widespread, Rangel makes no excuses. He attributes his group's successes to putting its own spin on Saul Alinsky's community-organizing model: identify the powers that be and join forces with them rather than fight them. In essence, he believes working with the machine is the optimal path to immigrant empowerment for the Latino community. He does not endorse "symbolic representation" unless it comes along with government largesse.

UNO is far closer to the Chicago political machine than is the ICIRR. In fact, Rangel supported the machine-sponsored white ethnic candidate over progressive Latino candidates in the race for the Third Congressional District in 2009. The first time a local Chicago Latino immigrant ran for Congress was when Jorge Mújica, a Mexican immigrant, longtime union organizer, and a champion of immigrant rights, challenged the powerful incumbent, Representative Daniel Lipinski. While Mújica's campaign helped to register seventy-five thousand immigrants in the district and received the support of most elected officials in the Illinois Latino Caucus, as well indirect support from the ICIRR, Pilsen Neighbors, the Resurrection Project, and the Asian American Institute, his campaign fell short. Given that Congressman Lipinski had been a staunch supporter the Sensenbrenner Act and opposed the DREAM Act, Rangel could only explain his support for Lipinski this way: "We are all about winning and supporting those candidates that can deliver the goods even if that means going against a Latino candidate."

UNO ratcheted up its cozy relationship with the Chicago political establishment a notch when Rangel revealed he would serve as Rahm Emanuel's campaign co-chairman for the mayoral election in 2010, despite the fact that two prominent Latino candidates also sought the office: Gary Chico, the former Chicago Public Schools president, and Miguel Del Valle, the city clerk and former state senator. Again, Rangel believed that he should work within the machine, not against it.

The ascendancy of UNO in Chicago's political establishment is not surprising and can be attributed to the success of its in-house Metropolitan Leadership Institute (MLI). The MLI was created in 2001, with the goal of increasing the advocacy capacity of Chicago's Latino immigrant community. By training the next generation of Latino leaders in civics, politics, business, and networking, the MLI has seen many of its graduates go on to play vital roles in city government. These include current First Ward alderman Joe "Proco" Moreno; former Chicago Transit Authority president Rich Rodriguez, now the UNO Charter School Network board chairman; former First Ward alderman Manny Flores, currently a high-level state government official; and State Representative Silvana Tabares. It is important to note that these elected officials were front and center in supporting the city's efforts to accept the *matricula consular* as well as the state's legislative push for driver's licenses for undocumented immigrants. The MLI is credited with helping to establish greater political agency for Chicago's Latino communities with regard to progressive immigrant initiatives. For Rangel, "MLI was the missing political link that connected Chicago's growing Latino immigrant community to the power apparatus of the city's governing structure."

In 2014, however, UNO's close link with the Chicago machine led to serious difficulties for the organization. With support from the Speaker of the Illinois House, Michael Madigan, a close ally of UNO's president Juan Rangel, the State of Illinois allocated $98 million for UNO to construct new charter schools. Many of the contracts went to companies owned by brothers of UNO's senior vice president, Miguel d'Escoto. Discovery of this relationship led to charges from the SEC that UNO had defrauded bondholders from whom it had raised capital funds and resulted in Rangel's firing, leaving the organization in disarray and no longer managing its charter schools (Mihalopoulos 2014).

While not nearly as prominent as the ICIRR and UNO, several other citywide coalitions have also emerged around immigrant issues. One is the Coalition of Limited English Speaking Elderly (CLESE). Partnering with the Illinois Department on Aging, CLESE helps twenty-two community-based ethnic groups provide services to seniors in a great variety of languages. Another example was the now-closed Coalition of African, Arab, Asian, European, and Latino Immigrants of Illinois (CAAAELII), born of a concern that Chicago's immigrant communities were too balkanized. As Dale Asis, past executive director of CAAAELII, put it, "I was concerned that the location of immigrant services and their organizations was serving as a barrier . . . preventing greater cooperation on matters affecting a lot of immigrant neighborhoods." CAAAELII procured a state grant to unify immigrant organizations around citizenship-training courses that linked more than twenty different immigrant-serving organizations around Chicago. For Asis, this brought together organizations that otherwise would not have communicated or collectively engaged the political process. Yet its influence paled before that of UNO or ICIRR.

Variation in Suburban Responses

The suburbs of Chicago have given immigrants a much more varied reception than the city itself. As described in chapter 2 and noted in Wilson and Svajlenka (2014), Chicago's foreign-born population fell slightly in the city itself between 2000 and 2013 but rose by more than 271,000 in the suburbs, leaving 63 percent of the region's immigrants, or more than 1 million, living there. (An ICIRR report on research by Rob Paral and Associates [Paral 2014] estimates that about 276,000 of them are undocumented.) This continues a trend under way since 1990. For example, the foreign-born population has risen by more than 200 percent in Kane, Lake, McHenry, and Will Counties.

These counties are now home to more than 483,000 immigrants, with about an equal number also in the suburbs within Cook County (Paral 2011). In 2009, immigrants made up more than 30 percent of the population in eight of the twenty municipalities in the suburban region with the largest number of foreign-born. The question of receptivity toward immigrants is thus being posed in many suburban settings. The arrival of immigrants presents both challenges and opportunities for municipalities to design programming and other initiatives that help integrate these new populations into civic life.

While the City of Chicago has adopted strongly pro-immigrant stances for the reasons given, and the state has echoed these stances on a number of occasions, many suburban jurisdictions have provided a much cooler reception. While some localities have embraced their immigrant populations, others have been unapologetic about supporting greater policing and enforcement measures. For example, in 2007, at the behest of then-mayor Richard Hyde, the Waukegan City Council voted 8–2 to reconfirm its previous vote in favor of 287(g), allowing Waukegan police to initiate deportation proceedings against immigrants who commit serious crimes. Only the two Latino aldermen, Tony Figueroa and Rafael Rivera, were dissenters. This response was fueled in some measure by the enormous growth of Waukegan's Latino immigrants, who had reached 40 percent of the population, creating resentment among its white residents. (In response to this measure, the ICIRR organized a naturalization and registration campaign that contributed to Hyde's upset defeat in the next election; but Waukegan continues to report to ICE undocumented immigrants arrested for minor infractions.)

Such actions led important Chicago organizations such as the ICIRR, UNO, and the Instituto del Progreso Latino to make Waukegan the suburban epicenter of the immigrant-rights marches in the summer of 2007.

Similarly, as suburban Carpentersville, a blue-collar town of thirty-seven thousand, became 48 percent Latino and 40 percent white, immigration created a wedge between the groups and a public-relations nightmare. In 2006, the village board proposed an ordinance modeled on one passed in Hazelton, Pennsylvania, that would deny business permits and government contracts to employers who hired undocumented workers; it also sought to fine landlords for knowingly renting to illegal immigrants (Keilman 2010).

Initially, the proposed ordinance drove some Latino immigrants away, dampening the prospects for commercial and real estate growth in the declining town. In the end, the local business establishment's opposition to the ordinance forced the village board to reverse course and suspend the measure. The town engaged in a long public-relations campaign to cultivate a more welcoming atmosphere for immigrants in search of greater socioeconomic opportunities.

Unlike Cook County, the neighboring counties of Lake, Will, and McHenry have all engaged in ICE's Secure Communities initiative to cross-check in federal immigration databases those arrested locally, although Lake County's sheriff has lately grown critical of the program (*Frontline* 2011). As with similar measures across the country, advocacy groups and legal experts have become increasingly concerned about the merging of federal immigration enforcement and local police, which they fear will reduce immigrant cooperation with the police.

In spite of the immigrant backlash in these counties, some towns are attempting to promote immigrant integration. The blue-collar town of Cicero, located seven miles outside Chicago, is a case in point. Unlike Waukegan and Carpentersville, Cicero has been supportive of its growing Latino immigrant population, who have helped to revitalize, both economically and culturally, a community that had been in decline. In fact, many Latino immigrants have been attracted by Cicero's affordability and public services (Aguilar 2010). According to Frank Aguilar, Cicero's director of community affairs and special projects, "the town is cognizant of the many contributions immigrants have brought to Cicero; we know they are here to work and to make Cicero their home, and as such, [town] President [Larry] Dominick is responding in kind." Cicero has developed bilingual programs in areas of real estate and business, assisting Spanish-speaking business owners with translation on procedures and regulations for becoming licensed.

Similarly, the town of Elgin, about thirty-five miles northwest of the city, has sought to tap into existing resources to connect Spanish-speaking residents to civic life. The Hispanic Heritage Coalition of Elgin has been at the forefront of cultural diversity programming. Each fall, it hosts the "Fiesta Salsa," with Latinos and non-Latinos participating in the planning committee. The event brings attention to the Latino immigrant community and forges social relationships among the town's residents. The Elgin Unified School District has also supported bilingual education in its primary schools and high school. Such outreach efforts have made the immigrant community feel welcomed. As one lifelong resident, Francisco Castelan, reflected, "When my father arrived as an immigrant thirty years ago to open a business, these efforts were nonexistent, and unlike neighboring towns, Elgin has chosen to embrace rather than exclude its immigrant population."

The northern suburbs have found it more challenging to respond as they have become new destinations for immigrants. A 2008 *Chicago Reporter* story examining thirty-one North Shore municipalities found that most if not all were ill-equipped to handle the socioeconomic needs of their immigrant populations. Only five municipalities translated government documents into Spanish, while only two required that their protective and social service employees participate in language and cultural training. Fewer than half had human relations and housing commissions. Only Evanston and Aurora had elected foreign-born residents to local office.

City-Suburban Partnerships

While some North Shore towns have taken constructive approaches toward immigrant integration, under former Mayor Daley's leadership the City of Chicago sought to organize positive regional approaches to immigrant integration. In 1997, Daley initiated discussions that led to the formation of a Metropolitan Mayors Caucus. In 2007, Daley asked this metropolitan-wide forum for mayors, civic groups, and city council members to discuss strategies and solutions to deal with immigrant integration efforts and to find ways in which the twenty-two hundred nonprofit health and human services organizations in the Chicago metro area could work together to address the needs and aspirations of immigrant communities.

This initiative brought together the mayors, civic and faith leaders, immigrant-serving nonprofits, and foundation representatives, as well as the Latino Policy Forum and the Center for Metropolitan Chicago Initiatives of the Institute for Latino Studies at the University of Notre Dame, to discuss four models of service provision that would facilitate immigrant integration in the metro region. These include a community-based organization, a one-stop social service collaborative, a school-community partnership, and a faith-based initiative. Of these, the one-stop collaborative received attention because it might consolidate numerous services with one visit.

In 2011, the mayors' caucus surveyed the 237 suburban municipalities concerning their immigrant integration programs and received responses from 109. The resulting report (Milld 2012) indicates that municipalities are aware of their growing immigrant populations and beginning to respond to them, most frequently by providing translation for emergency services, but also lack staff and resources to develop adequate responses. The report highlighted a number of model programs, such as the Palatine Opportunity Center, which brings together fourteen providers to train personnel and deliver a range of social services.

Such efforts suggest that the work of the Metropolitan Mayors Caucus is bearing some fruit. While the discussions of its Diversity Committee have helped municipalities share best practices around such cross-cutting issues as translation and interpretation services and cultural competency training, the work of developing a bigger service infrastructure is just beginning, and many local responses remain in the realm of symbolic recognition and "know your neighbor" events.

Mayor Emanuel and the New Immigration Agenda

The 2010 election of Rahm Emanuel, the first new mayor since 1989, ushered in a new era of political leadership for Chicago. President Barack Obama's former chief of staff, Emanuel inherited a city facing difficult economic and budgetary challenges, including pension reform, a struggling educational system, and a budget that could not keep up with the delivery of important social services to residents. On the political front, he was faced with keeping together the key sectors of Mayor Daley's electoral and governing coalition, including business, labor, and racial and ethnic minorities, in particular blacks and Latinos. The immigrant communities and the organizations that serve them wondered how the new mayor would respond to them, given that he had not been an advocate of immigrant rights while in the White House.

Incorporating Immigrants

Mayor Emanuel did not take long to indicate that he would indeed continue to embrace the platform of immigrant receptivity set forth by his predecessor, for similar political motivations. Emanuel had already taken a first step in cementing his credibility as an advocate of Latinos and Chicago's immigrant communities by appointing UNO's CEO, Juan Rangel, as cochairman of his 2011 mayoral campaign. After winning the election, Emanuel reached out to the various non-profits and political groups that serve and represent these communities, including the ICIRR, UNO, the Latino Policy Forum, and the Chicago and Illinois Hispanic Legislative Caucuses. He affirmed policies aimed at improving the political and entrepreneurial opportunities for Chicago's immigrant communities.

On June 6, 2011, Mayor Emanuel established a Mayor's Office of New Americans (ONA), which leads his Chicago New Americans Initiative, a comprehensive municipal effort to assist eligible immigrants become U.S. citizens in collaboration with the State of Illinois and the ICIRR's Uniting America Campaign. Like his predecessor, Emanuel says that promoting naturalization will enhance the economic competitiveness and cultural vitality of the city and region and has vowed to make Chicago the most immigrant-friendly city in the United States (Chicago 2012).

The aim of the New Americans Initiative is to help ten thousand immigrants in Chicago become U.S. citizens. To reach this goal, the New Americans Initiative works closely with the ICIRR to host regular citizenship workshops and numerous smaller citizenship assistance efforts to help legal permanent residents through the complicated and expensive process of becoming a citizen. It conducts outreach in public schools, city colleges, libraries, park field houses, and city service centers. It also makes these spaces available to host English-language and citizenship classes.

Like similar offices in other cities, the Mayor's Office of New Americans seeks to (1) establish a centralized language access policy for the City of Chicago; (2) expand opportunities for immigrant business owners and entrepreneurs; (3) enhance coordination between city government and community organizations; (4) expand immigrant parent engagement throughout the Chicago Public Schools; (5) expand English-language educational resources and opportunities in community settings; (6) support the launch of the Illinois DREAM Act; and (7) promote U.S. citizenship. The 2012 Chicago New Americans Plan outlined twenty-seven policy initiatives in the areas of economic development, youth and education, and community development.

While the Chicago New Americans Initiative helps to promote advocacy for immigrant integration, it also builds links between pro-immigrant organizations and city hall. By the summer of 2012, ONA had hosted workshops on entrepreneurialism, and the New Americans Small Business Series organized quarterly events to foster small business growth in immigrant communities throughout Chicago. Emanuel attracted a diverse group of leaders from business, academia, and civic and community organizations to serve as an advisory board to help develop the new integration measures.

Mayor Emanuel took a further step in the summer of 2011 by pushing the adoption of a Welcoming City Ordinance, which develops basic protections for undocumented Chicagoans. It bars police officers from turning over illegal immigrants to federal agents if the immigrants do not have serious criminal convictions or outstanding criminal warrants (Thomas 2012). Also, it forbids police from detaining undocumented immigrants unless they are named in criminal warrants or have been convicted of a serious crime. In the words of the mayor, "this ordinance will make Chicago a national leader in welcoming those who play by the rules, contribute to our economy and help make Chicago the incredible city that was envisioned by its first immigrant settlers" (Chicago 2012).

With this proposal, the mayor made it evident that he wanted to enhance his standing among the growing Latino segment of Chicago's electorate. The new ordinance builds on the 2006 ordinance that disallows city agencies from asking or considering immigration status in applications for city services. According to Alderman Danny Solis, "These steps by Emanuel mirror those of the previous mayor in that he is looking out for opportunities that best serve the interests of our immigrant community" (Solis 2012).

However positive, these steps have not been pleasing to everyone, especially Chicago's black community. The mayor's outspoken support for greater Latino representation, more political inclusion, and charter school expansion, while simultaneously closing public schools in predominantly black neighborhoods, has elicited a high degree of anxiety in the black community. The matter is not helped by the fact that in the last redistricting, blacks lost a council seat while Latinos gained two seats.

While the City of Chicago was embarking on the New Americans Initiative in 2012, the Cook County Board of Supervisors also reconfigured the county's immigration policy. In September 2011, led by county board president Toni Preckwinkle and newly elected Seventh District commissioner Jesus "Chuy" Garcia, the board pushed through a historic pro-immigrant ordinance that refines the relationship between local law enforcement and federal immigration agents in dealing with the county's undocumented.

In doing so, the county board moved in the opposite direction of neighboring Will and Lake Counties. The board challenged policies that called for greater cooperation between the Sheriff's Department and U.S. Immigration and Customs Enforcement (ICE). Board president Preckwinkle had two concerns about the legality of the detainee policy set forth by ICE. The first was whether ICE had the right to force the county to detain suspected undocumented immigrants beyond the required forty-eight-hour period before being allowed to post bail. The second was whether, under federal law, the county sheriff's office was required to comply. ICE's view was that it had the authority to make these demands, while the county's position is that they were voluntary requests.

As a champion of immigrant rights, former state senator, alderman, and county board member Jesus "Chuy" Garcia argued against complying with ICE's detainer policy. He felt this arrangement violated the spirit of the county's historic standing as a sanctuary and argued that the policy did not distinguish between felonies and misdemeanors as justification for holding an undocumented person beyond the forty-eight-hour threshold (J. Garcia 2009). Commissioner Garcia and other members were concerned that racial profiling and police harassment might go unchecked. Supporters hailed the ordinance as a victory for immigrant rights, which not only saved county taxpayers $15 million annually but would uphold the rule of law (Benito 2012; Magee 2012).

The State of Illinois also inched closer to this position. Then-governor Pat Quinn withdrew Illinois from the ICE Secure Communities program. In echoing the sentiments of the Cook County Board, the governor asserted the program did not identify only individuals who had been convicted of serious criminal offenses, but that in Illinois, "more than thirty percent of those deported from the United States, under the program, had never been convicted of any crime," based on federal statistical data compiled through February 28, 2011 (Quinn 2011).

In 2013, Illinois took the unprecedented step of becoming one of four states to pass legislation that grants driver's licenses to undocumented immigrants. Senate Bill 957 was touted as a model for collaborative leadership on progressive immigrant legislation. The bill passed in the House by a 65–46 vote, with bipartisan support. Backers included former Republican governor Jim Edgar and other top state Republicans, Chicago's Mayor Emanuel, and City Clerk Susana Mendoza. This measure was hailed as a giant step for immigrant rights in Illinois, which had already approved its own DREAM Act in 2010 to create a privately funded scholarship program for immigrant students.

Shortly after signing it into law, Governor Quinn said the legislation would help "to ensure that every Illinois motorist will be properly licensed and empower more immigrants to become stronger contributors to our economy" (Foley 2013). ICIRR chief executive officer Lawrence Benito agreed that "passing the highway safety legislation in Illinois is an example of what can happen nationally and proves that both parties can put the politics of fear and scapegoating aside and work on practical solutions that keep our roads and families safe." In just the first two months of the program, the secretary of state's office had already issued fourteen thousand temporary driver's licenses to undocumented immigrants (*Fox News Latino* 2014).

Perhaps with the 2015 mayoral election in mind, Mayor Emanuel announced a new program to provide nearly twenty-three thousand city-funded internship, volunteer, and job opportunities for undocumented students in April 2014 (Chicago 2014a). The idea is that experience with agencies such as the Department of

Human Services, the Department of Family and Support Services, and the Office of New Americans will equip these students with valuable professional experience in city government.

Emanuel took another bold step during the humanitarian crisis of Central American adolescents arriving at the U.S. southern border in 2014. He announced that the "City of Big Hearts" would welcome and shelter as many as one thousand of these migrant children (Chicago 2014b). In addition, the mayor's office planned to tap the city's legal community to build what it described as a "broad-based pro bono campaign" to counsel the city's share of unauthorized immigrant children, a proposal hatched as federal authorities worked to boost the government's capacity to shelter and care for the unprecedented number of children arriving from Latin America (Chicago 2014b).

The 2015 Mayoral Election

While moves of this sort drew positive reactions from Latino elected officials in Chicago and Cook County, at least some of them began to think that the growing Latino vote might provide the basis for a challenge to Mayor Emanuel. And just as Emanuel had to defeat two Latino candidates in the 2011 primary, he faced a significant Latino challenger in 2015. County Supervisor Jesus "Chuy" Garcia mounted a sufficiently effective campaign in the February mayoral primary to force Emanuel into an April runoff election. This marked an important maturing point for Mexican-origin (as well as Puerto Rican and other Latino) voters, and the election raised the specter of whether Garcia could form an alliance among Latinos, African Americans, and white reformers broad enough to topple the Cook County Democratic Party's key figure, Mayor Emanuel.

The 2015 mayoral runoff presented opportunities as well as challenges for Mayor Emanuel in reinforcing his electoral coalition and strengthening his relationships with its key constituents, including labor, blacks, and Latinos. Garcia's strong primary showing and subsequent opinion polling suggested to some that the machine was becoming weak and less able to register, mobilize, and turn out its vote. Others (see Torres and Cordova 2015) saw cracks in the mayor's electoral and governing coalition between whites on the one hand and blacks and Latinos on the other, accusing the mayor of having focused only on his most affluent constituents. Emanuel had received 59 percent of the black vote in his initial 2011 victory, but only 42 percent in February 2015. In response, the mayor turned to his key black aldermen, such as Deborah Graham (Twenty-Ninth), Lona Lane (Eighteenth), and Walter Burnett Jr. (Twenty-Seventh), to help him reconnect with black voters, who were disaffected in part around school closings in their neighborhoods. The buzz of excitement and popularity surrounding the Garcia campaign in Chicago's Latino neighborhoods also led Emanuel to appoint Chicago's two most prominent and highly visible Latino elected officials as cochairs of his campaign: Congressman Luis Gutiérrez and City Clerk Susana Mendoza. The mayor hoped that with a history of being advocates of immigrant rights such as the Illinois DREAM Act, Gutiérrez and Mendoza would widen his appeal in Latino communities and ultimately help him maintain or increase his share of the Latino vote in April. That he might be able to do so was suggested by the fact that he had captured nearly 30 percent of the Latino vote in 2011 and even managed to take 33 percent in February 2015.

Garcia was a formidable candidate, and just as the Villaraigosa, Cisneros, and Pena campaigns had in LA, San Antonio, and Denver, he advanced the idea that a Latino candidate could lead a multiethnic coalition to victory. Not only was Emanuel accused of being "the mayor of the 1 percent," but his actions had upset blacks and unions, especially the Chicago Teachers Union and the SEIU local representing city-funded employees, as well as Latinos. As Emanuel's campaign gained momentum, Gutiérrez and Mendoza went on the attack as primary surrogates for him in narrating ads on Spanish-language outlets such as Univision and Telemundo. The ads, however, did not attack Garcia's immigrant rights agenda, given the broad appreciation of his advancement of immigrant rights legislation as alderman, state senator, and county commissioner (Dominguez 2010).

Despite his having lost the initial primary vote to Garcia in all the Latino wards, Emanuel's showing was good enough to suggest he could do better with help from council allies such as Danny Solis (Twenty-Fifth), Roberto Maldonado (Twenty-Sixth), Ed Burke (Fourteenth), and Joe "Proco" Moreno (First). As with black elected officials loyal to the organization, many members of the Latino political establishment wanted to maintain their share of the benefits that flow from city hall. In the end, they delivered an impressive 36 percent of the Latino vote in the April runoff. With this victory, Latino leaders reasonably expected that they would continue to play a major role in Emanuel's electoral and governing coalition.

The Latino vote was not Emanuel's only problem. A chasm had opened up between the mayor and black voters over the fifty schools closed in mostly black neighborhoods, and there was also vocal opposition from the Chicago Teachers Union. It became clear that a Garcia victory would depend on whether he could put together a black-Latino coalition, similar to the one that enabled Chicago to elect its first black mayor, Harold Washington, in 1983 and 1987. Financial backing and endorsements from the Chicago Teachers Union and the Service Employees International Union enabled Garcia to create some inroads among the black electorate, as did endorsements from Jesse Jackson Sr. of the Rainbow Push Coalition, former U.S. senator Carol Moseley Braun, Congressman

Danny Davis, and Bobbie Steele, the former president of the Cook County Board. Even Willie Wilson, a black candidate on the February ballot, tossed his support behind the Garcia campaign.

In the end, Garcia was unable to weld such a coalition together. Most members of the Latino and black political establishments stuck with the mayor, figuring Garcia probably would not win and that deserting Emanuel would put them at considerable risk if Garcia lost. Emanuel mounted a much better financed and focused campaign, as well. The mayor's PAC, Chicago Forward, worked hard to define Garcia as a tax-and-spend liberal who lacked the political vision, business acumen, or the experience to deal with the city's impending pension and financial crisis (*Chicago Tribune*, April 8, 2015). Outspent 3-to-1, Garcia was not able to get sufficient traction for his message of fiscal reform and neighborhood inclusion, especially with black voters.

In the city council elections, however, many insurgent candidates, with help from the SEIU, the United Working Families, and the Chicago Teachers Union, did beat those backed by the mayor and the Cook County Democratic organization. Some of Emanuel's most ardent supporters from the West Side and Southside were defeated, such as Lona Lane (Eighteenth), Deborah Graham (Twenty-Ninth), and Mary O'Connor (Forty-First). Latino-origin newcomers included former Univision reporter Milagros "Milly" Santiago (Thirty-First), schoolteacher Susan Sadlowski Garza (Tenth), Raymond Lopez (Fifteenth), and former ICIRR community organizer Carlos Ramirez-Rosa (Thirty-Fifth). These latter races pitted political newcomers against traditional Latino machine-backed incumbents. In the Northwest Side Thirty-First Ward, Santiago squeezed by veteran alderman and deputy mayor Ray Suarez by fewer than a hundred votes, thanks in part to the teachers union and the strong backing of Congressman Gutiérrez. The hotly contested Southeast Side Tenth Ward race pitted Sadlowski Garza against Emanuel ally John Pope. Strong CTU support, as well as the challenger's heritage as a daughter of a famous and respected steelworker union activist, put Sadlowski Garza over the top by a mere eighty-nine votes. Candidate Carlos Ramirez-Rosa benefited in the Thirty-Fifth from having served as a caseworker for Congressman Gutiérrez (who was front and center in endorsing him); as in the Suarez race, the mayor chose to remain neutral despite having supported a previous incumbent, in part not to undercut the congressman as his campaign cochair. Three of these new council members have joined with immigrant advocates to propose a six-point plan to strengthen the city's policies toward immigrant services and immigrant rights (http://www.aldermancarlosrosa.org/cityplan).

A detailed analysis of voting results by Scott Kennedy of Illinois Election Data showed three sources for Emanuel's victory. (These patterns were also mapped by the *Chicago Tribune* analysis; see Epton and Bordens 2015). First and foremost,

Emanuel increased his support among voters in majority-white precincts from 54 to 67 percent, with turnout in them also rising substantially (Kennedy 2015). Second, he boosted his support in majority-black precincts from 42 to 57 percent, with turnout increasing less than average in them. Finally, while Garcia increased his share in majority Hispanic precincts from 57 to 67 percent, and increased turnout there above average, that was not enough to offset Emanuel's gains elsewhere. Indeed, it was impressive that Emanuel retained one-third of the vote in Latino areas against a popular Latino candidate. As a result, Emanuel's overall share rose from 46 to 56 percent and his margin over Garcia from 58,000 to 73,000 votes (all numbers from Kennedy 2015).

While some parts of the greater Chicago metropolitan area continue to present challenges for integrating immigrants, immigrant advocates have achieved a great deal. The local political characteristics, cultural norms, and organizational capacities that made such gains possible, however, remain unevenly distributed. The City of Chicago has adopted a strongly pro-immigrant stance, and Cook County's importance in state politics, along with the political prowess of the Illinois Coalition for Immigrant and Refugee Rights, led the State of Illinois to do the same. Moreover, the Metropolitan Mayors Caucus has at least initiated conversations in many suburbs about best practices. Yet pockets of anti-immigrant reaction persist, especially in the more suburban and conservative counties, which have only recently experienced a rapid immigrant influx. The anti-immigrant hysteria in Waukegan and Carpentersville provides clear examples. At the same time, inner-ring suburbs like Cicero and Elgin, with support from the Metropolitan Mayors Caucus, have been more welcoming.

Chicago mayors Daley and Emanuel both made including immigrant Latino communities within their broader electoral coalition a central strategy. To get the backing of these communities, the mayors supported public funding for immigrant services and immigrant advocacy, all filtered through ward-level influence over public and nonprofit services. The Latino challenge in the 2015 mayoral election shows that they had good grounds to be concerned about binding the allegiances of the growing immigrant-origin voting blocs.

In the end, Garcia's challenge to Mayor Emanuel in the 2015 election did not alter the relationship between city hall and immigrant-serving nonprofits. To the contrary, Mayor Emanuel has reinforced and extended this relationship as a means of solidifying his governing base. His Welcoming City Ordinance and Office of New Americans insulated him from criticism that he was not sufficiently responsive to immigrant issues. Making immigrant-rights champions such as Congressman Gutiérrez and City Clerk Mendoza his campaign cochairs eliminated the notion that he would abandon Latino- and immigrant-friendly initiatives. Some Latino leaders expect he may even groom Mendoza to be next in line as a mayoral candidate.

In a city electorate traditionally divided between black and white, the growing Latino immigrant population will increasingly make Chicago a tripartite city. The non-Hispanic white share of the electorate continues to fall, and the black electorate is declining as well. In the redistricting following the 2010 Census, blacks lost a council seat for the first time since the ascension of Harold Washington as mayor. Given that Mayor Emanuel has forged a close relationship with Juan Rangel of UNO, Alderman Danny Solis, former city clerk Miguel Del Valle, and current city clerk Mendoza, Latinos will expect him to continue to respond to their needs. At the same time, as the combined African American and Latino voter base becomes an increasing majority, the possibility that an ambitious political leader will fuse them to challenge the white plurality in the political establishment cannot be ruled out. Of course, this will require that the Latino elected leadership convince African Americans that Latinos are not the enemy and that a biracial coalition can be built around matters that are important to both communities, such as reducing urban violence and increasing affordable housing, neighborhood economic development, and civic and political participation.

5

MOVEMENTS MATTER

Immigrant Integration in Los Angeles

Manuel Pastor, Juan De Lara, and Rachel Rosner

The most recent Census data indicate that one-third of LA County residents are foreign-born, a quarter more were born in the United States to a foreign-born parent, more than one-third of its workforce is immigrant, almost two-thirds are immigrants or children of immigrants, and more than three-fifths of its voters in the 2012 presidential election were immigrants or their children. This underscores what Angelenos have long known: the ways in which the region is integrating its immigrants and their children is largely determining its future. But knowing that immigrants are a major part of a region's future does not mean that all of the region's civic leaders will welcome them warmly. The future, after all, can be scary, particularly for members of previously dominant but now declining groups who worry about their position being undermined by cultural and demographic changes, economic displacement, and shifting political winds.

As the opening chapter of this volume suggests, regional receptivity to recent immigrants depends on many factors, including the history of immigration in past generations, the degree and rapidity of contemporary change, the composition of new immigrant groups, the underlying calculus of political entrepreneurs, and perhaps on the metropolitan area's experience in developing regional responses to common problems. Los Angeles is distinctive because its long histories of migration from and interconnections with Mexico and parts of the Asia-Pacific region, but also because massive immigration picked up so recently, dating to the 1980s. The size of this wave was surely a surprise to the region initially, but one that has been wearing off since the region's foreign-born share has been declining in recent years, something that cannot be said of any of the other cases discussed in this book. Nonetheless, the high concentration of immigrants and their descendants gives them a regional cultural, social, economic, and political weight that tends to shift politics in a pro-immigrant direction, just as it has in New York and to a lesser degree, Chicago.

The immigrant presence in Los Angeles has manifested itself politically not simply through the traditional means of electing immigrants to public office, but in another and perhaps more fundamental way: immigrant communities have been at the center of a strong multiethnic progressive alliance that has asserted itself across a range of issues and become integrated into local institutions. Once known as the "wicked city" for its avowedly antilabor politics, LA is now the epicenter of a revitalized labor movement whose new momentum derives largely from organizing immigrant workers (Milkman 2006). Immigrants and the progressive alliance have also changed the city's racial and political geography, as Latino immigrants and their offspring have transformed the heart of black LA in South Central, leading to the formation of new organizations rooted in interethnic commitments to social justice, which have essentially eclipsed older black organizations such as the NAACP and the Urban League (Pastor 2014).

In short, LA's receptivity to new immigrants must be understood within an overall framework of social movement building, or the ongoing work of creating and nurturing coalitions that reframe narratives and transform systems of political influence (Pastor and Ortiz 2009b). This is not to say that other actors have not also made important contributions to immigrant integration: a local community foundation has created a Council for Immigrant Integration, the Los Angeles Chamber of Commerce has worked to support the DREAM Act and comprehensive immigration reform, and LA's political leaders, including its last two mayors, have promoted immigrant integration even as some conservative political figures, including one county supervisor (Frank 2014), have sought to warn of the economic and social costs of "illegal aliens." But what makes the LA story distinct in the context of this volume is the presence, strength, and breadth of social movement organizing. These organizations are building a broader movement—one anchored in coalitions and cross-cutting alliances—that has made the struggles faced by immigrant communities a central element of the work. Indeed, many of the social-justice organizing advances in the areas of labor, community development, and environmental remediation, and on other issues, have resulted in tangible gains for immigrants in the region.

Nevertheless, Los Angeles may be underperforming relative to other metro areas in terms of how much local government has institutionalized policies to foster immigrant integration. Until recently, for example, the city's Office of Immigrant Affairs was relatively dormant, and the far-reaching changes in institutional practices documented in the New York case are not matched by municipal authorities in this Southern California metropolis. A recent study comparing immigrant integration practices and outcomes in California determined that Los Angeles was securely in the middle of the pack, with San José far outpacing the rest of the state (Pastor et al. 2012). This suggests that LA's social movement actors and immigrant rights activists need to better translate their political potential into implemented policy and institutional changes.

This chapter examines how community advocates, labor unions, and immigrants themselves have tried to forge changes in immigrant integration in two contrasting locations in Los Angeles County: the big City of Los Angeles and the small inner-ring suburb of Maywood.[1] These subareas differ greatly in size, but social movements have been prominent in both. While the City of Los Angeles has been the launching point for the region's most dynamic immigrant and social justice organizing groups, social movement organizers settled into immigrant-rich Maywood—located in a swath of southeast Los Angeles that includes several other similar cities (Pastor 2013)—to see whether they could foment civic engagement that would better shape immigrant integration in Southern California's smaller jurisdictions, especially the inner-ring suburbs.

Of course, this selection of two cases does not encompass the full range of the larger Los Angeles region—which includes not only the San Fernando Valley, but Orange County and all its diversity, such as the city of Costa Mesa, a site of significant anti-immigrant sentiment and laws (Harwood and Myers 2002), and Santa Ana, the top large city in the United States (population above 250,000) in terms of households where a language other than English is spoken in the home.[2] We are also not covering the fascinating immigrant Chinese "ethnoburbs" in the San Gabriel Valley—where business, residential, and educational preferences, not a desire for political empowerment, have driven the growth of new populations and changing municipal policies (see, for example Li 1999; Zhou, Tseng, and Yim 2008). Likewise, we do not tackle the sprawl of the Inland Empire—another chapter in this volume looks at that adjoining metro region separately. Our choice here to concentrate on two spaces in LA County helps us keep the focus on the importance of social movements in the dynamics of immigrant integration in the region; while we believe that this helps us lift up a central element of the story, we realize that the focus comes at some cost in terms of not fully capturing the diversity of the immigrant experience in this sprawling metro.

The chapter begins by reviewing Los Angeles's demographic transformation and its implications for the landscapes of immigration integration. We then analyze the makeup and dynamics of the social movement ecosystem and how it has influenced policy and social change in the region. We focus in on the changing dynamics and policies in the City of Los Angeles, noting that while Los

Angeles institutions have learned to accommodate the city's new inhabitants, a prominent and politically influential network of social movement organizations helped and sometimes pushed them along. We explore in depth the context of that movement, as well as immigrant integration struggles in two key arenas: policing and education.

We then turn to Maywood (with a much shorter review; its population is, after all, less than 1 percent that of the City of Los Angeles). Despite the size, it is more fascinating and somewhat archetypical, as it is one of a band of industrial suburbs that were once set up to house the white working class and have seen the demographics shift dramatically as a result of deindustrialization and mass migration. In that context, immigrant activists saw an opportunity to transform a city politics that had previously been characterized by policies tilted against undocumented immigrants. This effort, like the anti-immigrant drives profiled elsewhere in this volume, reflected another version of political entrepreneurship or opportunity seeking, with activists seizing the reins of government and declaring Maywood as a "sanctuary city." Of course, sanctuary is tough when a city is very under-resourced, and so impact has been less than ambitious.

Both cases suggest that social movement organizations have not been able to create the full range of policies and programs they might have wanted, even where they established a strong toehold in community organizing. The next stage in immigrant integration in greater LA, therefore, will not simply be a matter of building movements for change but creating institutions that can effect change—and there is some evidence that this is now happening.

The Immigrant Landscape: Demography and Geography

Los Angeles has been a churning demographic cauldron since its inception. Spanish and Mexican settlers displaced the Tongva and Chumash peoples during the late 1700s and early 1800s. White prospectors pushed the Mexicans aside in turn during California's mid-century integration into the United States, especially as rail service was established after 1876. During the Depression era, Los Angeles bore the brunt of the nation's first massive deportation or "repatriation" campaign targeting Mexican Americans (Sanchez 1993). The economic boom during the World War II period attracted large numbers of African Americans from the western part of the South and whites from the Midwest (Flamming 2006; Sides 2006). Over the second half of the twentieth century, Latin American and Asian immigrants transformed Los Angeles from a majority white city and county into a region where no ethnicity commands a majority. Meanwhile, the African American and white populations are declining as shares. These demographic shifts have triggered social, economic, and political forces that have allowed—and forced—Angelenos to reinvent their city (Gottlieb 2007).

What does the latest iteration of Los Angeles look like? The city and region's immigrant population grew steadily since the 1980s, although the data in chapter 2 indicate that the share of foreign-born is now on the decline. While the dominant discourse—as depicted in the media and by some anti-immigrant politicians—portrays nearly all immigrants as Mexican, LA's immigrant population is surprisingly diverse. The region's proximity to Mexico has cultivated deeply rooted transnational and binational communities in LA, shaping the identities of U.S.-born Latinos and Los Angeles's culture. But this "Latino-ized" view of the immigrant community often fails to see the region's diverse immigrant population. Mexicans account for only 30 percent of those immigrants who migrated to Los Angeles County since 2000, while more than a third of those in that recent cohort are Asian and Pacific Islanders.

One of the most striking features of the new immigrant Los Angeles is that nearly 60 percent of all children in Los Angeles County have at least one immigrant parent; indeed, one in five children has an undocumented parent, while over 80 percent of even this cohort are U.S.-born citizens (Pastor and Marcelli 2013). This means immigrants are generationally interwoven and are likely here to stay (Pastor and Ortiz 2009a). Indeed, demographer Dowell Myers and his colleagues find that "at age 25–34, fully 86.2 percent of Latinos and 82.5 percent of Asian and Pacific Islanders who were California born remained living in the state in 2007, rather than move elsewhere in the U.S., compared to 75.7 percent of black and 62.1 percent of whites" (Myers, Pitkin, and Ramirez 2009, 2). Immigrant integration, in short, is about the future of the entire region, with significant implications for long-term approaches to education, health, and civic engagement.

Los Angeles's immigrant population is not only increasingly diverse; it is also increasingly geographically dispersed, as figures 5.1 and 5.2 depict. Immigrants no longer concentrate in historically ethnic enclaves like Boyle Heights, East Los Angeles, Chinatown, Mid-City, and East LA, but have shifted in significant numbers into suburban areas, including the San Fernando Valley (technically a part of the City of Los Angeles but always thought of as a suburb within the city). Some new and relatively well-off immigrant suburbs have emerged, such as Monterey Park (Li 1998), along with poorer inner-ring suburbs like the one discussed later. Many immigrants to LA have moved beyond the urban core to San Bernardino, Riverside, Orange, Ventura, and San Diego Counties, seeking new jobs and cheaper housing.

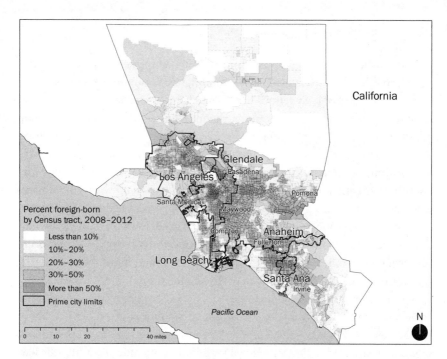

FIGURE 5.1. Percent foreign-born by Census tract, 1980, Los Angeles

Source: 1980 Decennial Census, Census TIGER/Line, and ESRI.

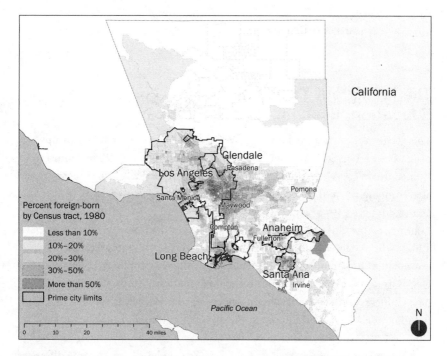

FIGURE 5.2. Percent foreign-born by Census tract, 2008–2012, Los Angeles

Source: 2008–2012 American Community Survey (Ruggles et al. 2011), Census TIGER/Line, and ESRI.

Local institutions have adapted to this shifting ethnic landscape by developing new mechanisms to engage and serve immigrant communities. For example, policy makers and police agencies have expanded their constituent services and community-relations efforts in neighborhoods with rapidly growing immigrant populations. New ethnic tensions and challenges have also emerged in areas of the city where immigrants replaced other groups as the new majority. The rapidly growing Latino population and shrinking African American community in South Los Angeles is one example. The area's racial makeup changed dramatically between 1980 and 2008–2012, falling from 70 percent African American to 30 percent, as the Latino numbers rose from 23 percent to 64 percent. Meanwhile the foreign-born population rose from 18 percent to 36 percent, a slower pace, suggesting that some of those who moved in were immigrants, but most were U.S.-born (or the U.S.-born children of those immigrants).[3]

This rapid transformation illustrates that the urban core retains a significant concentration of immigrants but it is now expanding past the old neighborhood gateways of East Los Angeles and Westlake. Outside the city, working-class immigrants are settling in formerly white middle-class inner-ring suburbs like Maywood, Bell, Bell Gardens, and Huntington Park (Pastor 2012). Like South Central, these suburbs have become extraordinarily Latino, heavily immigrant and noncitizen, and quite poor—with Maywood topping the charts in terms of linguistically isolated households.

The Immigrant Landscape: Education, Economics, and Politics

This geographic diffusion of immigrants has not always been matched by upward progress in education and earnings. Of the immigrant population older than twenty-five in LA, 37 percent do not have a high school degree, 20 percent graduated from high school, 19 percent have some college or an associate's degree, and 24 percent have a BA or higher. This varies considerably by country of origin. For example, 62 percent of Mexican immigrants older than twenty-five do not have a high school degree, and only 4 percent have a bachelor's degree; for Koreans, those figures are 7 percent and 54 percent respectively. Moreover, contrasting the U.S.-born and immigrants in four main population groups (Mexicans, Filipinos, Chinese, and Koreans), the U.S.-born are generally much better educated, with Filipinos showing the smallest gap between immigrants and natives in Los Angeles County.

The education difference by nativity helps to explain some income differentials. For example, analysis of the 2010–2012 combined ACS sample shows that native-born Asian and Pacific Islanders (APIs) had household incomes that were nearly $15,000 higher than for immigrant APIs. Similarly, household incomes were approximately $16,000 higher for U.S.-born Latinos than their immigrant counterparts. Differences exist across groups as well. Immigrant APIs earned higher household incomes than either immigrant or U.S.-born Latinos—in fact, more than $22,000 more than immigrant Latinos. At the same time, APIs and Latinos both show similar progress over the longer haul—but APIs show progress much faster. And since immigrant Latinos generally arrive with lower skills than immigrant Asians and earn lower incomes, the dollar level of the income gaps between immigrant Latinos and Asians rises over time even if the percentage gain is similar.

In any case, if Los Angeles's long-term success depends on the ability of its children and their parents to make progress over time, these trends in education and income are critical indicators. Moving the needle of the factors that will promote economic integration would seem to be less of a political challenge in Los Angeles because of the nature of the political leadership. The previous mayor, Antonio Villaraigosa, and the current mayor, Eric Garcetti, both come from (and boast about) immigrant backgrounds, as do many other local elected officials. Four of Los Angeles's fifteen city council members are of Mexican descent, while several of the eight white council members are also children of immigrants. At the county level, the five-member Board of Supervisors includes only one Mexican American, Hilda Solis (a former U.S. secretary of labor) who succeeded Gloria Molina, an East Los Angeles political activist; Solis is known as a champion of immigrant issues. The sole African American member has taken pro-immigrant stances—partly because of his own political inclinations but also because the South Los Angeles area he represents has changed so dramatically.

It is not surprising that local political leaders have close personal ties with immigrant communities. After all, about 45 percent of the voters in the Los Angeles metro area (defined as LA and Orange Counties)—and nearly half the voters in the principal cities—are themselves immigrants or children of immigrants. Nevertheless, Los Angeles still has fewer immigrant-origin elected officials than cities like San José. But while immigrant leaders have not landed as many elected positions, they have forged an extensive array of institutionalized relationships with policy makers. For example, it was relatively easy for immigrant advocates to access the mayor's office under Villaraigosa, not only because he was sympathetic, but because he also hired many people with social movement experience and progressive backgrounds.

Of course, some of the increasing interest in immigrant issues was driven by increasing Latino political power. Over the course of the 1980s, grassroots political engagement helped double the number of Latino representatives over one decade and change long-standing political power dynamics (Brackman and Erie 1993). In 1985, for example, community activists in Eastside Los Angeles brought "insurgent" candidate Steve Rodriguez within four votes of unseating incumbent city council member Arthur Snyder (Aragon 2010). In the early 1990s, following lawsuits by the Mexican American Legal Defense and Education Fund (MALDEF) over redistricting, grassroots support propelled Gloria Molina, a city council member at the time, to become the first Latino on the Los Angeles County Board of Supervisors in over a century (Brackman and Erie 1993).

But the most striking feature of the political landscape is the social movement and multiracial character of the coalitions that have put officials in office. The political transformation of Los Angeles that was marked by Villaraigosa's election as mayor in May 2005 was powered by a progressive coalition anchored by labor unions and African American, Asian, Latino, and white liberal organizations—and Villaraigosa himself was careful not to be depicted as the "Latino" candidate, something that actually may have limited his latitude in dealing with immigrant issues as mayor (Sonenshein and Pinkus 2005). This embrace of a progressive multiculturalism was not a new phenomenon: Tom Bradley, the second African American to be elected mayor of a major city, held on to office for five terms starting in 1973 with the help of a broad-based multiracial coalition. Jackie Goldberg—an open lesbian and self-described progressive—served as a city council member and assemblywoman for a majority Latino constituency until she was termed out in 2006; a veteran of the Free Speech movement at UC Berkeley, she left a legacy of coalition building and progressive policies that includes the 1997 living wage ordinance that benefited many immigrant workers. Assemblyman Gil Cedillo—a former labor leader—championed legislation that would allow undocumented immigrants to obtain driver's licenses and in 2013 was elected to the Los Angeles City Council. Cedillo's successor in the Assembly, Kevin de León, is a longtime community organizer who helped plan mass protests against the anti-immigrant Proposition 187; he has now become a state senator representing Los Angeles's central core—and the California Senate's president pro tempore as of 2014.

The list could go on—the connection between electoral power and progressive organizing is both unusual and distinctive. While activists do not always get their way, the critical fact is that a significant share of the political actors in and around Los Angeles have a progressive social movement—rather than purely political—background. This has created a set of ties that allows for a particular kind of access and influence by activists. It has been matched by a lessened influence for business (which, of course, has been a subject of concern and complaint for business interests). We do not mean to overstate the case: business leaders are still influential, particularly when the economy slows and every municipality is courting investment; but the current situation is a far cry from a past period

when a small group of businessmen dictated the future of the city and the re
The reasons for the decline of their power reflect the abandonment of Los Angeles by Fortune 500 companies as much as the rise of progressive organizing, but
the scenario is different today: progressive, not just liberal; movement, not just
money; and activists, not just advocates.

Has the region's progressive political climate and immigrant-sensitive voting
bloc led to greater institutional receptivity to immigrants? It depends on whom
you ask—and where you are looking. The City and the County of Los Angeles have
long had human relations commissions; interestingly, each grew out of moments
of violence, with the county's being set up in the wake of the Zoot Suit Riots of the
1940s (formally incorporated as a commission in 1958) and the city's set up in the
wake of the Watts Riots in the mid-1960s. The city's human relations commission
established an Immigrant Advisory Committee (IAC), composed of forty different advocacy groups, to serve as an institutional mechanism for the inclusion of
immigrant voices into policy decisions. The committee allows access to government officials by various immigrant constituent groups, such as the Coalition
for Humane Immigrant Rights Los Angeles (CHIRLA), the Council of Mexican
Hometown Associations (COFEM), the Koreatown Immigrant Workers Association (KIWA), the National Association of Latino Elected and Appointed Officials
(NALEO), and the Mexican American Legal Defense Fund (MALDEF). While the
IAC has built stronger ties between the city and immigrant communities, there is
frustration that its mission hasn't been inserted into all city departments.

The city also has a Mayor's Office of Immigrant Affairs (MOIA), a fact that
suggests that immigrant integration is being addressed at an institutional level.
The MOIA, created during the previous mayoralty of James Hahn, floundered in
the first few years of the Villaraigosa administration because it lacked adequate
staffing and funding. This may not have been entirely accidental: Villaraigosa
came out early for immigrant rights, during his first year in office, speaking to
a crowd estimated at more than half a million at the 2006 Los Angeles march
for immigrant rights. However, he and his advisers worried that as a Latino
politician, he might get overly identified with one ethnicity—a constraint that
other contemporary mayoral supporters of immigrants, such as Richard M.
Daley of Chicago or Michael Bloomberg of New York, and even Villaraigosa's
successor, Eric Garcetti, do not face (see also Sterngold 2006). Indeed, one con-
fidante noted that in a meeting about attending the march, a mayoral adviser
suggested that "you can't be going out there and speaking to all of these immigrants that have come to City Hall, because you are the mayor of all the people,
not the Latino mayor. As soon as you go out and embrace this issue you are going
to be isolated. You are never going to be the mayor for everyone." The mayor
reportedly responded by telling his staff that he needed to take a strong stand

on immigration because it was a question of long-standing principles and basic integrity for him. At the same time, Villaraigosa allowed the Office of Immigrant Affairs to wither, although it became more active after 2008. Conversely, Villaraigosa's successor Eric Garcetti emphasized his Latino identity to signal his solidarity with the immigrant community, an asset afforded him by his mixed Jewish and Mexican ancestry. Upon election in 2013, Garcetti not only coordinated the revival of the Office of Immigrant Affairs and appointed Dr. Linda Lopez, the daughter of Latino immigrants, as its chief, but also championed this initiative as a demonstration of Los Angeles's support of comprehensive immigration reform and proactive approach to immigrant integration.

Compared with other cities with sizable immigrant populations that have made strong commitments to formal immigrant integration measures, like New York and Chicago, Los Angeles may seem less systematic in its efforts. But fortunately, there has been a strong social movement working to keep the city administration honest and ensure that political, economic, and social equity for immigrants remains a key feature of the regional policy agenda. Some of these organizers and organizations are from the immigrant rights tradition and others from labor and multiethnic community organizing groups. This political landscape also facilitated Mayor Garcetti's revival of the city's Office of Immigrant Affairs. Most significantly, social movements have envisioned a far broader version of immigrant integration than is occurring in many regions: the regional, coalition-based, and progressive orientation of active grassroots and established organizations has succeeded in integrating concerns of often low-wage immigrant communities in terms of labor, education, environmental justice, and other policy areas. Some of the most recognized immigrant rights organizations have established their power not necessarily by singular wins in terms of institutionalizing immigrant integration, but by representing the experiences of often marginalized undocumented immigrants in political activism (Pastor 2015). The number and diversity of players involved may make it harder to pin down the institutional mechanisms supporting immigrant integration, but that has ensured that immigrant rights are inextricable from broader progressive policy change. In addition, the breadth of the movement has created multiple pathways and opportunities for immigrant communities to exercise civic and political power.

Movements Matter

California's infamous Proposition 187—a 1994 ballot initiative intended to cut off public benefits to undocumented immigrants and remove undocumented children from the public school system—was a clarion call for the immigrant community. Los Angeles emerged as a hub for the immigrant rights movement in the struggle to oppose the proposition, partly because of the region's heavy immigrant population but also because of the presence of a multiracial social movement that includes strong civic institutions, labor, and community-based organizations. Indeed, in many ways, pro-immigrant advocates have gone beyond immigration issues per se, understanding that immigration reform and citizenship rights may create policy-level opportunities for enfranchisement, but that the ability to secure good jobs, healthy communities, and quality education requires immigrants to become engaged citizens who effect social change through collective action (Pastor 2015).

While the struggle against Proposition 187 was a turning point, it must be seen in the context of Los Angeles's post-1990s progressive political revival (Goodno 2005). The Los Angeles civil unrest of 1992, following the acquittal of Los Angeles police officers in the beating of African American Rodney King, was a pivotal moment in the region's class and ethnic politics. In response to the turmoil as well as the economic backdrop that had been one factor in the unrest, many new grassroots groups and alliances were formed to address social and civic inequality—and immigrants were often at the core of the issues that were raised.

These new groups and alliances include the Los Angeles Alliance for a New Economy, a labor-based group that has pushed for living wages, community benefits agreements, and so much more; the Bus Riders Union, a project of the left-leaning Labor/Community Strategy Center that organized the users of the county's bus system to insist on better service for the largely immigrant and African American working poor clientele; Strategic Concepts in Organizing and Policy Education (SCOPE) in South LA, a group that led a fight for jobs when the city was going to subsidize the building of a new film studio and which since has led a struggle for better employment as part of a municipal effort to retrofit buildings to reduce greenhouse gas emissions; and many, many others (Gottlieb, Freer, and Vallianatos 2005; Pastor 2001).

Unions are one example of how social movements have both reframed immigration as an economic justice issue and woven together immigrant energy and worker organizing. Around the early 1990s, groups representing immigrant communities had also been critical in reenergizing the labor movement in Los Angeles—and placing the concerns of immigrant workers at the center of these new efforts. While some argue that Latino workers have played a key role in Los Angeles labor unions for a long time (M. Garcia 1995; Sanchez 1993), it is undeniable that something new was afoot: organizing drives over the last several decades by the Hotel and Restaurant Employees Union (HERE), and by the Service Employees International Union (SEIU) for the Justice for Janitors campaign, were signs that labor unions were willing to embrace what had been considered an unorganizable worker population, especially the immigrant Latinos who are most likely to be undocumented.[4] These efforts preceded the broader AFL-CIO's shift to incorporate immigrant workers, which would not have been possible without the "social movement unionism" approach taken by SEIU and HERE to link with emerging immigrant community-based groups, as well as clergy and local civic leaders. During the 1980s, the Los Angeles County Federation of Labor was also the first AFL-CIO body to provide immigration-related services and support and to address the needs of Asian and Pacific Islander workers (LA County Federation of Labor, AFL-CIO 1990). Indeed, some observers suggest (convincingly, in our view) that the American labor movement reinvented itself in Los Angeles by embracing immigrant-worker organizing in key service sectors (Milkman 2006).

What defined some of the earliest successful work of these emerging organizations and coalitions—a strong focus on reducing economic inequality, a "pragmatism in policy objectives," a dedication to multiracial coalitions, and a strong effort to build a "mass base"—came to characterize the immigrant rights and service organizations that emerged during this period (Pastor, Benner, and Matsuoka 2009, 108). It is within this broader context of movement organizing that the immigrant rights movement has "grown up" in Los Angeles. Within regional political conversations, the main organizations in Los Angeles that compose this movement are not spoken of as solely immigrant rights organizations or outside the context of their broader work for social justice. As a result, the left-leaning and multiracial Coalition for Humane Immigrant Rights of Los Angeles has a more visible political presence than, say, the Mexican American Legal Defense Fund. Even MALDEF is actively engaged in worker justice, education, and leadership development issues and not simply immigration or civil rights issues per se. Also noteworthy and unusual is the fact that many organizations started from a grassroots organizing approach and then built out more traditional service and advocacy capacities. For example, the Central American Resources Center (CARECEN) began as a grassroots organization advocating for the rights of refugees from El Salvador, Guatemala, Nicaragua, and Honduras in the early 1980s and helped push Los Angeles to be declared a sanctuary city in 1989. Only later did the organization expand to include legal and social services, while remaining a key player in efforts for workers' rights, education, and immigrant rights.

This holds true beyond Los Angeles's Latino immigrant communities. The Koreatown Immigrant Workers Alliance (KIWA) is one of the most recognized among organizations serving Asian immigrant communities, partly because of its alliance with labor organizations and the broader progressive movement in Los Angeles. KIWA began originally as the *Korean* Immigrant Workers Association but shifted from a Korean-based identity to redefine itself as a multiracial group with a base of Korean and Latino immigrants who work in the central Los Angeles neighborhood known as Koreatown. Asian Americans Advancing Justice—Los Angeles (or, simply, Advancing Justice), formerly the Asian Pacific American Legal Center of Southern California, has long used legal strategies to advocate for civil rights; but it, too, expanded its work to integrate more organizing and movement-based strategies. The South Asian Network (SAN) was formed in 1990 but gained special significance in the period after the September 11, 2001, attacks on the United States. The growth of antipathy against Muslim, Arab, Middle Eastern, and South Asian communities and civil rights abuses against them in the name of national security and counterterrorism led many South Asians to be concerned about racial profiling and civil rights. Moreover, many recent South Asian migrants work in relatively low-skill and low-wage jobs, such as taxi driving, and SAN has been part of the effort to organize these workers.

One remarkable aspect of the effort to promote immigrant integration in Los Angeles is the relationship between immigrants and African Americans. A few of our interviewees broached this topic by addressing some of the tensions that emerge from multiracial organizing in transitional urban areas. This was particularly true in areas where Latinos and other ethnic groups have moved in large numbers. Several of the interviews touched on the importance of pointing to African immigrants as a way of bridging an understanding of the foreign-born. Two African American–led organizations simply suggested that an increased Latino and immigrant presence meant that established organizations had to embrace new constituencies. One leader noted, "I don't care what color people are, this is our neighborhood and we are going to organize whoever lives here" (Dupont-Walker 2010). Meanwhile, some groups—like the Community Coalition (CoCo) and SCOPE/AGENDA in South Los Angeles—responded to demographic changes by identifying themselves as black-brown organizations that focus on economic and social justice. They are very intentional about their multiracial identity; as one interviewee said, "Once you start doing that type of organizing intentionally . . . it's like second nature to just own being African American and Latino, and making sure that we're representing those constituencies" (Walton 2010), and that, in part, means lifting up immigrant as well as economic and neighborhood issues.

Some Latino immigrant rights organizations have also embraced multiracial alliances. In an interview, CHIRLA's director indicated that it was very important for immigrants to include members of the African American community in the debate on immigration reform (Salas 2010). The Center for Community Change is developing a curriculum that will help CHIRLA build interethnic bridges in the San Gabriel Valley, in this case between Latinos and Asians, both immigrant and native-born. CHIRLA also mentioned the use of the Crossing Borders Curriculum at the national level.[5] It is important to note that two prominent African American leaders expressed that if Latinos expect African American support on immigration reform, they need to do a better job of giving black immigrants a role at the negotiating table. The point—and one quietly echoed by some of the Asian groups—is that the immigration debate is often framed by Latino-dominated organizations, and other immigrant groups' voices do not always get heard.

In keeping with the social movement theme, leading immigrant-based organizations, like CHIRLA and Advancing Justice, have built upon their direct engagement and leadership development to "scale up" and become active participants in national efforts to achieve comprehensive immigration reform, such as the Reform Immigration for America campaign. Los Angeles is also home to the National Day Labor Organizing Network (NDLON), which built from intensive community-building and leadership development work to create a forty-member organization network that has been an active, progressive voice in state and national conversations on immigration (NDLON 2015). The youth organizing arms of many of the most active immigrant rights organizations, such as CHIRLA and CARECEN, have also worked in strong coalition with issue- and neighborhood-based groups like Community Coalition, Communities for a Better Environment, and the Eastside's Inner City Struggle (ICS), signaling that the most recent generation of Los Angeles organizers are beginning their training in a context of multiracial, multi-issue organizing (Pastor and Prichard 2012).

Immigrant rights organizations have also considered churches as active allies in these coalitions. For example, the Catholic Archdiocese of Los Angeles has championed immigration reform and immigrant integration issues. The connection between social justice and religious organizations has been crystallized in the multidenominational, interfaith group Clergy and Laity United for Economic Justice (CLUE), an extensive network of faith-based leaders who are involved in worker justice and have participated in various campaigns that directly affect immigrant workers and their families. For example, CLUE leaders built a black-brown alliance that brought together African American and Latino (many of them immigrant) churches in South Los Angeles in an effort to build multiracial alliances for economic justice. Other faith-based organizations, like One LA—an organizing project associated with the Industrial Areas Foundation, one of several national interfaith organizing groups—have been involved with organizing in Maywood, South LA, the Mid-City area, and even the more suburban San Fernando Valley. As will be discussed, others, like the PICO affiliate LA Voice,[6] have been active in successful campaigns to prevent the towing of cars taken from undocumented drivers.

Most important, many of these coalitions for economic, political, and social justice—whether led by youth, faith leaders, or multiracial coalition builders—raise the concerns of immigrant communities within a broader context. Partly as a result, their strategies have included pushing for particular policy and institutional changes, but also securing long-term gains by developing civic power and helping get progressive candidates elected (Gottlieb, Freer, and Vallianatos 2005). Perhaps because of these broader ties and efforts at power building, local opposition has not been able to effectively tap into the sort of anti-immigrant sentiments displayed in other parts of the country. With strong allies, respondents feel that while nothing is easy, they have the numbers to exert a voice and exercise some power to influence policy and practice.

It is important to note that this movement strength can mask some underlying weaknesses. Among these, once you move beyond the city core of the Los Angeles region, the immigrant organizational infrastructure is far weaker and less rooted, a problem taken up in the chapter on the Inland Empire but also seen in the San Fernando and San Gabriel Valley suburbs that adjoin the City of Los Angeles. And as noted above, there are fewer visible immigrant integration institutions that can help expand the scope of economic and social equity for immigrant communities. But in looking at two issue areas more closely, namely policing and education, we can see the ways in which many of the threads in Los Angeles's movement-building that we have noted—grassroots leadership development and organizing, multiracial and multi-issue working partnerships and coalitions, and an orientation toward tangible policy change *and* building long-term political power—tie together to shape the prospects of immigrant integration in the region.

Immigrant Integration in Los Angeles: Examining Progress

We have suggested that a vibrant network of social movement organizations in Los Angeles has embedded immigrant issues into everyday social justice efforts and that immigrant organizations have embedded broader social concerns into their work. Nonetheless, more traditional immigration issues like legal reform and enforcement continue to shape immigrant experiences and advocacy efforts. At the same time, groups like CHIRLA, MALDEF, Advancing Justice, and others have also shifted their focus onto leadership development, political integration, and improving the daily lives of immigrants, partly because hopes for legalization and reform have faded and partly because these are the everyday realities that affect immigrants and their families.

Below, we discuss the efforts around immigrant integration in two key areas where the everyday "rubber" of leadership development, organizing, and coalition and movement building has had to "hit the road" and lead to visible change in the lives of immigrant populations: local law enforcement and education (with the latter being a particular challenge for the economic progress that we outline above). In both cases, advocates have been better able than before to direct their efforts toward shifting both specific policies and the broader orientations of public institutions responsible for these areas. While they have, of course, met mixed results, by mobilizing multiethnic, cross-neighborhood coalitions in sustained activism, the movement has secured tangible local changes, some of which are now beginning to reverberate to state-level governance. Where policies have been slow to be implemented, these groups have worked to apply continued pressure and integrate the voices of immigrant communities into the policy-making process. They are helping to ensure that schools, police departments, and other public institutions do not stand as roadblocks—and instead perhaps eventually become assets—to immigrant integration.

Local Police Enforcement

In June 1990, a mostly immigrant janitorial workforce seeking a union contract peacefully marched through Century City—and was met by a baton-wielding Los Angeles police force that arrested forty and injured two dozen, an action that drew condemnation from many and a rebuke from the mayor (Baker 1990). Nearly two years later, the LA civil unrest triggered by the verdicts in the Rodney King trial brought its own set of tensions with immigrants: during the unrest, the LAPD patrolled the riot areas with officers from the Immigration and Naturalization Service on the grounds that the police did not have enough Spanish-speaking officers, and handed suspected undocumented residents directly over to immigration authorities (Pastor 1993). And it is not just ancient history: a May Day immigrant rights march in 2007 was brought to an end by a melee that left 246 protesters and journalists as well as eighteen police officers injured (an incident we discuss in more detail below; see Winton and Helfand 2007).

Thus, it is striking that there was a general consensus among our interviewees that the Los Angeles Police Department has rebuilt its relationships and image with the immigrant community. The change was a result of institutional restructuring that focused on improving services and more effective community policing. Some of these changes where a direct result of immigrant organizations that successfully lobbied for police reform, and others were due to broader social movement efforts to reshape relationships between local police and communities of color. Some of the immigration groups—CHIRLA, the city and county human relations commissions, and local churches—have even institutionalized their relationships with local enforcement as a direct result of these reform efforts. As research has demonstrated, police practices vis-à-vis immigration can only partially be explained by the broader political orientation of city hall (Lewis and Ramakrishnan 2007). However, in 2012, Lewis and colleagues found that immigrant-friendly cities tend to shape policing through local bureaucratic reforms. This makes sense in the City of Los Angeles, where community organizations both partner with and push city departments, including the police, to shift their policies.

Nationwide, bureaucratic restructuring and reform in police departments are strongly linked to changes in police policy toward immigrants (Lewis and Ramakrishnan 2007). Urban police chiefs, in some instances, have sought to reframe the police force as professionals with a particular mission of serving the community, and some chiefs now acknowledge that crime prevention efforts can be effective only with input from and positive relationships with the community (Skolnick and Bayley 1988). In Los Angeles, these reframing and prevention strategies are, of course, not just generated inside the police department but respond to sustained, organized pressure from local social movement groups and advocates, as was the case both before and after the 1992 civil unrest and the 1999 Rampart police corruption scandal (Rice 2012). As in other sectors of movement organizing in Los Angeles, organizations themselves have at times assumed an outsider role and at times worked in partnerships with law enforcement and other civic institutions to produce change (Pastor, Benner, and Matsuoka 2009; Pastor and Ortiz 2009a).

Given that, some changes within the LAPD that benefited immigrants were part of a broader strategy to improve community relations across the board, and some were directly linked to concerns of the immigrant community. For example, since 1993—a year after the unrest—each policing district (basically organized around police stations) has had a Community Police Advisory Board, composed of select community members, which meets on a monthly basis to discuss community issues. The LAPD, along with several other California municipal police departments, has also enacted a number of policies aimed at improving its service and its relationship with immigrant communities (Lewis and Ramakrishnan 2007). Among these measures, the department accepts IDs that are issued by the Mexican consulate as valid forms of identification. The department also implemented a policy in the late 1990s that created salary incentives for officers to learn a second language, as the city's changing demographics and mounting political pressure forced the department to make changes. The LAPD now dedicates ninety hours to language training as part of its educational curriculum. Groups like CHIRLA have also worked with the LAPD to hold a community-policing academy in which public agencies and community advocates review police officer training programs.

Making use of its discretionary power, the LAPD has improved relationships with immigrant groups through its implementation and enforcement of Special Order 40, a rule that prohibits officers from asking about immigration status during the course of a routine stop. Adopted in 1979 under the direction of Chief Daryl Gates, the order was suspended in practice during the civil unrest, something that clearly poisoned relations at that time. One of our interviewees framed Special Order 40 as part of a broader community policing strategy that allowed the department to build strong ties with the Latino community (Romero 2010).

In 2008, anti-immigrant forces rallied in the wake of a high-profile murder of an African American seventeen-year-old involving an undocumented immigrant suspect to push the city council's Public Safety Committee to repeal Special Order 40 by arguing that it protects violent undocumented criminals from possible deportation (Blankstein and Winton 2008). In the 2008 hearings regarding Special Order 40, numerous current and former police leaders spoke up in favor of keeping the order intact, and CHIRLA, the juvenile justice reform group Youth Justice Coalition, and other community groups, including those representing African American constituents, mobilized supporters to provide a voice for immigrant communities affected by the order. The relationships that community groups had established among each other and with the police bore fruit: the effort to amend Special Order 40 at the council level was quickly defeated, and movement organizations successfully challenged attempts by anti-immigrant groups (and mainstream media) to paint the issue as one of black versus brown communities.

Two of our interviewees from the police force confirm the argument that Special Order 40 is largely misunderstood by both the public and by rank-and-file officers. Former chief Bernard Parks stated that the special order does not prevent officers from doing their job (Parks 2010). Captain Rigoberto Romero, former Latino community liaison for the chief of police, told us that the special order does allow officers to use documentation status as an enforcement tactic if suspects are involved in violent felonies or high-degree misdemeanors (Romero 2010). Still, both Parks and Romero independently stressed the same point: local police should not act as immigration enforcement agents if they wish to maintain trust with the immigrant community. Both men believe immigrants would be less likely to report crimes and cooperate in investigations if they fear possible deportation by the police.

While most of our interviewees acknowledged that the LAPD has improved its relationship with various immigrant communities, both city officials and community advocates pointed out that several key incidents damaged public perception of how the police department interacts with the immigrant community. One was the aforementioned 2007 May Day rally, an event in fact organized by the Multi-ethnic Immigrant Worker Organizing Network, which CHIRLA and KIWA helped lead. At the rally, which took place in MacArthur Park, located in a Central American immigrant neighborhood, police officers used force to control what they considered to be a hostile crowd. This resulted in numerous injuries and several lawsuits against the city. Municipal leaders, including then-mayor Villaraigosa and police chief Bill Bratton, were quick to admit that officers made critical errors in judgment and deployment tactics. An internal investigation revealed problems with improper training and assigned some of the blame to faults in leadership. But interestingly—and of profound importance—a number of our interviewees, including representatives from the police department, claimed that the police reaction was not related to race.

Finally, while interviewees acknowledged the greater transparency and community involvement of the LAPD, some contended that police leadership does not yet reflect Los Angeles's ethnic diversity. More representative police leadership has been seen to lead to healthier relationships between police and immigrant communities (Decker et al. 2009). As one prominent community leader mentioned, no Latino officers were considered for the open chief position after Bratton left the job in 2009: "Given the significant amount of interaction and the size of the immigrant community and LAPD, it would've been terrific if it was an immigrant—or a child of immigrants—Spanish-speaking police chief candidate who had a serious opportunity to get that job. Such a person would understand why it's important to maintain good relations with the immigrant community" (Saenz 2010).

Perhaps as a direct response to these sorts of criticisms, the newly selected police chief, Charlie Beck, prioritized his relationship with the immigrant Latino community and appointed an immigrant—Captain Rigoberto Romero—to serve as his community liaison. Chief Beck and Captain Romero both cited Special Order 40 as a "core value" of the LAPD, one that is aimed at building stronger relationships with the Latino immigrant community, and Beck affirmed his support in a meeting at Dolores Mission Catholic Church in East Los Angeles just a month after his appointment. In March 2011, Chief Beck met a key demand of immigrant rights activists when he announced a change in a previous policy in which LAPD impounded the cars of unlicensed drivers stopped at sobriety checkpoints—even if they were sober. The new policy allowed the driver to arrange for a licensed driver to take the vehicle, saving close to $1,200 in impoundment fees (Rubin and Bloomekatz 2011). The result was a 39 percent decline in the number of cars impounded by the LAPD in just one year, although the LA Superior Court deemed that this impoundment rule undermined the authority of the state vehicle code, and it was therefore rescinded. Chief Beck responded by encouraging police officers to consider less-severe impoundment options, such as those that do not require a thirty-day holding period (Rubin 2013).

Beck's decision did not emerge simply out of his goodwill: it was due in large part to the sustained pressure of a multiyear campaign against the checkpoints, led by interfaith groups like LA Voice and the grassroots Southern California Immigration Coalition (Daily News Wire Services 2011). The effort provided a precursor for a statewide bill passed later that year, authored by progressive (and movement-raised) assemblyman Gil Cedillo, to ban the practice of towing unlicensed drivers' cars at checkpoints, so long as the car could be handed to a licensed driver or registered owner; through the Free Our Cars Coalition, activists have continued to mobilize to ensure these policies are followed where police have failed to comply (Linthicum 2013).

The Los Angeles Police Department has also worked to implement policies that limit its officers' role as immigration enforcement agents; and in July 2014, the city-level LAPD announced that it would no longer honor ICE detainers—that is, requests to hold immigrants who have been arrested but would otherwise be released. But Los Angeles County signed a 287(g) memorandum of understanding with ICE in February 2005. This is particularly striking, given that only thirty-seven counties nationwide signed such an agreement, codifying what are often informal police relationships with ICE (Decker et al. 2009). Under the agreement, Los Angeles sheriff's deputies that have been trained are able to question detainees about their immigration status, consider evidence to support deportation, prepare detainers, administer immigration oaths, take sworn statements from detainees, and prepare notice-to-appear applications (Coalition for Humane Immigrant Rights of Los Angeles 2008). The LA Sheriff's Department referred 10,840 people to ICE for possible deportation between February 2005 and June 2008 (Gorman 2008).

CHIRLA and other immigrant advocates had hoped that a new Department of Homeland Security administration under President Obama would give them momentum to repeal existing 287(g) agreements, but they initially made little progress. Immigrant advocates used new policy language that the Obama administration issued as an opportunity to lobby county supervisors to consider a different approach to any new memorandum of understanding. Los Angeles County supervisors Gloria Molina and Mark Ridley-Thomas supported efforts to limit participation in the 287(g) program, but immigrant advocates were unable to convince pro-enforcement supervisors, who were led by Supervisor Mike Antonovich. Ultimately, it was federal budgetary considerations that led to the end of the quite-costly 287(g), which was phased out and replaced by the Secure Communities initiative in 2012. This limited the relationship with ICE but mandated that police departments send fingerprints of anyone booked under criminal charges to ICE to cross-check with immigration records, a program adopted by nearly all U.S. jurisdictions (Immigration and Customs Enforcement 2013).

Eventually, sustained activism at the local and state level from CHIRLA, the Southern California Immigration Coalition, DREAMer organizations, and others cracked the sheriff's department's intransigence in this area. In 2013, Sheriff Lee Baca announced his agency would limit its participation in Secure Communities and no longer send ICE fingerprints for what were considered "low-level" cases (Hesson 2013).

More recently, in 2013, immigrant rights and broader social justice organizations, thanks to their long-term regional power-building efforts, were able to press successfully for the passage of the state-level TRUST Act, coauthored by Los Angeles's state senator Kevin De León. The act prohibits law enforcement agencies from placing individuals on ICE holds. Pressed by established groups including Los Angeles–based NDLON, Advancing Justice, CARECEN, and CHIRLA, as well as grassroots immigrant youth organizing groups, the city council passed a resolution supporting the act and took a key role in the successful statewide coalition.

Where policy changes have been slow in coming, local immigration groups have challenged the harmful effects of federal immigration policing through other strategies. A surge in immigration-related raids led organizations in Los Angeles to form rapid-response networks between 2006 and 2010. Worker centers and other advocacy groups created information networks through SMS (text messaging) to help gather community support against raids as they occurred. CHIRLA created a network of lawyers and community organizations that developed a "Know Your Rights" campaign, which led to more receptive relationships with both local law enforcement and the Department of Homeland Security (DHS), as well as an enforcement forum cosponsored by CHIRLA and DHS. The forum provided a space for participants to discuss their concerns about enforcement practice and policies.

The picture then squares with what we were suggesting before: long-term coalitions anchored in social justice have had a significant impact on policing policies within the City of Los Angeles, but a much more limited effect in the rest of the county. The geographic pattern both results from and is complicated by the patchwork of policies and political attitudes toward immigrants across the region (see, for example, Lewis et al. 2012). And the varying response by locality matters more than ever in a context where the Obama administration conducted a record number of deportations (438,421 deportations in fiscal year 2013, as compared to 391,597 in 2009 and a low of 165,168 in 2002; see Gonzalez-Barrera and Krogstad 2014). Because these deportations often target immigrants with no criminal record, local advocacy groups have worked hard to ensure that law enforcement wields its discretionary power and bureaucratic autonomy to protect immigrant communities. At the same time, the geographic

limit of such changes in policing indicates the need to develop movement organizing infrastructure outside the central city core, a fact that has not been lost
on advocates.

Education

Education is, of course, a vehicle for immigrant integration because of its long-
term effects on economic and social mobility—and education and immigrant
social justice organizing has a long history in California that dates back to the
1946 case of *Mendez v. Westminster*, which began a national fight against school
segregation. Moreover, immigrants and children of immigrants make up a large
share of Los Angeles's students: in 2010, for example, 41 percent of all students in
the elementary schools in the Los Angeles Unified School District (LAUSD), the
nation's second largest, were classified as English learners.[7] One would wish success for these students—but the data suggests that they are not doing well. Using
the academic performance index, an accountability measure used by the state
of California, Asians in LAUSD slightly outperform non-Hispanic whites, while
African American and Latinos measure 29 and 25 percent below whites, respectively. Unfortunately, we can only break this data out by ethnicity, since nativity
is not collected; however, English learners perform 31 percent below whites.[8]
And the performance measures account only for those who are still in school: in
the LAUSD, the high school dropout rate for Latinos is 32 percent and for African Americans 37 percent, while for Asians and whites, it is 12 and 18 percent,
respectively.[9] It is easy to see how dropout rates affect young people immediately
after the supposed age of graduation. For those between the ages of nineteen and
twenty-two in Los Angeles County, nearly 70 percent of whites and 80 percent
of Asians are enrolled in a postsecondary program, with very little difference
between U.S.-born and immigrant Asians. The postsecondary enrollment rate
for African Americans is 52 percent, nearly identical to that of U.S.-born Latinos.
Bringing up the rear are immigrant Latinos—with a postsecondary enrollment
rate of 25 percent. While part of this disparity is due to a large number of recent
arrivals that are in the labor force only, it also highlights a special challenge for
immigrant Latinos in Southern California's school systems.[10]

It is perhaps little wonder then that Mayor Villaraigosa adopted education
reform as a key goal for his administration, including an initial effort to take
over the whole school system—à la Mayor Bloomberg in New York and Mayor
Daley in Chicago. After running into significant resistance, he instead began running his own candidates for the school board in 2006 and then, with the new
leadership, worked to take over some of the district's lowest-performing schools
through his Partnership for Los Angeles Schools. According to key staff members,

the mayor was so keen to reform local schools because he believes that the city's prospects for increased employment and prosperity depend on them.

In tandem with, and in fact preceding, the former mayor's work to reform Los Angeles's educational system, a number of community organizations brought students and parents together, regardless of race or nativity, into multiethnic campaigns to press for increased educational quality and postsecondary access. In the early 2000s, a coalition of youth and parent-led groups organized to ensure that all LAUSD schools provide and require students to complete the "A–G" courses required to attend any of California's public universities. The campaign was spearheaded by the South Los Angeles–based Community Coalition, which first cut its teeth trying to prevent liquor stores from reopening after the Los Angeles civil unrest in 1992; the East Los Angeles education and equity group Inner City Struggle; and more than twenty other groups from Central, East, and South Los Angeles (Inner City Struggle 2014a). Students surveyed literally thousands of their peers to find that, contrary to popular perception, low-income youth of color were interested in attending college but were getting neither the required courses nor other resources to achieve this. After six years, in 2005, students and parents succeeded in pressuring the LAUSD board to adopt the "A–G Life Prep" resolution requiring all schools to provide these courses and to make these categories standards for graduation.

Student advocates did not stop there: these organizations pressed for a 2008 internal audit to see if schools were meeting this mandate, finding that numerous schools were far from delivering on this promise, particularly in the neighborhoods that needed it most. Advocates continued to press for concrete budgets and plans to increase access to and help students understand the importance of this college prep curriculum. In 2012, advocates pushed the board to further codify the A–G courses as part of graduation requirements, mandating that all students earn a C or above to pass (Blume 2012).

Social justice groups, educators, and former mayor Villaraigosa also sought to deal with the contentious issues of racial conflict between Latino (often immigrant) and African American students. This is important because many schools have undergone dramatic demographic transformations: the eight main high schools in South Los Angeles (Crenshaw, Dorsey, Fremont, Jefferson, Jordan, Locke, Manual Arts, and Washington) went from being 86 percent African American and 13 percent Latino in the academic year 1981–1982 to being 69 percent Latino and only 30 percent African American in 2008–2009.[11] The mayor's office deployed the Human Relations Commission to work with the LAUSD on training for staff and students in schools where racial tensions erupted between different groups, to diffuse racial conflict. However, this training is conducted on a site-by-site basis and is not part of a comprehensive curriculum.

According to our interviews, some of the tensions can be attributed to a decline in school infrastructure. In a district where, until the 2000s, a new high school had not been built for over thirty years, crowded schools and poor classroom conditions led to racialized debates about the distribution of public resources. Since the early 1990s and California's Proposition 187, anti-immigrant groups have framed the debate by blaming immigrants for declining school resources, particularly in the context of Los Angeles's shifting economy (Johnson, Farrell, and Guinn 1997). Some U.S.-born residents feel that immigrants are taking resources away from citizens—which can be especially problematic for black parents who already feel shortchanged by the system. For example, in 2009 at John Ritter Elementary in Watts, African American parents were angry when summer school classes were canceled because of a shortage of funds—but money was available from separate sources for summer school classes that targeted English-language learners. As in the aforementioned case of the tensions over Special Order 40, cross-cutting alliances among organizations have been important in helping immigrant and U.S.-born residents see their common interests and giving them a space to work together to change policy.

There have been significant moments where the mayor's office, the school board, teachers' unions, and social justice advocates have aligned toward resolving some of the issues that underlie these racialized tensions. In 2008, various advocates, the mayor's office, and the board of education coalesced around a county-wide measure to grant LAUSD a $7 billion bond to build more schools, upgrade facilities, and increase technology district-wide. This furthered a continual effort by advocates since 1997 to pass a series of bonds to end the district's more-than-thirty-year-long freeze on the construction of new schools. In a matter of a decade, the district has succeeded in building or adding to over 180 facilities, benefiting students across the district (Duchon 2009).

Social justice groups, city hall, and teachers' unions have also come together around locally controlled education under the "pilot schools" model, which in some ways serves as an alternative to charter schools in Los Angeles. Developed by a coalition of over forty groups, which includes immigrant organizations in central Los Angeles, these first pilot schools were launched in 2007 at the new Belmont High School site in the heavily Latino immigrant neighborhood of Pico-Union. Pilot schools are typically a group of small schools on one campus; they include a focus on particular areas like leadership, arts, or technology and share a "community schools" model that brings a range of services together under one roof (Reason Foundation 2009). At the Belmont Pilot Schools, one of the small pilot schools, Civitas, includes leadership training operated by CARECEN and gives youth opportunities in social movement activism. CARECEN was also instrumental in a more than ten-year-long effort to have the new Belmont school built in the first place, as many of the immigrant students in the neighborhood had to be bused miles to the San Fernando Valley and other locations (CARECEN-LA 2014). Inner City Struggle and other East Los Angeles groups also organized to have the new Esteban E. Torres High School follow the pilot schools model (Inner City Struggle 2014b).

Models of grassroots leadership development and organizing were also applied to engage immigrant parents through the Parent University, a program launched by SEIU Local 1877 (the same local behind the Justice for Janitors campaign), in which janitors who are parents of school-age children are taught about parents' rights, school governance, English-language classification, college prep, and other issues relevant to helping their children and holding schools accountable. Launched in part because a poll of union members showed they ranked children's education even above immigration reform, it squares with careful empirical work that demonstrated that social movement union activism can also produce parents who are more engaged in school advocacy (Terriquez 2011; Terriquez et al. 2009).

Similar patterns of parent engagement can be found at a more formal institutional level. For example, district-based Language Assessment Committees have become important civic participation vehicles for immigrant parents of English language learners (ELLs). Youth and parent-led groups like ICS, CARECEN, and Students for Education Reform representing immigrant communities have also stepped in to include immigrant parents in LAUSD's rollout of the Local Control Funding Formula (LCFF), which disburses millions in new funds from California's Proposition 30 sales tax to public schools throughout the state through a participatory budget process (Alagot 2014). Advocates have sought to ensure LCFF funds will serve ELL and low-income students who continue to face high dropout rates.

Research has shown that oftentimes administration and leadership in school districts in suburban areas will take direct, bureaucratic action to serve immigrant students, often with little backing from municipal government (Jones-Correa 2008b). In the case of Los Angeles, though, the landscape is far more complex: it is social justice advocates from immigrant and nonimmigrant communities—in collaboration and sometimes in conflict with city hall, the LAUSD board, teachers' unions, philanthropic foundations, and business associations—that have shaped the way schools serve immigrant youth. The case of education is also particularly complicated by the fact that the LAUSD reaches far beyond the bounds of the central core or even the City of Los Angeles, including over one thousand schools that run the gamut from high-immigrant suburban cities like Maywood to wealthy, mostly native-born areas such as Marina Del Rey. This has spurred protracted tensions over the decades—and efforts from different, mostly wealthy groups to break the district apart—but it also means that the efforts of social justice groups in the central core have wide reverberations for immigrant families throughout the county.

The key point here—one in keeping with our "LA Story"—is simply how much the educational reform efforts owe their momentum and scope to social movement organizing. Such organizing has been anchored in cross-community coalition building, focused not only on policy change but also on implementation, yet it has not obscured the particular concerns of immigrant communities. Many of the youth involved in these efforts for reform earlier in the decade have also gone on to other efforts, including direct advocacy for immigration reform as part of the DREAM movement (Terriquez and Patler 2012). Immigrant students have developed their own strong regional and national networks around the DREAM Act and access to higher education, leading to the Obama administration's 2012 implementation of Deferred Action for Childhood Arrivals (Nicholls 2013). Education reform has been a key site to reshape the prospects of immigrant youth—while also inspiring a new generation of advocates who have taken the helm of the immigrant rights movement beyond the boundaries of Los Angeles and cast a broader vision of immigrant integration.

New Immigrant Spaces: Maywood and Southeast Los Angeles

As noted earlier, Los Angeles's immigrant population is more dispersed than it was thirty years ago. Few areas have been more affected by this transformation than the industrial inner-ring suburbs of Southeast Los Angeles, places like Bell, Bell Gardens, Commerce, Cudahay, Huntington Park, Maywood, South Gate, and Vernon. Southeast Los Angeles once served as the heart of Los Angeles's industrial manufacturing (Rocco 1999). Industrial giants like Bethlehem Steel and Chrysler operated plants on Slauson Avenue, one of the area's major thoroughfares. Ford operated a plant in Pico Rivera, and General Motors made Pontiac, Oldsmobile, and Buick cars in South Gate. Firestone opened a large tire plant in South Gate sometime in 1928. This was by design: as urban planner Bill Fulton points out, "Cars and tires went to the lowlands, creating an industrial belt south and east of downtown, along the Los Angeles River and the major rail lines that followed the river from the rail yards south to the ports near Long Beach" (Fulton 2001, 72).

Communities like Maywood, Bell, and South Gate—as well as communities to the south like Lynwood, Compton, and Carson—functioned as a mixed-use development path that provided space for both industrial growth and residential expansion; indeed, the idea of an "industrial suburb" was a marketing scheme that promised bountiful employment close to single-family homes with lush private lawns. The concept was appealing, and as major manufacturers moved into the region, a steady stream of white working- and middle-class families settled in Southeast Los Angeles (Nicolaides 2002). But the post-1970s deindustrialization that transformed Los Angeles's economy—every single one of the plants mentioned above is no longer operating—led to the out-migration of most white families. They were quickly replaced by a wave of Latinos—a large share of them immigrants—who moved into the region with many of the same hopes for a better future that white families possessed a generation earlier. By the mid-1980s, immigrants had transformed southeastern Los Angeles into a mostly Latino region.

To track through the change—and response—in one location, we look at Maywood. Incorporated as a city in 1924, Maywood covers roughly one square mile and has a population of approximately twenty-eight thousand, making it the densest city (in terms of population per square mile) in California. Like other cities in the southeastern LA region, Maywood, in its early rise as an inner-ring suburb, was closely tied to blue-collar and middle-class white suburbanization—and its demographic transformation paralleled a process of deindustrialization and white flight. The 1970 Census reported that Maywood was 97 percent white and about 16 percent foreign-born (although 36 percent of the population was Spanish-speaking; in the 1970 Census, race and Spanish origin were not separated), which implies, given that there were only seven black residents, that the city was nearly two-thirds non-Hispanic white.[12] Today, 98 percent of the population is Latino, 47 percent is foreign-born, and 92 percent of its residents older than five speak a language other than English at home (with nearly 40 percent of households considered to be linguistically isolated, meaning no household member fourteen years or over speaks English "very well").[13] And while white flight may have opened up opportunities for new Latino and immigrant residents, they seem condemned to low-wage employment, given that per capita income levels are equal to about 42 percent of the county average.

What distinguishes Maywood from other cities in Southeast Los Angeles is that an organized immigrant base used the city's demographic transformation as an opportunity to build a vibrant civil society that managed to elect a pro-immigrant mayor and city council. While the nearby city of Bell has become the poster child for Latino political corruption—having experienced an infamous scandal first exposed in 2010 in which the city manager and city council apparently conspired to pay themselves excessive salaries—Maywood suggests that a movement built on pro-immigrant civic engagement can provide a broad platform for immigrant rights.[14] More important, as our interviews revealed,

Maywood's political transformation was part of an intentional geographic strategy to appropriate space by capturing a local jurisdiction in order to transform it into a platform for pro-immigrant regional organizing—a story in keeping with our emphasis on social movement pressures and realities in Los Angeles.

Reframing Immigrant Politics and Integration in Southeast LA

A series of recurring police DUI checkpoints in the early 2000s sparked a political revolution in Maywood (Glover and Lait 2007). Immigrant activists claimed that the owner of a local towing company was using political contributions to garner support for the checkpoints from Maywood's city council—and that the young and university-educated U.S.-born Latinos who controlled the city council were using checkpoints as a personal and public revenue stream. Funds obtained from the seizing of cars were reportedly used not only for private gain but to hire more police officers and thus expand the capacity of the city to conduct more checkpoints; immigrant dollars were being used to further expand car seizures.

Community activists, many of them involved with the Mexican immigrant community center Comite Pro Uno, argued that the checkpoints were effectively dispossessing Maywood's immigrant population by seizing cars from unlicensed drivers. Maywood residents, native-born and immigrant alike, actively protested the checkpoints. A coalition of community organizers and residents set up an elaborate system that subverted police efforts by warning drivers about the location of impending checkpoints. This led to a series of confrontations between police and pro-immigrant activists that escalated as Maywood officials increased the frequency of the checkpoints, with police routinely holding checkpoints every Friday and Saturday evening.

Mounting public scrutiny—including a series of articles in the *Los Angeles Times*—and pressure from Maywood's immigrant community leaders eventually induced Maywood to change its policy in 2003 (Del Olmo 2003). It also led California's attorney general to investigate the police department for possible discrimination and corruption, and eventually forced a restructuring of the Maywood Police Department (Glover and Wagner 2009). Interestingly, Maywood's experience proved a groundbreaking precursor to the aforementioned changes in Los Angeles and California state policy on checkpoints. But more important than all the specifics: the fight over police checkpoints led to the emergence of a vibrant civil society composed of a highly organized network of new community-based organizations.

Comite Pro Uno, for example, became a key player in Maywood politics, and Padres Unidos de Maywood (United Parents of Maywood, or PUMA), which later became one of the city's most politically influential community groups, was formed as a direct response to the police checkpoints. Other groups involved in this network include Maywood Unidos (Maywood United) and the United Students of the Southeast Cities (USSC). Maywood Unidos was formed by homeowners, many of them immigrants, who opposed proposals by the Los Angeles Unified School District to demolish homes in order to make way for the construction of a new high school. The United Students of the Southeast Cities—a group of immigrant high school students from Bell, Maywood, Huntington Park, and Southgate—was also formed and mobilized support for AB 540 and the California version of the DREAM Act, two pieces of legislation that have made it easier for undocumented immigrant students to attend and pay for college in the state.

By 2005, this network of immigrant-based community organizations transitioned from outsider oppositional politics to an integration-focused movement when they successfully ran candidates for city council. PUMA and other groups tied to Comite Pro Uno targeted Maywood's two biggest voting blocs—Latino senior citizens and young families, many of them recent citizens. Pro-immigrant groups were ultimately successful in electing Felipe Aguirre—a Comite Pro Uno leader—because they were able to increase voter turnout. Maywood's new political leadership declared it effectively a "sanctuary city" for immigrants—that is, a location in which local authorities would not check for documentation status as part of regular operations. As a result, anti-immigrant activists descended on the city and attacked the new leadership. VDARE.com, an anti-immigrant web-based news service, called Maywood "occupied America." Anti-immigrant forces like the Minuteman Project and FAIR routinely attacked Maywood for its stance.

While Maywood's newly elected city leaders inserted themselves into the raging immigration debate, their political platforms were largely defined by more local and nontraditional immigrant rights issues. For example, Comite Pro Uno leaders told us that their involvement in local grassroots organizing transformed the organization's political and geographical perspective. Comite Pro Uno was founded as an organization that provided services to the immigrant community, but its leaders were also very involved in Mexican national politics. All this changed as a direct result of their local organizing, which anchored Comite Pro Uno's political work in everyday social justice issues—like schools, police enforcement, housing, and the environment—that shaped immigrant life in Maywood.

Much as has been occurring in Los Angeles more broadly, immigrant issues became fused with concerns like democratic governance, environmental justice, education, and the historical legacies of class and race that took root during the region's earlier industrial age. As one Maywood leader noted,

> So there were a lot of good union paying jobs here when the population was mostly Anglo in Maywood. And when a lot of these companies ended up closing in the late seventies, early eighties, a lot of those people started to take off, and then the people that came in to start to clean up all the previous society's mess, environmentally and otherwise, [were] the Latino immigrants. Because we cleaned up all the environmental waste that was left by companies like Bethlehem Steel and National Glass, Anchor Hawking, this became a Superfund site. And we were cleaning a lot of these sites that were for previously prosperous societies. We were cleaning it with our bodies. (Aguirre 2010)

Immigrants are rebuilding southeastern Los Angeles; but they face a tough road ahead. Many cannot rely on the well-paid industrial jobs that once provided the region's families with middle-class lifestyles. As one Maywood leader said, "We've gone from union jobs to Walmart jobs" (Alvarado 2010). Immigrants have also inherited a city that is constrained by very limited resources. In 2010, for example, the city laid off all its employees and contracted out virtually all city services, including its police department, as a way to avoid bankruptcy (Vives, Gottlieb, and Becerra 2010). The fact that so many low-income immigrants live in such a small jurisdiction limits the amount of revenues the city is able to collect. As one city leader put it, "We basically have to live off of whatever the state sends back to Maywood and whatever amount [of] money that the federal government gives out to Maywood, which in reality is based on the low Census count that we had last time" (Aguirre 2010).

Despite the challenges, Maywood is important because it shows how immigrants can capture political power without significant contributions from labor unions or from the Latino arm of the Democratic Party—an important third way, given our earlier discussion about the relative lack of elected immigrant leaders in Los Angeles. Grassroots leaders—most of them immigrant—were able to create a mobilization apparatus that included local churches and was tied to Comite Pro Uno but also managed to maintain a certain level of independence. Again, a social movement theme dominates, but a warning is relevant here as well: in much the same way that the takeover of municipal leadership by many black political figures in the 1960s came just as big cities were on the skids, the gaining of a significant political voice in a set of inner-ring suburbs plagued by low incomes, a shrinking tax base, and the environmental wreckage of past industrial practices is not necessarily a winning strategy.

Immigrants and their children are as much a part of Los Angeles as Hollywood or sunshine. The city and county have long been meccas for migrants from every corner of the globe—and every state in the Union. While there is certainly a history of exclusion—Los Angeles was an epicenter of the mass deportations of Mexicans during the Great Depression, a focal point of the mass assembly of Japanese Americans during the wartime internment, and a stellar example of the sort of redlining and racially restrictive covenants that partitioned postwar America—the contemporary period has been much more marked by receptivity than by repulsion.

We have suggested that while some of this can simply be traced to the longtime presence of immigrants and the way this affects the calculus of political figures, another important element has been the strength of social movement organizing in the region. Los Angeles has been reborn as a bastion of progressive politics, and it is this multiracial cross-class commitment to "everyday social justice" that seems to drive much of the agenda. Immigrant integration is one part of this, and immigrants themselves are concerned about a whole host of issues, including educational progress, labor rights, and environmental remediation. And as has been discussed, this agenda could not be realized without the everyday work of leadership development, organizing, and coalition building—and sensitivity to regional inequalities—that has not only grown dynamic movements, but also tangibly reshaped the political and policy landscape.

We do not mean to say that other non-movement sectors are unimportant to the challenges of immigrant integration. Business owners, so reliant on immigrant labor, have also been supportive, and the Los Angeles Chamber of Commerce, not known for its progressive views on issues like living-wage laws, has been a local leader in the fight for the DREAM Act and has been actively involved in efforts for education reform that could benefit the children of immigrants. But business seems to play a somewhat lesser role than it does in places like Charlotte, New York, and San José, partly because Los Angeles business leaders are not an especially well-organized force overall; it is also hard to gauge how much their choices to support immigrant rights are predicated on the ways in which progressive movements have made the needs of immigrant communities inextricable from political discussions in the region.

As for the philanthropic and civic sector, the California Community Foundation (inaptly named, since it is really just the community foundation for Los Angeles County) has brought together an inter-sectoral Council for Immigrant Integration. The council includes people from business, labor, city government, police, immigrant rights groups, and others and has created a forum for at least deriving shared principles and shared communication strategies. While the commitment of the foundation to this topic represents an important turn for a long-standing civic institution, it may be telling that it occurred under the watch of a president who was the former executive director of the Mexican American Legal Defense Fund and was herself involved in immigration issues—movement again seems to be lurking just behind the surface. And philanthropy has also been important in forging the sort of alliances between social justice and immigrant organizations that give the immigrant integration effort its movement roots.

Such roots are also evident in the public sector. Mayor Antonio Villaraigosa, in particular, came from a movement background, and the current mayor, Eric Garcetti, has ties—less close but still there—with various movement actors and immigrant advocates. The result is a proactive and cooperative politics that aims at integrating immigrant issues into daily governance and policy decisions, although it is sometimes a bit more timid than activists would like. One interesting nuance has been the way in which Garcetti has moved to institutionalize immigrant integration in a way that Villaraigosa did not; this reflects not only the different temperament of the two leaders (Garcetti has stressed getting city government to provide effective services and generally seems more interested in the day-to-day workings of the municipality) but also the fact that Garcetti is less easily tagged as an ethnic politician, something that squares with the way in which the deracialization of immigrants has facilitated integration efforts in other metro regions. In any case, the basic message here remains: the fact of a strong movement provides any mayor with political cover for friendly policies, and that has spilled over into a more favorable set of relations between the local police and immigrant communities.

Maywood's politics can be classified as both proactive and conflictual. A political crisis over towing led to new forms of engaged citizenship in this majority Latino and immigrant community, and the resulting political leadership has embraced policies that support immigrant integration (sanctuary city, ending police checkpoints, supporting parents' groups on education issues). But Maywood has also become a lightning rod for anti-immigrant forces within the Los Angeles metropolitan region. Maywood advocates intend to use their new civic platform to develop a regional immigrant-based political movement in Southeast Los Angeles. But some key U.S.-born Latino politicians have also criticized Maywood's leadership for building its own immigrant-based political machine that sometimes refuses to play ball with the established Democratic Party structure.

At the same time, Maywood offers a cautionary tale about how the increasingly diffuse immigrant population in Southern California, in a highly fragmented metropolitan landscape, will have to redefine and pursue integration. Maywood was able to organize an immigrant base of grassroots leaders to influence local policies by transforming the potential of changing demographics into real political change. But like many other small cities, Maywood faces a dire financial situation that threatens any long-term policies that can adequately address issues related to immigrant integration.

In general, however, the tale here is that social movements have shaped integration by providing political pressure for social institutions to change their receptiveness toward immigrant communities. Immigrant-serving and immigrant rights organizations built power alongside multiracial neighborhood and issue-based grassroots organizations, and this has ensured that immigrants are integrated into the ways in which social justice movements speak about and work to shift labor, police, educational, and other policies. There is certainly room for improvement: some of our interviewees believe that the movement would benefit from the inclusion of more Asian and African immigrant groups—and a number of African American leaders believe that the sphere of the immigrant rights movement is too small and that existing leaders are reluctant to include new groups or build ties with existing civil rights configurations (Dupont-Walker 2010). But this simply seems to reflect a need to step up the game: Los Angeles is basically an example of how immigrants have claimed the mantle of engaged citizenship by helping to build strong unions, community organizations, and a revived civil society.

At the same time, our findings suggest that a vibrant pro-immigrant civil society and sympathetic progressive political leadership have not always resulted in institutionalized policies and practices to promote immigrant integration. Even where policies do change, as in the case of policing practices, immigrant rights and other movement organizations have had to spend significant energy ensuring implementation. When there is political fallout (as with Villaraigosa) or fiscal stress (as in Maywood), constraints will bind, and policy progress will be stymied. Movements may matter, but institutions are important—and making more measurable progress on the things that count, such as educational and economic achievement, is likely to require engaging other sectors of the regional leadership, as has been done in San José, New York, Charlotte, and elsewhere. Still, those areas may also have something to learn from a place where a highly mobilized and integrated immigrant population—in this case, integrated in a broad social justice movement—has been able to reshape the debate and begin to reshape the policies that structure both immigrant lives and the very future of the metro region.

6

THE LAST SUBURB

Immigrant Integration in the Inland Empire

Juan De Lara

On July 1, 2014, several dozen people gathered on the streets of Murrieta, a small city in southwestern Riverside County, to block three buses from delivering unaccompanied minors from Central America to the local U.S. Border Patrol station. Many of the protesters held American flags or signs that read "Stop Illegal Immigration" and shouted slogans like "Send them back." Local and national camera crews rushed to capture the drama that erupted when protesters planted themselves directly in front of the Border Patrol buses and refused to budge. The media attention made Murrieta into a flashpoint in the national debate about immigration.

Immigration officials eventually ordered the buses to turn around. But tensions continued to rise over the next several days as pro-immigrant activists converged on Riverside County to challenge what they characterized as a hostile and racist reaction. Angry exchanges between pro- and anti-immigrant sides harked back to the contentious politics of immigration that dominated California elections in the 1990s. Scenes like these were no longer supposed to happen in California—not when a March 2013 poll showed that 72 percent of registered voters supported a path to citizenship and 53 percent agreed that undocumented immigrants have a mostly positive effect on the state's economy.[1]

Unlike Arizona and states in the South, California was thought to be more comfortable with and accommodating to the immigrants that have transformed the state's ethnic makeup. Southern California in particular had emerged as an iconic immigrant landscape leading up to the turn of the twenty-first century. Nonetheless, what happened in Murrieta showed that the state's old political conflicts, which gave life to strident anti-immigrant propositions like 187 and 229, have not completely disappeared into the shadows (Calavita 1996).

This chapter moves far to the east of Los Angeles into the Inland Empire to examine how something like the events in Murrieta could happen. While Los Angeles's transition to an immigrant metropolis in the post-1990s period is well documented, relatively little has been written about how the inland counties of Riverside and San Bernardino emerged as Southern California's newest settlement gateway during this same period. In fact, California experienced a great inland migration during the first decade of the twenty-first century, as more than 450,000 Los Angeles and Orange County residents pulled up stakes between 2000 and 2006 to pursue more affordable housing, new jobs, and less dense suburban living (Johnson, Reed, and Hayes 2008).

The new arrivals—including a large number of immigrant and native-born Latinos, and Asians—created an ethnic plurality that posed new challenges to the mostly white existing political establishment. While the region has historically served as a refuge for white conservative politics, impending demographic changes signal the potential for a more diverse political leadership. This chapter provides a brief demographic overview and sets the context for how immigrant integration has been framed in the region's political discourse and policy arena. It also examines how stakeholders have mobilized around integration issues and explains why local institutions responded to immigrants by either extending or limiting access to public services and civic institutions. The chapter concludes with a brief discussion of the prospects for immigrant integration in the region.

Demographic Context

Riverside and San Bernardino Counties offered employment and housing opportunities at a time when rising rents and exorbitant home prices pushed people out of the Los Angeles metropolitan core. The region's relatively cheap land and favorable growth policies, as well as lax mortgage-financing practices, provided developers with the impetus to expand beyond the saturated, higher-priced coastal county real estate markets. As a result, the Inland Empire's population exploded from 2.5 million residents in 1990 to more than 4.35 million by 2012. According to some, the move inland provided a geographic solution for Southern California's aspiring middle class, many of whom could not afford to purchase a home and raise a family in Los Angeles (Kotkin and Frey 2007). The sprawl was widespread: most of the population lies to the south and west of the San Bernardino Mountains, but these counties extend far into the desert, to the Nevada state line.

Inland Southern California has often served as a development frontier for those wishing to escape certain elements of urban Los Angeles. For example, during the late nineteenth century, thousands of white families moved to the area and built a regional citrus industry that made the Inland Empire one of the most important agricultural centers in the country (Zierer 1934). Citrus farms required a large agricultural workforce, and landowners turned to Latino and Asian labor as a solution. The result was a stratified social system in which a white agricultural elite held political power over a highly racialized labor class (Alamillo 2006; Matt Garcia 2001). The World War II period triggered a second round of migration, when a manufacturing surge, led by Kaiser Steel, expanding rail yards, and new military bases, drew a new wave of migrants. Thousands of African Americans, Asians, Latinos, and working-class whites moved into the region during and after the war years in order to find work and buy homes. Like the earlier wave of agriculture-driven migration, this manufacturing boom forged a particular brand of politics that was deeply embedded in the region's racial and class divisions (Davis 1990).

The most recent wave of inland migration, which occurred between 1980 and 2012, was decidedly different. To begin with, the sheer number of people not only eclipsed earlier migration figures, but made the Inland Empire into one of the fastest-growing metropolitan regions in the United States. The most spectacular growth period occurred during the 1980s, when the Inland Empire's population grew by 66 percent, or more than one million people. While whites accounted for 45.9 percent of this growth, Latinos made up 38.4 percent of the boom. The next decade's growth rate, 26 percent, did not match the previous decade, but it did mark the ascendancy of Latinos as the largest in-migrating ethnic group, representing 80 percent of all new Inland Empire residents. As figures 6.1 and 6.2 show, these trends drove the immigrant share of the region's residents up sharply between 1980 and the present.

The population surged once more between 2000 and 2010. While Latinos maintained their nearly 80 percent share of the total growth, Asian and Pacific Islanders (APIs) grew at a faster clip, rising to 13 percent of the total population. No other major metropolitan area gained more Latinos in this period. Additionally, the region ranked third for API growth (Frey 2010, 55). Not all ethnic groups expanded; in fact, out-migration and low birth rates resulted in the loss of more than 72,000 white residents. Immigrants were among those who moved into the region in large numbers. The immigrant population expanded to approximately 933,000 in Riverside and San Bernardino Counties by 2010, giving the Inland Empire metro area the ninth-largest foreign-born population in the country (Singer 2010). By 2012, immigrants made up 21.4 percent of the total population, up from just 7.8 percent in 1970 (figure 2.3). Among the foreign-born population, approximately 69.9 percent are Latino, and nearly 18.5 percent are APIs (2010–2012 ACS).

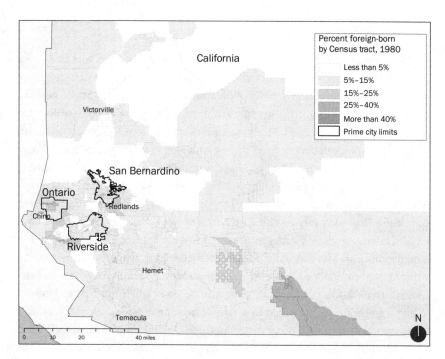

FIGURE 6.1. Percent foreign-born by Census tract, 1980, Inland Empire, CA

Source: 1980 Decennial Census, Census TIGER/Line, and ESRI.

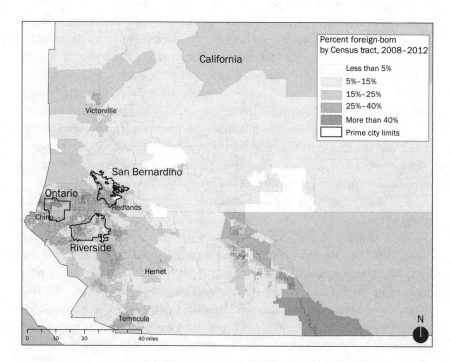

FIGURE 6.2. Percent foreign-born by Census tract, 2008–2012, Inland Empire, CA

Source: 2008–2012 American Community Survey (Ruggles et al. 2011), Census TIGER/Line, and ESRI.

These regional demographic changes did not apply evenly across the entire Inland Empire. Riverside, San Bernardino, Fontana, and Ontario have relatively large and well-established Latino populations; only Riverside, at 49 percent, does not have a Latino majority. Meanwhile, the fast-growing cities of Rancho Cucamonga, Temecula, and Murrieta all have rather large white populations. These cities are located away from the region's older core and have openly marketed themselves as upscale white-collar communities. Some cities in southwestern Riverside County—Temecula and Murrieta, for example—often identify with their whiter and more affluent neighbors in Orange County. Another group of fast-growing and outlying cities, Moreno Valley, Corona, and Victorville, have larger Latino populations. African Americans are most heavily concentrated in San Bernardino, Moreno Valley, and Victorville. Meanwhile, APIs tend to be concentrated in Rancho Cucamonga, Corona, Temecula, and Murrieta—all cities that have relatively large white populations and smaller numbers of Latinos. While segregation, as measured by a Hispanic-white dissimilarity index, is relatively low compared with other metro areas, the Inland Empire ranked eleventh out of the top fifty metropolitan areas with large Hispanic populations in terms of the increase in the index between 1990 and 2010, likely contributing to a sense of increasingly separated communities.[2]

In any case, segregation is part of the geographical legacy of race and power in Southern California. As Richard Wright and his colleagues argue, "Some forms of racial concentration signal isolation and lack of access to important resources. Other forms of segregation (e.g., white self-segregation in certain metropolitan areas) proclaim just the opposite" (Wright et al. 2014, 174). Accordingly, white flight and post–World War II suburbanization provided white families with a spatial solution. Suburban living became a way for some groups to access resources while locking others out. Even if suburban life was often more complicated than the ideal it was given in the national imaginary, dominant narratives of the American dream in the urban fringe became a powerful cultural force that motivated many to migrate into the suburbs.

Immigrants moved to the Inland Empire during the 1990s and 2000s for many of the same reasons that attracted earlier white migrants. As a spokesman for San Bernardino Republican congressman Jerry Lewis noted during an interview: "The Inland Empire generally, San Bernardino County particularly, has seen a huge migration of people out from the Hispanic suburbs of LA County. They came for the same reasons that almost everybody else comes out there. The housing is much, much cheaper. The school districts tend to be a little less chaotic. There are large numbers of people who are either first or maybe even up to third generation U.S. citizens who moved out of those areas and into the Riverside–San Bernardino County area" (Specht 2010).

Nonetheless, even if the more recent migrants shared many of the same aspirations as earlier arrivals, they faced very different challenges. Perhaps the greatest threat to the ideal of an American dream came toward the end of the 2000s, when the boom that dramatically reshaped the Inland Empire's ethnic landscape was replaced by an economic crisis that threatened many of the region's more recent arrivals. Tens of thousands lost their jobs as the Great Recession of 2008 decimated the housing market and idled a local economy that owed much to the logistics industry and its movement of goods from the ports to the warehouses in the Inland Empire and then on to the rest of the country. Migrants who had invested their time and money in establishing new homes were suddenly faced with ballooning mortgage payments and devalued property. Median home prices for San Bernardino County dropped from approximately $370,000 in 2007 to $155,000 in 2010; in Riverside, median prices plummeted from $410,000 to $200,000. Partly because so many of the earlier purchases were financed through subprime loans, foreclosures skyrocketed: Riverside and San Bernardino trailed only the Stockton and Las Vegas metro areas in the percentage of total housing units that were in foreclosure during the third quarter of 2008. Even as some immigrants fled the economic devastation, most stayed behind and tried to piece together a plan for an uncertain future.[3]

Politics and Immigration

Demographic change introduced a number of factors that began to tip the old balance of political power in the region. Most significantly, rising numbers of Latinos and more liberal coastal-county transplants began to chip away at conservative white political power. Earlier waves of white migration, especially during the agricultural booms of the late 1800s and post–World War II suburbanization, had contributed to a decidedly conservative electorate. More recently, inland Southern California, like the Central Valley and parts of Orange County, has functioned as an electoral refuge for the state's shrinking Republican Party, even as conservatives lost control of coastal jurisdictions and statewide offices. For example, the Inland Empire's share of California's registered Republican voters jumped from 7 percent in 1978 to 13 percent in 2012.[4] As a result, California politics is essentially divided into a liberal coastal zone and a much more conservative inland zone.

Even as the region's demographics shifted and the white population declined, white voters maintained a disproportionate share of the regular voting base. While native-born whites with native parents represented 32.9 percent of Inland Empire adults in 2012, they made up 41.6 percent of the voters in the

2012 presidential election, larger than any other group (November 2012 Current Population Survey). Given these numbers, it is easy to see how a staunchly conservative and overwhelmingly white Republican political leadership has fought to maintain control over most of the Inland Empire's major legislative offices. Of the ten supervisors who govern the two counties, all but one are white Republicans. This power balance may ultimately shift as Latinos, blacks, and more-liberal coastal transplants continue to grow in numbers. In fact, Democrats gained a numerical majority among registered voters on the eve of the November 2008 elections in San Bernardino County; they managed to hold on to this advantage leading into the 2012 general election cycle. Yet Riverside County is an entirely different story. Even as the Obama election motivated a more diverse generation of voters to register for the 2008 and 2012 cycles, Republicans managed to hold on to their numerical edge.

Both the Democratic Party and Latino civic organizations like MALDEF hoped that the region's shifting demographic numbers would encourage the California Citizens Redistricting Commission—a body charged with redrawing the state's political boundaries in 2011—to create new seats that would make it easier for Latinos to get elected. The commission's final electoral maps—which include three congressional seats, one state senate seat, and three assembly seats—added only one additional Latino district. However, the new maps did cause two long-time conservative Republican congressmen to retire from office rather than pursue one of the new seats. As a result, Democrats took control of three out of the six congressional districts after the 2012 elections. And a Democrat narrowly won in the 2014 election to take over retiring Republican Gary Miller's Thirty-First District seat.

Even as demographics and redistricting altered some parts of the Inland Empire's political landscape and enabled Democrats to gain new positions, county-level politics changed little. Democratic efforts to unseat a Republican from the powerful Riverside County Board of Supervisors fell short during the June 2014 elections. Republicans will need to manage their brand to maintain political power in the foreseeable future, particularly if Democrats win more offices; and in that context, the struggle over immigrant integration will continue to be a contentious issue in local policy debates. Perhaps in awareness of long-term demographic shifts, however, the Republican supervisors of Riverside County did favor a resolution backing comprehensive immigration reform in February 2013.

Still, striking up an honest conversation about immigrant integration is tricky, because many local actors frame their responses to immigrant issues with a focus on border enforcement and repatriation. Additionally, anti-immigrant activist groups have found fertile soil in the region's conservative voting base. Some of these groups have cultivated close relationships with local political leaders. Joseph Turner is one example. Turner founded the anti-immigrant group Save Our State and served as the western region representative for the Federation for American Immigration Reform (FAIR). Both groups oppose immigration, and Turner himself gained national notoriety in 2006 when, as a member of the San Bernardino City Council, he championed a local ordinance that would bar landlords from renting to people who could not prove their legal immigration status. He was ultimately unsuccessful, and his career as an elected official was relatively short, but Turner eventually took a position as senior staff member for a San Bernardino County supervisor and as an adviser for a local police union. Other groups like the Minuteman Project and various neo-Nazi offshoots, while small, function as a vocal counterpoint to immigrant integration efforts.

By contrast, pro-integration forces have little to no leverage over local policy decisions because they lack close relationships with elected officials (Ramakrishnan 2007). Maybe the shifting political landscape will alter this imbalance, but several of our informants mentioned that many Democratic elected officials have shied away from pro-immigrant stances because they fear that this might alienate the region's large share of independent and conservative voters.

The mix of conservative leadership and vocal anti-immigrant sentiment—especially in relatively white jurisdictions—means that politicians often use immigration to sharply distinguish themselves from the rest of Southern California. Evidence of this division can be found in the symbolic support or condemnation of Arizona's SB 1070 law, also known as the "show me your papers" bill. While Los Angeles, San Francisco, and numerous other municipalities chose to boycott Arizona after it passed SB 1070, Inland Empire cities like Hemet, Lake Elsinore, and Highland passed supporting resolutions. Support for anti-immigrant laws isn't purely symbolic. Several inland cities have enacted ordinances that specifically target the immigrant community (Kohout 2009). For example, five Inland Empire cities passed laws requiring all local businesses to check the legal status of new employees via the federal government's E-verify system (Lovett 2011). Efforts are under way to implement a similar policy across all of Riverside County.

Of course, given the region's size and spread, this political climate does vary somewhat geographically. Not all Inland Empire cities have embraced an anti-immigrant stance, particularly in jurisdictions with a more diverse political leadership. Ontario, the only large city that has elected a Latino mayor, refused to endorse or condemn Arizona's SB 1070 when pressured by regional anti-immigrant groups to take a stand. In San Bernardino, the region's second-largest city, a multiracial political coalition of African American, Latino, and white liberal and centrist leaders took control of the city council in 2006.[5] Led by Mayor

Pat Morris, a self-identified Democrat, this new council majority opposed Joseph Turner's anti-immigrant ordinance. Several of our interviewees told us that while the new council majority supported issues important to the immigrant community, Mayor Morris (who stepped down in 2014) was not willing to publicly support pro-immigrant campaigns. As one activist noted, "He has said that it's not something local government can fix—it's up to the federal government" (Amaya 2010).

Similar changes have also rocked the more conservative southwestern part of the Inland Empire. For example, controversy over the construction of a mosque in Temecula highlighted how race and immigrant integration are often central if silent issues in local policy debates. In January 2011, Temecula City Council members voted to approve plans by the Islamic Center of Temecula Valley (*Valley News* 2011). The vote came after contentious opposition from a group calling itself Concerned American Citizens, which cited traffic concerns as its main reason for not wanting to see the mosque built. Mosque supporters, including the Interfaith Council of Murrieta and Temecula Valley, claimed that the issues were really religious freedom and cultural inclusion. The fact that opponents called themselves Concerned American Citizens suggested that they meant to preclude local Muslims from identifying themselves as legitimate citizens—and the fact that the group also expresses sharp concerns about the spread of Sharia law is in line with the xenophobic undertones in the debate. Such undertones were hard to ignore, especially in a city bordered by Murrieta, the previously mentioned anti-immigrant hotbed, and the northern San Diego County municipality of Fallbrook, once home to Tom Metzger, a self-proclaimed grand dragon of the Ku Klux Klan. Nonetheless, the Temecula council's support for building the mosque, and Ontario and San Bernardino's pro-integration political openings, suggest that change is possible even in the region's more conservative jurisdictions.

Inland Empire politicians have also promoted the adoption of anti-immigrant legislation at the state and national level. For instance, San Bernardino Republican state assemblyman Tim Donnelly, from District Fifty-Nine in the northwestern part of the county, introduced a bill modeled after Arizona's SB 1070. Donnelly has also pushed for ending in-state tuition for immigrant students. His efforts failed to gain traction in the Democratic-controlled state legislature. Democrats responded to calls for reform by successfully passing legislation that gave undocumented immigrant students access to private and public financial aid.

This rift between Donnelly and California Democrats points to a major paradox within the modern Republican Party in California. Some Republicans have supported comprehensive immigration reform as a political survival strategy. They argue that if Republicans continue to support anti-immigrant measures, they will alienate and mobilize the state's growing Latino electorate. Republicans from inland agricultural areas have spoken the loudest in support of immigration reform. While Republicans from agricultural areas receive support from farmers who stand to benefit from an increase in potential workers, the Inland Empire's exurban residential communities do not share the same need. Though Central Valley Republicans like Jeff Denham and David Valadao have joined Democrats in supporting comprehensive immigration reform, Inland Empire representatives like Ken Calvert and Paul Cook have supported staunch enforcement-only policies. One local exception has been Jim Brulte, former California State Senate Republican leader and San Bernardino assemblyman, who told a group of influential business and political leaders at a 2010 Inland Action meeting that unless the Republican Party stops attacking Latinos and immigrants, it will become irrelevant in California politics.

Institutional Receptivity

Given the hostile political landscape, it is easy to see why immigrant-related politics are often oppositional rather than accommodating. Immigrant advocates told us that the region's unreceptive political environment forces them to spend most of their time on defensive maneuvers rather than on long-term integration. Nevertheless, immigrant organizers did begin to shift the debate away from enforcement and toward economic and social justice in 2008 and 2009 by focusing on education, good jobs, and healthy communities. Along with the demand for comprehensive immigration reform, these issues became components of a sustainable integration agenda championed by a coalition of labor, community, and faith-based groups. But even with this new focus, enforcement policies and cuts to public resources continue to dominate the region's immigration debate.

Some institutional stakeholders have played a more accommodating role in the immigrant integration process. One example is the San Bernardino Mexican consulate, which uses mobile service units to extend its constituent services to the expansive immigrant population in the Inland Empire, including the issuance of consular identification cards (*matriculas*). Local agencies, including the Riverside and San Bernardino county sheriff's departments, recognize *matriculas* as a valid form of identification. Immigrants can also use these *matriculas* to open accounts at a number of national and local banks. However, these efforts did not go unchallenged. Anti-immigrant groups, led by the Minuteman Project and the FIRE Coalition, demanded that the consulate stop providing off-site services, and actively protested mobile services (Olsen 2008). These protests inspired Corona-based U.S. congressman Ken Calvert to sponsor a bill that would bar federal agencies and banks from recognizing *matriculas* as valid forms of identification.

Local Effects of Enforcement-Only Policies

Congressman Calvert's position reflects how many of the region's most influential governing bodies have responded to immigrant issues—that is, by focusing narrowly on enforcement and deportation. The Riverside County Board of Supervisors responded to the growing immigrant population by mobilizing local law enforcement agencies to apprehend, detain, and deport people who were unable to verify their legal status. Its members rationalized this law-and-order approach by deploying a narrative of immigrant criminality. The spokesman for San Bernardino County congressman Jerry Lewis illustrated this connection when he told us that immigration-related enforcement policies—like 287(g) agreements—maintained public safety by helping to get rid of dangerous criminals (Specht 2010).[6]

Alfonso Gonzales (2013) writes that the link between immigration anxiety and crime-related panic provided the backdrop for Riverside County's debate on participating in the U.S. Immigration and Custom Enforcement's 287(g) program. When concerns were raised about local taxpayers having to bear the costs of increased policing, Supervisor Jeff Stone argued that residents would gladly pay because further deportations ensured a safer climate. He said, "In plain English, I fully support [the effort] to identify and return illegal aliens, especially those that commit crimes, back to Mexico" (Gonzales 2013, 87). Supervisor Stone's statement not only backed deputizing local law enforcement as border enforcement agents, something not normally under the purview of police officers, but portrayed all undocumented immigrants as Mexican.

Of course, categorizing immigrants as lawbreakers is a common narrative tool used to justify such policing practices. However, given the regional context described above, this tends to racialize the discourse about all Latinos. A number of interviews touched on this point. Republican congressman Jerry Lewis's office connected race to immigration and policing when his spokesperson argued that as Latinos moved into the region, sometimes to escape the perceived problems of Los Angeles, they brought urban criminal elements with them (Specht 2010).[7] According to this logic, increased local police enforcement, including programs like 287(g), were critical to protecting public safety. When local prosecutors began targeting Mexican drug cartel activity, some political leaders drew direct connections between the rising immigrant Latino population and transnational gangs.

This racialization of the immigration discourse was captured by one community organizer with the Inland Congregations United for Change who said, "Because of the demographic change, there's a supposition that most [Latino] people are undocumented—meaning illegal—meaning criminal—meaning should be treated like criminals. This serves as a justification for abuse."

Laura Liu (2000) argues that any attempt to understand contemporary social relations must acknowledge that racial frames are applied to immigration. Policy makers and anti-immigrant advocates have used racialized terms to describe social services and public institutions linked with the region's growing U.S.-born Latino and immigrant population. For example, Riverside County supervisor Bob Buster suggested that fiscal constraints flowing from the economic crisis of 2008 should raise questions about public spending on programs that might benefit immigrants. According to Buster, "With the recession, everybody's watching the dollar [and debating which] people we should be spending money on" (Gorman and Connell 2009). This logic treats public spending on education and community health as a threat to governmental prudence rather than an investment in the region's future. While most public figures have been careful not to directly stereotype U.S.-born Latinos, several of our interviewees felt that criticisms of immigrants implied that even Latino American citizens are suspect.

Increased police expenditures have not come into question. As Riverside supervisor Jeff Stone pointed out, local jurisdictions have happily increased formal and informal cooperation with federal immigration agencies in order to neutralize perceived threats to public safety (Stone 2010). Such cooperation was on display in 2008 and 2009, when the Riverside office of the U.S. Border Patrol carried out a series of raids across the region. According to local immigrant advocates, raids increased when the Border Patrol implemented a quota system that provided incentives for agents to boost apprehensions and deportations. As a result, Border Patrol agents undertook regular sweeps of day labor centers, bus stops, and predominantly Latino neighborhoods. Community advocates accused local police departments of participating in coordinated multiagency sweeps, something they say violates the intent of 287(g) agreements.[8] Localities also participate in ICE's Secure Communities program, which automatically matches anyone being booked in local jails with the Department of Homeland Security immigration database. Local police agencies turn anyone listed as undocumented over to ICE. Even as some police leaders (including in nearly Los Angeles) have been critical of programs like 287(g) and Secure Communities, contending that they undermine trust with immigrant communities, Riverside County sheriff Stanley Sniff defends them. In fact, Sniff was a leading opponent of the TRUST Act, a bill passed in 2014 by the California legislature that limits police ability to deport arrestees.

That has not stopped police departments from implementing their own policies that target the region's immigrants. The San Bernardino, Moreno Valley, Ontario, and Coachella police departments have used sobriety checkpoints to stop and impound cars from thousands of unlicensed immigrant drivers.[9] While police officials justify this as a public safety measure that reduces drunk driving, the immigrant advocates we interviewed claim that the checkpoints and impoundments function as de facto anti-immigrant policies. Until 2015, undocumented immigrants were unable to acquire a valid driver's license in California. As a result, unlicensed immigrant drivers were subject to traffic citations and impoundment, sometimes for an automatic thirty days; many of those who lost their cars found it difficult or impossible to pay towing and impoundment fees—and, of course, this was a big flashpoint in Maywood, as recounted in the Los Angeles chapter. Indeed, data from the Riverside and San Bernardino sheriff's departments show that most checkpoints are conducted in communities with large Latino populations. For example, Moreno Valley police conducted thirty-seven checkpoints between 2007 and 2009 in three voting districts containing large concentrations of Latinos. Meanwhile, only five checkpoints were conducted in the city's remaining two, mostly white, districts (McKinnon 2010). Police officials claim that checkpoint locations are decided by traffic levels and dismiss accusations of racial bias. Nonetheless, immigrant and Latino leaders see the checkpoints as an attack on their communities. Some Moreno Valley residents, including an elected school board official, mounted protests against ongoing police checkpoints. Residents in a number of other communities eventually forced some Inland Empire police agencies to change their impoundment policies. For example, community pressure persuaded Cathedral City to end automatic impoundments; instead, it now gives unlicensed drivers fifteen to twenty minutes to arrange for a licensed driver to take possession of their vehicle.

Education

While most of our policy discussion has focused on enforcement and deportation (partly because they serve as good signals of underlying attitudes), several of our interviewees pointed out that schools and jobs are the key to long-term immigrant integration. Community advocates at Inland Congregations United for Change argue that education issues cannot be separated from immigrant issues (Timpson and Dolan 2010). In fact, the Inland Empire's future is now closely tied to immigrants and their native-born children. Young people, both immigrant and citizen alike, represented a significant part of the population growth that transformed the region between 1990 and 2010—and 41 percent of all Inland Empire children have at least one foreign-born parent (Pastor and Marcelli 2013, 38).

Of course, racial differences complicate the task of seeing the commonality between the old and the young. As Frey (2010) and others have pointed out (and as discussed in chapter 2 of this volume), when a graying white baby boomer population confronts a mostly Latino and Asian young population, a cultural generation gap ensues. This definitely holds true in the Inland Empire, where recent Census data show that 76 percent of the children in Riverside and San Bernardino Counties are nonwhite, while about 65 percent of the senior population is white.[10] This gap places the Inland Empire in the top 5 percent of the 150 largest metro regions in terms of the racial generation gap—and complicates the politics of the region.

Clearly, whatever the social distance, a large number of youth have immigrant parents, and, as elsewhere, local schools are key to the future of immigrant integration. Unfortunately, the local schools are also among the worst in the state. For example, 58 percent of schools in the San Bernardino City School District ranked below average on California's Academic Performance Index when compared with similar schools throughout the state; the below-average figure was 74 percent for the Colton Unified School District. Additionally, 402 of the region's schools were placed on the No Child Left Behind sanctions list for failing to bring all student groups up to federal standards (Klampe 2011). Many of the region's poor-performing schools are in low-income neighborhoods where 80 percent to 90 percent of the population tends to be Latino, African American, and in some neighborhoods, Vietnamese.

The many immigrant and second-generation students classified as English language learners (ELLs) face problems. The number of ELLs grew from 93,162 in 1995 to 182,652 by 2010, a growth rate of approximately 96 percent.[11] More than 94 percent of the Inland Empire's English learners speak Spanish as their first language. Two district administrators separately told us that there had been difficulties with adequately training teachers to meet the needs of ELL students (Valdez 2010; Navarro 2010). The majority of teachers in local schools have not earned state-mandated English-language teaching credentials (Valdez 2010). Even so, ELL students in Riverside and San Bernardino outperformed their peers on the 2010 California English Language Development Test. Thirty-eight percent of San Bernardino County ELLs and 39 percent of Riverside County ELLs performed at the advanced or early advanced levels; the statewide average was 37 percent.

School performance data suggest that regional leaders have their work cut out for them. Some policy and business leaders are beginning to pay more attention. Influential regional economist John Husing made a direct connection between immigrant integration and regional economic health when he asked during an interview, "How do we in fact create educational opportunity that's for people who need upward mobility, many of whom are first- and second-generation immigrants?" (Husing 2010). Husing and others believe that better educational opportunities can improve long-term prospects for the region's large number of poorly educated blue-collar workers; approximately half of the region's adult population earned only a high school diploma or less. Immigrants face steeper educational challenges. Approximately 42 percent of the foreign-born population above the age of twenty-five did not have a high school diploma in 2012, compared with only 12 percent of their native-born peers (see chapter 2). Yet others have tapped into the region's pervasive anti-immigrant narrative to claim that immigrants and their children place a greater burden on local schools. These resource-conflict claims can seem very real in a region with crowded and over-burdened schools.

The Integration Ecosystem

If the Inland Empire is going to move beyond the discourse of enforcement and deportation, then pro-integration forces will need to challenge the narrative and change the power imbalance. A loose coalition of community, labor, and faith-based organizations has responded to the region's anti-immigrant climate. For example, they formed the Justice for Immigrants Coalition and the Rapid Response Network in the mid-2000s in response to the policing practices and immigration raids mentioned earlier. These are relatively new organizations. In contrast to the movement-driven integration story told in this volume about Los Angeles, immigrant rights advocates in the Inland Empire have not had much impact on policy-making decisions.

Emerging Immigrant Networks

Among the most active regional networks was the Justice for Immigrants Coalition (JIC), which gained attention for its efforts to roll back deportations linked to federal enforcement programs like 287(g).[12] Local advocates pressed for changes in the 287(g) program's implementation as the Obama administration revised the memorandum-of-agreement renewal process with police agencies in 2010. Catholic auxiliary bishop Rutilio del Riego—a key leader in the JIC— encouraged local police leaders to withdraw from the 287(g) program. Advocates eventually concluded that outright rejection of 287(g) was unlikely and instead pushed to modify existing agreements. JIC members called for a public stakeholder committee with oversight on enforcement, removal of non-felons from the program so that only post-conviction felons would be screened, and greater public transparency. None of these proposals were ultimately adopted, but JIC members used the process to establish regular communication with law enforcement, something that remains relatively new for the immigrant community in this region.

JIC members also used their work on 287(g) renewal to establish better regional coordination among themselves. Such networking and relationship building provided valuable space for new alliances and partnerships to develop. For example, members of the JIC used the network to connect Pomona Habla—a community-based organization in eastern Los Angeles County—to fledgling groups in Cathedral City, Moreno Valley, Coachella, and San Bernardino, all of which were organizing around the effects of police checkpoints on immigrant communities. This yielded capacity-building exchanges via training and joint organizing activities. When a number of service providers and day labor leaders joined forces to document enforcement abuses at day laborer sites throughout the region, they had learned how to use video footage to support their claims that local police agencies were violating the intent of established 287(g) agreements.

The Rapid Response Network (RRN) was formed in the aftermath of a 2008 immigration raid on a Palm Springs–area bakery. A coalition of service providers and community organizations, RRN documented the effects of immigration raids on local families. Through an elaborate communications network, RRN members deployed mobile response teams to places where they knew a raid was going to take place; enforcement agencies sometimes informed RRN members of an impending raid. During one such mobilization, the rapid response team prepared day laborers for an imminent raid by informing them of their rights and instructing them on how to respond if confronted by a Border Patrol agent. According to an RRN member, most people were able to avoid arrest because they exercised their legal rights. Network members used such experiences to organize against further sweeps and worked with the Mexican consulate to pressure enforcement agencies into reducing the volume of deportations. These activities were eventually successful in curbing the number of Border Patrol raids. RRN members also provide legal advice and support services for families and communities who are affected by immigration raids. The network's Know Your Rights workshops teach immigrants how to respond if and when they are questioned about citizenship status.

While the Rapid Response Network and the Justice for Immigrants Coalition have many of the same members, they differ in organizing philosophies and tactics. One member of both alliances noted the difference by claiming that the JIC is a faith-based initiative with a particular audience and strong leadership from the diocese. The RRN, on the other hand, is more of an activist-based organization driven by community and labor organizations. Differences between the two groups' strategies were at issue when church officials questioned the more confrontational approach sometimes taken by RRN-led protests against the Border Patrol. RRN members also played lead roles in organizing May Day marches and other social justice events, something seen as more controversial by church leaders. These differences point to a bigger debate about what constitutes immigrant integration and some of the limits posed by accommodation policies that do not deal with underlying relationships of power. For some community activists, the idea of integration without social justice can sound dangerously like old assimilation arguments.

The Catholic Church

The appointment of Bishop Gerald Barnes as head of the San Bernardino Diocese in 1996 is the biggest reason why the local Roman Catholic Church emerged as a key voice on immigrant rights. Bishop Barnes gained national recognition for his work on immigrant rights during his tenure as chairman of the U.S. Bishop's Committee on Migration and Refugee Services. He continued this work in the Inland Empire by appointing Auxiliary Bishop del Riego to create a Ministry Formation Institute for lay members that included immigrant issues in its training curriculum. The institute and committee aimed at incorporating immigrant issues across the diocese's ninety-four churches, with a total of 1.2 million members. According to church staff, Bishop Barnes was so committed to expanding immigrant issues and services that his was the only diocese in California to employ a full-time person to work on immigrant justice projects.

As Bishop Barnes built this infrastructure, he developed alliances with immigrant advocates outside the church. In fact, several interview respondents credited the church with lending legitimacy to the Justice for Immigrants Coalition and for holding the coalition together. Additionally, the diocese worked with the U.S. Department of Labor and the Mexican consulate to support a program called Empleo, which serves as a hotline for workers (including immigrant workers) to report mistreatment in the workplace. More than one million assistance calls had been processed at the time of our interview.

Nonetheless, even with Bishop Barnes's strong leadership, church leaders struggled to implement his pro-integration message across all the Inland Empire's parishes. Church officials told us that only a few parish leaders adopted the pro-immigrant message. Diocese staff believe that many priests are reluctant to take a pro-immigrant stance because they fear a negative reaction from their conservative congregations. Tensions between the church's pro-integration position and more conservative anti-immigrant congregations emerged in 2005 when a relatively white and wealthy Riverside parish was entrusted to priests from the Philippines. According the parish priest, many of the white congregants complained about the new priests' accents. These same members also objected to the increased presence and influence of Asian and Latino immigrants within their congregations. Tensions boiled over when the church began to expand its Spanish-language services in order to accommodate immigrant parishioners, who make up an estimated 25 percent of its congregants. Eventually, a number of the most influential donors and volunteers left the parish. Unfazed by the exodus, the new priests continued their campaign to remake the church as a space that reflected a growing Latino and Asian population. Some of the white parishioners returned, but the hostile reception highlighted some of the challenges faced by the church and the region.

The Roman Catholic Church isn't the only faith-based institution with an interest in integration efforts. For example, the Inland Congregations United for Change (ICUC) is a faith-based community organization that is part of the national congregation-based People Improving Communities through Organizing (PICO) network. It has been active in the San Bernardino, Riverside, Palm Springs, Cathedral City, Coachella, and Mecca areas. The ICUC strives to connect local parishes with community issues. Some of its work in the Inland Empire has involved immigration and education. Clergy and Laity United for Economic Justice (CLUE), a statewide organization, has also been active in the Inland Empire, where it has built relationships between unions and local congregations around labor rights issues. CLUE has struggled to maintain a full-time organizational structure in the Inland Empire, but it has been able to incorporate immigrant worker issues into the faith-based community's integration efforts.

Organized Labor

CLUE's connections to organized labor helped fill a major gap between local unions and immigrant rights groups. Inland Empire labor unions have been relatively absent from both immigration enforcement reform efforts and longer-term integration issues. Community organizers from the RRN told us that local labor leaders refused to advocate for immigrant workers even when their own union members were being affected. Some of the reluctance was attributed to the conservative and racial makeup of the region's union leadership, which is mostly white and conservative. When compared to labor councils in other regions with large numbers of immigrant workers, particularly Los Angeles, the joint labor council that acts as the regional governing body for Riverside and San

Bernardino has not championed immigrant worker organizing. In fact, it gave little or no support to two recent organizing drives that specifically targeted the region's immigrant workers. While some of the distance reflects people's true beliefs, it is also the case that labor leaders seem to believe that their members will benefit from taking moderate stances and forging close relationships with the region's conservative political leaders.

Even without much local union support, a number of national labor unions launched organizing campaigns that put residential construction and warehousing workers, many of them immigrants, on the political radar. This pro-immigrant labor voice was expressed in at least two significant ways. First, by engaging in direct actions and public organizing campaigns, immigrant workers introduced the idea of economic justice into the debate on regional development. It was an important intervention in a region where most leaders clamored for more jobs without a serious discussion about living wages and community benefits. Workers were able to craft a pro-integration vision for the future by framing jobs and economic development as a long-term strategy for economic mobility.

Second, the organizing campaigns enabled national unions like Change to Win (CTW) and the Laborers International Union of North America (LiUNA) to team up with grassroots immigrant-based organizations like CLUE and the National Day Laborer Organizing Network (NDLON). Union staff members also took active roles in organizations like the Justice for Immigrants Coalition. Members of the coalition felt that union participation in immigrant organizing efforts provided a tremendous boost to the network. A few of the community advocates we interviewed expressed initial distrust of organized labor's more recent interest in immigrant workers. But they also acknowledged that sustained labor participation could strengthen the immigrant social justice movement by providing resources including funding, organizers, and campaign knowledge. Community advocates specifically mentioned that labor unions were instrumental in pushing a regional organizing model.

The new labor-immigrant coalition was stymied by the Great Recession of 2008. Most of the union staff who participated in the immigrant network were employed by the national organizing office. For example, even though LiUNA has Inland Empire locals, its national organizing staff took a leadership role in conducting citizenship fairs for the immigrant community. When unions began cutting their national staff, that reduced their participation in regional immigration coalition work. Some labor organizations, like the Warehouse Workers United, continue to participate. Overall, the general sentiment among labor and immigrant organizers was that this alliance should be a key part of any effort to implement a more strategic integration agenda.

Education and Youth Organizing

Several groups have formed in response to the education challenges reviewed above. Like the immigrant coalitions that have developed, youth-centered organizing has begun to push school performance measures and immigrant integration to new levels, in part by introducing concepts like social and restorative justice. Groups like the Moreno Valley Parents Association, the ICUC, the Catholic Diocese, the Asian American Resource Center, the Latina and Latino Roundtable of the San Gabriel Valley and Pomona Valley, along with many other informal ones, have demanded a seat at the education table. Several of the leaders we interviewed claim that immigrant parents and their U.S.-born children have very little influence over education policy decisions in the Inland Empire. As a result, their efforts to improve local schools deal not only with performance standards but also with parent and student empowerment. Representatives from the Catholic Diocese and the Moreno Valley Parents Association claimed that building parents' capacity to act as advocates for their children must be part of a broader plan to deal with systemic education failure.

Some education activists believe that existing policies can provide vehicles for parental engagement in decision making, something especially important for undocumented parents who cannot cast a vote in local school elections. Education officials and community advocates alike mentioned that state-mandated District-Based Language Assessment Committees (DLACs) allow parents of English language learners to participate in school-based decisions. School board members from the cities of San Bernardino and Moreno Valley told us that DLACs provide important opportunities for immigrant parents, especially women, to participate in educational governance. The San Bernardino School District has also developed a Parent Institute that trains many immigrant parents on how to effectively deal with the American public education system.

Parental involvement in curriculum decisions may also be affected by the same demographic shifts that have altered the region's political landscape. Some of the most inclusive and forward-thinking integration policies have been implemented in school districts where Latinos have been elected or appointed to key positions. For example, within the San Bernardino City Unified School Board, Latinos now hold a majority. This was not the case as late as 1997, when African Americans held two of the seats, four were held by whites, and one was held by a Latino. By 2010 these numbers had changed; four seats were held by Latinas, two by whites, and one by an African American (although the composition has shifted once again, and now there is less Latino representation; as of 2015, there were two Latina, two African American, and three white board members). The new majority expanded services to English language learners. District officials also developed a master plan that maintained bilingual education at a time when nearby districts were systematically rooting out support for bilingual students. Fixing the education system will be a daunting task, but as became evident from our conversations with local leaders, a standards-based approach to reform that doesn't include specific strategies for immigrant communities, including ELL students and second-generation children, will shipwreck the economic future of the region.

Business

Finally, while the business community is deeply implicated in questions about jobs and education, it has been absent from immigrant organizing efforts. Unlike in San José and Charlotte, the local business class has not used pro-integration projects to advance its economic interests. This is a significant departure from earlier periods, when local growers advocated for immigrant farm labor. Local farmers even defended immigrants against white populist attacks (Matt Garcia 2001). So why has the Inland Empire's business community been slow to take a public lead on immigrant integration?

Local business leaders cited two main reasons for their hesitancy. First, the business class is not well organized and thus does not function as a group that pursues collective interests; while business leaders have tremendous individual influence, they have not built formal institutions to channel their power. Second, even those business leaders who favor comprehensive immigration reform have not taken a public stand on the matter because they worry about possible backlash in a hostile conservative political climate.

Some business leaders have taken steps to address their lack of formal organization. To this end, the Inland Empire Economic Partnership (IEEP), which represents businesses, local governments, and educational institutions, underwent a major restructuring in 2010 with the intent to craft a regional economic agenda. IEEP staff conducted more than one hundred interviews with regional business leaders to identify problems and possible solutions. Business leaders apparently told IEEP staff that they felt disconnected from the local political establishment and from regional policy decisions. Some of this disconnect is tied to global changes in the economy that transformed the local business landscape in the post-1990s era when national and international business interests flooded into the region. According to the economist John Husing, "When corporate America took over, and it's Walmart and it's Target, those people do not exist here, they exist in a corporate culture. They're here today, they're gone tomorrow. They don't know about the local issues, they don't care" (Husing 2010).

In response, the IEEP took steps to connect local and nonlocal business leaders with regional policy makers. More specifically, it formed the Inland Empire Business Council and the Inland Empire Business PAC. Both are attempts to give business "a voice" and to "support a jobs agenda," according to the IEEP's chief executive officer, Paul Granillo. The IEEP leaders have also taken steps to integrate the growing ranks of ethnic entrepreneurs into their leadership structure. The head of Cardenas Markets, for example, was appointed to the newly configured IEEP Board of Directors; Cardenas is a regional grocery chain that caters to Latino clients. Company executives have also played a key role in the Inland Empire Hispanic Leadership Council. The company also sponsored events to increase Latino participation in the 2010 Census.

When asked about how the business community is addressing the economic needs of first- and second-generation immigrants, business leaders pointed to a number of education and job-training initiatives in the region. Perhaps the most successful example is the Coachella Valley Pathways to Success program— organized by the Coachella Valley Economic Partnership, local high schools, colleges, and businesses—which links high school students to internships and jobs in key sectors like health care and alternative energy. IEEP leaders stressed the importance of higher education, and they cited the Esperanza program in the city of Ontario as a model for increasing the number of college-educated workers. Local Latino business leaders established the Esperanza program as a way to encourage college education by teaching parents and students how to succeed in college.

Education and economic development seem like less controversial issues for business leaders to support when compared with immigration reform. Business leaders are loath to, as one of our interviewees put it, "rock the boat," especially because they fear that taking a public stance on immigration reform would cause a political backlash. As one of our interviewees noted, when asked about business support for comprehensive immigration reform, "the hotel people said it needs to happen, certainly the farmers said it needs to happen, and we heard from some business owners that I would never have imagined being supportive of comprehensive immigration reform who said, this just needs to get fixed." Will these business owners come out from the shadows to support immigrant issues? Community and business representatives told us that if local ethnic entrepreneurs did emerge with a pro-immigrant voice, they would likely become the leading voices. It's also clear from other cases in this volume that such a regional business voice would provide the cover for other forces to more adamantly pursue and support immigrant integration policies and rhetoric.

State of Movement-Building in the Inland Empire

Whether it is education, jobs, or civic life, the region's hostile environment toward immigrants undeniably shapes the everyday experience of these immigrants and their families in the Inland Empire. This comes as a surprise in a state like California, where the anti-immigrant political battles of the 1990s seem like ancient history. Yet as the demographic overview suggested, other parts of California were transformed by demographic changes much earlier than the Inland Empire, and so the growing pains those areas experienced back then are now in full evidence in the desert environs of the Inland Empire. But it's not just demographics that explain the entire story of California's evolution into a more pro-integration populace. Demographic change, political calculations, and economic factors certainly play a role in shaping everyday opportunities, but we know from examples in places like Los Angeles and Chicago that a deep social infrastructure and vibrant social movements can play a big role in how immigrants are integrated into and help to redefine particular places.

For the most part, immigrant organizations in the Inland Empire don't have a seat at the decision-making table. Because of this outsider status, organizers believe that they must move beyond—but not abandon—the politics of protest if they want to strengthen their political position. As one of the Inland Empire's leading immigrant rights leaders told us: "Demonstrating will not be enough—the way to make real change is by getting our own people elected. Doing things like voter registration and public education of the political process in their communities, not just for immigrants, but minorities in general" (Amaya 2010).

If immigrant advocacy organizations want to effect social change, they will need to overcome a number of challenges. This includes a lack of organizational capacity, poor regional coordination, and weak alliances with other stakeholder groups. Several of the Inland Empire groups we interviewed listed organizing capacity as a major barrier to success. Accordingly, a number of them, including the Warehouse Workers United, the Center for Community Action and Environmental Justice, and the Inland Congregations United for Change, devote significant institutional resources to leadership development. On the resource side, most of the community advocates we interviewed expressed frustration with current funding streams. In particular, local organizations seem stuck in a funding paradox in which foundation program officers express a desire to provide more resources but are hesitant to do so until the region gains adequate social infrastructure.[13] As one of our interviewees asked, "How can we develop infrastructure if funders don't help?"

Some funders circumvented weak organizational capacity by funding Los Angeles organizations to develop projects in the Inland Empire. National organizations like Reform Immigration for America have reached into the Inland Empire to conduct a number of training sessions and informational meetings about comprehensive immigration. While these efforts can be helpful, they do not directly contribute to local leadership development. Suzanne Foster, executive director of the Pomona Day Laborer Center, touched on this tension between local and external groups: "I think it's good to be connected, but I also think the Inland Empire has to do it on their own, to build their own capacity, to be able to get to a point where LA is at. LA can't do it for us" (Foster 2010). Resource competition is another tension point between Inland Empire and LA groups. As Emilio Amaya told us, "Sometimes it's an issue when groups with resources come to work in the area, but once the resources run out, they leave. . . . We should help local community groups develop" (Amaya 2010). Nonetheless, the financial and institutional resources that outside groups like NDLON, CLUE, and various unions have invested in Riverside and San Bernardino Counties have helped form important mega-regional connections between Los Angeles and the Inland Empire.

Immigrant social movement organizations have not been able to build multiracial alliances including African Americans and Asians. Members of the Justice for Immigrants Coalition acknowledged that they have very weak relationships with African American community leaders and with the growing Asian immigrant community. When the JIC approached a prominent Pomona-based African American pastor for his support of a march on May 1, 2008—International Workers' Day—he expressed initial support for the event's economic justice themes. But he withdrew his support because organizers chose to link the march to immigrant rights. According to JIC members, the pastor felt that the immigration focus would exclude African Americans.

Rather than blame the African American pastor for not supporting immigrant rights, one key JIC leader told us that this episode highlighted the need for deeper connections with the black community. There are some indications that this is beginning to happen. The Latina and Latino Roundtable recently cosponsored a Martin Luther King Jr. church event, and African American church members participated in a farmworker pilgrimage march. According to José Calderon, a cofounder of the Roundtable, these interactions and relationships allowed the groups to articulate a common frame; African Americans and immigrants found solidarity in shared stories of lost jobs and foreclosed homes, but they also discovered unity in hope for a better future. As a result, Pomona-based African American and Latino groups have supported each other's issues and have collaborated on funding campaigns, something Roundtable members would like to extend to other parts of the Inland Empire. Immigrant advocates have been less successful in building relationships with non-Latino immigrant communities. For example, Asian immigrants are virtually absent from regional organizing efforts.

What awaits these immigrant organizations if they manage to build their capacity and strengthen alliances? Evidence from Chicago and Los Angeles suggests that a strong immigrant-origin voting base and robust community organizations can create political space for both Republican and Democratic policy makers to support immigrant-friendly initiatives. The idea is that as social movement organizations build political power, they can push policy makers, regardless of party. But outside of a few small jurisdictions, the Inland Empire's current conservative climate and weak civic infrastructure have prevented this from happening. Some local activists question whether the growing Democratic Party strength is a solution. Gil Navarro, a San Bernardino County Board of Education member, claims that the Inland Empire Democratic Party structure has excluded Latinos and Asians from recruitment and fund-raising efforts. According to Navarro, the San Bernardino County Central Democratic Council consistently failed to address immigration reform (Navarro 2010). Navarro was so disenchanted with local Democratic Party leadership that he formed the Inland Empire Latino Caucus in 2010. The split made at least one thing clear: the Democratic Party, like other local institutions, is a contested field, and struggles to define its agenda will ultimately shape the future integration politics.

Finally, the region's size and jurisdictional fragmentation have hampered regional social movement coordination. In short, the area is big, fragmented, and lacks centralized organizational capacity, factors that make it difficult to organize at the mega-regional level. There are signs that social movement organizations are learning how to mobilize across counties without losing their local roots. One example is the statewide mobilization project launched in 2010 by California Calls. The Los Angeles–based organization developed regional partnerships with community-based organizations across the Inland Empire and provided them with resources and training to develop get-out-the vote campaigns. More important, the organization created links between African American groups, labor, and immigrant-based organizations. Eventually, California Calls and its network of community-based organizations would like to enact tax and fiscal policy reforms that they believe would improve educational and economic opportunities for their members. Like many of the other examples listed in this chapter, this alliance is new, and it is difficult to assess its long-term prognosis.

If regions manage to build networks, they must do so knowing that funding for civic engagement and immigrant integration is relatively limited. Most nonprofit funding supports direct service provision and not the type of grassroots organizing needed to push for long-term integration. For example, the San Bernardino–based Asian American Resource Center is one of the few organizations that serves the region's Asian immigrant population. Its leadership would like to adopt a more civic-minded social movement platform that advocates for Asian immigrants across the region, but the organization is concerned that more direct action would endanger existing service-oriented funding. Limited funding and geopolitical challenges often mean that there is little time or resources to organize at the regional level. Time will tell if immigrant groups, who sometimes fly under the radar of more mainstream and service-oriented nonprofit funders, will have the resources to expand, but it is clear that immigrant integration will depend on whether work is done to shore up the region's social movement infrastructure and organizational capacities.

Most Californians might like to believe that they have left behind the divisive and contentious immigrant politics of the 1990s. It is easy to think that they are way ahead of Arizona or some southern states that are still coming to grips with their new demographic realities. But the protests in Murrieta in the summer of 2014 revealed that parts of California have yet to sort out the complex politics of immigrant integration. While California as a whole is often said to represent the demographic future of the United States, the state includes places like the Inland Empire—and the problems and politics in those locales require closer attention.

This is particularly so because the Inland Empire was supposed to be California's new frontier, a refuge for the state's growing Latino, Asian, and immigrant families. Yet instead of accommodating the new arrivals, local political leaders responded by adopting pro-deportation policies and by limiting access to public goods. Even more pervasive was the deployment of an anti-immigrant narrative that linked the region's growing Latino population—native and foreign-born alike—to a perceived tidal wave of undocumented immigrants. As a result, a number of our interviewees told us that political leaders who are open to pro-immigrant approaches often remain silent because they fear a conservative backlash.

Recent attempts to build a regional immigrant rights network may be a sign that things could change, but early efforts have been sluggish. The region's scattered geography and jurisdictional fragmentation are just two of the challenges that limit cooperation. Advocates believe that demographic changes and recent organizing initiatives will provide new winds to the sails of pro-integration efforts. Business also needs to step up, although it seems to be in a bit of a bind: companies are dependent on immigrant labor and often quietly favor reform but don't want to lead in a region where more conservative lawmakers control both local rule making and local rhetoric.

In the end, what happens in Riverside and San Bernardino Counties will reflect on California's ability to provide a sustainable, just, and comfortable home for a new generation of immigrants who rushed to the Inland Empire to pursue their American dreams, only to witness an economic collapse that devastated the region. How will the growing immigrant and Latino majority react to the widening gap between hope for a better tomorrow and despair over the harsh reality of a highly racialized economic disorder? Will they create a vibrant civil society that transforms the Inland Empire's democratic fabric, or will they be subjected to a racial and economic order that casts them as a chronically disenfranchised underclass?

7

"THE KINDNESS OF STRANGERS"

Ambivalent Reception in Charlotte,
North Carolina

Michael Jones-Correa

Charlotte, North Carolina, grew spectacularly over much of the last three decades, emerging as one of the winners following federal banking and energy deregulation in the 1980s and drawing a wave of newcomers. These new residents sought the jobs promised by the region's expanding economy and came not only from across the country, but from abroad. Like the rest of North Carolina in the 1990s and 2000s, Charlotte became a new destination for Latino and other immigrants seeking work in the booming areas of construction, light manufacturing, and services that accompanied and fueled North Carolina's growth. Many of these migrants were low-skilled workers from Mexico.

The native-born residents of Charlotte are, and remain, deeply ambivalent about this trend. As in Phoenix, many of the new immigrant residents did not arrive in the United States legally, and North Carolina's political context, like Arizona's, was not supportive of integrating these newcomers. The sociocultural climate in North Carolina was not as welcoming as that in San José, California, but neither was the reaction as virulent and hostile as that taking place in Arizona. Instead, Charlotte, like North Carolina as whole, took a middle path between acceptance and outright hostility, reacting at least initially with denial. As the issue of immigration became too visible to ignore in the 2000s, Charlotte's leaders attempted to strike a balance between expanding services, directly and indirectly, and increasing enforcement.

After the immigrant marches in the spring of 2006, the failure of national immigration reform later that year, the implementation of 287(g) in Charlotte's Mecklenburg County in 2007, and the national (and regional) recession that was well under way by 2008, that balance may have temporarily tilted the city toward greater hostility toward immigrants; but Charlotte, and North Carolina, still occupy a middle ground among new receiving destinations, and Charlotte has recently moved explicitly to signal a welcome to newer arrivals. The following chapter is divided into three parts: it outlines the economic and social context of the city and county (the two cannot be discussed separately, as they provide certain services jointly); it then describes moves made by local government and service providers to respond to and integrate new immigrant arrivals; and finally, it assesses the backlash against immigrants after 2006, expressed through the implementation of a 287(g) accord between Mecklenburg County and the Department of Homeland Security, and the recalibration in the county's response since.

On the whole, the story told here is of a city and region that took economic growth as a given and gave little thought to its consequences, particularly in terms of how it would change the city's demographics. As the sizable and growing noncitizen immigrant population residing in the city and county became apparent, local leaders have taken different stances—some more accommodating, some more hostile. Overall, however, the region is attempting to achieve an ambivalent balance, offsetting negative responses with a concern for projecting a "New South" image of entrepreneurial harmony.

Local Context and Environment

As late as 1980, textile and furniture manufacturing dominated the Charlotte regional job market. In 1980, 13 percent of all jobs were in textile manufacturing, with no other sector accounting for more than 5 percent. By 2000, however, banking and energy were clearly the dominant sectors. Banking deregulation in the 1980s permitted Charlotte's local banks to evolve into national actors: NationsBank became Bank of America; First Union became Wachovia (though Wells Fargo acquired it after it failed in 2008). Duke Power, which began as a local utility provider, expanded with energy deregulation into a variety of energy-related ventures throughout the country, and energy has become a greater economic focus since the 2008 financial crisis.

The fact that these and other Fortune 500 companies developed in Charlotte and remained headquartered there gave their executives a sense of commitment to the city and region. Interviews suggest the presence of a "tight-knit private-sector philanthropic economic growth machine." Key executives at each of these corporations—beginning with Hugh McColl (NationsBank, later Bank of America); Edward Crutchfield (First Union Bank, later Wachovia), and Bill

Lee (Duke Power)—worked with city and government leaders to develop Charlotte's downtown. One of the city's current business leaders said, in an interview: "These leaders had a vision, worked in great collaboration with government, and kept their eye on their vision for decades. . . . They had a vision for Charlotte to become a first-class city." Another interviewee from the city's chamber of commerce noted that "there were at that time [in the 1980s] enough CEOs that were powerful enough to make this happen—that . . . was important. . . . All three key people were local. . . . Those three built buildings, but they also created the policy infrastructure. . . . They not only served as leaders, they set the template for the private market stepping up. They took the risk." The interviewee went on to say: "Our [Charlotte's] past public-private partnerships would not have worked today" (interview conducted by Mai Thi Nguyen, 2009).

One city official commented that "everything in Uptown [Charlotte's downtown] was paid for by Bank of America." It might be more accurate to say that Bank of America (formerly NationsBank) was the driving force behind Charlotte's downtown revitalization.[1] In Charlotte, Bank of America underwrote Corporate Center, Founders Hall, and the Blumenthal Performing Arts Center, to create a community center gathering place in the central business district. It leased a large, centrally located parcel of land for one dollar a year to the city to create the transit system hub. When citizens voted down a referendum to build a sports arena, leaders of the two major banks and the power company built the complexes instead, putting together $100 million in financing, paid for in part by a city hotel and motel tax (BRR field report, economics team). The business sector in Charlotte, particularly the banks headquartered there, saw the continued growth of the region's finance industry and the success of the city's downtown as intertwined. "Success of the redevelopment of downtown by the banking industry created a lifestyle suitable for attracting talent, while the growing banks [aided by flexible state banking laws] created upper-management jobs in banking, back-office services, and clerical level jobs" (interview conducted by Mai Thi Nguyen, 2009).

The fact that corporate leadership was local shaped the banks' corporate philanthropy in the city. In Charlotte, government leaders described a clubby partnership where business and government work more closely than almost anywhere else in the country, and where accessibility of the business leaders to their government officials (and vice versa) is only a 24/7 phone call away, enabling government to deal directly with these key private-sector leaders. One respondent described how "the chamber of commerce is responsible for securing votes for bond issues. When the county commission and city council want something, then they make calls to the business community and ask them, 'Can you get this done?' Our purpose is business" (interview conducted by Mai Thi Nguyen, 2009).

The shift to banking and finance as the city and county's primary economic base in the 1980s continued through 2014, though it consolidated after the 2008 financial crisis. (Wells Fargo's acquisition continued Wachovia's activities in Charlotte and made it the bank's East Coast operations center.) One consequence of this shift was burgeoning service and construction industries that provided employment for the wave of immigrants arriving in Charlotte in the 1990s and 2000s.

Immigration

Charlotte was a boomtown from the 1980s through 2008. The region's broad economic growth drew an increasing number of migrants, domestic as well as international. The region's black population, for example, increased substantially in recent decades: "While nationwide employment of African American workers increased 14 percent between 1990 and 2000, it grew by 20.7 percent in the Southern 'magnet' states and 40.5 percent in Mecklenburg County" (Deaton 2008, 5). The state's and the region's Latino populations grew rapidly as well. Between 1990 and 2000, North Carolina registered the highest rate of increase in Hispanic population of any state—from 76,726 to 378,963, or 394 percent. During the same period, the Hispanic population in Mecklenburg County, of which Charlotte is the county seat and largest city, rose from about 6,000 to almost 45,000—an increase of 620 percent. By 2010, Mecklenburg's Hispanic population had grown even more, to 112,000—an increase of 1,766 percent since 1990 (U.S. Census, 2010, American Fact Finder).

Immigration to the city and county took place almost entirely after 1990, and largely since 2000: there were very few immigrants in Charlotte in 1980. One respondent who came to Charlotte as an immigrant herself, and who grew up in the city during this period, recalled the broad outlines:

> There's always been a Latino population. I remember growing up through elementary and middle school [that] there was this small niche . . . [of Latinos] from all over the place—South Americans, Mexicans, and stuff like that. But it was like certain pockets. You knew down South Boulevard and the certain duplex complex, that's where everybody kind of lived. And even if we'd buy homes or something we'd stay in that general area. It is not as compared to now . . . in almost every sector of the city now you see some kind of Hispanic or Latino influence, or some kind of immigrant influence. (Author's interview, April 15, 2009)

Twenty years ago immigrants to the region were largely invisible. Today the signs of immigration in Charlotte are inescapable.

While immigrants to Charlotte hailed from countries across the globe, a majority of new arrivals were from Latin America, and a plurality from Mexico. In the 2000s Latinos made up one in four of the region's new residents (Deaton 2008, 2). As described in chapter 2, Latino migration transformed the local workforce: by 2000, immigrants made up 22 percent of the county's construction trade, 15 percent of building and grounds cleaning and maintenance workers, and 12 percent of food-preparation workers. Attracted by the booming local economy, initially these new immigrant arrivals were, on average, more likely than the native-born to be young, male, and unmarried—characteristic of migration in its early stages. By the 2000s, though, the migrant stream had become increasingly female, and Latinos in Charlotte included rising numbers of families with children, perhaps the unintended consequence of federal immigration policies that made it increasingly difficult for short-term migrants to cross the border (Massey, Durand, and Malone 2003).

Residential Concentration and Inequality

Immigration to Charlotte entered a spatial terrain almost entirely defined by white-black racial segregation, in which immigrants were, and are, a relatively small share of the total population (the lowest of all our cases). While the importance of the black-white dynamic is, of course, not entirely absent in the other cases (Chicago, New York, and Los Angeles, for example), the dominance of this white-black narrative, and its historical resonance in the South, give the interplay of race and immigration a peculiar resonance.

One indication of the intersection between immigration and race can be seen in the spatial distribution of immigrants and native-born blacks. The foreign-born population is somewhat clustered around the Uptown central business district in the center of the region, with denser concentrations to the southeast and southwest (referred to in Charlotte as the "Eastside" and "Southwest side" of the city). The Eastside is the more "established" Latino and immigrant community, having expanded from a small Asian immigrant settlement that was in place as early as the 1980s, but "established" should be understood in the context of a very recent immigrant population (Smith and Furuseth 2008). Figures 7.1 and 7.2 show this dramatic spread of foreign-born residents between 1980 and the present.

Understanding black-white segregation patterns in Charlotte is essential to understanding the pattern of immigrant settlement in Mecklenburg County. Blacks in Charlotte are concentrated to the north of the city, embracing Uptown. The city's older white residential neighborhoods are to the south of Uptown, forming a triangle of census tracts pointing toward the city's central business

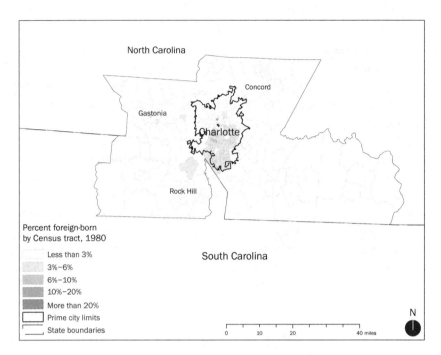

FIGURE 7.1. Percent foreign-born by Census tract, 1980, Charlotte, NC

Source: 1980 Decennial Census, Census TIGER/Line, and ESRI.

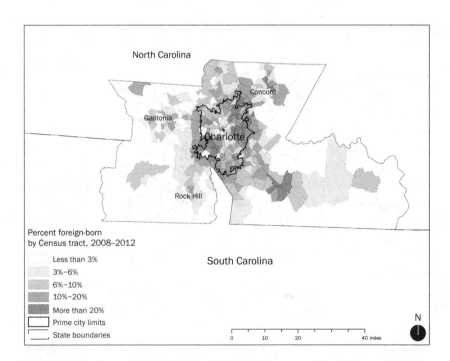

FIGURE 7.2. Percent foreign-born by Census tract, 2008–2012, Charlotte, NC

Source: 2008–2012 American Community Survey (Ruggles et al. 2011), Census TIGER/Line, and ESRI.

district. The predominantly black tracts radiate from the west of the central business district around to the northeast. The largest concentrations of the new, largely Latino, immigrant population reside in "buffer areas" between black-majority and white-majority tracts.

This description, however, does not fully capture the dynamics of demographic change in the city and county. First, Latinos are still a minority, even in the tracts where they are concentrated. Latino neighborhoods are not strictly Latino—they are multiracial. As Smith and Furuseth point out, in 2000 "only one Census tract, Census Tract 53.04, with a Latino population of 44.7 percent, [came] close to meeting the higher benchmark set by Lobo, Flores, and Salvo (2002) wherein a census tract must have at least 50 percent Hispanic residents to be classified as a Hispanic neighborhood" (Smith and Furuseth 2004, 225).

Second, Latino immigrants increasingly overlap residentially with native-born blacks in tracts to the west and north of the city, leading to greater opportunities for both conflict and cooperation. Third, neighborhoods closest to Uptown on Charlotte's Eastside and Southwest are also gradually being gentrified by non-Hispanic whites seeking proximity to downtown. Fourth, the triangle of white tracts to the south of Uptown are losing population as the residents age and younger white families move elsewhere. These areas are likely to become more racially/ethnically diverse in the near future. Fifth, wealthier whites are now moving to the far north of the city and county, and indeed into adjoining counties, skipping the city's core and near suburbs entirely.

It is no surprise that these patterns of immigration and segregation should also show up in measures of inequality. Foreign-born Latinos have significantly lower median incomes than native-born whites (with median household incomes roughly similar of those of native-born blacks). Asian immigrants have household incomes that are comparable (though just slightly lower) than those of native-born whites. Spatial sorting to some extent reflects a preference for co-ethnic proximity—Latinos, for instance, making decisions to live close to other Latinos (Smith and Furuseth 2004). But neighborhood sorting reflects economics as well as race: Latinos settle where real estate prices are cheaper and where there is access to transportation to jobs. This often means settling in neighborhoods that are predominantly African American, or buffer zones between black and white residential spaces. These are transitional neighborhoods, with some observers noting the substantial amount of turnover in apartment housing, even month to month (author's interview, April 18, 2009).

Race Relations

The influx of immigrants is leading to a gradual restructuring of race relations in the region (Hanchett 1998). This is a complex process. It has taken the form of an increase in tensions between blacks and Latinos around competition for common resources, as well as racial stereotyping (Matthews 2007; see also Deaton 2008; Marrow 2007; McClain et al. 2006). Karen Johnson-Webb (2002) found, for instance, competition between Hispanics and blacks for employment opportunities in North Carolina. In her study of employer recruitment in the hospitality sector in the Triangle region, she determined that employers actively recruited Hispanic workers as opposed to other ethnicities because they perceived Hispanics as having a greater work ethic and found it easier to recruit labor through ethnic social networks (Johnson-Webb 2002, cited in Matthews 2007, 6–7). Johnson-Webb's research echoes findings by Roger Waldinger on the ethnic preferences of (largely) white employers for recent immigrants in New York and Los Angeles (Waldinger 1999). White employers' preference for immigrant labor creates the setting for resentment by black workers.

Black resentment was evident in some conversations. An African American council member, for instance, speaking at length about illegal immigration from Latin America, said the view of blacks "in the coffee shops and the ice cream parlors and the bars" is that they are sick of illegal immigrants: "They are taking our jobs. I'm out of work, but I can't get a job at a place I want to get a job at: everybody there is from somewhere else. That brings on race tensions and the next thing you know you have retaliation, next thing you know you going [to] get more crimes being committed where folk up there are attacked and hurt. . . . [People] are targeted, are discriminated against." An African American minister voiced similar concerns: "In construction [Latinos] are doing 90 percent of the work. There are a lot of African Americans who would love to do some of those jobs. There is a perception that Latinos get jobs over African-Americans because they are willing to work for a lower wage and they desire to work. . . . That's how the African-American community sees this. This is what we have to overcome" (interviews quoted in Deaton 2008, 14).

Blacks have some resentment as well toward Latinos' use of social services, particularly for their children in the areas of health and education. The black council member complained that illegal immigration had an

> effect on taxpayers, locally that is. You're talking about the school impact, you're talking about overcrowding, you're talking about increasing the number of schools, you're talking about tutors, you're talking about paying someone to translate. [All] those additional costs for the great state of North Carolina. We say that if you're in this state, whether you're illegal or not, our state charter says that we have to educate you. And that child has to attend school. So those children go to school and we have to educate them. And we can't speak their language, they don't understand our language, and we have to hire or get additional help in

those classrooms to assist those teachers, and that's a cost. It's not free. So you've seen that increase, you've seen the increase in [the demand for] social services, you've seen the increase of welfare, you've seen the increase of assistance, whether it be through WIC, whether it be through food stamps, or whether it be just medical. (Author's interview, April 16, 2009)

Channing Matthews's study (2007, 11) quotes an African American resident who says, "If I was born here, and cannot even get [health] insurance, why should they, if they aren't even citizens?" The director of the Charlotte-Mecklenburg Community Relations Committee recalled the misperceptions he had heard from other black residents in Charlotte: "I had an opportunity a while ago to attend [a meeting] that was attended mostly by African Americans, and we were talking about what is going on in the Hispanic ... community, and I was amazed [at] the number of people at that particular meeting who were of the impression whenever Hispanics came to the United States the government gave them each $25,000 to get started in life, and for the first five years that they worked they didn't have to pay any federal income tax!" (author's interview, April 13, 2009). The perception among some black residents and community leaders—based on a mix of reality and rumor—that immigrants have undeserved access to services and benefits, and place undue strain on the taxpayers who fund those programs, seems broadly shared.

Schooling, too, is an area of some tension. The influx of Latino children into public schools, which had begun in the 1990s, accelerated in the 2000s. This coincided with the school district's transition to a neighborhood-school model, as court-ordered busing, a system that had been put in place to enforce racial desegregation, was dismantled under legal challenge in 2000. As the transition to neighborhood schools coincided with an influx of (largely Latino) immigrants into the school system, the school district (mandated by the federal government to provide instruction for students not proficient in English) dramatically increased the number of English as a Second Language (ESL) programs in neighborhood schools. The expansion of ESL in the district increased the visibility of the immigrant children in schools and the resources—mostly state and federal—allocated to these children.

Crime, of course, was another problem associated, however unfairly, with the new immigrants: "There is a racial aspect to crime and law enforcement as well. One black city official noted how [because Latinos] did not believe in banks ... blacks were making Latinos ... targets. There was a black and Latino crime sort of thing. It was not black-on-black crime like it used to be" (author's interview, April 14, 2009; and author's interview, April 13, 2009). African Americans also perceived Latinos as responsible for increasing gang violence. "Perceptions [are that] all gang members in the community are of Hispanic descent," one black city official noted (author's interview, April 13, 2009). On the enforcement side, the city police force and county sheriff's department are overwhelmingly black or white, but an increasing number of those incarcerated are Latino. The Mecklenburg County sheriff's department, for instance, has 1,500 employees (including 800 detention officers and 350 sworn officers). Half are African American. Only a very small fraction—the county sheriff did not volunteer a number—are Latino. About 18 percent out of approximately twenty-four hundred inmates (as of the date of the interview) were Latino (author's interview, April 16, 2009).

The combination of rapid demographic shifts, changes in ethnic residential patterns, job competition, and perceived jockeying for public services has reportedly led to increased tensions, particularly between foreign-born Latinos and native-born blacks. Smith and Furuseth note that "the rapid in-migration of Hispanics into neighborhoods that have only recently transitioned from predominantly white to bi-racial, or mostly visible minority, is both opportuni[ty] and tension generating" (2004, 233).

These tensions coexist, however, with concerted efforts at dialogue and cooperation among native-born blacks and immigrant Latinos. Blacks and Latino immigrants sense some commonalities, and opportunities may exist for cooperation: as one African American pastor interviewed volunteered, "I think African-Americans are more equipped to learn to understand and get along with immigrants than whites are. We've been down that road. We know what they are going through, and it should be easy for us to reach out and accept them. We don't have as much to lose as white Americans do" (quoted in Matthews 2007).

The African American executive director of the Charlotte-Mecklenburg Community Relations Committee described how the city began to partner with Latino organizations, in particular the Latin American Coalition, beginning in the mid-2000s: "There was a perception in the community that there were major tensions between the African American community and the Latino community. What we did was we pulled the leadership of the African American community and the Latino community together to have a conversation about . . . these tensions. . . . What we found out is that [these tensions were] just a perception, but perception drives reality for some folks, so it was still a good idea that we sit down and talk" (author's interview, April 13, 2009).

In 2009, almost two hundred people attended an African American–Latino Community Unity Summit organized by the Latin American Coalition together with the Community Relations Committee. Latino and African American elites began making these efforts at dialogue in the context of the election of the city's first African American mayor, a Democrat, in 2009. The small core of Hispanic voters in the city supported his election, easing some tensions.

Immigrant Arrival and Flashpoints

The increase in immigration elicited negative reactions from the native-born who felt threatened, but there were only intermittent flashpoints. The former director of Charlotte-Mecklenburg Police Department's Immigrant Relations Unit from 2006 to 2008 described the community's reaction to the increase in immigration:

> I think [feelings about immigration are] probably under the surface, and when it comes to the surface it is usually [after] some high-profile incident. It usually involves a DWI incident where it turns out the person is not here legally and didn't have a license and things like that. . . . You know, you will have a DWI-related death involving a person that is here legally, and it barely makes anything in the paper. It kind of explodes when there is . . . a more dramatic expression of "here is someone that was here illegally." But from day to day there is not a lot of . . . obvious expressions of concern over [immigration]. (Author's interview, April 19, 2009)

But according to the same former director, there were no overt hate crimes and only occasional friction over use of public space, such as taco trucks popping up in parking lots. He also described tensions over quality-of-life issues, particularly overcrowding in housing—a common avenue for concerns about immigration to get expressed (Light 2006). "There was some concern that came up through the media about too many people in a residence. And they were looking at passing an ordinance relating to limiting the number of people that could live in a single structure. I don't think that went anywhere, but that was kind of focused on the immigrant community" (author's interview April 19, 2009).

What is striking, however, in the Charlotte narrative is how, at least through the mid-2000s, these tensions seemed manageable and were to some extent being addressed through existing institutions.

Immigrant Integration

The initial official response to immigration in the city of Charlotte and Mecklenburg County was tentative and largely ad hoc. The region's politics were, for the South, and for North Carolina, relatively liberal. The general attitude toward immigrants and immigration in the 1980s was, if not exactly welcoming, at least neutral or benign. Immigration had already been under way for at least two decades before the city's political institutions began to respond in a concerted way, conducting reports, implementing strategies, and debating policy responses.

Until then, local responses were largely bureaucratic, designed and conducted by agency administrators and service providers, and largely below the radar (Jones-Correa 2005a, 2008b; Lewis and Ramakrishnan 2007; Marrow 2009).

The Political Context

The political environment encountered by immigrants to Charlotte/Mecklenburg was a kind of liberal conservatism peculiar to the South. North Carolina has a more expansive social service network than many southern states and greater commitment to education, including a highly regarded network of publicly supported community colleges and universities. As for immigrant integration, until the mid-2000s, driver's licenses could be acquired without proof of citizenship. This more open approach was partly the result of Democratic Party officeholders staying in place even as the state was increasingly voting for Republican candidates for president and Congress (although the state did vote for Barack Obama in 2008). But the relative inclusivity of cities like Charlotte or Durham is also due to a desire to project an inclusive or progressive image, as these cities opened up to new global industries and welcomed a new professional and managerial class looking for the amenities urban areas could offer, while avoiding any concomitant tensions.

This was particularly true for Charlotte. The partnership between elected leaders and corporate actors sought to project an image that would foster development. That partnership is reflected to some extent in the region's governing framework. Some regional organizations exist (Charlotte's council of governments is called Centralina, and the regional partnership for economic development is the Carolinas Partnership), but the city and county councils govern the region. (Consolidation of the two bodies following the Nashville model has been discussed off and on but has not come about.) Political decision making is split: the city has a mayor-council structure, while board of commissioners runs the county. The county plays a key role in the region and in some ways exercises greater authority than the City of Charlotte because of its primacy in health, social services, and policing—areas important to the region's immigrants.

Pat McCrory, a Republican, served as mayor of Charlotte from 1995 to 2009, the period of greatest immigration growth. He oversaw the consolidation of banking as the city's dominant industry, the substantial population increase, the downtown redevelopment, and the exponential rise of immigration. Anti-immigrant sentiment also increased during his tenure, as evidenced by the establishment of Mecklenburg County's 287(g) program in 2006, which deputized the county sheriff's department to enforce immigration law, and a 2007 county report exploring cuts in services to immigrants. The city's second African American mayor, Anthony Foxx, a Democrat, succeeded McCrory in 2009. His election introduced a new political dynamic into the city's racial/ethnic relations, defusing some of the anti-immigrant sentiment that had led to the establishment of Mecklenburg's 287(g) program. However, the county continued to participate in the 287(g) program even after Foxx's election. (In 2013, President Obama named Foxx secretary of transportation. His successor, African American city councilor Patrick Cannon, was convicted of bribery, and the city council appointed the current mayor, former state assemblyman Dan Clotfelter, to the office in April 2014.)

Like elected leaders in many of North Carolina's jurisdictions, the Mecklenburg County Board of Commissioners has been split on the issue of immigration, but it steadily tilted toward a more hostile stance toward new arrivals in the 2000s, particularly those that are in the United States illegally. Jennifer Roberts, who was chair of the county's board of commissioners in 2009, noted that "when I became a commissioner, in 2004, I began to hear from some of my colleagues some concern about illegals—of course I think it's not illegal to be a human being and so 'undocumented' is a better term. But there is a law-and-order perspective in [much of] the public sector, and this was being voiced very loudly by some of my colleagues and by the community" (author's interview, April 17, 2009). As Roberts described it, the county board was split between those who wanted the county to take a harder line against undocumented immigration and go to the limits allowed to local authorities in the enforcement of immigration statutes, and those who saw immigration enforcement as largely a federal issue. Roberts placed herself in the latter group:

> I followed the Hazelton, Pennsylvania, case, I followed the Texas cases and the California cases and the propositions and all that, and realized that what usually happened was that they either got reversed [when] some of the housing laws were proved unconstitutional or they sparked a series of lawsuits that became very expensive for that county or that state or whoever. So, my goal in office became one of continuing to thwart or vote down bad proposals by those who were afraid that we were providing too many services to undocumented immigrants, who [they felt were] taking resources that could have [been] used for citizens. (Author's interview, April 17, 2009)

Apparently, this view dominated through much of the 2000s as Charlotte/Mecklenburg kept a relatively open policy toward immigrants.

The tenor of the local political debate on immigration began to change after 2006, with the failure of federal immigration reform efforts that year and the large immigrant marches around the country; as is seen in other cases in this volume, the national tone can affect the local debates. Almost immediately, county commissioners began to propose legislation that would prohibit the county from doing business with anyone who employed undocumented immigrants. If employers were going to get a county contract, they would be required to follow federal immigration law. The first big debate, Roberts recalled, was in December 2006, over whether the county could require agencies and employers to take on the role of asking for and verifying documentation about their employees' legal status (author's interview, April 17, 2009). A second debate in 2007 was over a proposal to deny county services to people who were undocumented. That proposal failed, mostly because services such as emergency room care are federally mandated. In any case, it is worth noting that even in the less favorable climate around immigration, Charlotte/Mecklenburg did not pursue draconian anti-immigrant policies.

Public Services for Immigrants

The agnosticism of local government toward withholding services to immigrants did not translate into active expansion of services, either. Demographic change is often more rapid than institutional change, yielding "institutional mismatches" (Jones-Correa 2005b). And it is not just immigration; as one Charlotte respondent noted, "Mecklenburg County is not ready for the boom that we are having. I see in Mecklenburg County what I saw fifteen years ago in Houston, Texas. There is a lack of services everywhere—jails, hospitals, schools, public services. It's because . . . we are getting people from everywhere . . . looking for a better life" (author's interview, April 24, 2009). However, there was very little in place in terms of immigrant-specific or Latino-specific services before 2000. The manager of the trial court interpreters for the city noted, for example, that "the interpreting program did not start until 2000 here in Charlotte. Once we started here in Charlotte, in about 2001, 2002, the state kind of took over and used Charlotte's as the [model] program for everyone else in the state. Prior to that it was basically anyone who said they could speak a little bit of Spanish could come in and interpret" (author's interview, April 15, 2009). In another instance, the Charlotte-Mecklenburg Police Department had (in 2009) only 64 bilingual employees (and 46 Hispanic employees) out of a workforce of about 1,647—just under 4 percent of its workforce. These were the figures after twenty years of sustained Latino immigration to the city, and even with the city offering financial incentives for bilingual staff and officers (author's interview, April 18, 2009).

As one step toward developing a more systematic response to the region's changing demographics, Mecklenburg County put together a report in 2000 developing a strategic plan for diversity for the county, and created a staff member to help implement that plan in 2005. Much of his work was to persuade city and county departments to respond to the region's increasing demographic diversity and to develop measures for diversity, track the county's responses to diversity, and report the results on a "corporate scorecard." New policies were also attempted, including additional pay as an inducement for public employees to acquire bilingual language skills. The police department also began to use these incentives as well:

> We have folks that earn a language incentive, and they are through- out the department in both sworn and non-sworn positions. We have telecommunicators that speak a foreign language and receive a salary incentive for that. We have dogcatchers, animal-control folks that have language skills as well that are non-sworn people. We have people in our records department that speak a foreign language and are paid for that. So we have sworn and non-sworn folks that get a language incentive for not only Spanish but for several other languages as well that are in primary need. (Author's interview, April 18, 2009)

Such incentives provide a way for the county to promote the hiring and retention of bilingual staff. By and large, however, these responses in the public sector still have an ad hoc nature, even when they have become institutionalized. Agencies have protocols in place to deal with language minorities, for instance, but many still do not have bilingual staff. One interviewee noted, for example, that in 2009, "I would guess that probably . . . most agencies have somebody they can call even if . . . most don't have bilingual employees . . . so it might be one of those resource centers calls family services and says 'can you send yours over, I need them right now.' I suspect they have worked it out" (author's interview, April 24, 2009). The manager of Charlotte's trial court interpreters noted that the courts' interpreta- tive services were set up simply by an administrator's individual initiative, not in response to any legislative initiative or mandate from the city: "He had noticed the need. He is very into . . . having the courtroom accessible to everybody. . . . He actually did the research . . . about how much it would cost to become a member of [the National Center for State Courts] and have them do the testing and all of that. He was able to provide [the Charlotte/Mecklenburg courts] information and documentation as to how to get grant funding" (author's interview, April 15, 2009). The manager described, too, how the availability of bilingual services encouraged more Latino residents to come into the courts:

> We've seen an increase of family law things like custody, visitation, divorces, where Hispanics come in and try to get that paperwork final- ized, while before they kind of just waited until they really needed the stuff. So they are more proactive. . . . In juvenile [court] before it used

to be that the juvenile would get in trouble, the parents would show up. ... The parents would never understand completely as to how the system worked and how they can also have an impact as to what the judge decides. Now ... parents are being more vocal, knowing what to say and knowing what to ask for. (Author's interview, April 15, 2009)

The trial court manager also did a lot of outreach on her own, particularly after recognizing that many immigrants perceived the courthouse as unfamiliar territory. Again, greater public outreach to immigrant arrivals seemed largely the result of individual, ad hoc efforts.

The Charlotte-Mecklenburg school district has been aware of the issues around increasing demographic differences across schools, which accelerated after the end of court-ordered school desegregation in 2001 and with the accelerating arrival of immigrants through the 1990s and 2000s (American Institutes for Research 2005; Burger 1971; Godwin et al. 2006). One response has been to expand bilingual programs in schools particularly affected by the arrival of the children of immigrants. Bilingual programs and services have generally become more entrenched in the schools, particularly since schooling is a legally protected right for all children, regardless of legal status.[2] Charlotte-Mecklenburg's school district has been offering ESL classes since the 1970s, though it took some prodding (and a citation from the state's Office of Civil Rights. The director of the Charlotte-Mecklenburg school district's ESL program noted: "So we have a long history of ESL and providing English-as-a-second-language services to students coming from other countries. Since then we have grown. In 1995 we had one high school ESL program. ... Now in 2009 we have ESL programs in every school, and we have 174 schools in the district" (author's interview, April 14, 2009).

The expansion of ESL programs has followed from the growth in foreign-born or second-generation children in the public schools: Charlotte-Mecklenburg Schools reported a tripling of Latino student enrollment from 2000 to 2005, and in 2006, 13 percent of children in the public schools were Latino (UNC Charlotte Urban Institute 2006, 9). School officials did not see any push-back on ESL from the larger community: "There has not been any controversy or issue around funding ESL programs specifically" (author's interview, April 14, 2009), in part because the federal courts have upheld the principle of providing different treatment to ensure equal access. Responding to English language learners, emphasizing "cultural competence," and reaching out and engaging children's parents continue to be the foci of educational initiatives in the region (Charlotte-Mecklenburg Schools Task Force 2013).

On the whole, surveys indicate the region's new immigrant arrivals like the services they receive. A 2006 survey of Latinos in the county found that, aside from schools, immigrant residents had the greatest contact with the Mecklenburg County Health Department, the Charlotte-Mecklenburg Police Department, and the Mecklenburg County Department of Social Services. A large majority of Latino residents rated these agencies as providing either very good or good services (UNC Charlotte Urban Institute 2006). It is worth keeping in mind, however, that other research on immigrant attitudes indicates that initially positive assessments—in which new arrivals are essentially comparing their present circumstances with their experiences in their countries of origin—decline over time and across generations (Michelson 2000).

Nonprofit Service Provision for Immigrants

Service provision through the nongovernmental sector is still nascent in the Charlotte region. Smith and Furuseth (2008) write that there are different levels of institutional networks in place, with concomitant service provision: "Eastside Charlotte has a more fully integrated Latino service infrastructure with the widest range of Latino oriented businesses and a complete range of Spanish language services offered and more immediately available there. In Southwest Charlotte, Latino oriented retailing and services certainly exist but they are broadly scattered across the cluster area and interspersed among the larger mainstream commercial and service landscape." The North Charlotte neighborhood, where Latinos overlap the most with African Americans, has the fewest service providers, and in sizable portions of the rest of the city and county there are no services at all for Latinos (UNC Charlotte Urban Institute 2006, ix).

Many of these local nonprofit service providers receive some funding from the city or county. The county commission chair noted that these funders often provide services regardless of legal status, or certainly without inquiring directly about legal status: "We have a lot of community partners that we fund partially, and we don't ask them [about the legal status of their clients]. The Latin American Coalition, for example . . . they're trying to get people hooked up with jobs and housing and that sort of thing, but they don't ask for immigration status, and they'll tell you that most of theirs are undocumented. . . . There's another group that we fund . . . Mi Casa, Su Casa, which runs health clinics, and again mostly [for the] undocumented" (author's interview, April 17, 2009). So although legal guidelines and restrictions prevent some public agencies from providing services to illegal aliens, the county and city apparently turned a blind eye to the fact that many of the nonprofits it was funding were providing similar services to these same undocumented residents. But the chair of the county commission noted that organizations that provide such services indicate immigrants are often afraid to apply for them, or, in cases like that of the Crisis Ministry program, nonprofits that receive federal funding and have to document the use of their services to fulfill federal guidelines may not be able to offer their services to those without legal status (author's interview, April 17, 2009).

In the 2006 survey of Latinos in Mecklenburg County, while majorities of respondents had generally good opinions of local nonprofit organizations serving new immigrants, fewer than 16 percent of respondents said they had had any contact with any of these organizations (UNC Charlotte Urban Institute 2006, 24). That is to say, none of these organizations have successfully reached out to more than a fraction of Latinos in the county. Latino residents in the county are much more likely to have had contact with public agencies (health, schools, police) than with nonprofit organizations offering services.

Immigrant Political Participation

Two-thirds of Charlotte's immigrants are not citizens and hence not eligible to vote (American Community Survey 2010–2012). Without a political voice, the region's new immigrants are acutely aware of their position on the social margins. A survey of Latino residents in Mecklenburg County indicated that the top three challenges/barriers they perceived were, in descending order, language barriers (37 percent), discrimination (16 percent), and undocumented status (16 percent) (UNC Charlotte Urban Institute 2006, 23). Nonetheless, some researchers have found that Latino families and the emerging entrepreneurial and business leadership have begun to speak out on a variety of issues, most notably educational opportunities and crime and safety issues. These early efforts toward civic engagement and activism are likely to expand and play out on a variety of fronts (Smith and Furuseth 2008).

Some examples of emerging Latino service providers include Mi Casa, Su Casa, a service provider active since 2000; the Latin American Coalition; a Latino Citizens Committee, organized to work with the region's police department; and the Latino Issues Forum (Batista 2009). Three Spanish-language FM stations broadcast in Charlotte, and one Spanish-language newspaper, La Noticia, has been publishing since 1995 (Postelle 2009). At least seven semiweekly Spanish-language newspapers serve the region (author's interview, April 18, 2009). In addition, some non-Latino community organizations have been active in promoting cross-ethnic/racial interactions. Among these has been Charlotte Helping Empower Local People, which is affiliated with the Industrial Areas Foundation and the United Way. However, these recent homegrown immigrant or immigrant-serving organizations are stretched thin in trying to serve the broad spectrum of needs of the fast-growing Latino population in Charlotte. One activist noted bluntly that "with so many day-to-day problems, we don't have time to learn how to provide services better. We address all problems. Obviously we are growing and satisfying needs, but not getting better preparation for satisfying those needs. . . . It's hard. We don't have time" (quoted in Deaton 2008, 8). Nonetheless, more of these organizations are likely to emerge and become more rooted over time.

Turning Points

Through the early 2000s, local government agencies often acted on their own to respond to the region's recent immigration and the needs of these new residents. The region's official response began to shift in the mid-2000s—in part by formalizing earlier informal bureaucratic responses, and in part by exploring local alternatives to immigration enforcement in a state and national climate that was taking a turn to a harder policy on immigration. While the Charlotte region has continued to navigate a course somewhere between Arizona's hostility and San José's efforts at integration, this balance shifted somewhat toward a more punitive stance in reaction to the 2006 immigrant marches held in Charlotte and around the country and the accelerating economic downturn after 2007.

The 2006 immigrant rally in Charlotte, which attracted tens of thousands of marchers, dramatically raised the visibility of the Latino community. Native-born residents took notice, and the tone of commentary around immigration became increasingly negative, at least for a time. One Latino community leader said that after the 2006 marches "some radio stations started talking like we are the problem. . . . Discrimination has been worse since the rallies. People didn't know so many Latinos were here. Before, they thought of Latinos as a problem. . . . After the rallies, they saw us as a big problem" (quoted in Deaton 2008, 11). An interview with an African American city council member seemed to confirm this view: "Personally as an American I was offended when illegal immigrants that we know are illegal and do not have proper documentation take to the streets, some flying the flag upside down; some burned the flag . . . some marched in Washington screaming they wanted fair and equal rights—well, you have no rights, you're in this country illegally" (author's interview, April 16, 2009). Soon after the marches in 2006, the state legislature changed the state driver's license procedure to require anyone seeking to acquire or renew a license to show proof of a valid Social Security number or a visa. But the single biggest shift was the region's approach to policing.

At the local level, policing and law enforcement in the region is split between the Charlotte-Mecklenburg police and the Mecklenburg County sheriff's office, and the two departments have a close working relationship. As the county sheriff described it, the "Charlotte-Mecklenburg police have countywide jurisdiction. They respond to all 911 calls and investigate all crimes related to those 911 calls. We [the sheriff's department] in turn operate the jail and the arrest process, and I guess the relationship is they are our biggest customer, as far as bringing arrestees in and housing folks. . . . I would say probably 90 percent of [our inmates] are arrest-related or investigations from Charlotte-Mecklenburg police" (author's interview, April 16, 2009). In general, the police carry out "on the beat" functions, while the sheriff's office runs the county jail.

The relationship between policing and the region's immigrants had been relatively uncontroversial through the 1990s. However, anti-immigrant sentiment was building and with it the pressure to use police for local enforcement of immigration law. Some of the cooperation between local police and the Immigration and Customs Enforcement (ICE) branch of the Department of Homeland Security could be seen as stemming from the lack of local expertise. This how the Mecklenburg County sheriff saw it: "It was in 2005 that we started noticing a larger number of Hispanics, in this case in our jail, and we were having difficult identifying who they were. We had no idea what their history was. We have some bilingual officers but not nearly enough, and when they were giving us their name and whatever . . . the only mechanism we had at that time [to verify who they were] was to contact . . . the ICE headquarters database . . . and it would take a couple of days to get that information back" (author's interview, April 16, 2009). However, the 287(g) agreements signed between ICE and local and state enforcement agencies, leading to the joint identification and apprehension of undocumented immigrants, went beyond this. Section 287(g) originated in the 1996 Immigration and Nationality Act but expanded significantly after 2006 (Immigration and Customs Enforcement 2005). By 2009, ICE had sixty-six active memoranda of understanding with various local and state law enforcement agencies; of these, only four existed before 2006 (Immigration and Customs Enforcement 2009).

According to the county sheriff, 287(g) got started in Mecklenburg in part by happenstance but quickly picked up local support:

> The sheriff then had gone to a conference [of] county sheriffs, and in the airport he was talking to a sheriff from California, and the sheriff mentioned the 287(g) program. And we realized when we started researching it, there wasn't a whole lot known about it, in fact the local ICE people didn't know much about it . . . it was not used much. And so we started looking into it and found out that if we could get that program implemented here and do the fingerprint and the photograph quick-checks, we could actually accurately identify these individuals in

about two minutes as opposed to waiting for a couple of days. (Author's interview, April 16, 2009)

The sheriff at the time, Jim Pendergraph, pushed hard to make Mecklenburg County the first department on the East Coast to sign a 287(g) agreement with ICE and persuaded the county commissioners to go along in 2006. (He left in 2007 to take a position in the Bush administration's Department of Homeland Security promoting such agreements but left in less than a year.) By 2009, ICE not only had a 287(g) agreement with Mecklenburg County but had established a regional detention removal unit and an investigative group based in Charlotte, as well as a federal immigration court.

Although the city needed the immigrant community to cooperate in day-to-day contacts to address crime in Charlotte, city officials were fully in favor of 287(g). Even more liberal members of the Mecklenburg County Board of Commissioners voted for the implementation of 287(g), mostly because of the frustration local law enforcement expressed about not being able to track criminals effectively. But while the frustration may have been real, and the problem of undocumented migration significant, 287(g) implementation was problematic. A county commissioner noted: "Unfortunately, if you don't [exercise] control, there are people . . . who are likely to profile and who all of a sudden have a new tool to do it with, or an excuse. Then you can see what happened in our community . . . people stopped for a driver's license expired or a tag expired" (author's interview, April 17, 2009).

The implementation of 287(g) changed policing in Mecklenburg County and to some extent across North Carolina. By 2008, law enforcement agencies in eight counties or municipalities in North Carolina had signed 287(g) memoranda with ICE. About one hundred undocumented Latinos were being brought in to the Mecklenburg county jail every week "by ICE on roundups and stuff like that," with some arriving from other counties (Mecklenburg's jail is one of three in North Carolina that ICE has authorized to hold ICE detainees). Since ICE pays for housing inmates, "there's no cost to the citizens for operating 287(g) because that housing that they pay for offsets all the costs for the deputies and everything else, so it's just a revenue source. So it's kind of a 'well, it offsets the cost so you don't have to worry about it'" (author's interview, April 16, 2009). The arrest process was changed by 287(g) as well:

INTERVIEWER: And when you're processing somebody at the jail, what types of identification documents do you ask for from that person?
COUNTY SHERIFF: We ask two questions: I guess that's the best way to start. We ask them if they were born in the United States and if they are a

citizen of the United States. If there's a language barrier there, that is a clue, and we further ask questions. If they say they are a citizen, they were born here, we ask them questions. If they are a naturalized citizen we ask for that . . . documentation. Once we get that, they're not interviewed, they don't even go through the 287(g) program. If they are holding visas . . . we ask for that, and if they've got that we don't go any further with it either because that's . . . enough. But if they have nothing, that's when we check them on 287(g); 287(g) is a fingerprint check and a photograph, and it hits the ICE database in about two minutes. It will tell us if they have ever had contact with immigration before, if they've been detained, if they've been deported, if they are a fugitive, or if they have been given a citation to appear at an immigration court but did not [appear]. . . . Then essentially we notify ICE, and they're considered state inmates until their state charges are satisfied. That could be through a court appearance . . . or making bond. . . . We operate under ICE regulation, so if ICE wants us to detain them, we detain them . . . and then we turn them over to ICE. Usually within a couple days ICE comes and gets them. (Author's interview, April 16, 2009)

Police officials were adamant that the process changed only for those arrested. A key officer in the process asserted that police don't get involved in ICE operations, though "they cooperate if they have arrest warrants." However, it is less clear whether the implementation of 287(g) in Mecklenburg County led police officers to arrest individuals for minor charges that would not have led to arrest before, as a precursor to checking their legal status.

One officer interviewed, who had directed the International Relations Unit with the Charlotte police in the early 2000s, noted, for instance, that while a person could not be arrested simply for not having ID while walking down the street, not having an ID while operating a motor vehicle would lead to arrest and, if the arrestee's legal status was verified while arrested, then to deportation: "If we can't identify you by other means, we can't write a ticket just based on who you want to say you are that day; we have to arrest you to positively identify you. If you happen to be here illegally and you get arrested, then 287(g) kicks in, so you have a lot of people saying they are getting deported just for not having a license or minor offenses" (author's interview, April 18, 2009).[3] It seems probable, then, that 287(g) implementation has led to increased arrests and deportation of immigrant drivers for violations that in the past might only have led to a citation.

The Latino community echoes this concern. The director of the service provider Mi Casa, Su Casa complained that "the ends to which [287(g)] is put to are completely inappropriate. [It was designed] for specific situations to detain people who were not following the law or who were delinquents, committing crimes. That's why the law was created"[4] (author's interview, April 17, 2009). The director's comments reflect the Latino community's considerable mistrust of the 287(g) program and the Charlotte-Mecklenburg police.

Police officers interviewed indicated that the implementation of 287(g) had a deleterious effect on law enforcement and may have led to the underreporting of crime by immigrants. As one officer put it:

> We were hearing kind of anecdotal stories about people not reporting robberies, not calling 911 when they needed the police and just kind of not calling us at all. Our sense was that a lot of crime was going unreported. We are so data driven in this department—we use crime mapping and stuff to see where problems are happening, and that is where we deploy resources—so when we have people that don't report crimes in the first place, the red dots don't show up on the map, and so officers . . . don't drive to where the dots are, so more crime happens because there is no police and no one is reporting it. It is a real issue, and that is one of the things that we have tried to explain the importance of calling the police and the fact that we are not interested in their immigration status and things of that nature. It has been a tough sell. (Author's interview, April 18, 2009)

The police department in Charlotte is essentially pursuing strategies that pull in two different directions—on the one hand, it needs the cooperation of the immigrant community to reduce crime in the city. For this strategy to work, the police have to be seen as neutral, providing a service to all. On the other, the county's 287(g) agreement results in the increased arrest of adult immigrants, and their likely deportation, leading to less cooperation overall from the immigrant community. Indeed, according to Lacour (2014), between late 2006 and 2014 the jail identified 24,232 foreign-born arrestees and referred 13,187 for deportation.

The Democrat who succeeded Pendergraph (a Republican who was perhaps the North Carolina equivalent to Sheriff Arpaio in Arizona) as sheriff noted his predecessor "was pretty passionate" about illegal immigration, but he himself, on the other hand, took a more dispassionate stance: "I never have been that passionate about whether somebody was in the country illegally or not. I mean, I don't see it causing any problems from a crime standpoint. I can't say it too loud, but I didn't have many problems with it, they're . . . doing what they do" (author's interview, April 16, 2009). The issue cooled somewhat following the transition in leadership. In 2009 the sheriff indicated that he met regularly with members of the immigrant community to talk about concerns they have, and . . . we try to do that periodically to exchange information. [They] know where I stand on [undocumented status]: my basic tenet is, if they're not arrested, I don't worry about it. I don't worry about immigration. . . . None of [my deputies] has ever gone out with ICE to homes to look for illegals: we don't do it. The police department does sometimes, generally as it's related to gang investigations and things like that. [But] even the police department doesn't ask [about legal status]. The only way we find out is if somebody is arrested. That's the only way we find out. (Author's interview, April 16, 2009)

In 2009 the metro region's police department helped form a Latino Citizen Committee, which brings a group of about twenty faith, business, and neighborhood actors together to work with the police to address issues and defuse tensions (Cowman 2010). According to one participant, the committee was only partly successful:

One of the things we tried is using one of our outreach groups, the Latin American Coalition in Charlotte, to have them host a meeting and then us attend rather than [say] 'Hey, come out to the police meeting' and listen to the crickets chirp. They would hold a meeting, and we would essentially be their guests and have their stamp of approval. Typically in the IRU [International Relations Unit] we would show up in plainclothes, not in uniform, and that kind of thing, to try and set folks at ease. It was still a real challenge to get folks to come out. I think there was a general sense [in the community] of not wanting to be engaged . . . out of fear just not knowing what was going to happen. I think they had seen things and heard things and just didn't know what was going to happen if you came out to a meeting and the police were there. (Author's interview, April 18, 2009)

The decline in cooperation with police is one indicator that the pervasive fear and uncertainty among recent Latino immigrants as a result of programs like 287(g) diminish civic participation among Latinos overall (Jones-Correa and Fennelly 2009).

Like the other new receiving areas addressed in this volume, the Charlotte region has changed rapidly, economically and demographically, since 1980. Not the least of these changes has been in the transformation of the city's central business district and business model, engineered by the local finance and energy industries. This transformation attracted a great many new immigrants to low-skilled service and construction jobs. The large majority of these immigrants have arrived since 2000 from Latin America, and a large share of adults are undocumented.

These immigrants settled in areas overlapping or adjacent to majority working-class black neighborhoods, increasing friction between the two groups, though there is also collaboration at the leadership level. Local public service providers have worked to adjust to the influx of non-English-speaking immigrants and have initiated a "bureaucratic incorporation" of new immigrants. However, there is still a significant institutional mismatch between the services that public and nonprofit organizations provide and the needs of the immigrant population receiving services. Institutions have not kept up with demographic change (particularly in terms of language capacities), immigrant organizations are still in their infancy, and there are no local representatives elected from among the new immigrants or their descendants.

Local service providers have been on the defensive, negotiating not only increased demands from a new immigrant population, but negative reactions from native-born white (and black) residents. For example, the report on provision of services for immigrants commissioned by the mayor of Charlotte in 2007 veers in tone from suspicion of the legitimacy of new arrivals' claims to services to a bureaucratic accounting of the legal basis for providing services for immigrants by the city and county (Mayor's Immigration Study Commission 2007). The date of that report may be no surprise: 2006 marked a turning point in the local government's relationship with immigrants, reflecting the failure of national immigration reform, the immigrant marches in Charlotte and across the country, and the search by key local actors to find a way to respond to rapidly increasing undocumented migration in the region. The county's 287(g) agreement with ICE adopted in 2007 dramatically changed the relationship between law enforcement officials and immigrants and arguably dampened immigrant integration.

In short, the region's response to immigration was markedly ambivalent: welcoming when the numbers were small and the policies quiet, but less so when the numbers became more apparent and the needs more pressing. However, Charlotte seems to be taking yet another turn: in 2009 the city elected its first African American mayor, Anthony Foxx, a Democrat, whose policies reflected a more open stance toward new immigrant arrivals, and his successors have followed his more-welcoming approach. And in 2013 the city council chartered a new Immigrant Integration Task Force that is tasked with making recommendations on how to incorporate immigrants into the city's social and economic fabric.

It was no accident that the new task force is situated in the city's Office of International Relations, which sees its role as "promoting international business and communities" and is itself part of the city's Economic Development division.

As always in Charlotte, economic development and immigration are never far apart—and the region's civic and business leadership, always interested in promoting the metro area as part of a tolerant "New South," is eager to turn the page on the recent spate of less-welcoming policies and practices. As a result, the recommendations of the Immigrant Integration Task Force, finalized in 2015, call for supporting the growth of immigrant businesses, easing the strains between police and the community, creating a community ID card along with a city office and advisory council for immigrant services, promoting citizenship, and widening language access (Immigrant Integration Task Force 2015).

While the tone around new foreign-born arrivals in Charlotte-Mecklenburg became more negative since 2007 with the onset of both the economic downturn and reactions elsewhere against illegal immigration, the region never adopted the more punitive response taken by the North Carolina legislature, which acquired a Republican majority in 2010, or the neighboring states of South Carolina and Georgia. The region's reaction has been tempered by Charlotte's history of economic growth and opportunity, the role of its civically engaged business community, and a generally liberal political culture. The tone is shifting again in a more positive direction, but the end of the story is not entirely clear. Charlotte remains, then, relatively tolerant, even if sometimes distracted and neglectful, toward its recent immigrant residents.

8

CHILL WINDS IN THE VALLEY OF THE SUN

Immigrant Integration in the Phoenix Region

Doris Marie Provine and Paul G. Lewis

Phoenix is unusual, and perhaps unique, among metropolitan regions in this study in its entanglement in an intense and polarized debate over how to respond to unauthorized immigration from Mexico. To a significant degree, issues associated with immigrant integration and empowerment have been overshadowed, and sometimes displaced, by the furor over unauthorized immigration. Nevertheless, immigrants are a large and growing proportion of the area's population, and Latinos are an important voting constituency in several municipalities in the region, including Phoenix itself. A growing collection of advocacy organizations, service providers, and Latino elected officials does attempt to speak for the interests of immigrants. But newcomers and their advocates frequently find themselves on the defensive in this metro area.

One immigrant group, however, finds a warmer welcome: refugees. The state of Arizona ranks fifth in the number of refugees it accepts, outranked only by much more populous states: California, Florida, New York, and Texas. The vast majority settle in Phoenix, making it a leader among American cities in terms of the proportion of refugees to its population.[1] Most refugees are from Africa, the Middle East, and Asia. Their presence tends to be accepted by a curious public largely naïve about the conflicts and process that brought them to the United States for resettlement. The publicity-grabbing efforts of anti-immigration political "entrepreneurs" at the county and state level have so far ignored this population, focusing instead on the "invasion" from the south.

Popular hostility, then, is at least somewhat nuanced, directed almost entirely toward immigrants from Mexico and Central America, who are presumed to have no legal right to be in the area. There is a pervasive sense that uninvited immigrants are an affront to Arizona hospitality, reduce the quality of life, are dependent on public assistance, and represent a kind of takeover of the state. Refugees, who may have no more education or skills than unauthorized Mexican immigrants, do not arouse the same sense of fear and dislike. This may in part be because states can determine the number of refugees they want to accept, and because the federal government defrays the costs of their settlement. Haines and Rosenblum (2010) suggest that the pattern in Arizona is common elsewhere. Refugees evoke a sense of American goodness and thus carry a positive moral valence in receiving communities (Haines and Rosenblum 2010).[2] The prevalent attitude toward Mexican immigration could hardly be more different, with hostility toward unauthorized immigrants bubbling over in some minds into suspicion of Latinos in general.

The response of metropolitan Phoenix to the rapid growth of its Mexican-origin immigrant population, and questions of regional resilience more generally, require inquiry into the demographic, economic, and political structure of the state of Arizona as a whole. While Phoenix is by far the largest city in the state, as well as the state's capital, it often feels the impact of an intrusive state legislature determined to control the city's perceived excesses. The state's politics, driven by suburban and rural interests, thus shape life in metro Phoenix. This is particularly true in the realm of immigration, where urban efforts to integrate immigrants into the economic and political mainstream are often met with hostile legislation arising out of the state government. This chapter therefore takes an approach to the issue of how immigrants are received in Phoenix that is both multijurisdictional and focused on state-local relations.

Geopolitical and Demographic Background

Phoenix is the sixth-largest municipality in the United States, with a population just over 1.5 million. The metropolitan area, which is largely contained within the geographically huge Maricopa County, is the twelfth most populous in the country, with 4.4 million residents.[3] Maricopa County dominates the state, with more than half of Arizona's residents and a land mass greater than that of seven states. Phoenix is also the county seat. For most residents, Maricopa County effectively defines the metropolitan area, a region often called by its nickname "the Valley of the Sun," or simply "the Valley."

Within Maricopa County there are twenty-five municipalities, but the city of Phoenix is by far the largest. Geographically very extensive (517 square miles), Phoenix contains 40 percent of the county population. Although this political geography is less complex than that of many other metropolitan regions, the Valley is by no means a regionalist's ideal case. Maricopa County government, though large and powerful, lacks a regional perspective. Its five-member board of supervisors is elected by district and sometimes is at loggerheads with the incorporated cities. The regional council of governments (the Maricopa Association of Governments) concerns itself primarily with transportation issues and is not a major political player.

Nor does the city of Phoenix dominate the county as a whole. Rather than providing a strong center, Phoenix shares the county with several very large suburban municipalities that serve as political counterweights. Chandler, Gilbert, Glendale, Mesa, and Scottsdale each have a population over 200,000, with Mesa's population exceeding 450,000; Tempe and Peoria each have more than 150,000 residents, and several suburbs have substantial concentrations of businesses (see also Lewis 2004 for more on large suburbs as political counterweights to central cities).[4] Phoenix is also poorer than most of the nearby suburbs, although it contains many affluent and middle-class neighborhoods. Unlike the county as a whole, which is a GOP bastion, Phoenix leans Democratic.

There is a transient quality to the Phoenix region, which has been among the fastest growing metropolitan areas in the United States in recent decades. More than 55 percent of the native (that is, nonimmigrant) residents of Maricopa County were born in one of the other forty-nine states.[5] Individuals and families arrive—and often later leave—in search of economic opportunities, affordable home ownership, warm weather, or simply a place to start their lives over. Many of these residents come from areas of the country, such as the upper Midwest, with little experience of immigrants or of ethnic diversity. The explosive growth of metro Phoenix and its lack of a collective history are manifest in the presence of relatively few civic institutions, foundations, big locally rooted corporations, corporate headquarters, or other institutions that might push for intercultural dialogue and immigrant integration.

Arizona is known as a state attractive to retirees, yet Maricopa County has a younger age profile than the national average, due in part to the presence of (largely youthful) immigrants and their children. Phoenix, the central city, is an immigrant hub, with the sixth-largest immigrant population among American cities. No other large southwestern city has experienced such a dramatic increase in its foreign-born population. The proportion of the state population consisting of Latinos born or naturalized in the United States has also been increasing rapidly. The old/young Anglo/Latino axis creates what could be considered an ethnic and political divide, as Pastor and Mollenkopf discuss in chapter 2. In short, the Hispanic population of Arizona, in comparison to non-Hispanic whites, is skewed toward youth, a situation that magnifies differences in electoral strength (McConnell and Skeen 2009).

In Maricopa County, 15 percent of the population is foreign-born, a slightly higher proportion than the national average (13 percent). In racial/ethnic terms, 30 percent of the county's population is Hispanic/Latino, 6 percent is black, and only 4 percent is Asian.[6] In comparison with the county as a whole, the city of Phoenix has a higher percentage of immigrants (20 percent) and of residents who identify as Hispanic/Latino (41 percent), but about the same proportions of blacks and Asians as the county (7 percent and 3 percent, respectively).[7] This reflects a long-term settlement pattern, with Latinos tending to cluster in the central city, the area of earliest settlement, while many Asians have moved directly to suburbs.[8] Figures 8.1 and 8.2 show the rapid growth of the region's foreign-born population between 1980 and the present, with growing immigrant presence both within and outside the city of Phoenix.

The Hispanic and foreign-born shares of the population have increased substantially over the past two decades or so, fueling angst among the Anglo population, many of whom are themselves recent migrants from the Midwest,

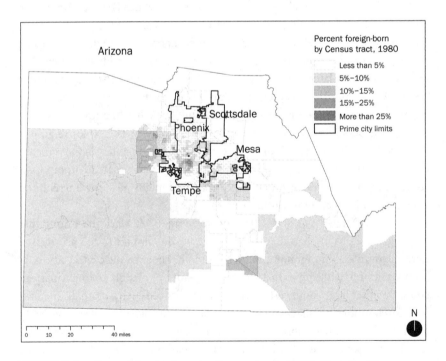

FIGURE 8.1.   Percent foreign-born by Census tract, 1980, Phoenix, AZ

Source: 1980 Decennial Census, Census TIGER/Line, and ESRI.

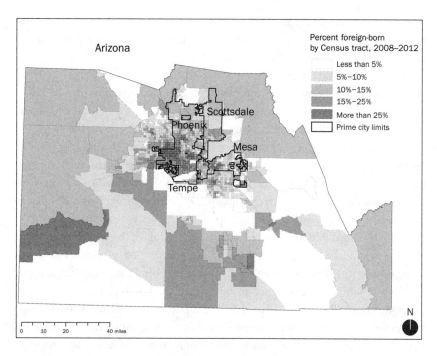

FIGURE 8.2.   Percent foreign-born by Census tract, 2008–2012, Phoenix, AZ

Source: 2008–2012 American Community Survey (Ruggles et al. 2011), Census TIGER/Line, and ESRI.

California, and other parts of the United States.[9] In Arizona, "immigrant" often is taken to mean "Latino immigrant" and specifically "Mexican immigrant," given the area's proximity to the border and the fact that 55 percent of the foreign-born in Maricopa County hail from Mexico.[10] Many of the recent Mexican arrivals are poor and poorly educated, with an estimated 51 percent below the poverty line (Oberle and Li 2008). Poverty, lack of education, and lack of diversity of immigrant backgrounds may have limited the amount of bridge building and coalition formation in support of immigrant integration that would otherwise have occurred. The persistent problems of crime and violence in Mexico, not surprisingly, have heightened anxieties.

Federal border policy has had a key impact on the Phoenix region. The decision to increase federal resources to block unauthorized immigration into more populated areas in California and Texas in the late 1990s pushed border crossings toward the Arizona deserts. Only 160 miles from the border with Mexico, Phoenix has become a flashpoint for the nation's frustrations with border control. There are roughly four hundred thousand to five hundred thousand immigrants without legal status in the state, around 8 percent of the population. The intense focus on legal status of these residents, critics charge, is a cover for anti-Latino prejudice (see, for example, Plascencia 2013).

Unauthorized immigrants, who by some estimates make up about one-tenth of the Phoenix-area population and workforce, tend to keep a low profile. Black-market activities connected to human smuggling, however, became a major political and law-enforcement issue during the economic boom of the 1990s and 2000s when large numbers of unauthorized immigrants were entering Arizona on their way to jobs across the United States. Criminals sometimes took over these smuggling operations, holding immigrants prisoner at "drop houses" to demand payment from U.S.-based relatives. Phoenix police officials claimed to have investigated 359 such cases in 2007 alone. A department spokesperson at the time described Phoenix as the "kidnapping capital" of the United States. This claim proved to be wildly exaggerated (Immigration Policy Center 2010), but not until after the department had hired several hundred new officers, about one hundred of whom were assigned to investigate crimes associated with human smuggling (Gordon 2010b).[11] The nationwide publicity generated by the kidnapping claims and the intense local media coverage of drop house raids contributed to the hothouse, crisis atmosphere around immigration and helped to cement an association between unauthorized immigrants and crime, even though in these cases unauthorized immigrants were themselves the crime victims.

State Legislative Context: Emphasis on Enforcement

Current-day Arizona was once Mexico, becoming part of the United States with the conclusion of the Mexican-American War in 1848 and the Gadsden Purchase in 1853. Mexicans residing in the new territory were offered American citizenship, but that did not reduce the potential for conflict. Violence between Mexican and white residents was common in this period. Mexicans worked in Arizona mines at less than half the Anglo wage, provoking strikes and labor unrest. Anglo residents of the Arizona Territory even went to war with Mexico, enlisting in the various armies fighting Mexico during the Mexican Revolution (1910–1920).

The legacy of separate and unequal citizenship continued until well into the twentieth century. Segregation by race was legal in Arizona until 1953, when the Arizona Supreme Court declared such laws unconstitutional. In the Phoenix area this involved segregation of swimming pools, public schools, theaters, restaurants, and churches. Residents of Mexican descent and African Americans were forced into the basements of churches, the balconies of theaters, and inferior schools, and limited to public pools and dance halls one day per week. They lived in enclaves in the South Phoenix neighborhood (not annexed by the city of Phoenix until the 1960s, despite its close-in location) and other areas with few social services. Segregation was maintained by racially restrictive covenants in deeds. Certain areas were off-limits, except for work, until the 1940s. Well-paying jobs were unavailable, and the minority presence at the state's universities and in the professions was minimal. Arizona maintained an anti-miscegenation law banning marriages between persons of "Caucasian blood" and those of "Negro, Mongolian, Malay, or Hindu" blood until 1959, when it was declared unconstitutional.

The return of Mexican American soldiers after World War II helped to raise the economic fortunes of their neighborhoods. A few years later the demise of legal segregation and rising concern about civil rights and racial discrimination changed the rules, but not the attitude that Anglo culture must remain dominant in Arizona. The state legislature made English the state's official language in 1988, but a state court declared the law unconstitutional. As the civil rights of Mexican Americans became better established, the focus shifted toward unauthorized immigrants. Early in the new millennium most of the state legislature's efforts to impose limits on such immigrants' employment and their use of services were vetoed by Governor Janet Napolitano, a Democrat who served from 2003 until resigning in January 2009 to accept a post as U.S. Secretary of Homeland Security. In 2004, however, a solid majority of voters adopted Proposition 200, limiting access to public benefits and the vote by requiring proof of citizenship. In 2005 Napolitano signed a bill imposing sanctions on employers who knowingly hire unauthorized workers. Employers can lose their business licenses for a second violation. Despite its name, however, the employer sanctions law has been deployed almost entirely against immigrants, not employers.

Soon additional restrictions were enacted, mostly through a process of initiative and referendum. In 2006 large majorities agreed to deprive residents without legal status of in-state tuition in higher-education institutions, access to state welfare services, including adult English-language classes, and access to bail in serious criminal cases. The bail provision, which had been favored by 72 percent of the voters when it was adopted, was declared unconstitutional by the federal courts.[12] A similar fate awaited a 2005 law criminalizing human smuggling.[13] Andrew Thomas, the county attorney of Maricopa, had interpreted it to render those smuggled into the state equally culpable as "coconspirators" in their own smuggling.[14]

The 2006 changes included a ballot measure making English the state's official language and requiring that it be given priority in all government communication. This version of the English-only law has survived without effective challenge. Spanish nevertheless continues to be included on many documents, including voting materials and driver's-license instructions, because of federal requirements and safety concerns.[15] The state courts continue to provide foreign-language assistance in all cases, without cost, as a matter of constitutional obligation, and translation services are sometimes provided at public meetings. The passage of the English-only law and the symbolic reassurance it provides may have taken the spotlight off language policy. There have, however, been efforts to make non-English speakers pay for translation services in civil cases.

For decades controversy reigned over whether non-English-speaking children would receive public education in their own language, and for how long. The state's official policy is "structured English immersion," which sets considerable limits on instruction in languages other than English and a tight time frame for readying English learners for regular classes. Critics claim that the policy is underfunded and fails to meet the needs of these students. After extensive litigation about this policy, including an appeal to the U.S. Supreme Court, the matter appears settled. The Court decided against advocates of a more costly and expansive program for English learners, leaving the matter to local school discretion. The local schools, strapped for resources and bound to state policies, have adapted and are not actively engaged in attempting to change the law.

The teaching of ethnic studies has been another political battleground. In 1997 the Tucson Unified School District established a Mexican American studies program as part of a settlement over legal claims that the district discriminated against minority students. But the program was controversial and strongly opposed by the state superintendent of public instruction, Tom Horne, a Republican. At his urging the legislature passed HB 2281, which prohibits any program that, in the state superintendent's estimation, promotes resentment against a race or class of people, advocates ethnic solidarity, or promotes the overthrow of the U.S. government. Soon afterward Horne was elected state attorney general. He promised litigation to force the district to scrap the program, and the Tucson school board complied, to avoid losing nearly $15 million in state funding. Diane Douglas, elected state superintendent of schools in 2014, continued to press for changes in the Tucson program, claiming that two songs in the curriculum promote resentment and advocate ethnic solidarity.

The place of Latinos in Arizona is also at stake in the continuing controversy over the role of local law enforcement in federal immigration control. The issue took shape through the activities of Maricopa County sheriff Joseph Arpaio, who was among the first to sign up his deputies for immigration-enforcement training sponsored by the federal government. Federal Immigration and Customs Enforcement personnel managed the training, which was dubbed the 287(g) program after its location in the federal Immigration and Nationality Act. The sixty Maricopa County deputies who received training were soon deployed in public-safety raids that focused on Latino neighborhoods and hangouts. The deputies arrested scores of persons suspected of being unauthorized, which frequently resulted in their deportation. To assist in the effort, the sheriff's office established a hotline where residents could anonymously report suspected unauthorized immigrants.

Critics of the raids argue that they compromise community safety by making immigrants (legal and illegal) afraid to report crimes to the police or serve as witnesses. As one local mayor observed, "The community is out there, seeing what the police can't see. That's why it's so harmful when the sheriff is doing what he is doing, because it creates fear in the same community we are trying to build up" (Lopez Rogers 2010). Another interviewee involved in K–12 education related how a sheriff's raid in a Phoenix neighborhood, coming on the heels of the passage of employer sanctions legislation, led to a situation in which several hundred schoolchildren in one elementary district failed to return to school after the winter holiday break; some of these students never returned.

The raids became notorious, particularly after one of them occurred without warning at midnight in the municipal library in Mesa, a city within Maricopa County that has its own police department and at that time had a city policy against such raids.[16] The controversy over the sheriff's actions in this and other cases eventually resulted in a federal decision not to renew his 287(g) authority to arrest suspected unauthorized immigrants. His only remaining authority was to assist federal authorities in the booking process at the county jail. The sheriff responded by pledging to use his authority under state law to pursue unauthorized immigrants.

Arizona's 2010 Adoption of Senate Bill 1070

The sheriff, unbowed by federal disapproval, continued his raids. He soon received a boost from the state legislature with Senate Bill 1070. The bill was signed into law in April 2010 by Republican governor Jan Brewer, previously the secretary of state, who under Arizona law became governor when Napolitano resigned. The announced policy of SB 1070 was "attrition through enforcement," to be achieved through a potpourri of provisions, all directed toward the removal of unauthorized immigrants from the state. Knowingly transporting an unauthorized immigrant was criminalized, for example, as was solicitation of work by residents without legal status. Arguably the most significant provision was the requirement that law enforcement officers, in their stops and arrests, question all persons suspected of lacking legal status. Failure to implement this policy would expose a police department to a civil suit by any concerned Arizona citizen.

Race and ethnic appearance were not supposed to be criteria for making the determination of when a person might be undocumented, but it was unclear how police were to implement the policy without taking these characteristics into account. Legal permanent residents and other noncitizens with secure legal status were required to carry papers, presumably to make this requirement easier to implement. Failure to do so would not only violate state law, but risk detention until legal status could be determined. Warrant requirements were waived so that those who could not prove their right to remain could quickly be turned over to federal authorities.

The law immediately sparked a surge of protest locally, nationally, and even internationally, dramatically expanding the visibility of Phoenix as a site of struggle over immigration, and exposing the state to boycotts protesting the legislation. The new law drew concern not only among immigrant-advocacy organizations and immigration lawyers, but also among civil rights groups, individual police officers, municipalities, and the federal government. Seven lawsuits were filed, including one by the U.S. Justice Department. The Justice Department won a preliminary injunction from an Arizona district judge. Later, in the U.S. Supreme Court, the federal government largely prevailed in its argument that four key sections of Arizona's statute infringed on national authority to set and control immigration policy. However, one crucial section requiring police to inquire about immigration status during stops and arrests was allowed to remain, with the caveat that the stop not be prolonged to check immigration status.

The politics behind this saga of adoption and failed implementation bear at least brief discussion. SB 1070 represented a culmination, of sorts, of anti-immigrant legislation in Arizona. It established clearly for the first time that the state policy is "attrition through enforcement." Many of its provisions had been floated in earlier bills, but a Kansas anti-immigration lawyer with a national following, Kris Kobach, helped to write the final version. Phoenix-area business groups were able to exert some influence on the parts of the bill that most concerned them, those that would have toughened employer sanctions, but otherwise seemed ill-prepared for the storm of controversy that would accompany the passage of SB 1070 (Sanders 2010).

Sheriff Arpaio applauded the new law. Governor Brewer, who was not popular as an unelected governor in an economically troubled state, received a major political boost in her vocal support for the law. She gained enough momentum to outflank GOP primary opponents who had been viewed as more conservative and to defeat her highly experienced Democratic challenger in the general election.[17] Municipalities and their police departments, on the other hand, were completely left out of the legislative discussions. Flagstaff and Tucson, the core cities of smaller and more liberal metropolitan areas than Phoenix, sued to prevent implementation of the law.

Phoenix's mayor at the time, Phil Gordon, criticized the new law but was unable to persuade his city council to bring suit. The mayor asserted that the majority of the council was critical of the new law but that many of those representing outlying, Anglo districts were reluctant to be seen as supporting a lawsuit against the state: "The majority of the council has decided to sit out on the sidelines. . . . It has become more of a political concern for those who prefer to guard their political office rather than advance things" (Gordon 2010a).[18] He also suggested that city programs and infrastructure improvements that had historically been targeted at improving low-income, disproportionately Hispanic neighborhoods had begun to meet with opposition from council members who preferred a less targeted approach.

For the municipalities of Arizona, SB 1070 essentially created an unfunded state mandate. It required them to harden their policies toward unauthorized immigrants without being compensated for the increased costs involved.[19] SB 1070 also attempted to reshape the relationship between local police and their immigrant residents. In the past, cities in the Phoenix region had taken varied approaches to involving their police in immigration enforcement, with some emphasizing community policing ideals in encounters with police that did not involve serious crimes.

Pressure to make policies more stringent, however, had been building. In 2008, for example, the Phoenix Law Enforcement Association (PLEA)—a fraternal association of police officers—lent its support for a tougher policy in handling encounters with suspected unauthorized immigrants. The city abandoned its prior, less-stringent policy, which had been supported by its police chief and (at least implicitly) by the mayor.[20] Still, some of the more conservative leaders in the Phoenix police union apparently found this approach too "soft" on illegal immigrants; one of our interviewees suggested that PLEA had a major hand in pushing for the introduction of SB 1070. The police chief's vocal opposition to SB 1070 may have cost him his job. He was forced to resign in this period after a career rising through the ranks of the department to become its chief.

Neither the complaints of municipalities and police chiefs nor the successful federal suit to block SB 1070's implementation prevented Arizona from garnering widespread political support for its stand, including look-alike legislation in several states. With assistance from the Center for Immigration Studies (CIS), a Washington, D.C.–based group that favors reductions in legal immigration, Arizona had become a laboratory for the effort to reframe immigration policy from the local level. For a time it looked as if this situation would continue indefinitely. The state senator who had proposed SB 1070, Russell Pearce (of Mesa), was elected president of the Arizona Senate, and Republicans strengthened their hold on the statehouse in the November 2010 elections. Pearce floated bills to deny birth certificates to babies born in the state whose parents lack legal status and to force schools to identify which of their students lack legal status. Senator Pearce and Governor Brewer painted a picture of a state under attack from Mexico, both in terms of violent criminals in the drug and people-smuggling trades and, more insidiously, in the numbers of people from that part of the world who were "invading" the state to seek employment.

Fears of a "Mexican invasion," however, sat uneasily with the commitment on the part of the state and various local governments to increased trade with Mexico and the incentives provided by the North American Free Trade Agreement. The business community, which ordinarily preferred to work quietly behind closed doors, took the unprecedented move of drafting a letter signaling its disapproval of further immigration-enforcement legislation. The metropolitan area's leading business owners and managers signed on, and it was delivered to every legislator. At about the same time, immigration activists, with the implicit support of the business community, undertook another unusual effort: a recall campaign to remove Senator Pearce from office and replace him with an individual with moderate views on immigration. To the surprise of many, this effort was successful, sending a message that appears to have been heeded that further enforcement-oriented legislation would carry risks for reelection. Thus by 2012, cities were in a better position than in the previous few years to shape their efforts to attract foreign business and integrate immigrants without intervention from the state government.

Governor Brewer roiled these calming waters in responding to President Obama's June 2012 announcement of Deferred Action for Childhood Arrivals program (DACA), a program that defers enforcement against young immigrants who came illegally to the United States as children and offers work permits. Brewer, almost alone among U.S. governors, responded by denying DACA youth access to driver's licenses. This time the strategy of challenging federal authority with independent state action to stymie undocumented immigrants received a less favorable response from the local media and almost no response from local political leaders. The political climate seemed clearly to have shifted toward more tolerance for these residents. By 2015, when the newly elected attorney general, Mark Brnovich, appealed the federal court's decision requiring the issuance of driver's licenses to DACA recipients, he met with this headline from the *Arizona Republic*, the state's leading newspaper: "Brnovich Wasting Money, Time on Misguided Appeal" (*Arizona Republic* 2015a).

The situation in metro Phoenix nevertheless remains perilous for immigrants who lack legal status. The Maricopa County sheriff has maintained an aggressive enforcement posture, legitimated by the legislature's adoption of SB 1070 and the public support it received. Many Phoenix police officers also support aggressive enforcement; internal controls that would force them to take a more nuanced approach are weak. Only 12 percent of Phoenix's police officers are Latino, while over 40 percent of the city's youth are Latino. Throughout the state, municipal governments remain under pressure to allow their police to query immigration status when they stop or arrest individuals, because the federal government did not challenge the part of SB 1070 allowing citizen-initiated lawsuits to punish a department's failure to embrace "attrition through enforcement," which remains state policy.

The situation was exacerbated by the Secure Communities program, a nationwide data-sharing program aimed at enlisting local jails in federal immigration enforcement. Lacking meaningful protections against racial profiling, this federal initiative left much to the individual officer to decide, and those decisions vary. Some individual police officers have called for this new "tool," while others strongly resisted the new duty. Not surprisingly, there were many anecdotal reports in metropolitan Phoenix of stops and racial profiling to achieve immigration removal. These reports came not just from recent immigrants, but also from people who have lived in the United States for decades, from middle-class homeowners, and from native-born students. In the wake of persistent criticism of the Secure Communities program, in November 2014 President Obama ended it, in conjunction with the announcement of a series of executive actions that offered temporary relief from deportation to a broad array of unauthorized immigrants.

The problem of unconstitutional stops and arrests by the Maricopa County sheriff's deputies, the subject of litigation for years, also moved toward at least a tentative resolution with the October 2013 decision of federal district judge Murray Snow that Sheriff Arpaio's policies and practices amounted to unconstitutional racial profiling. The court ordered the sheriff's office to collect data on race and ethnicity in all phases of law enforcement and put the sheriff's office under the supervision of a court-appointed monitor, at a cost, Sheriff Arpaio estimates, of $21 million to taxpayers. In civil contempt proceedings associated with the case, Arpaio admitted and apologized for his failure to abide by Judge Snow's orders. Still at issue is whether the sheriff is guilty of *knowingly* violating the court's orders (Roberts 2015).

The Politics of Immigration in Metropolitan Phoenix: Actors and Issues

The politics of ethnicity and immigration in Arizona were not always as inflamed as in recent years. In 1974, Mexican-born Raul Hector Castro, a veteran Tucson-area politician and former judge, was elected governor of Arizona—one of the very few Latino immigrant governors in American history. The 1970s, according to one of our interviewees—the period of awakening of the Chicano movement—was the peak of the alliance between mainstream Anglo politicians and Latinos in Arizona, coming as it did soon after the civil rights movement. Hispanic Democrats achieved positions of power in the state legislature and served as close advisers to Governor Bruce Babbitt.

But soon a new wave of poorer and more monolingual Latino immigrants began arriving in the Southwest, and the mutual embrace of Latino and white leadership began to slacken. A 2006 article in the *Arizona Republic* described Latino leadership in the state as "waning" (*Arizona Republic* 2006).[21] Today, however, a minor resurgence appears on the horizon. The 2012 general election, which revealed growing Latino clout at the national level, brought five more Latinos to the state legislature, for a total of thirteen, out of ninety in the state house and senate.[22] There is a Latino caucus in both houses of the legislature. And in 2013, the number of Latinos on the Phoenix City Council, which had varied between zero and one in recent decades, grew to three in a council of nine.[23]

Phoenix's current mayor, Greg Stanton, a Democrat in a position that officially is nonpartisan, treads a fine line between the political necessity of support for border security and the economic necessity of enhanced business ties with Mexico. Arizona exports to Mexico much less than other border states, a source of unhappiness to local businesses (Gardiner 2013b).[24] Stanton's strategy is to urge business leaders to educate the state legislature about the economic benefits of immigrants and good relations with Mexico, while he takes steps to welcome Mexican investment. In December 2013 he announced that the city would open an office of trade and tourism in Mexico City to spur trade relations and enhance goodwill. Yet on the contentious issue of harsh immigration enforcement actions by Phoenix police against Mexican nationals, he has avoided taking a position. He tries to distance the city from SB 1070, which continued to depress convention bookings by as much as 30 percent in 2012, as compared with 2009, just before it was adopted. As he told a group of event planners, "What you may have read about our Legislature, don't hold against the rest of us. The rest of us, we're normal. We like diversity" (Gardiner 2013a).

Although the city of Phoenix has over one-fifth of the state's population, it carries little weight in the rural- and suburban-dominated state legislature. The increasingly Latino and urban face of the state's Democratic Party reinforces an ethnic political divide. Hispanic voters, in part as a result of the federal Voting Rights Act, have been effectively packed into "safe" electoral districts, giving legislators from other districts little incentive to listen to Latino voices or concerns. In safe Republican legislative districts, where primary elections tend to be decisive, challenges from conservatives and Tea Party favorites have given GOP legislators strong incentives to move further to the right on immigration. Low voter turnout also weakens the Latino cause, sometimes due to problematic political leadership. Hispanic lawmakers have been accused of slipping into personal agendas and petty rivalries, having "too much time and too little power."[25] Even among would-be leaders of the pro-immigrant and Latino groups in the state, splits and jealousies have sometimes erupted, with some organizational leaders accused of profiteering from their activities (see, for example, Irwin 2007).

Among pro-immigrant Latino activists, however, a generational transformation is occurring. Several interviewees referred to the "new generation" of activists and organizers with a different take on how change can best be achieved. The older generation of leaders, whose names are familiar in Arizona, carry memories of the overt anti-Hispanic racism of the pre–civil rights era. Some of them recall being belittled or slapped by teachers if they dared to speak Spanish in school. Many of this generation came from humble backgrounds to achieve much in politics, social services, education, and business. These include former state senator and gubernatorial candidate Alfredo Gutierrez and former mining executive Roberto Reveles. Many in this elite group were raised in mining towns in the mountains of rural Arizona and attended segregated schools but later won scholarships from the mining union to attend one of the three state universities in the 1960s and 1970s. Propitiously, at that time, large businesses and law firms in the state were seeking to increase their hiring of Latinos and other minorities to achieve diversity goals. Some of these "mountain people" were attractive hires, and they rose through the corporate ranks, entered management, founded nonprofits, or sought political careers as part of the nascent empowerment of Arizona Latinos (Nowakowski 2010). They are comfortable rubbing shoulders with Anglo power brokers and opining for the media.

Other leaders in the older generation are oriented more toward street organizing and Chicano empowerment in the civil rights tradition of Cesar Chavez. Salvador Reza, a longtime crusader for the rights and culture of indigenous populations, organized many demonstrations against Sheriff Arpaio's roundups of unauthorized immigrants and helped organize a day labor hiring center in north Phoenix. As both the more elite and the more openly activist wings of the elder

Latino leadership have felt the sting of the anti-immigrant activism of recent years, some alliances have formed. The Somos America (We Are America) coalition, formed in Phoenix in 2006, was an attempt to institutionalize these alliances between sometimes-conflicting advocacy groups.

Still, protest and self-defense against racism appear to be the main modes of activism for the older generation, and the tone is often (understandably) angry.[26] By contrast, the younger generation of activists often focuses more on political action, the creation of alliances, and advocacy for specific legislation. "If you go to Somos America, at every meeting they have they discuss a raid that's happened, and a demonstration that's going to happen," one of our younger interviewees said. "But they have never had a meeting on what is going to be the voter registration strategy, for example." And this respondent complained that during a major anti–SB 1070 march on Memorial Day weekend in 2010, no one at the microphone during three hours of speeches mentioned that a voter registration effort was under way at the event.

This newer generation prefers to view SB 1070 and Arpaio's raids "not as a racial issue, but as an issue of justice," in the words of one of our informants. Two interviewees compared the new wave of Latino leadership that emerged in the wake of Arizona's anti-immigrant legislation to the mobilization of Latinos after California's passage of Proposition 187 in 1994. They observed that a wave of "cultural production" (poetry, street posters, etc.) has appeared in Phoenix around the defense of immigrant rights. The "Legalize Arizona" T-shirt design was one example of this cultural production, and it went mainstream, with many non-Hispanic young people wearing it. High school students have also been part of this movement, demonstrating their opposition to SB 1070 by leaving school to march in protest.

Many of the younger Latino activists come from a background of union organizing, and some were active in the Obama campaign. They tend to be well educated and alert to ways to effectively pressure officials for change. Randy Parraz, a lawyer and political organizer for the Laborers' International Union of North America, often speaks to Valley audiences about immigrant empowerment and immigration reform. He cofounded Maricopa Citizens for Safety and Accountability (MCSA), an upstart group that organized a broad informational campaign and media events regarding violations and shortcomings of the sheriff's office in the county. Although the MCSA was unsuccessful in getting the Maricopa County Board of Supervisors to rein in the sheriff, the repeated visits to board meetings drew significant media attention and energized immigrant activists. Later Parraz joined forces with others in the successful effort to recall Senator Pearce. The skill set of the younger leaders, often including effective use of online social media, complements the marching and civil rights orientation of older generations of activists, though sometimes there are conflicts over strategy. As one younger activist asked: "How many times [through marches] do we have to show how many we are?"

The younger activists tend to focus on specific political goals. Puente Arizona, a grassroots immigrants' rights group, organized in 2007 to combat the sheriff's 287(g) enforcement authority. In 2014 Puente turned to the courts, suing to end the sheriff's campaign of workplace raids. As noted above, it was successful in getting a permanent injunction to end the practice. Promise Arizona, launched in 2010 from the ashes of the Reform Immigration for America campaign, recruited and trained eight hundred volunteers from around the state to conduct a long-lasting vigil at the state capitol against SB 1070. The group also launched an intensive and ongoing social media effort to gain congressional votes for the DREAM Act and comprehensive immigration reform. Promise Arizona registered about thirteen thousand new voters during 2010, its first year of operation. The voter registration effort then continued, reaching thirty thousand new, mostly Latino, voters by 2013. Between 2008 and 2012 Latino voter registration grew by 26 percent and turnout increased by 37 percent, a significant gain, and almost enough to have elected Latino Democratic candidate Richard Carmona to the U.S. Senate in 2012 (America's Voice and Latino Decisions 2014).

One of the best-organized groups of younger activists is the Arizona DREAM Act Coalition, which has an organizational structure, a constitution, and a meeting etiquette. The largely college-age membership also actively seeks out non-Hispanics to join, making the case for the DREAM Act as a matter of justice and de-emphasizing accusations of anti-Hispanic racism. Members described some of the tensions in the immigrant organizing movement in metro Phoenix. While the older generation of immigrant rights leaders used the appealing DREAM Act as leverage in their campaign for comprehensive immigration reform, they were reluctant to back it strongly on its own. The younger group was also more devoted to "organizing from the back of the room" rather than the classic approach of following a single charismatic leader. One described a march in Glendale, with about one thousand young people in attendance to support the DREAM Act, when a few elder Latino leaders went to the front and engaged in civil disobedience to get arrested, thus "stealing the show from the march."

Against the backdrop of changing Latino activism, the city's appointed officials and public administrators with immigrant-heavy clienteles tend to keep a low profile to avoid possible political repercussions. An exception cited by a number of interviewees is Phoenix Union High School District superintendent Kent Paredes Scribner, who has assured parents that the legal status of students in the district's schools will not be an issue. He frequently partners with Latino-oriented community organizations to conduct forums, training sessions, and citizenship and voter registration drives at school events. The 220-square-mile district is 79 percent Hispanic and 9 percent African American, with small percentages of Asian and Native American students; 47 percent of students come from homes where Spanish is the primary language spoken. Its seven-member governing board includes well-known Latino politicians and community leaders who are sophisticated advocates for Latino empowerment. Most other public administrators, even if they serve a largely immigrant clientele, cannot count on this level of political support and insulation from state politics.

The former principal of a local public charter high school is an example. Undocumented students at her school were taking joint-enrollment courses for community college credit, which required that they pay out-of-state tuition because of the strictures of Proposition 300. The principal sought private funds to defray the students' tuition costs, and donors supported her efforts. But some told her that she "couldn't say where this money came from, because it [was] going to ruin their political career" (Anonymous 2010). Indeed the controversy caused by this principal "going public" about the strictures that the state was placing on these students ultimately played a part in her dismissal.

Another cautionary example for public administrators occurred in Mesa, a generally conservative city, where former chief of police George Gascón sought to open lines of communication between police and immigrant residents. To foster trust, he instituted a limited-enforcement policy regarding unauthorized immigrants, along with other community-oriented policies. The political costs to Gascón and to elected city officials in Mesa were significant, as the council eventually required the police to increase their cooperation with ICE, and the city manager undermined the chief's authority. Gascón ultimately resigned to become police chief in San Francisco, where his community policing philosophy presumably would receive a warmer welcome.

In many of the smaller cities in metro Phoenix, the police chief is able to effectively set the tone for how officers will handle contacts with unauthorized immigrants. In Avondale (population 79,646 in 2014), for instance, under a Latina mayor and a community policing–oriented chief, police leaders have spoken from the pulpit at immigrant-heavy churches and at neighborhood meetings, attempting to build lines of communication. The chief also sends a Latino officer each year to the Hispanic Leadership Institute hosted by the Phoenix nonprofit Valle del Sol. City police in Avondale do not cite day laborers if they are in a public right-of-way, although they will cooperate with property owners in moving day laborers away from area businesses. The fact that the Maricopa County sheriff has overlapping jurisdiction in the city, however, complicates matters.

The metro area's business groups, like most of the civic leadership in the Phoenix area, have tended to avoid openly criticizing the stance that the sheriff and the state legislature have taken toward immigrants, though they have taken steps to protect undocumented workers. The local chamber of commerce was at first able to prevent an employer sanctions law, arguing that enforcement is a federal preserve; but with the failure of comprehensive immigration reform at the national level, that argument lost traction. Feeling intense political pressure from their core constituencies, several moderate Republicans in the legislature who typically supported the business position told the chamber "we just can't vote no" (Sanders 2010). About the same time, business interests lobbied the state legislature to institute a guest worker program that would bring short-term workers from Mexico to Arizona industries in need of labor. Then-governor Napolitano was interested if noncommittal, but most legislators refused to go along.

At times the metro business community has seemed oblivious of the impact of the legislature's harsh policy agenda. All indications are that the business community was not really prepared for the visceral national reaction to SB 1070. Before its passage, the bill was not on the chamber of commerce's list of legislation to watch. The boycotts and lost business in the hospitality industry, a major component of the local economy, helped focus the attention of business organizations on immigration-related legislation, such as Senator Pearce's effort to create special birth certificates for citizen children of unauthorized immigrants born in the United States.

Compared to the heft of business groups, labor unions are generally weak in Arizona, which is an open-shop ("right to work") state. Labor-friendly Democrats have rarely been in power. The Service Employees International Union (SEIU) has funded some immigrant-empowerment activities, and some of its organizers have been "lent" to immigrant-rights organizations, but the union's political clout is limited. The Laborers' International Union (LiUNA) is also active and firmly progressive on immigration-reform issues, but the severe decline in construction jobs in Arizona during the Great Recession weakened LiUNA's leverage. Meanwhile, the AFL-CIO finds it difficult to speak out on the issue, given the wide mix of worker groups it represents—including some U.S. Border Patrol workers—and the hostility of some traditional blue-collar groups to the entry of more immigrant workers.

Efforts toward Political Incorporation and Empowerment of Immigrants

An important shift in strategies has occurred among groups favoring a more immigrant-friendly, cosmopolitan metro area and state. The immigration marches of the mid-2000s have given way to a mixed strategy that includes, on the one hand, direct action to block deportation of immigrants caught in the web of aggressive local enforcement efforts, and on the other, a major effort to reshape the political base that governs Arizona. Base-changing tactics include getting more Latinos registered to vote and prepared to use the ballot. The continued concentration of many poorer Latinos in the central city makes Phoenix a logical focus for electoral change, but the state legislature, because of its hostility to immigrants, is another target. Activists rely on two Latino-serving newspapers, *La Prensa* and *La Voz*, to maintain contact with the ever-more-dispersed middle-class Latino population.

An important part of the political project is to help legal permanent residents become citizens and thus eligible to vote. Raquel Terán, a longtime activist in the realm of immigration reform and opposition to SB 1070, has spearheaded this effort through her leadership of the Arizona chapter of Mi Familia Vota, which is part of a multistate network of such groups, funded largely by the SEIU. Supported by a large group of volunteers, Mi Familia Vota holds citizenship preparation sessions that regularly attract several hundred potential citizens. An earlier campaign focused on achieving a more accurate count of Latinos for the 2010 Census. On the heels of the passage of SB 1070, there were concerns that unauthorized immigrants would not be counted because of their fear of contact with any representatives of the government.

Political office is also increasingly a goal for young Latinos in metro Phoenix, and, as noted earlier, there have been some successes. The Democratic Party, although clearly the minority party in the region, is seeking to attract Latino leaders at all levels. The division between the two parties is sharp on issues related to immigration; nearly all Democrats in the state legislature voted against SB 1070, while all Republicans favored it.

In municipal (though not county) government in the Phoenix area, all elected offices are officially nonpartisan. Even though the party leanings of mayors and council members are usually fairly easily identifiable to those who follow their city's politics closely, nonpartisanship in municipal elections may allow for more opportunities for Democrats and Latinos in local politics than at the state level and may enable more cross-ethnic collaboration among officeholders. In recent years there have been two suburbs with Latino mayors, both individuals with long roots in their communities. In the city of Phoenix the impact of the unprecedented election of three Latino members of the city council remains to be seen. For a time the city manager of Phoenix was Latino and reportedly did what he could to boost Latino city employees. The one long-serving Latina member of the county board of supervisors was an outspoken advocate for immigrant rights, often butting heads with Sheriff Arpaio.

Marie Lopez Rogers, a Latina who served as mayor of Avondale from 2006 to 2014, described how she had been recruited into local politics in the 1990s by an officeholder who had seen her volunteer work and group leadership in the community. At that time, there had never been a Latina on the city council. "In the Hispanic community, traditionally women are not the ones who go into politics. . . . Traditionally the woman is a matriarch of the family . . . and everything else comes after that." But, she added, women in large Latino families often have to be mediators and consensus seekers—a political role. And so to her, Avondale residents are an extended family, "and when they hurt, I hurt." She does not fear rapid growth and ethnic transition in her city because, she says with a laugh, "in a family, you always take in new people, because somebody gets married" (Lopez Rogers 2010).

Partially at her behest, a few years ago the city government initiated a Department of Neighborhood and Family Services, with a bilingual staff. This department refers residents in need of help to social service agencies or nonprofit providers to get the services they need. A former social worker, Lopez Rogers saw it as "crucial to the city to help the family holistically," and recalled from her days before elected office that she had worked with groups who said "people . . . want to help us, and then they come in, tell us how to live, and then they go away. And to me, government should not be doing that" (Lopez Rogers 2010). Mayor Lopez Rogers got the opportunity to become a national spokesperson for this perspective when in 2013 she was elected president of the National League of Cities.

At the metropolitan or state level, there is little discussion of policies designed to foster immigrant incorporation or to increase civic participation by immigrants. Individual programs and personalities on Spanish-language radio stations do sometimes focus on immigrant activism and rights, although the one full-time Latino news-and-talk station, KNUV-AM, signed off in mid-2008 when its investors pulled out, finding it hard to keep a forty-five-person newsroom financially afloat (D. Gonzalez 2008). The Mexican consulate aids Mexican nationals throughout the area but must keep a relatively low profile in its responses to state and local policy. Many of the major cities in the region have appointed human relations commissions, but these low-visibility commissions tend to concentrate more on fostering positive intergroup relations and studying the diversity of the municipal workforce rather than on increasing the involvement of underrepresented groups in civic affairs.[27] Divisions by economic class in the Latino immigrant community tend to discourage overarching alliances around the issue of political incorporation. Thus the Hispanic Chamber of Commerce and local nonprofit Chicanos por la Causa attract some well-off, assimilated Latinos to leadership roles and promote political engagement, but their numbers are small. Valle del Sol runs a Hispanic Leadership Institute, but the

$1,000 fee for enrolling in this program would seem to target Latinos who are already relatively advantaged.

Poor immigrants are a much larger segment of the Latino population, but they have not had much political voice, nor do they seem poised to achieve it soon. The only notable political mobilization has been occasional street demonstrations and marches, most spectacularly in 2006 when Phoenix experienced its largest march ever in favor of immigration reform and immigrant rights, an event that attracted over one hundred thousand people. On a much smaller scale in 2010, some immigrants and their supporters participated in prayer vigils, demonstrations, and civil disobedience near the state capitol in Phoenix as the legislature debated SB 1070 and the governor considered whether to sign it. Most recently a few dedicated young activists have risked arrest in their attempt to block the local immigration office from carrying out deportations.

Immigrants without substantial means benefit from several organizations devoted to their interests. Stand for Children, an advocacy organization for public schoolchildren, with offices in several states, opened shop in Arizona in January 2010. It has focused considerable effort on helping immigrant parents advocate for their children's education by organizing teams of about twenty to thirty members in particular schools and districts. Team coordinators receive weekly training on public speaking, persuasiveness, and the use of electronic resources for organizing. The group focuses on "winnable, achievable" goals, such as educator effectiveness, with its organizers targeting particular school districts and legislative districts where they feel knocking on doors could make a difference in policies or elections.[28] Although Stand for Children focuses on education needs rather than immigrant rights, its organizing efforts have potential for positive spillovers. When parents achieve success—as they did in contacting voters to help ensure passage of a budget override in the Phoenix Union High School District—"they learn that Spanish-speaking voters are important, and that the undocumented can participate effectively in the political system. . . . They are feeling empowered; they are doing something that marches are not doing for them . . . that community forums are not doing for them, which is taking action, in the way that a citizen would" (Avila 2010).

Promoting civic participation by residents lacking legal status is a key component of the reform effort for other groups as well. A principal of a charter school with a largely immigrant student enrollment, for example, described a volunteer effort in which twenty-five high school freshmen were trained by an immigration lawyer to assist at a naturalization workshop in their neighborhood. Instead of the usual types of voluntarism pushed on students, such as trash pickup in parks, "we need to do something where these kids really feel they are of use and of service. . . . In that moment, it just transcends everything else. They are not undocumented anymore, and they are empowering someone else" (Watterson 2010).

A similar effort has been undertaken by several area religious leaders, including both Anglo and Latino clergy, generally leaders of individual congregations, or some of the more liberal individuals affiliated with the Valley Interfaith Project, which has participated in many immigrant rights activities. Clergy of some predominantly African American congregations have actively supported immigrant rights, hosted rallies and forums on immigration issues, and worked to convince their congregations of the justice issues involved in immigration reform. Predominately white evangelical churches are also playing a small role in rallying poorer immigrants to consider their rights, but so far most of the energy has come from a few committed ministers, not from mobilization by immigrants themselves. Evangelicals are also frequently uncomfortable working in an ecumenical setting with other faiths and secular groups on such issues, preferring to operate as a congregation. One young leader who works at an overwhelmingly Latino Protestant congregation in inner-city Phoenix sums up his perspective:

> An attrition strategy by the government toward human beings cannot reconcile with a Christian philosophy. . . . And this is the first sentence in SB 1070 [and] pretty much the governing strategy of governing leaders in Arizona today. . . . And it doesn't match up with any sort of Christian philosophy. It basically says we are going to make this place so horrible for you—not only more horrible than the place you escaped, which is probably pretty bad. But we're going to try to drive you out. [But] we say . . . you're not alone, God is . . . going to fix this, and we're going to join Him. So if you want to join in this team, let's start liberating the oppressed. . . . This is what we say to our students, to our families. And we get a lot of traction. (Danley 2010)

By contrast, higher-level leadership of the Roman Catholic and Latter-Day Saints churches in the area have not taken an active role. One interviewee who is both an observant Catholic and active in immigrant rights said, "Personally, it's disappointing. Sometimes you think, if anyone should take a stand . . . it should be them [the church]. . . . But on a local level . . . my own church has a priest who is welcoming to organizing, getting together, discussing. So again it's down to neighborhood-level communication. . . . He's not out there banging a drum; he's pastoral."

The Roman Catholic bishop of Phoenix, Thomas J. Olmsted, does not participate in prayer vigils or demonstrations regarding the plight of immigrants, though as one respondent noted, he does attend rallies against abortion and gay marriage. The church's reaction has been to appoint an auxiliary bishop who is

Hispanic and to feature Spanish on the diocese web page.[29] Some of the clergy of large suburban Protestant mega-churches have been quietly supportive. An interviewee active in the immigrant civil rights movement observed: "A lot of these pastors will tell you the same thing a politician will tell you behind closed doors: 'I agree with you, but I can't say it.' They could lose their jobs, just like a politician could."

The formation of cross-ethnic alliances may not come naturally to the Latino population in Arizona, given both its dominant size compared with other minority groups and its historic tradition of self-help and mutual aid in the face of Anglo oppression (Rosales and Marin 2009). There is an Asian Chamber of Commerce, which is active in the community, but its emphasis is on improving the situation of its own membership and developing alliances within local and state government, not on ameliorating the political isolation of poor or unauthorized immigrants.

As Latino activists in Phoenix and other Arizona cities moved toward shifting the makeup of the state's political establishment, Republicans in the state legislature responded with legislation that, the activists argue, will suppress Latino voting. The issue came to a head in the closing hours of the 2013 legislative session, when after urging from the national Republican Party, the legislature passed HB 2305 to take occasional voters off the permanent early voting list and forbid the practice of ballot collection by get-out-the-vote volunteers. Although these changes were couched as measures to enhance efficiency and ballot security, opponents of HB 2305, including the Arizona affiliate of the American Civil Liberties Union, the League of Women Voters, the Democratic Party, and several churches, were able to garner widespread support for overturning this law. With over eighty-five thousand valid signatures, groups opposing HB 2305 were able to get the law suspended pending a referendum on the measure at the November 2014 election. Rather than face the referendum, the legislature acted to repeal the law in 2014. The strength of this pushback, especially in a case where the anti-immigrant aspect of the bill was not apparent on the surface, reflects the growing sophistication and determination of the pro-immigrant coalition that is emerging in Arizona. Concern about voting access and reducing the under-registration of Latinos, who lag almost 20 percentage points behind Anglo voters (America's Voice and Latino Decisions 2014), is high on many organizational lists. Both state affiliates of the ACLU and the National Organization for Women, for example, have made voting rights an element of their strategic plans. Republicans, however, have not given up the fight. In the 2015 legislative session there was an effort to revive a key element in HB 2305, the prohibition on gathering early ballots cast after the mail-in deadline. Violators would face a felony charge. The bill died when an alliance of Democrats essentially filibustered the bill in the House, which effectively prevented the Senate from voting on it in the closing hours of the legislative session.

Economic Integration and Service Provision to Immigrants

In a state as strapped for resources as Arizona, debate about economic mobility for immigrants is not on the public agenda. Behind the scenes, local immigrant-assisting agencies, such as the Department of Neighborhood and Family Services in Avondale, provide many services to those seeking jobs and assist immigrants in acquiring certifications for advancement. Cities like Avondale and Phoenix, with Latino populations of over 40 percent, participate in Worldfest, Cinco de Mayo, and Day of the Dead celebrations. Even municipalities less populated by immigrants and with less outreach, such as the town of Gilbert, support world culture days and similar events that make a show of their cosmopolitan interests and suggest their bona fides regarding immigrant integration, provided the immigrants have legal status.

The oldest metro-wide agency serving newcomers is Friendly House, which was founded in 1920 to serve poor Mexican and Chinese immigrants. Maintained mostly by government grants, Friendly House employs 130 people and runs its own school, as well as offering other kinds of assistance. Another important non-profit is Chicanos por la Causa (CPLC), which despite its name and its origin in the Chicano power movement of the 1960s is now a relatively mainstream, pragmatic service-providing NGO (Rosales and Marin 2009). The *Arizona Republic* has referred to CPLC as a "far-flung Latino bureaucracy" (de Uriarte 2005). Valle del Sol is yet another well-known, established nonprofit that disproportionately serves immigrant clienteles. Each receives federal and state government contracts and support in carrying out its functions, specializes to a degree in certain services, and loosely collaborates with its counterparts.[30] Refugee-serving agencies, stretched for resources, also make jobs a priority for their clients but do not appear to be engaging in public debate for more resources. Most such groups are based in Phoenix and lack much presence in the suburbs. Mesa, the area's second-largest city, has little if any engagement with immigrant-serving organizations, although it did elect its first-ever Latino council member in 2014 (after he was appointed to fill a vacancy in 2013).

Proposition 300, passed by voters in 2006, prohibits nonprofits that receive state funding from providing services to unauthorized immigrants. Probably because most of these organizations are dependent on state support, they do not actively oppose this restriction. Rather, these NGOs tend to keep out of the public eye, working collaboratively with local and state government officials to maintain their grant funding. However, as the state's position toward immigrants became harsher, some of these nonprofits appear to have rethought their political passivity. Friendly House, despite its links to state funding sources, became a plaintiff in one of the suits against SB 1070.[31]

Even city governments, because of the provisions of state law, are hindered in efforts to help immigrants economically. "As a creature of the state, we have a difficult time offering benefits," said former Phoenix mayor Phil Gordon. "City employees can get sued individually for offering benefits. . . . Now any provider of services must assure that there is no provision of services for unauthorized immigrants" (Gordon 2010a).[32] In this environment, immigrant-serving agencies and organizations tend to go about their work quietly. The state's reaction to unauthorized immigration has forced them to keep their distance from any organization that forcefully advocates the human rights of unauthorized immigrants, however sympathetic they are to such arguments. As one advocate told us, "The other issues are important—they're just going to have to wait. For me, we can't do workforce development work on the back of a broken immigration system. . . . So we're kind of waiting, or trying to build power in the meantime, so we can get on with the real problems. . . . Immigration has become so dominant in Arizona . . . that we're ignoring real issues that need attention."

The Exceptional Case of Refugees

Arizona was one of the last states to join the refugee resettlement effort because of fears that any degree of visibility for the program would kill it. This fear, it turned out, was unfounded. As Arizona has become a leader in refugee work, city and state agencies and the general public have proven quite welcoming to these immigrants. Three agencies of roughly equal size operate in Phoenix to aid refugees: Lutheran Social Services, the International Rescue Committee, and Catholic Social Services. These agencies are not small—Lutheran Social Services, for example, has thirty-two full-time staff, offices in both Phoenix and Tucson, can work in thirty-five languages, and has a certified paralegal program that allows it to take cases to the Bureau of Immigration Appeals. Together these three agencies settled about thirty-three hundred refugees in 2010, about 20 percent less than their all-time high in 2008 (Thoresen 2010). Although most of their support comes from federal grants, they work closely with churches and other agencies, as well as volunteers who assist refugees in shopping, in learning English-language skills, and other cultural basics.

Each local resettlement agency maintains strong links with its parent national organization. These national voluntary agencies (or VolAgs, in agency vernacular) work with the federal government through the U.S. State Department. The resettlement process, which is set forth in the 1980 Refugee Act, involves a yearly report to Congress on the status of refugees around the world and results in a quota set by presidential decree after consultation with Congress. Cases begin to flow after this annual quota is set, with the VolAgs sending files to cities for their consideration and acceptance, which is typically forthcoming. A city or state can request fewer cases, as Arizona did beginning in 2008 because of strained local resources.

The state government distributes federal money for the initial resettlement through the Department of Economic Security and picks up costs that the federal government does not cover, taking responsibility for up to five years for immigrants who cannot support themselves. These expenses tend to involve welfare benefits, housing, and medical care. Local government is also deeply involved in the resettlement process. The City of Phoenix offers significant assistance, much of it in in-kind services. Valley Metro, the region's transit agency, offers heavily discounted transit passes and regular training on how to use the bus and rail system. Local public school districts accept many over-age refugees. Community colleges offer free English classes. Hospitals and the local police cooperate with the effort. Twenty to thirty local landlords offer rentals with no application fees and no security deposits.

Most of this activity occurs in the city of Phoenix rather than in outlying areas. The central city has the inexpensive housing, convenient public transit, and entry-level jobs that refugees need to find their footing. There is, however, a regional dimension to this effort. About fifty to sixty local churches and a few mosques and synagogues participate in resettlement work, with individual congregations often sponsoring families. Nondenominational fundamentalist churches are major supporters. These organizations, many of which are located in suburban areas, do much of their work in Phoenix. A well-appointed center for the young Sudanese refugees known as the Lost Boys of Sudan opened in 2003 near the state capitol. It is thought to be the only such community center in the nation.

The needs of refugees tend to be great. Many come with only a suitcase after years, even a decade or more, of life in an isolated refugee camp where there are few educational or work opportunities. There are exceptions, however. Phoenix has resettled wealthy Iraqi and Iranian doctors and professionals who come with their laptops and smart phones. As Lutheran Social Services executive director Craig Thoresen explained: "We get refugees that are rich and poor, rural and urban, educated and uneducated, and all of the above." Thoresen, who came to

Phoenix from Chicago, sees in Phoenix "a tolerance that you don't see in other areas" (2010).

Education as an Arena of Immigrant Integration

Interestingly, while the cost of educating often illiterate refugees who are above normal school age is considered unproblematic, the costs of educating unauthorized migrants from Mexico is widely regarded as a significant burden on local taxpayers. This is true despite the fact that Arizona ranks last among the states in its support for K–12 education, having spent just over $7,200 per pupil in 2013, according to a Census Bureau report; the national average was $10,700 that year (U.S. Census Bureau 2015). For a time there was interest in requiring schools to document the number of children without legal status and in challenging *Plyler v. Doe* (1982), the Supreme Court decision that requires states to support all students through high school, regardless of legal status. For educators strapped for state and local funds, the issues include dealing with the special needs of immigrant populations, implementing the state's constraining English immersion requirements, managing the concentration of immigrants and English learners in particular schools and districts, and dealing with the lack of resources for language and social needs. The Tempe Elementary School District, for example, has sixty-three foreign languages represented, including Native American dialects (Tate 2010).

School administrators view the state as hostile to schools and teachers and always concerned about the schools wasting money. There are concerns also about state-reporting requirements under Proposition 300, which outlaw services for unauthorized immigrants and require state personnel to report attempts to receive them. With many schools providing social services like assistance for homeless youth and a "clothes locker" and free breakfasts for needy students and their parents, this is a significant concern. Arizona's embrace of charter schools and open enrollment does offer some opportunities for motivated and well-informed immigrant families to enroll their children in schools more tailored to their needs, or to leave struggling districts to enroll in schools in neighboring districts. But the issue remains how to serve youths without legal status in a state determined to eliminate support whenever possible.

The state legislature's Republican majority has been consistent in its determination to minimize resources for unauthorized students, and uninterested in immigrant students generally. This position has been carried forward into school administration by the State Department of Education in its commitment to structured English immersion and abandonment of traditional bilingual education. The statewide organizations for teachers and school administrators have not spoken forcefully on immigrant-related issues, leaving advocacy and supportive arrangements to individual districts, school boards, superintendents, and principals, who tend to work individually and to stay out of the public eye.

The needs of Latino students in the state are undeniable. Standardized testing reveals a significant lag in reading and math skills that begins in the elementary grades and persists through high school. From 1992 to 2009, in fourth grade, for example, there has been a steady 22-point to 32-point achievement gap each year between white and Latino students in reading and mathematics. The gap persists through high school and is similar for African American and Native American students, both groups with high rates of poverty similar to those of Latinos. Over 70 percent of Latinos in K–12 are eligible for free lunches (as opposed to less than a third of whites). Language is another barrier. Twenty-nine percent of Latino students enter the elementary grades classified as English language learners (Hemphill, Vanneman, and Rahman 2011). Fewer than 70 percent graduate from high school, and fewer than 10 percent finish college. Preschool education might help to reverse this education gap, but it is unavailable to the vast majority of Latino children. As one educator noted in describing these statistics, "The education system in Arizona appears to be built, not for the near-majority of minority students in the public schools, but for other people's kids" (E. Garcia 2015).

The state law that denies unauthorized immigrants in-state tuition at state universities and community colleges creates a different set of problems for educators, particularly since the Obama administration's DACA initiative that gave young people a two-year window of opportunity to continue their education without fear of arrest or deportation. Even before that program was announced, there had been some push-back from local DREAM Act advocates and from at least one university administrator. Arizona State University president Michael Crow, in alliance with Chicanos por la Causa and local Latino elites, organized a drive to raise private funds to pay for scholarships to defray the costs of out-of-state tuition, which is three times higher than the in-state rate. Although about $10 million was raised, the funds have been fully expended. Crow was warned by state politicians that under the strictures of Proposition 300, absolutely no university facilities or staff time could be used in this effort. A similar face-off occurred when the Maricopa County Community College system announced that it would provide in-state tuition rates for DACA students. In-state tuition at these community colleges is one-fourth the out-of-state rates. The state's attorney general at the time (and former state school superintendent) Tom Horne responded with a lawsuit to end this practice, but a college spokesperson promised to continue the policy until a judicial ruling (Faller 2013).

Metropolitan Regionalism and Immigrant Integration

A regional approach to the integration of immigrants requires more than a favorable distribution of governmental entities and population. Metropolitan Phoenix is an excellent case in point, with a metro area largely contained within a single county and a diverse central city that contains 40 percent of the county's population. Compared to Frostbelt metros and some of the other regions in our comparison group, Phoenix has relatively few "suburbs per capita," though those that do exist tend to be large and relatively independent. But as Alba and Nee remind us, "institutions structure incentives and specify the rules of legitimate social action" (Alba and Nee 2003). Marrow's (2009) research makes a similar point. She found that bureaucrats served Hispanic newcomers in hospitals, schools, and service agencies, not just out of professional duty, but also with reference to external government policies that exert both direct control over the "rules of the game" and also indirectly influence behavior "by shaping their conceptualizations of their professional roles and responsibilities" (772).

In Phoenix, aside from services to refugees, there is little governmental support for helping immigrants adjust to their new surroundings. Nor is there much regional thinking on any topic. The county government has never been regional in its outlook, nor is the district-based system for electing its board of supervisors conducive to regional thinking (though it does allow for one "Hispanic seat" out of five on the board). The sheriff discourages regionalism by pursuing an aggressive enforcement policy that does not sit well with most cities in the county. The county supervisors and the sheriff are seriously at odds, but neither works effectively with Phoenix city government. The regional council of governments, as in most U.S. metro areas, is weak and relatively invisible. And a "regional leadership class" on immigration issues does not really exist.

Arguably, the most visible regionally known politician is Sheriff Arpaio, who is famously repressive toward immigrants. Lacking fiscal or other inducements to cooperate, cities within the metro area compete to attract businesses and have also sporadically argued about transportation funding priorities. They tend to face their difficulties with immigration on their own, as has been the case with day-labor centers and policing policies. Another factor working against regional cooperation is that the city of Phoenix is growing noticeably poorer and more nonwhite than its surrounding areas.

School districts are also fragmented within Maricopa County. For historical reasons (cities can annex land, school districts generally cannot), school district boundaries do not line up with municipal boundaries. In fact, the city of Phoenix alone has more than twenty school districts operating within its boundaries. This proliferation tends to concentrate immigrant students and their needs in certain districts, while separating these needs from tax resources. On the other hand, the inner-city school districts are a rare, though resource-strapped, institutional source of power and self-governance for immigrant and Latino populations, as we noted in the case of the Phoenix Union High School District.

Nearly all the nongovernmental groups that are active on regional issues or involved in immigrant-supportive activism are located within the city of Phoenix or concentrate their activity there. This is true even of the volunteer activity associated with refugee integration, which often begins in the suburbs but nearly always occurs in the city. Interviewees who worked on behalf of immigrant integration readily admitted that their activities in suburbs are hit or miss, with advocates seeking out potentially supportive locations and partners but sometimes not finding any. Advocates are so preoccupied by the state government and the county sheriff's activities that they do not appear to have given much attention to region-wide cooperation. Nor is there much of a regionalist movement in business or civic groups; so there is no one to spur ethnic and immigrant organizations to think along these lines.

The Arizona legislature has shown no inclination toward regionalism and little interest in the integration of immigrants. Its unrelenting hostility toward unauthorized immigrants overshadows any concern it might otherwise have with integration of newcomers. The state government also appears hostile to its metropolitan areas, including by threatening to take away tax revenues that have been shared with local governments, in order to deal with yawning budget deficits during the recession. The adoption of SB 1070 was a blow not just to immigrants, but to city governments that desired to pursue a different path with residents who might lack legal status.

Part of the reason that there is little thought of metropolitanism lies with the rapid growth of the Phoenix area. Developers often have major sway in local politics and have resisted statewide or regional growth management, feeding tendencies toward centrifugal development. The newness of the area also explains why there are few well-funded civil-society groups or foundations that might address immigrant integration. Phoenix illustrates, in extreme form, the approach to immigrant integration that the federal government has taken, which Bloemraad and de Graauw (2012) label "laissez-faire integration." For immigrants it can often be a geography of isolation, and for those without authorization, a harsh landscape indeed.

The way local politics is conducted in the Valley of the Sun places obstacles in the way of effective advocacy for immigrants at the local level. Municipal elections are mostly held on isolated dates in the spring, drawing low turnout; and city governments follow the Progressive-reform-era traditions of nonpartisan elections and council-manager government, somewhat depoliticizing local politics. Although the mayor of Phoenix is directly elected, significant authority is vested in the city manager, who is appointed by the council.[33] Nor is there reason to expect that the municipalities that make up the Phoenix metro area will combine energies to improve services for immigrants. Local governments mostly either contract out social services or leave them to the county government, making negotiations over coordinated delivery more difficult. The Maricopa Association of Governments (MAG) does have a human services coordinating committee of local elected officials that deals with certain state social service grants and discusses domestic violence and homelessness, among other issues, so immigrant needs do come up, although the discussion rarely makes it to the broader regional council that governs MAG.

Phoenix is an interesting case because it could conceivably be a welcoming place for newcomers of all nationalities. Land and housing are relatively cheap. Entry-level jobs were, until the Great Recession, abundant, and are perhaps becoming abundant again. There is adequate public transportation to navigate the area without a car, though this is not easy in the more low-density districts. The relatively easy absorption of refugees through coordinated public and private action illustrates the potential for a more progressive approach. The reception of refugees also indicates that Phoenicians can welcome newcomers, even when those newcomers differ sharply from the local mainstream in religion, dress, race, and culture.

To be more broadly successful in the integration of immigrants, two major institutional changes would have to occur at levels beyond the metro area. The state legislature would have to adopt policies that encourage cities within its metropolitan areas to work together toward common goals. There are many goals, beyond immigrant incorporation, that could be targeted, including economic development policy and more coordinated delivery of health and police services. The other change would have to occur at the national level if Hispanic immigrants are ever to feel welcome in Arizona. Immigration would have to be generally understood as controllable and organized, as it is in the case of refugees. Financial support for the local costs of immigration would have to be forthcoming, even if it did not cover all such costs, as in the case of refugees. The failure of the federal government to acknowledge the state and local costs of immigration may be what started Arizona on its path of harsh restrictionism.

Were these changes to occur, there would be room finally for the discussion Arizona needs to have about its role as a border state. Metropolitan areas would push for a more transnational sensibility that businesses, universities, cultural organizations, ethnic communities, and many others would welcome. There would be opposition to this outlook, as there has been in California and other states. But at least metro Phoenix would have an opportunity it does not currently enjoy to focus on its nascent cosmopolitanism and the benefits of a more inclusive, regional approach. It is encouraging that advocates for a more inclusive approach to immigration appear to see the problem in these terms and are increasingly prepared to fight the electoral battles required for legislative and political change. An example is a movement, which took shape in 2015, to create a Phoenix municipal identification card, a strategy for immigrant inclusion that is under way in a number of other cities around the country. The municipal ID movement projects itself in broad terms, as a civic engagement and public safety issue, providing a way to help the elderly, the homeless, children, and other people who experience difficulty identifying themselves to police and other public authorities. The activists most associated with the effort to create this new form of identification, however, are focused on unauthorized immigrant residents in the community and the many difficulties they experience in establishing their identity to police, banks, landlords, and others with whom they come into contact in their day-to-day lives. An April 2015 proposal to the Phoenix City Council from municipal ID advocates resulted in a split vote and a decision to study the matter further. Opponents rejected the public safety argument and argued that the municipal ID is an immigration policy appropriate for the federal level (see, for example, *Arizona Republic* 2015b). Will Phoenix eventually follow the California pattern, in which determined advocacy in urban centers with high numbers of Latino residents eventually brought the state firmly into the immigrant-friendly category? Many signs are favorable: increasing voter registration and participation, the growing number of well-educated activists supported by local and national organizations, and the removal of some of the most ardent anti-immigrant activists from positions of power. Much of the most draconian anti-immigrant legislation that the state adopted in the first decade of the new century has been overturned by the federal courts, and there is a perceptible lessening of enthusiasm for anti-immigrant laws since SB 1070.

Nevertheless, the obstacles are daunting. Minority populations in Arizona tend to be poor. While Latinos have gained some sway within Democratic Party politics in Arizona, that party clearly remains the minority party (in both senses of the term) in the state. The large numbers of retirees in Arizona, many of whom vote regularly to keep taxes low, means that the investments in education and social services required to help these populations close the gap in educational achievement will not occur until Latinos somehow force the issue. Discrimination in access to jobs and promotions remains an issue. But minority populations are growing, a transformation that is especially evident in the school system, where nearly half the students have Latino surnames. This ineluctable demographic trend will eventually have a political impact, but Arizona's conservatism regarding public investments and its interventionist, rural- and suburban-dominated state legislature will slow that process, pointing to a much longer road for immigrant and Latino political empowerment in the state than in California next door.

9

OUT OF MANY, ONE

Collaborating for Immigrant Integration in San José

Manuel Pastor, Rachel Rosner, and Jennifer Tran

San José is a city of firsts—the first capital of California, the first major U.S. city to elect an Asian to be mayor, and one of the first places where local governments actively embraced the term "immigrant integration." Given its role as the commercial center of Silicon Valley, a hotbed of invention, innovation, and immigration, it perhaps follows that the city and the region are also among the most inventive with regard to new approaches to incorporating immigrants. It is a place where immigrants from across the skill spectrum have received a warm welcome and become part of the region's political fabric.

San José's receptivity reflects in part the fact that many of its immigrants are highly skilled, with engineers, software developers, and others streaming from around the world to participate in a high-technology cluster that the rest of the world longs to emulate. Who would not want to attract such talent? But the region does not roll out the carpet only for Indian and Chinese scientists and investors: Santa Clara County, which surrounds and contains San José and which provides a home for such firms as Google, Facebook, and Apple, has developed a range of innovative programs for a diverse range of immigrants, exemplified by the Children's Health Initiative, a program that seeks to provide health insurance coverage for all children, regardless of immigration status. A cooperative effort between a health care provider, an interfaith grassroots organization, the county board of supervisors, and a public policy institute, it has successfully provided access to health care for thousands of children—especially undocumented children through the locally funded Healthy Kids program.[1]

This program would be a political hot potato in many other settings; Silicon Valley takes pride in it. Many constituencies in the Valley take pains to point out how its immigrants make positive contributions: Working Partnerships, closely affiliated with the region's Central Labor Council, has extolled the virtues of immigrants, while the annual social indicators report issued by Joint Venture: Silicon Valley Network, a business-based collaborative, highlights the rising share of the foreign-born as a strong plus for regional competitiveness. In short, this is definitely not Arizona.

Why such a positive reception? It cannot be explained, as in New York or Chicago, by a long, storied, and consistent history of being an immigrant gateway. Audrey Singer (2004) aptly characterizes San José as a reemerging immigrant gateway region. While there was a strong immigrant presence in the city at the beginning of the twentieth century, that population dwindled over time until the 1970s, when the region reemerged as an immigrant destination. And then it did so in force. While San José is a smaller metro area than the mature gateways of this study, it has a larger share of the foreign-born than any of them, and the foreign share has grown the most rapidly, as reported in chapter 2. The warm regional reception provided to these immigrants is all the more remarkable precisely because this change has been so rapid. Nor can we explain San José's relative receptivity by a vibrant set of local social movements; community organizing has played a role, but, unlike in Los Angeles, such movement-oriented immigrant-rights and other groups are not the only part of the civic ecosystem that has made a difference.

We argue below that several interweaving factors have led to the positive regional tone. First, the vibrancy of Silicon Valley is rightly credited to the central contributions that foreign-born individuals make to the synergies of the Valley's intellectual capital and social networks (Saxenian 1996). The region's research universities (particularly Stanford and Berkeley), the strong regional presence of defense spending and its impacts on technology, and the development of deep pools of venture capital have nurtured the region's innovations in information technology, biotech, and medical devices. Immigrants have contributed to all of these dynamics. As a result, immigrants figure far differently in the popular imagination than in the other regions; those made uncomfortable by their growing presence therefore have far more difficulty in casting them as a drain on public coffers or racializing them negatively, and their supporters have a far easier time framing them as an asset to regional vitality.

Second, while many immigrants came to the region primarily for higher education, employment, and business formation, they and their children have become voters and active participants in the political process, establishing an electoral voice in many of Santa Clara County's cities, particularly San José. Indeed, Santa Clara County ties with Los Angeles County and slightly exceeds the New York metro region with 23 percent of the voters in the 2012 presidential election being foreign-born and only slightly lags LA in having another 18 percent who are native-born children of immigrants (November 2012 Current Population Survey). Immigrants and their allies have also developed a broad network of community-based organizations that is itself a base of political influence and which provides organized resistance to any anti-immigrant rhetoric and initiatives that might emerge.

Finally, business, labor, and civic leaders (as well as public agencies) have made a significant public commitment to the idea of immigrant integration, in part, we speculate, because this metro area has stronger regional organization than any of the others in this study. Indeed, many observers consider the region's major business group—Silicon Valley Joint Venture—to be a model for other business-based regional collaboratives (Henton, Melville, and Walesh 1997, 2004), and its labor group, Working Partnerships USA, is a prime model for regional labor-community collaborations (Dean and Reynolds 2009). While these two groups may be at odds about specific issues (and about the relative balance between labor and business interests in economic policy), they do have a shared sense that thinking regionally is key. And the idea of stirring up division around growing immigrant communities within this regionalist context, rather than reinforcing the idea that the region needs to attract new talent, runs against the local (or rather metro) grain, with positive spillover effects in the arena of immigrant integration.

To better understand what has developed in San José—and to think about what lies ahead—this chapter begins with the history and demography of immigration in the region, then turns to the roles of politics and local government. We then consider the nature of immigrant organizing groups, particularly since the mid-2000s, as well as the effects of labor and business groups. We conclude by suggesting that the region's unique orientation facilitates collaboration across private and public sectors. This, coupled with the diversity of its immigrant population, results in positive receptivity. In any case, the San José metro area is ahead of the curve on immigrant integration and will continue to hold a leading place in the continuing national debates about comprehensive immigration reform and the intersection of national immigration enforcement with local policies and practices.[2]

The Immigrant Landscape

Immigrants played a vital role in the development of the San José area long before Silicon Valley emerged. However, recent immigration differs qualitatively from that of the distant past. San José was a relatively low-immigrant area in the early and middle parts of the twentieth century, and the decline of its immigrant population tracked that of other predominantly agricultural parts of California, such as Fresno. As the foreign-born share began to rise in San Francisco in the 1950s and in Los Angeles in the 1960s, it continued to decline in San José until 1970. At that point, however, it staged a sharp increase, on track with the similar rise in Los Angeles. Moreover, it continued to rise in San José even as it began to decline in Los Angeles after 2000.[3] Notably, the uptick in San José's foreign-born population differed from that of many other regions of California: the increases after 1970 included newly arrived Indian and Vietnamese immigrants, many of them coming to the Silicon Valley for graduate school or as refugees, respectively (Gleeson and Bloemraad 2011).

A complex history lies beneath this data, with the early migration reflecting Asian as well as Mexican farmworkers entering the region's agricultural labor market in the early twentieth century and again in the 1940s, under the bracero or guest-worker program. The early importance of agriculture may surprise those familiar with modern-day Silicon Valley; however, the San José metro area was once known as the "Valley of Heart's Delight" because of its many citrus fields. It was also home to a vibrant canning industry, a sector that peaked in 1954 and then shrank to a third its size by the late 1970s, stranding the immigrant farmworkers as long-term low-income residents (Pellow and Park 2002).

During the Second World War, San José transitioned into manufacturing as it became a major location for defense contractors. With the founding of the Ames Aeronautical Laboratory in 1939, now the Ames Research Center, NASA's leading supercomputing and information technology center, an aerospace industry also emerged. In the 1950s, IBM opened its first West Coast manufacturing plant in San José, helping to launch the high-tech cluster. NASA's demand for integrated circuits helped Fairchild (from which key personnel later left to found Intel) "learn by doing" on the government's expense (Terdiman 2007). That early high-tech explosion was accompanied by a decline in the percent of foreign-born, as the region initially attracted U.S.-born engineers. One author describes the region as "a new Mecca for the white middle class" and notes that by 1950, "San José had one of the lowest percentages of non-white residents of any major California city" (Pitti 2003, 129).

During the 1950s, San José's boundaries also grew greatly through the annexation of surrounding towns. When Norman Mineta was elected mayor in 1971—the first Asian American mayor of a major American city—he changed San José's twenty-year-old policy of rapid growth by annexation. The legacy of annexation, however, left San José with an odd suburban feel—more of a series of single-family neighborhoods with a sleepy downtown, a configuration that would eventually turn the city into a bedroom community for the rapid business development that would take place in the rest of the Valley.

Despite its 1950 characterization as a white region and a white central city, the city of San José and its metro area are now remarkably diverse. In 2012, the city's population was almost evenly distributed between Latino, Asian, and white—28 percent white, 33 percent Latino, and 33 percent Asian and Pacific Islander.[4] For the rest of Santa Clara County outside the city of San José, the breakdown is 42 percent white, 20 percent Latino, and 33 percent Asian, a pattern that suggests that even the suburbs are majority-minority, Asians are evenly distributed across the city and its suburbs, and the suburbs remain a bit whiter than the city. Figures 9.1 and 9.2 show the overall increase of the foreign-born share of the region's population and its spread to almost all parts of the county between 1980 and the present.

Not only are these numbers and geographic patterns striking, but so is the relative fluidity of interpersonal relations among groups. Santa Clara County, after all, had historically been marked by problematic race relations, including the exploitation of Asian and Mexican farmworkers, and San José is where Cesar Chavez, the founder of the United Farm Workers Union, earned his initial

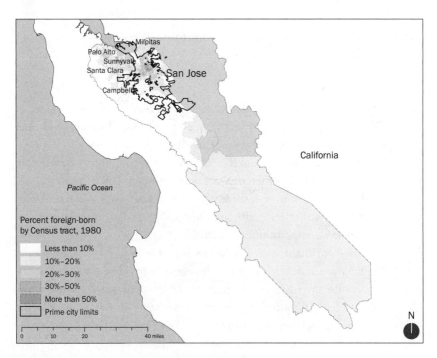

FIGURE 9.1. Percent foreign-born by Census tract, 1980, San José, CA

Source: 1980 Decennial Census, Census TIGER/Line, and ESRI.

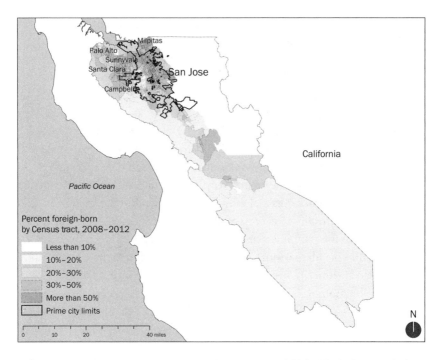

FIGURE 9.2.   Percent foreign-born by Census tract, 2008–2012, San José, CA

Source: 2008–2012 American Community Survey (Ruggles et al. 2011), Census TIGER/Line, and ESRI.

organizer chops working in the disadvantaged and disenfranchised east side of the city. Today, racial and ethnic diversity crosses religions, education levels, and economic class both in the city and the rest of the metro area.

On the other hand, results from the Social Capital Community Benchmark Survey, conducted in forty different U.S. communities in 2000, found the Valley had higher degrees of overall social trust, interracial trust, and friendships that crossed racial boundaries, although fewer that crossed class boundaries than in comparable communities (Koch and Miller 2001). While this class divide is critical for many issues, it means that members of the native-born elite are much more likely to interact with people from other ethnicities, making it (along with the widespread presence of highly educated Asians across the region) harder to negatively stereotype immigrants. In the Inland Empire, being immigrant is equated to being Latino. While Latinos have had a longer presence in Santa Clara County, the mainstream is also acutely aware of other immigrant groups.

Even given the higher level of integration than in many other metro areas, the west side of the valley tends to be more affluent and white, while the east side is more working class and immigrant, including some gateway neighborhoods, including the Mayfair neighborhood where Chavez did his first urban organizing. The surrounding towns of Mountain View and Sunnyvale also have pockets of working-class immigrants, mostly in the apartment complexes. Still, higher-income and better-educated immigrants have located throughout the suburbs, although none of these suburbs have the overwhelming shares of immigrants that mark LA ethnoburbs like Monterey Park, but instead retain many white residents.

The proximity of immigrants in the workplace and neighborhoods seems to contribute to the region's greater openness. One interviewee associated with the immigrant rights movement explained: "Here we aren't segregated. . . . We live in the same spaces" (Castellanos 2010). As noted, San José has had the most rapid increases in the share of the foreign-born and the largest share of immigrants—surpassing both Los Angeles and New York. This latter figure was 37 percent for the San José region in 2012, well more than doubling the 14 percent share from 1980. Immigrants and their children make up approximately two-thirds of the region's total population. They are a mix of immigrants and refugees; with refugees from Bosnia-Herzegovina, the former Soviet Union, Vietnam, Somalia, and Iran, the county is home to the top five refugee populations resettled in the United States. The city of San José alone has the largest Vietnamese population outside the country of Vietnam.

The region's foreign-born population mixes recent and longer-term immigrants. Over one-third migrated to the United States in 2000 or after, and just under 30 percent migrated in the decade before that. Of those migrating since 2000, the largest share came from India (21 percent), followed by Mexico (19 percent), China (12 percent), Vietnam (8 percent), and the Philippines (7 percent); this is the lowest share of Mexican immigrants for any of our cases, except for New York, and it speaks to immigrant diversity. About 16 percent of immigrants came to the country before the 1980s, the second-smallest share of the seven case studies; however, this is still a big base, since immigrants make up so much of the region's population. While there are many new immigrants, and the region has experienced rapid increases, this shift built on this original base. Nearly two-thirds (62 percent) of pre-1980s immigrants to San José speak English well or very well, but that falls to about half (46 percent) among those who migrated after 1999, although even this figure is high relative to the other metro areas (see figure 2.8). Nearly half (47 percent) of the foreign-born are between the ages of twenty-five and forty-five—that is, prime working age; of those who are employed, 19 percent are employed in the professional, scientific, and top-level management services, versus 15 percent for the native-born. While the share in manufacturing is also higher than for the native-born (23 percent compared to

15 percent), as is the share in hotels and restaurants (6 percent versus 3 percent), the overall pattern is one that bifurcates the immigrant labor force in terms of occupation and prestige.

Indeed, one interviewee describes the status of immigrants as "a definite pecking order, based on access to income and opportunity" (Hobbs 2010). There is indeed a remarkable achievement span: 47 percent of working-age immigrants (twenty-five years and older) in San José have a bachelor's degree or higher, while 21 percent have less than a high school degree. Nearly half of all BA holders or higher in the region are immigrants. At the other end of the educational attainment spectrum, immigrants make up 78 percent of those with less than a high school degree.[5] And the experience varies dramatically by country of origin: an extraordinary 89 percent of Asian Indians, 67 percent of Chinese, and 59 percent of non-Indian South Asian (for example, Pakistani and Bangladeshi) immigrants twenty-five years and older have at least a BA, while only 7 percent of Mexican and 28 percent of Vietnamese immigrants do. Filipino immigrants fall in the middle of the spectrum, with 47 percent possessing a BA or higher.

The achievement gap persists among children of immigrants: Latinos score lower than Asians (the data do not allow us to break out nativity) in elementary and secondary education measures in English-language arts and mathematics by gaps ranging from 32 to 42 percent (non-Hispanic whites perform just below Asian scores). Recognizing the severity of this problem, the City of San José, the Santa Clara County Office of Education, school districts, charter schools, colleges, and business and nonprofit community agencies created an educational initiative in 2009 to "eliminate the achievement gap by 2020" (Santa Clara County Office of Education and the City of San Jose 2011).

Given these varying degrees of educational attainment, it follows that incomes also differ by country of origin. The median incomes in 2012 of Mexican and Vietnamese immigrant households are substantially less ($51,600 and $65,300 respectively) than those of Chinese and Indian households, both which receive well above $100,000 per year, with Filipinos following at $102,100. By comparison, the median household income for U.S.-born, non-Hispanic whites is $93,900.[6] The relatively high incomes for many in the Asian immigrant population can obscure real differences within Asian immigrant groups. Seventeen percent of Chinese immigrants and 29 percent of Vietnamese immigrants live below 150 percent of the federal poverty level; these figures are lower than they are for Mexican-origin immigrants (37 percent) but much higher than for U.S.-born non-Hispanic white (about 10 percent) or U.S.-born Asians (about 11 percent).[7] According to one interviewee, "People are surprised that there's an Asian service organization—they are surprised that there are poor Asians in the area" (Im 2010).

The Political Landscape

Immigrants in San José have broken a great deal of political ground. Members of minority groups, many first-generation immigrants, began to take leadership roles decades ago. In 1967, Mayor Ron James appointed Norman Mineta to a vacant San José City Council seat. He was elected to office on his own in 1969 and ran successfully against fourteen other candidates for mayor in 1971. In this election, Mineta, of Japanese descent, won every precinct, with over 60 percent of the total vote, and became the first Asian American mayor of a major U.S. city. In the 1980s, Blanca Alvarado (now retired) became the first Latina to serve on the San José City Council and then the Santa Clara County Board of Supervisors. According to one council member, "The population is embracing inclusiveness. There are opportunities for [Asian] immigrants to become political players. On the council there is Taiwan, India, Mexico, China, and Vietnam represented. The opportunity is there" (Chu 2010).

Many of the other fourteen incorporated cities and towns in Santa Clara County have also elected immigrant leadership. The city of Cupertino has three Asian council members (a majority), and Michael Chang, the former mayor of Cupertino, now serves on the Santa Clara County Board of Education; he is also the founder of the Asian Pacific American Leadership Institute of Silicon Valley. In the city of Campbell, Evan Low was the first gay and Asian council member, and the other council members selected him to serve as mayor in 2009; he has since gone on to the California State Assembly. Sunnyvale, Saratoga, and Milpitas, as well as Palo Alto, also have a growing number of qualified immigrant candidates vying for and gaining council seats. Several San José Council members, like Madison Nguyen of District 7, started their political careers by serving on school boards. On the state level, Paul Fong represented California's Twenty-Second State Assembly District until he was termed out in 2014.

Immigrant-origin politicians are not the only strong advocates for immigrants: our informants often mentioned both Sam Liccardo (San José City Council and, as of 2015, the mayor) and Zoe Lofgren (Sixteenth U.S. Congressional District) as being important voices on immigrant concerns. Lofgren, ranking minority member and former chair of the House Immigration Subcommittee, consistently took up the issuance of H-1B visas to allow high-tech immigrants to work in Silicon Valley and also supported more general comprehensive immigration reform. Also representing the region in Congress is Mike Honda, chair of the Congressional Asian Pacific American Caucus; Honda was interned (along with his family) during World War II and is considered a stalwart defender of immigrant rights.

Politicians pay attention because a significant percentage of Santa Clara County's voters (as noted earlier, 23 percent in 2012) are immigrants.[8] Moreover, just over 60 percent of the population under the age of eighteen—the region's future voters—have at least one immigrant parent, suggesting that efforts to support immigrant integration can resonate into the political future. Still, some interviewees criticized the politicians who favored immigrants for not doing anything "game changing." Others worried that elected officials do not see immigrant issues as being distinctly separate from the concerns of all people of color, and so their particular needs get lost. In the words of one respondent, elected officials "don't specifically address the needs of the ethnic immigrants, if they are not being identified . . . and by taking a colorblind approach, sometimes [they] are not culturally sensitive" (Vuong 2010).

Interestingly, the County of Santa Clara seems to target more (positive) services to immigrants than does the city. Until June 2015, the City of San José did not have an office specifically dealing with immigrant issues—city leaders argued that they were all aware of how their policies and programs may impact immigrant communities, and that was enough (something that changed after Liccardo began serving). The county has historically done more. In some ways, this is surprising, given that the county board of supervisors is currently less diverse than the area's city councils, partly because immigrant communities are less concentrated within its larger districts. Still, the county board has been outspoken about protecting immigrants. When the Minuteman Project appeared on the scene, the board of supervisors passed a resolution on September 27, 2005, "to promote positive human relations and support immigrants and human rights." The resolution stated that "the Minutemen do not help with border security, but in fact, make it more difficult for the border patrol to do its job, and create a more dangerous, hostile environment for all immigrants who come here seeking work and a better life for themselves and their families" and called upon "local, state and national leaders to make the enactment of fair immigration policies a top priority."[9] This kind of support for immigrants partly reflects the fact that San José is a strongly Democrat region with a relatively progressive history, but its strength and early onset are still striking.

And it continues. In 2010, after Arizona's passage of SB 1070, County Supervisor George Shirakawa proposed that the county participate in lawsuits against Arizona's anti-immigration law. Shirakawa drew parallels between the Arizona law and the Japanese internment, arguing that the criminalization of individuals based on race would generate public mistrust and fear of government and be counterproductive. Only one county supervisor, Donald Gage, voted against the motion—he was also the lone dissenter in the early resolution condemning the Minutemen—but he did support the county's resolution in June 2010 that the county would not report anyone's immigration status when that individual was seeking county services, which passed unanimously. The resolution was framed as a public safety and public health matter and addressed the treatment of residents by county employees. County supervisors also acknowledged in the resolution that immigration law is a federal matter, not something that should be enforced by local government.

Congresswoman Lofgren and Congressman Honda have championed immigrant rights and issues at the federal level. When Democrats controlled the House, Lofgren chaired the Judiciary Subcommittee on Citizenship, Refugees, Immigration, and Border Security and worked with other members of Congress on a bipartisan comprehensive reform bill. Although her role is naturally focused on national-level issues, Lofgren's staff is in regular contact and communication with local immigrant communities. One interview observed that "their office tends to do things that most congressional offices do not; regardless of whether or not the issues brought to them are federal issues, they try to get residents in touch with the right resources to work through their issues." Community and advocacy groups spoke of their regular interaction with Lofgren's office and how her staff would respond to community concerns around Immigration and Customs Enforcement (ICE) raids and police checkpoints.

While fairness and humane treatment have been the major tropes of pro-immigrant advocates, other strategies have worked well in this region. The argument that local law enforcement can better maintain positive relations with immigrant communities by not acting as enforcers of immigration law has made headway (leading, for example, to the 2011 decision by the board of supervisors and the sheriff to nearly completely refuse to cooperate with ICE around the Secure Communities program). In June 2010, the board of supervisors unanimously passed a resolution that instructed all county employees to provide public services to eligible individuals regardless of immigration status and clearly delineated that employees are not to be involved in immigration-law enforcement activities. Supervisor Shirakawa said of the resolution, "The intent of this resolution is to get at three issues—All residents of Santa Clara County can and should trust their County health and safety agencies; this trust is predicated on the fact that County employees will not inquire into residents' immigration status—unless required; and the County does not enforce federal civil immigration laws."[10]

The business community has also been supportive. As one San José council member put it, "By not allowing companies to compete for talent we could put the region at a disadvantage in being able to create more companies and more jobs" (Kalra 2010). Advocates also play on the idea that "the region likes to think they're open-minded and forward thinking" (Kalra 2010). Regardless of the motivations, San José has supportive elected officials and business and civic leaders and so generally does not have to contend with organized opposition to immigrants.

Still, one interviewee told us that support from elected public officials does not always translate into results: "For any elected [official] to stand up and support [the] immigrant community has always been a tough issue. Unfortunately, immigration is that issue that really scares people. . . . Rhetorically, our representatives are supportive, but to what extent do we see that support translating into concrete leadership in trying to push forward policies that are really going to be helpful to the immigrant community? . . . How are we talking about immigrant issues in communities so that that fear isn't there? . . . [We need to dispel the fear because] it makes it very hard for elected officials to push policies that are a benefit to immigrant communities forward" (Sanchez 2010). Still, as another interviewee put it, "Local officials can't change the odds of CIR [comprehensive immigration reform], but they can develop policies that are not disproportionately harmful and that help benefit immigrants as part of our community" (Avitia 2010). This is exactly the spirit of this volume—that ultimately, immigrant integration is driven significantly by local and quotidian practices.

One way to keep up the pressure on elected officials and agencies is to develop motivated voters—and to shape the next generation of elected leaders. The publicly managed and county-sponsored Immigrant Relations and Integration Services (an organization discussed below) and the labor-affiliated Working Partnerships have set up leadership development training for immigrants. The latter is specifically focused on preparing people of color (including immigrants) to be effective leaders and serve in administrative and elected offices. These educational resources can be found throughout the county, providing services to promote naturalization, citizenship, and leadership.

Local Government Policies

While San José has a general history of progressive policy making (Trounstine 2008), the experience with regard to immigrant integration has been quite striking: this has been achieved partly through political leadership, partly through voter pressure, and partly because of a vibrant immigrant rights movement. Before turning to the movement, however, we first examine the actions of public agencies.

The 1996 welfare restructuring is a good place to begin. The implementation of the federal Personal Responsibility and Work Opportunity Reconciliation Act called for several things that seemed to threaten the well-being of legal immigrants: the legislation promised to dramatically limit benefits that legal noncitizens could access, remove cash assistance as an entitlement to families, and establish limits on the length of time families could receive benefits. Nationally, though immigrants were estimated to be only 9 percent of the public beneficiaries, they were slated to absorb 43 percent of the cuts. With its relatively large legal immigrant population, Santa Clara County was destined to be hard hit (Petsod, Wang, and McGarvey 2006, 48). Approximately 15,500 (roughly 4,500 of whom were children) of the county's legal immigrant residents would no longer be able to receive food stamps following the implementation of the legislation (Learmonth 1997).

In an effort to mitigate the impact of the 1996 law on the community, Santa Clara County developed an action plan called the Employment Support Initiative, which created a local safety net for legal county residents who no longer qualified for federal and state welfare aid. The board of supervisors also approved a Citizenship Initiative to allow low-income immigrants to reestablish eligibility (by shifting from lawful permanent resident status to that of a naturalized citizen) for federal benefits programs.[11] To implement these efforts instead of either allowing the cuts to go forward or developing its own social safety net, the county tapped into the existing network of community-based organizations already providing services to the immigrant and refugee community.[12] This strategy helped fortify an immigrant services infrastructure that has survived to the present day.

Another milestone in county involvement in immigrant integration came with the 2000 publication of *Bridging Borders in the Silicon Valley* (Santa Clara County Citizenship and Immigrant Services Program 2000), a study drawing on twenty-five hundred interviews, twenty-four focus groups, and other research. The findings were showcased at a meeting titled "Bridging Borders in Silicon Valley: Summit on Immigrant Needs and Contributions." Summit conveners stated that "our collective need to integrate, improve, and transform the lives of all residents of Santa Clara County depends upon our ability to integrate, improve, and transform the lives of immigrants and the need to re-think planning, policies, and practices. . . . The deep-seated needs of immigrants in Santa Clara County were assessed by community members, the Social Services Agency, and the Office of Human Relations and they were recognized by many entities and the Board of Supervisors in particular as assessed needs not only to be understood but to be addressed" (Santa Clara County Citizenship and Immigrant Services Program 2000, 21–22).

The summit led to a long-term program called Immigrant Relations and Integration Services (IRIS). Housed in the County Office of Human Relations, IRIS convenes stakeholders on multiple aspects of immigrant integration and has employed a range of strategies, from direct services to leadership development.

IRIS also leads the Citizenship Collaborative—an alliance that hosts the county's annual Citizenship and Immigrant Pride Day, provides resources and information to immigrants about the citizenship process in fourteen different languages, and encourages them to vote. The immigrant pride event focuses on how immigrants contribute to the region and promotes cultural awareness. The collaborative also launched the Save for Citizenship Program, an innovative project funded by the Opportunity Fund and the Knight Foundation to bring future citizens together with legal organizations throughout the region to determine eligibility for citizenship. Then, using an "Individual Development Account" model, the program provided financial education and set aside up to $1.85 million in matching funds for eligible citizenship applicants to pay for naturalization filing fees.[13]

IRIS offers cultural competency training for employers and hosts an online resource website, Knowledge of Immigrant Nationalities, intended for use by businesses, educators, students, community members, and immigrants. IRIS also runs an immigrant leadership course at San José City College to develop the leadership skills of immigrants and to address ongoing issues affecting the county's immigrant communities. Despite major cuts during the current fiscal crisis, IRIS has remained, albeit with dramatically reduced funding (Gleeson 2012).

The public sector's institutionalization of immigrant integration efforts should not be seen as driven just by public administrators or elected officials. According to one of IRIS's original staff members, "IRIS staff have come from community organizing backgrounds. . . . We learn with [the immigrant] leadership. . . . As government, we never thought we had answers. We acted more as a convener tapping into their knowledge by creating opportunities to express their knowledge and for participation" (Castellanos 2010). The importance of public-sector relationships with organizers can also be seen in the Children's Health Initiative's Healthy Kids program. A large portion of uninsured children in Santa Clara County were covered by Medi-Cal or Healthy Families, but a portion of them were not, owing to their immigration status. In response, a collaboration of community organizations—including Working Partnerships USA, People Acting in Community Together, the Santa Clara Valley Health and Hospital System, and the Santa Clara Family Health Plan—worked to allocate tobacco settlement funds to create the first program in the United States to provide universal health insurance for children in the region, regardless of immigration status.

Since it first started in 2001, the Healthy Kids program has been funded by a mix of local private and public sources, including tobacco taxes, city and county funds, and private foundation contributions, as well as tobacco settlement funds. Enrollments grew steadily until 2005, when reports suggested that the program had covered nearly 80 percent of those children who were uninsured in 2001 (Guido 2001; Howell and Hughs 2006; Trenholm and Orzol 2004, 2007).[14] Considered a smashing success, it is a model for other counties, even though the demand outpaced funding (going from $14.5 million from all sources in 2005 to $6.9 million in 2013). Demand for the program has decreased with the expansion of Medi-Cal for children—in many ways, Healthy Kids, alongside others, set the precedent for such federal shifts—but Healthy Kids remains the only program in the county to insure regardless of status.

In order to expand the program's scope to fully meet underlying demand, the county, as well as the Santa Clara Family Health Foundation, the Healthier Kids Foundation, and other nonprofit, 501(c)3 organizations that support the Healthy Kids insurance program, has worked to secure long-term funding for the program. In 2012, Santa Clara County voters, by a wide margin, passed Measure A, which raised the sales tax one-eighth of a percent over the subsequent decade and was expected to raise over $50 million annually (Kurhi 2014). Such an electoral victory reflects not only the hard work of organizers but also a local political climate responsive to immigrant rights. Indeed, with this support, the Healthier Kids Foundation is working to increase eligibility for Healthy Kids from 300 percent to 400 percent of the federal poverty level and to continue to respond to the ways in which the Affordable Care Act of 2012 fails to cover undocumented children (King 2014).

Philanthropy has also stepped in to fill the gaps in services for immigrants in the region and help answer their needs. In 2007, the Silicon Valley Community Foundation launched an Immigrant Integration initiative, providing funding that strengthens the legal services infrastructure for immigrants and increases adult English-language acquisition.[15] The requests for proposals in these work areas continued into 2014, although 2015 strategic initiatives suggest a movement in other directions, particularly education (which is, of course, important to the large number of the region's children who have immigrant parents).

Many agencies and workforce developers incorporate language and citizenship education into their programs. They use applied subjects for learning the language, including civic engagement, parental involvement, and domestic violence. Immigrants can access numerous adult education programs throughout the county. The Building Skills Partnership, an adult education program of SEIU Local 1877, started with work-site training and expanded to topics like health care and comprehensive immigration reform. The staff notes that through this program they "are able to reach people that would not otherwise be accessing adult school [with a] curriculum [that] includes financial and computer literacy" (Ascher-Webber 2010).

Immigrant Organizing and Mobilization

While Santa Clara County and its city governments have taken enlightened measures exemplified by the Children's Health Initiative, they have frequently been
assisted and propelled via a vibrant set of immigrant organizers and their allies.
As is suggested by the work of Cesar Chavez in the east side barrio of Sal Si
Puedes (in English, "Leave if you can"; the area is now known as Mayfair), San
José was a center for Chicano organizing in the heady days of the 1960s, and
several Chicano-led or -serving institutions, including the Center for Employment Training and the Mexican American Community Services Agency, date to
this period. In 1988, the La Raza Roundtable, a coalition of Latino and Mexican
American organizations, was founded—again reflecting a sort of ethnic politics.
But much of the leadership of the earlier movement was aging by the mid-1990s,
and the immigrant landscape was changing, with a new wave of Mexican immigrants and an increasingly Asian presence in the immigrant community.

Contemporary immigrant organizing came about through the 1994 mobilization to oppose California's Proposition 187, the Save Our State (SOS) initiative.
The initiative would have denied those without legal status many public benefits,
including health care and education. The Network for Immigrant and Refugee
Rights and Services—which later became a key immigrant-serving agency, the
Services, Immigrant Rights and Education Network (SIREN)—brought together
organizations in the region to protest the proposition at the federal building in
downtown San José. Though the voters passed Proposition 187, a federal court
later found it unconstitutional, and Governor Gray Davis refused to appeal the
decision in 1999. Even so, its passage sent shock waves throughout the state and
galvanized immigrant communities in San José and elsewhere in California, particularly in Los Angeles.

Shortly afterward, immigrant activists and their allies formed the San José
Coalition for Driver's Licenses. This is a key issue for undocumented residents
who may need to drive to work but cannot obtain a license because of their undocumented status. In 2004, the Santa Clara County Board of Supervisors voted to
support Assembly Bill (AB) 2895 introduced by assembly member Fabian Núñez
that would allow undocumented immigrants to obtain driver's licenses; Governor Schwarzenegger eventually vetoed the bill. The struggle around licenses
would later resurface in efforts to counter the use of checkpoints and lengthy
and costly vehicle impoundments against undocumented drivers, but the failure
to win driver's licenses also led activists to believe that they were "fighting for
something that was not going to solve the underlying problem" (Vital 2010).

A bigger platform and broader set of issues arose when HR 4437, the Border Protection, Antiterrorism, and Illegal Immigration Control Act of 2005,

passed the U.S. House of Representatives. Known as the Sensenbrenner Bill, after its Republican sponsor, it would have criminalized undocumented immigrants and organizations and individuals assisting them, given state and local governments the power to enforce immigration law, and created a mandatory system for employers to verify work-authorization status.[16] The bill's December 2005 House passage sparked unprecedented mass mobilizations of immigrant communities and their supporters nationwide, and the bill stalled in the Senate.

In San José, protesters voiced their opposition in marches throughout 2006. The first one coincided the celebration of Cesar Chavez Day in March, and thirty thousand people mobilized again on April 10, this time joined by representatives of the San José City Council and of Santa Clara County, their attendance in keeping with the political sympathies we outlined above (Vital 2010). The biggest event occurred on May Day, when a march to support immigrants drew an estimated 150,000 protesters, one of the largest in the country and an amazing feat for sleepy San José, a place that had never seen such a mass mobilization of the immigrant community and its supporters.

While not strictly a Latino issue, the enforcement threat implicit in HR 4437 was of particular importance to Latinos, and they had a leading presence. For example, though the marches received mainstream coverage in the *San Jose Mercury News*, it was the Spanish-language media that helped spread the word widely in the Latino community.[17] Still, the San José Immigrant Rights Coalition, made up of over eighty organizations, mobilized an effort that was characterized as multicultural, multilingual, and multiethnic. Indeed, the diversity of representation from unions, service providers, community-based organizations, faith-based groups, and activists was impressive. The Central Labor Council (CLC) was heavily involved; even though overall union membership is not largely immigrant in the San José area, labor support has also been central to immigrant-related issues (like Healthy Kids). The CLC also supported the local Service Employees International Union (SEIU) in its Justice for Janitors campaign aimed at a low-skilled immigrant workforce, and helped create the Interfaith Council on Race, Religion, Economic and Social Justice, now known as the Interfaith Council on Economics and Justice, a multi-faith effort that has taken up immigrant workers' rights in the hotel and service sector and focused on the intersections between health, employment, and immigration. The Diocese of San José participated in Justice for Immigrants, the U.S. Conference of Catholic Bishops' campaign for immigration reform. The diocese specifically designated immigrant integration as one of its key issues, and its representatives have been vocal in the media in informing the public about the church's position on immigration and to let people know how to get involved.

The 2006 marches likewise helped inspire a younger generation; as one organizer noted, "I was very happy to see a lot of young people that continue to be involved in San José" (Bustamante 2010). Energized by the marches, the Student Advocates for Higher Education at San José State University was founded to support undocumented students. Active in statewide and national coalitions to support the DREAM Act and comprehensive immigration reform legislation (which spurred the Obama administration's Deferred Action for Childhood Arrivals), the coalition has also raised over $20,000 in scholarships for undocumented youth.[18]

In an effort to also tap into the energy created by the marches, the Silicon Valley Alliance for Immigration Reform (SVAIR) was formed to allow organizations to continue working together (Castaneda 2010). SVAIR now meets on a monthly basis, has determined a shared purpose, and is building basic working principles and a common agenda for comprehensive immigration reform (Olvera 2010; Payne 2010). In short, the marches of 2006 set off a round of immigrant organizing and mobilizing that has continued to reverberate across generations and lines of difference in ways that connect directly with the collaborative, regionally oriented ethos that has defined Silicon Valley.

Immigrants and Enforcement

While the fight for comprehensive immigration reform has continued to preoccupy immigrant rights advocates, much of the local organizing that has emerged post-2006 has touched upon many of the issues that affect most San José residents—housing costs and foreclosure, health care coverage, and quality and cost of education. One issue that has also attracted significant attention is excessive use of force and arrest by police. Indeed, while SVAIR has immigration reform at its policy heart, it co-hosted a 2011 conference, "Immigration and Immigrants: Causes, Criminalization and Contributions," held at Santa Clara University.

Interactions with police are central to the immigrant experience—and not simply for those who are undocumented. These interactions provide many opportunities for cultural miscues between an older police force and emerging immigrant communities. Most areas in the United States have some history of tension between the police and local communities of color, creating an uncertain base for integration. San José is no exception—but in a way, this tension with police is an exception in a region in which immigrants have been generally welcomed and integrated in recent decades. Interviewees pointed to community-police relations as one of the biggest challenges and characterized the San José

Police Department (SJPD) as one key regional player that is out of sync with other local entities on the issue of immigrant integration.

The issues with the SJPD were described as not necessarily specific to the immigrant community, but rather more broadly concerning relations with communities of color. Nevertheless, immigrants in particular have been central to several controversial incidences of excessive use of force by the police in recent years. In 2003, a mentally ill Vietnamese woman who spoke limited English was shot and killed by an SJPD officer in her home, as he reportedly mistook her vegetable peeler for a cleaver. Then, in 2009, SJPD officers were called when a mentally ill twenty-seven-year-old Vietnamese man cut his brother's neck. When the man refused to drop his weapon, officers shot and killed him. Later that same year, SJPD was again accused of using excessive force when witnesses captured video footage of officers beating and using a Taser on a San José State University international student from Vietnam while he was lying face-down on the ground, unarmed (Jayadev 2009).

The SJPD has been criticized by the public for disproportionately setting up traffic stops in low-income, immigrant Latino neighborhoods. For those who cannot get a driver's license, often because of their immigration status, this can be a disaster: when stopped, they are likely to have their vehicle impounded. California law requires towing companies to hold impounded vehicles for thirty days under many circumstances, with the owner incurring a storage fee often exceeding $1,200. Accrued costs of losing one's means of transportation may also include interference with getting to work, loss of pay, and other difficulties. In response to activism from immigrant rights organizations and faith-based groups, in early 2011 the SJPD officially changed its policy of impounding cars of unlicensed drivers, allowing someone else to pick up the car (Webby 2010). The Human Relations Council also started exploring diversion programs to remove misdemeanors that can result from these offenses. One advocate explained that "this will benefit immigrants (especially if immigration reform happens); misdemeanors . . . will [likely] blow their chances at becoming citizens" (Olvera 2010). These issues, along with the findings that Latinos and African Americans were disproportionately overrepresented in the SJPD's arrests for public intoxication and resisting arrest, galvanized a broad base of community members calling for the police department to reform its practices (Webby 2008).

Some interviewees say the police department has been receptive to learning how to improve its practices, especially when dealing with those with mental health issues and language barriers. One council person commented that the "police department has been more responsive—partly because of community outcry, and partly because the city council is willing to look at actions of department and criticize practices" (Kalra 2010). In 2008, San José City

Council member Sam Liccardo and District Attorney Dolores Carr formed the County Task Force on Law Enforcement and Immigrant Community Relations, cochaired by the PACT organization, a local grassroots organizing effort. This body has also connected with direct service providers such as Catholic Charities, SIREN, and advocated for comprehensive immigration reform. As a result, the community secured commitments from the SJPD and the county sheriff's department to refrain from participating in non-mandated ICE activities and 287(g) agreements.

Concerned about the implications of linking ICE and local police, particularly with 287(g)'s evolution into the sweeping federal Secure Communities program, the county responded with a powerful refusal of ICE's local authority. Under the widely adopted Secure Communities, local police were supposed to submit to ICE, for a cross-check with federal immigration records, the fingerprints of any persons booked; ICE then could issue detainers to hold a person for immigration procedures if he or she was found in violation in the database. Santa Clara County, however, passed legislation asserting it would not honor detainers if the person was found not guilty, if the person was a juvenile, if the person did not commit a specific list of "serious" and "violent" felonies. Likewise, County Supervisor George Shirakawa, the head of the Public Safety and Justice Committee, pushed for an amendment to the legislation such that "ICE agents shall not be given access to individuals or be allowed to use County facilities for investigative interviews or other purposes, and County personnel shall not expend County time or resources responding to ICE inquiries or communicating with ICE regarding individuals' incarceration or release date" (Perez and Jayadev 2011). In other words, ICE was effectively shut out of interfering in law enforcement processes, to an extent not seen in any other U.S. county at the time.

Around this time, when significant questions were being raised about how to rebuild trust between law enforcement agencies and immigrant communities, the Santa Clara County District Attorney's Office announced it would now consider and attempt to minimize "collateral consequences"—in particular, possible deportation consequences for a minor conviction—when negotiating plea agreements (Jayadev and Cobarrubias 2011). A poll of county residents by the *Silicon Valley De-Bug* found that local residents highly supported such efforts to de-link immigration and law enforcement, reflecting the immigrant-oriented social and political climate. Eighty-eight percent of the over five hundred immigrants and nonimmigrants surveyed supported Santa Clara County's work to keep ICE out of the local jail systems, and eight out of ten respondents thought that policies like Secure Communities weaken trust between immigrants and law enforcement (Flores and Domingo 2013).

Worries about profiling and the targeting of immigrants—and people of color more broadly—also shaped the 2011 appointment of a new police chief, which received significant attention in the press and in diverse communities.[19] The Coalition for Justice and Accountability (CJA), a multiethnic community-based coalition, had been working on police accountability issues since 2003 and became a central voice in the process.[20] In 2011 the coalition released the results of a community input survey funded by the Santa Clara Community Foundation. The survey, which had been distributed in three languages and filled out by three thousand respondents, asked what kinds of skills were required of the next police chief, in order to develop a "clear and measureable profile" to be used for selection and evaluation. The city also sent out a similar survey to collect input on the appointment. The results of both emphasized the need to respect diverse communities, though the CJA report was much more explicit about what this means. The report stated that the chief "must acknowledge that there has been real (not just perceived) problems with racial profiling, use of force, and arresting practices with the San José Police Department, and has exampled both a history that points to his/her ability to deal with this reality and a commitment to work to eradicate these problems" (Coalition for Justice and Accountability 2011).

The resulting selection, Chris Moore, was hired from within the police force, making some advocates wary. But within weeks, Moore revised the racial profiling policy of the department to cover not just bias in terms of the initial stop but also to work against bias in treatment of anyone stopped (Hollyfield 2011). In 2011, Chief Moore expanded the definition of racial profiling to "allow for scrutiny during the entirety of police interactions, rather than just the initial stop" (Shore 2011). To enable all immigrants regardless of status to give feedback on policing, individuals could file complaints in Spanish to the city's Independent Police Auditors who came once a month to the Mexican consulate. The city's IPA never asked about immigration status.

Moore retired from his position after two short years, in 2013, primarily because of disputes around police funding with the city council. However, the new police chief, Larry Esquivel (another hire from within the department), further concretized these profiling policies. As of the end of 2013, San José police must record every instance where they stop and detain a person—whether it yields an arrest or not—and provide data on the identified race of the person stopped, and the reason, result, and type of stop. The latter is meant to track "curb-sitting" stops: community organizations in the region have documented the ways in which young men of color are frequently stopped and forced to sit on the pavement, handcuffed, in a policy along the lines of New York City's "stop and frisk" (Salonga 2013).

Thanks to the interactions and collaboration among local elected officials and different community groups, including neighborhood, faith-based, and advocacy organizations, local police have slowly aligned their policies with the broader regional focus on immigrant integration. Such pressures, exerted through different bodies spanning the public and community-based arenas, have led county-level law enforcement to break from national trends and dramatically limit the influence of ICE, with the city police slowly following suit to address long-standing grievances from immigrants and communities of color. Contrary to much research on the relationship between local police and immigrants in immigrant-destination cities, this policy innovation has not been led by the internal, bureaucratic leadership of the police department (Lewis and Rama-krishnan 2007). These changes, which extend to racial equity questions more broadly, in fact reflect the collaborative efforts of municipal officials and social justice organizations, which are pushing police to integrate more fully with the broader regional environment of immigrant rights.

Immigrant Organizations and Collaboration

While de Graauw, Gleeson, and Bloemraad (2013) rightly note that San José's ecosystem of local immigrant-serving organizations ranks below that of a more established gateway city like San Francisco in breadth, sophistication, and the normative belief that immigrants have a claim on city resources, this may provide an incentive for collaboration. In a reemerging gateway like San José, one community leader notes, "the immigrant community in the county is old enough to know that we need to work together, but young enough that we don't have political baggage that makes it harder to collaborate" (Castellanos 2010).

Collaborations focusing on immigrant issues usually involve a mix of immigrant service organizations and immigrant rights groups. For example, the Refugee and Immigrant Forum is a group of approximately thirty service providers that have been meeting monthly since 1994 as an informal way to exchange information and share resources. Its original purpose was to figure out how to avoid competing with one another for county funding, but it has since evolved into a setting where service providers can discuss issues affecting their respective communities and assist one another. It has been an important venue for engaging new immigrant and refugee communities, such as Iraqis and Afghans, who are not yet organized. The Eastern European Service Agency noted that through this forum, it has been able to develop a mentoring relationship with the African Community Health Institute. The Minority Senior Services Providers Consortium, which was started by the Japanese community organization Yu-Ai Kai, has also been recently transformed. The nine-member consortium is intended to provide language assistance for patients and hospitals. When there is a patient who does not speak English, the hospital can contact the consortium, and the consortium will dispatch the appropriate agency to go to the hospital to provide translation.

The API Justice Coalition, headed by Asian Americans for Community Involvement (AACI), started in 2006. The AACI joined with the Asian Law Alliance, the Asian Pacific Bar Association, and the Japanese American Citizens League of San José to form a network to connect API-focused organizations into a unified voice for advocacy in the Silicon Valley. According to a staff person, "We support issues that may not necessary just benefit one community—the coalition understands that we're all impacted" (Im 2010). Another interviewee observed that the "Muslim community better understands the value in coalition work, and building relationships with other immigrant communities that have essentially suffered through similar discriminatory targeting as the Muslim community is suffering now" (Qureshi 2010).

Despite the generally collaborative environment, there are sometimes divisions between and within immigrant groups. For example, immigration status can affect the degree and type of engagement on comprehensive immigration reform. Latino groups are often focused on the issues of legalization and immigration reform, while comprehensive immigration reform does not directly affect refugees from countries like Ethiopia and Somalia. High-tech professionals tend to be more focused on influencing H-1B visas. Generally, the Vietnamese are more interested in family visas. One interviewee said,

> Many [APIs] have a Social Security number if they came in a long time ago. Their concerns are that they cannot go back for funerals, can't take vacations outside of the country, and can't keep on losing jobs (even though they have a Social Security number, with more e-verify systems they have to show other kinds of identification). So that point of mobilization doesn't work with the API community. . . . All of the campaigns, organizing, and resources are so focused on mobilizing through family unity and stabilization of communities that it bypasses the middle- and upper-middle-class API community. (Pedigo 2010)

There are also divisions within immigrant groups, particularly in the broad and highly diverse category of "Asians." One interviewee noted that "from the outside, [mobilizing] looks united. The challenges come from bringing native-country politics here. For example, the Vietnamese are divided between those who identify with the Republic of Vietnam and those that were communist. With the Chinese there are divisions with the communists, the nationalist Taiwanese, and the pro-independence" (Chu 2010). In 2008 this kind of tension erupted in the highly controversial naming of a Vietnamese neighborhood. One faction of the community pushed to use the name "Little Saigon," suggesting that this would signal defiance to the Vietnamese government. The council member representing the area, Madison Nguyen, opted to support "Saigon Business District" because it was more politically neutral. Opponents then attempted to recall her from her post and still point to this decision years later.

Organizing efforts are often dominated or driven by a particular group or groups, although there are some important examples of cross-race or cross-ethnic collaboration. Police enforcement incidents spurred the Vietnamese and Latino communities to work together, and the International Children's Network (ICAN), an organization that was formed to help Vietnamese children, has a working relationship with Somos Mayfair, a group in the largely Latino neighborhood of Mayfair in San José. According to ICAN staff, they are "starting to see that they can leverage each other's voices and build power" (Vuong 2010). And Somos Mayfair reaches out to its Vietnamese neighbors through the Mexican tradition of *teatro*, using theater to bridge cultural communication and understanding. Most interviewees recognized the need for more cross-race, cross-ethnic, and cross-nationality organizing, and one even characterized it as the last organizing frontier.

Despite the generally positive picture of working together, it should be acknowledged that there are also differences in institutional strength and power. For example, while the Latino voice seems to be quite strong in the context of organizing, Gleeson and Bloemraad (2011) suggest that nonprofits primarily serving or rooted in the Mexican-origin community seem to be underrepresented compared with other groups. De Graauw, Gleeson, and Bloemraad (2013) also contend that immigrant organizations based in the city of San José receive far more institutional support from local authorities than do organizations based in local suburbs, something in keeping with the patterns suggested in other cases in this volume. Still, the spirit of collaboration that seems to have made the Valley as a whole famous seems to be characteristic of the immigrant ecosystem as well.

Does Regional Collaboration Matter?

If collaborative efforts to shape a region's character and promote its strengths have gained ground anywhere, it is in the Silicon Valley. The Valley is, after all, a perfect example of a regionally clustered industry—high tech—whose competitive strength relies on the relationships developed through social structures and institutions (Saxenian 1996). Indeed, as important as the celebrated entrepreneurs of Silicon Valley are, they have succeeded by learning from each other through informal communication, collaboration, and cross-firm learning practices (Benner 2003). In a parallel way, diverse immigrant groups are actively shaping the "constellation of resources," including organizations and networks, that define this regional cluster (Gleeson 2012).

Does this collaborative spirit among employers spill over to other concerns? Silicon Valley hosts two leading business groups: the Silicon Valley Leadership Group (SVLG; formerly the Silicon Valley Manufacturing Group) and the Joint Venture Silicon Valley Network (JVSVN). These regional entities have brought business leaders together to address issues critical to the region's vitality, including education, workforce development, economic development, and disaster preparedness. Founded in 1977 by David Packard, SVLG is the older of the two. Representing three hundred companies and priding itself on the region's "can-do" civic spirit, SVLG has developed a legislative and advocacy agenda dealing with workforce, housing, education, and federal policies like health care reform and loosening restrictions on H-1B visas.

The JVSVN was formed in the early 1990s as a response to economic challenges posed by defense spending cutbacks. Its vision—"to build a community collaborating to compete globally"—pretty much says it all (JV:SVN 1995, i–2). It has valued collaboration among firms and with governments as the basis for innovation and growth, seeking to point out how social capital, human capital, and venture capital can all go together. Each year, the JVSVN releases the Silicon Valley Index, an indicator project that attempts to suggest how the region is doing. The index reflects the view that flows of people and ideas have been essential ingredients to the region and that it needs to coordinate efforts to attract talent to keep Silicon Valley competitive in a changing global economy. The index profiles immigrants and frames them as a regional asset. The report tracks the migration of foreign talent into the region and notes that the growth of the Chinese and Indian national economies has slowed the flow of immigrants into the region. The 2010 report noted with concern that the percentage of the region's population that speaks a language other than English at home slightly declined, by 1 percent, in 2008 from the previous year, something that had not happened since 2004.[21] Needless to say, we would not expect such an unusual local reaction in Phoenix.

Part of the openness to immigrant integration may stem from the fact that that business leaders encounter immigrants in their everyday working lives. While immigrant business owners and entrepreneurs are in the local neighborhood markets and nail salons, they are also in the executive board rooms of the technology sector, with immigrant-run companies depending on ethnic resources while integrating into the mainstream economy (Saxenian 2002). Moreover, a significant share of the engineering talent is foreign-born, and the Silicon Valley companies, often engaged in outsourcing production and coding, rely on the links of immigrants to facilitate such connections.

Indeed, the ability of the immigrant professionals to integrate into the business community, while maintaining their identities and even making transnational connections, is testimony to the openness of the region. Immigrants themselves, particularly in the 1980s and 1990s, formed an array of ethnic professional associations (Saxenian 1999). Silicon Valley immigrant professionals certainly rely on their networks for entrepreneurial purposes, including support and connections, but the degree to which they apply them to civic engagement outside their business network is less clear (Saxenian 2002). One activist, for example, notes the relative silence of a large Indian professional association in the area, Talent, Ideas, Enterprise (TiE; formerly the Indus Entrepreneur) since the aftermath of September 11, 2001 (Jayadev 2001). On the other hand, TiE was a collaborative partner (along with many of the community groups mentioned in the chapter and other business groups like the Silicon Valley Chinese American Computer and Commerce Association) of the Silicon Valley Collaborative for Reform, a group that works to engage communities about the issue of reform.[22]

Meanwhile, the overall spirit of regionalism seems to have influenced other, nonbusiness sectors as well. Under the initial leadership of Amy Dean, the county's Central Labor Council formed Working Partnerships USA (WPUSA), a public policy and research institute focusing on labor issues. Since its founding in 1995, it took a regional view in research, advocacy, and power building, partly as an outgrowth of a "Union Cities" strategy that had been adopted by the AFL-CIO but also because the WPUSA leadership recognized that the Valley's regionalist landscape required such an approach and wanted to serve as a counterweight to business efforts such as Joint Venture Silicon Valley Network. In any case, the WPUSA has tackled broad issues of land use, economic restructuring, and health care, and built new ties between labor and community groups, becoming a model for a series of other regionally oriented labor efforts that have now come under the banner of the Partnership for Working Families (Dean and Reynolds 2009).

The WPUSA was instrumental in the framing and passage of the Children's Health Initiative, as already noted. It has also produced publications with solid messages about the importance of immigrants and their contributions to the economy; the WPUSA report titled *The Economic Effects of Immigration in Santa Clara County and California* helped set an early tone by arguing that immigrants had not taken away jobs and suggesting that, on the contrary, places with more immigrants have lower unemployment (Auerhahn and Brownstein 2004). The executive director of the WPUSA up to 2013 was Cindy Chavez, a former San José council member who spearheaded San José's Strong Neighborhoods Initiative, a collaborative effort between the city, the San José Redevelopment Agency, and twenty different communities (many with large immigrant populations) to facilitate a process to organize and figure out their top neighborhood priorities. As Chavez indicated in our interview with her, "From the regional Bay Area labor perspective, the leadership truly understands and sees that immigrants and immigrant rights are integrated with the future of the labor movement."

Some of the community-based organizations have reached beyond the local boundaries to influence regional and even state policies and programs. SIREN has grown into being the key immigrant rights organization in the region, and a state leader. It is one of five coordinating partners of Mobilize the Immigrant Vote, a statewide effort to build the capacity of community-based organizations to register, educate, and mobilize their constituents for electoral participation.[23]

Some Silicon Valley community leaders, including those from immigrant communities, also participated in the Social Equity Caucus, a Bay Area membership group that uses regional strategies to support a comprehensive movement-building approach in support of low-income people and people of color. And one of the premier local community development efforts in exactly the neighborhood where Chavez organized, now called Mayfair, has an unusual regionalist twist to its mission. It says about the neighborhood and its organization, Somos Mayfair, "We are generations of immigrants, rooted in a vibrant community, who nurture healthy families and speak out for justice in Silicon Valley. We are working toward the day when all people of Mayfair believe our barrio to be a place where beauty, power, and dignity flourish and Mayfair is extensively connected to the region, valued for our contributions to society and engaged with the broader movement for justice."[24]

But just because many different sectors think regionally does not mean they all get along. In fact, one reason why labor "went regional" was to tackle the growing voice of business at that level. One interviewee characterized business support of immigrants as piecemeal: "On an individual basis, companies may have some support and some recognition of immigrants, but they are not invested in immigrant integration. Maybe they offered some ESL or [have] done some work on H-1B visas, but my sense is that they don't have a plan for it" (Castellanos 2010). But while the degree of business commitment can be debated, business clearly prides itself in being collaborative, and values its diverse workforce, setting a more positive overall tone than in other areas. And this regionalist tone is characteristic of other sectors as well.

Dionne Warwick's famous song—with melody by Burt Bacharach and lyrics by Hal David—asked "Do you know the way to San José?" Surely, many people interested in immigrant integration would like to know the secret behind the way *of* San José: few regions have experienced such a dramatic increase in the share of the foreign-born and done it with such minor conflict and with what appears to be a fairly happy ending. The process is not over, of course, but rather ongoing. In 2015, the City of San José finally followed the lead of Santa Clara County and institutionalized its approach to immigrant integration by establishing an Office of Immigrant Affairs, the third such office in California (the other two are in Los Angeles and San Francisco) (CBS SF Bay Area 2015; Rosenberg 2015). Community-police tension has been an issue, and surely other conflicts will arise in the years ahead. But while one might not want to paint San José as a completely untroubled location, the region's relative openness to immigrants is striking.

Some of the reasons for that receptivity are unique, but others offer lessons that might be transportable to other regions. The first is simply the diversity of the immigrants in the region: they range from undocumented and low-skill to properly visaed, highly educated, and bearers of venture capital. With the image of immigrants not simply that of the "huddled masses"—in this version, day laborers huddled in front of Home Depot looking for work—it has been much harder to racialize immigrants or define them as "other." What is also striking is that higher-skill immigrants have not simply tried to peal themselves off from the others and portray themselves as the deserving immigrants. So diversity counts—but so does the relative solidarity.

A second driving factor is the high level of voting power of immigrant citizens and immigrant-friendly voters. Politicians have found it to their advantage to appeal to the population, and political figures who might elsewhere find it advantageous to tap into anti-immigrant sentiment have not found enough voters with nativist feelings to make it worth their while. Still, the relative lack of resentment among white voters is striking, and it may be due to ongoing interethnic contacts in the workplace documented by studies of social capital in the Valley.

A third factor is the relative strength and flexibility of the immigrant-rights and immigrant-serving organizations. A bit less focused after the struggle against Proposition 187, these organizations really hit their stride in joining efforts with the local public sector to protect immigrants from the worst of the welfare-reform efforts of the late 1990s. This helped strengthen the immigrant service organizations, and their reaction against the harsh congressional bills in the mid-2000s further strengthened these organizing groups.

A fourth factor is the nature of the region itself. It is a place where intentional regionalism—efforts to develop a regional identity, promote the region, and coordinate efforts across sectors—has struck a real chord. Many analysts contend that the secret of the Silicon Valley is to have its highly competitive firms also accept that they need to share information, create porous relationships between firms, and pursue collective action for securing the necessary infrastructure.

Regionalist business organizations have taken deep root, and so have their labor and community counterparts. The region has a holistic identity and prides itself on being a crossroads of ideas, people, and investments. As such, it is less prone to nativism and isolation, if only because that works against its self-conception (as it did in Charlotte in an earlier era). In this fertile soil, immigrant integration has thrived.

Where else can one find a business organization that bemoans the lack of households speaking languages other than English? Labor working with small-business owners of immigrant origin? A Latino resident theater troupe performing a piece on biculturalism to a Vietnamese audience? Elected officials openly talking about their commitment to the immigrant community? County government crafting programming with immigrants in mind—and standing up directly to overreaching immigration enforcement? Even controversial issues, like police brutality and racial profiling, have resulted in ongoing dialogues between local leaders and residents to change leadership and practices.

San José is not without its difficulties. Opinions differ, and a host of problems confront residents, such as the high cost of housing. But one does not see the overt tensions, discrimination, and racial opportunism that is often present in other places. In a world in which immigrant issues are hotly and sometimes stupidly debated, Silicon Valley stands out for its regional approach to the challenge of immigration, the same perspective it applies to business development or land-use planning. It searches for solutions rather than places to lay blame, for collaboration rather than conflict. And there are lessons here for other regions that are seeking resilience and integration.

10

SYNTHESIZING THE RESEARCH
Themes, Challenges, and Opportunities

Manuel Pastor and John Mollenkopf

On November 11, 2010, a group of business, faith, civic, and immigrant leaders in Salt Lake City unveiled the "Utah Compact," an agreement to foster a more civil conversation about immigration issues in one of America's most Republican states. The compact, a valuable guide to discussing comprehensive immigration reform at a national level, recognized that immigrants make important economic contributions to the local economy; stressed that local law enforcement should focus on criminal activity, not civil violations of immigration law; emphasized the importance of supporting families, not breaking them up through enforcement; and argued that "Utah should always be a place that welcomes people of good will" (quoted in *New York Times* 2010).

It is hard to find a more dramatic and unexpected instance of a region working together to provide a warm welcome for immigrants. The fact that it emerged in Utah, one of the most Republican states in the union, with the chamber of commerce leading the effort—may at first seem surprising. But it actually squares well with many of the themes of our case studies. After all, while immigration is a relatively new phenomenon for Salt Lake City, the immigrant population there has not risen as fast as in, say, Arizona. It is also a slightly more diverse immigrant population than in Arizona, partly reflecting the work that Utah's Mormon population has been doing all over the world and the connections that have resulted. And while some local politicians in Utah have tried to mobilize sentiments against the new immigrants, other political actors, including the Church of Jesus Christ of Latter-day Saints, have overwhelmed them. Part of the reason: there is a strong sense of regional consciousness as evidenced by Envision Utah, a multi-jurisdictional private-public partnership that has been considered a model of metropolitan planning (Scheer 2012).

The example illustrates three things that we hope readers will take from the evidence provided in this volume. The first is simply to understand that there is an important *metropolitan* dimension to the challenge of immigrant integration and that it is changing as more immigrants flow into suburban areas. The foreign-born now live increasingly outside the metropolitan core, in areas with far less experience with immigrant communities, and sometimes far less acceptance of them. This leads us to conclude that immigrant-serving and advocacy organizations, usually based in the central city, must find ways to work beyond their normal borders.

The second takeaway is to recognize that metropolitan actors vary to a considerable degree in terms of whether they react negatively toward immigrants or seek to make immigrant integration work for them. This reflects in turn the complex interaction between economic, demographic, and political factors. Most conducive to a warm reception is a good fit between the skill and occupation mix and ethnic makeup of the immigrant population and the labor market and demographic contexts they are entering. So social-structural factors do matter greatly.

But our last observation and key takeaway is that, at the end of the day, political leaders and political deliberation determine the tenor of the overall reaction. Participants in this deliberation include the business community, civic leadership, elected officials, public-service providers, law enforcement, labor unions, the infrastructure of nonprofit organizations, and grassroots activists. Contextual factors do not determine the outcome; instead, they prepare the ground for the ways in which these metropolitan actors decide how to respond (or not) to the challenges and opportunities rendered by demographic change. In some of our cases, conservative populist political "entrepreneurs"—that is, individuals seeking to maximize political gain by playing to an eager crowd—took the initiative to mobilize public sentiment against immigrants. In others, growing immigrant electoral strength and a broad network of immigrant advocacy organizations provided political entrepreneurs on the progressive side of the equation with the motivation to push immigrant-friendly policies.

An America destined for more such changes in the immediate future will need both more understanding and more action—and we hope this volume contributes to both. In this concluding chapter, we briefly revisit these main themes, as well as the broad hypotheses about regional receptivity posited in the introductory chapter. We offer brief synopses of what we learned from each of our cases, summarizing some of the major threads of analysis and highlighting their implications for good policy and best practice at the federal, state, and metropolitan levels. We conclude the chapter—and the book—by returning to some of the implications for theory and research, particularly on ways to link the literatures on the new regionalism (particularly, regional governance) and immigrant integration more effectively.

Reviewing the Cases

This volume traverses the country from New York to Los Angeles via Chicago and from Charlotte to Silicon Valley via Phoenix and the Inland Empire. Our authors have advanced somewhat varied perspectives on these cases—although, as the introduction notes, we took some care to ensure they asked similar questions and used the same analytical prisms to consider and assess immigrant integration in these various locales. That said, here we offer our own take on what themes unify these cases and how we understand their implications for policy and research. We begin by reviewing the three traditional immigrant-receiving areas.

New York

In New York, Els de Graauw, Diana Gordon, and John Mollenkopf analyzed the contrasting dynamics in the region's central city and easternmost end, Suffolk County on Long Island. Reflecting New York City's long history as a major entry point for migration to the United States, it has become politically obligatory in the city to celebrate virtually every aspect of the immigrant experience. Despite this, the city bureaucracy does not always readily adapt to the needs of immigrants without organized efforts by those communities and their advocates, and New York City may well have the deepest and widest array of immigrant service and advocacy organizations of any place in the United States. These nonprofit advocates took up the issue of language access to public services for immigrant residents in New York City, and in 2003—following a five-year campaign effort—the city adopted a law to provide free interpretation regardless of language spoken at the agency that administers food stamps, Medicaid, and welfare benefits, and translated key government forms into six other languages (de Graauw 2015). Partly as a result of the strong immigrant-serving infrastructure, former mayor Michael Bloomberg directed city employees to not inquire about the documentation status of people with whom they were interacting and reaffirmed that undocumented immigrants were entitled to receive services (in stark contrast to Arizona SB 1070). Another example: by May 2009, thirty-nine agencies had filed language access improvement plans with the Office of Operations at an estimated cost of $27 million—improving accessibility to clients with limited

English proficiency across the city. Finally, Bloomberg's successor, Mayor Bill de Blasio, joined the new progressive majority on the city council to resist involvement with ICE in the city jails and adopt a new municipal ID card to provide documentation for all city residents, including those without federal authorization.

Sixty miles east of the city lies Suffolk County, but it is a world away in terms of receptivity. Given both its ongoing agricultural activities (shifting from potatoes to wine grapes) and the continual growth of its second-home and vacation sectors, it has been a magnet for low-skilled workers serving predominantly middle- to upper-middle-class landowners and builders. These market forces rapidly drew immigrant workers, with the number of foreign-born more than doubling since 1980. For a time, the former county executive and county legislators backed anti-immigrant local laws, including an attempt in 2004 (not passed) to deputize Suffolk County police to be immigration agents, and a requirement that county contractors demonstrate the legal status of their employees (passed). Several anti-immigrant hate groups emerged in the county, and a number of high-profile hate crimes took place on the island. In response, immigrant advocacy organizations founded the Long Island Immigrant Alliance (LIIA), an umbrella organization of nonprofit, social justice, labor, and religious organizations, some of which have connections with New York City.

Of course, the New York metro area is far more complicated than the contrast between the city and just Suffolk County might suggest. For example, the village of Port Chester in Westchester County has become an increasingly diverse microcosm, with the emergence of Latino political leaders, while South and East Asian communities have emerged in northeastern New Jersey. But the contrast illustrates our themes. The urban core celebrates its past and contemporary immigrant heritages—in part because the diverse groups that have settled in the city are becoming increasingly prominent parts of its electorate. The fact that they range from low-skilled workers, sometimes undocumented, to highly accomplished professionals means both that immigrants themselves need to form coalitions across national origin groups *and* that they are harder to racialize. By contrast, Suffolk County lacked the rich immigrant history, and the influx was disproportionately made up of low-skilled workers from Latin America. A former county executive saw the opportunity to stir up emotions, and the spark of opportunism met a tinder set by these structural factors. Yet partly because of the strong pro-immigrant focus in the central city and outreach by city-based philanthropies, nonprofits, and unions, and partly because of local leadership, these sparks did not ignite a fire.

Leadership thus matters. The city retains its current leadership role. Former mayor Bloomberg organized and serves as a cochair for the Partnership for a New American Economy, a coalition of mayors and business leaders pressing for national immigration reform. Current mayor Bill de Blasio has strongly advocated pro-immigrant measures and has joined with the mayors of LA and Chicago to promote support for President Obama's executive actions. After superstorm Sandy battered the East Coast in the fall of 2012, the new Suffolk County executive, prompted partly by the need to make emergency services more effective but also by rising pressures from immigrant rights activists, issued an order mandating translation support in county government offices (Altshuler and Oshiro 2012). Policy change in Suffolk County—one of the few suburban counties in the country to have such a translation provision—came about partly because of work initiated by immigrant rights groups based in the city, showing how suburban locales are sometimes dependent on services and organizing imported from areas with deeper experience with receiving immigrants. Owing to history, demographics, and politics, the New York metropolitan region is strongly receptive to immigrants, despite a political fragmentation that has sometimes allowed for the flowering of anti-immigrant sentiments in particular pockets of the region.

Chicago

Though it was, like New York, a major immigrant destination between 1880 and 1920, the Chicago metropolitan area newly reemerged as the locus of a large immigrant influx over the last decade. As chapter 2 indicated, more than one-third of the Chicago area's immigrants are of Mexican descent, many from the state of Oaxaca. Many immigrants have also moved to surrounding Lake, Will, McHenry, and DuPage Counties. As in other metropolitan peripheries, native-born suburban residents have been startled by the rapidity of the increase—but the suburban share of recent immigrants remains lower in the metro Chicago population than in New York or LA, or even San José or the Inland Empire. Moreover, Chicago's long and proud history of European immigration has helped to deracialize the contemporary immigration issue.

Indeed, the much-vaunted Democratic machine in the core city of Chicago has responded by accommodating immigrant populations, in part because it wanted to rely on the growing Latino voter base as an electoral bulwark against any potential African American challenge. (The share of immigrant-origin voters, however, is significantly smaller than in New York, LA, or even San José.) The city's mayor since 2011, Rahm Emanuel, has backed comprehensive immigration reform, although this is a policy that he argued to postpone when he was White House chief of staff in the Obama administration. City officials have cooperated with nonprofit organizations on health, education, and literacy initiatives, and immigrant advocacy organizations have built multiethnic coalitions. In 2010, the Chicago-based Illinois Immigrant Rights Coalition won the prestigious E Pluribus Unum Prize from the Migration Policy Institute for its work with the State of Illinois to implement an Immigrant Family Resource Program that reduces the barriers faced by low-income immigrants and their children when seeking public benefits and services; this effort is a model for cooperation between state agencies and the region's immigrant-serving organizations. The coalition also made inroads into suburban politics by pointing out to civic leaders that immigrants are a growing presence and a potential swing voting bloc.

Still, politics appears to be more of a factor behind Chicago's relatively supportive approach to immigrant issues than pressure from social movements, as is the case in Los Angeles, or the network of immigrant advocacy organizations, as in New York. In his chapter, Jaime Dominguez charts the rise of Latino influence within the Democratic machine, arguing that Mayor Richard M. Daley modernized that organization by incorporating Latino voters, partly as a way to offset challenges from black or white liberal independents (see also Simpson and Kelly 2011). While this led political figures to frame relevant policy issues in a generally pro-immigrant way, it also suggests that Mayor Emanuel and his supporters hope that any future increases in Latino empowerment will be accomplished through the machine, not by challenging the political establishment. The emergence of a strong Latino challenger in the 2015 mayoral election put that at risk, but perhaps led Emanuel to redouble his efforts to incorporate Latino constituencies, pushed by some new city council members. In any case, the broad political dynamic of incorporation has paved the way for immigrant-friendly policies, including at the state level. (In this respect, the influence of the Cook County Democratic Party on state politics, at least until the recent election of a Republican governor, provided a vector by which Chicago's immigrant advocates could multiply their impact.)

As in many other metro areas, the influence of the city's Democratic machine has been less evident in the suburban periphery, despite Chicago's role in creating a Metropolitan Mayors Caucus, which in turn established a diversity task force to survey immigrant integration practices in suburban jurisdictions. In the face of broadening migration, some suburban jurisdictions adopted local strategies to enforce immigration law, and others have threatened to cut bilingual education and English as a second language (ESL) classes that serve immigrant students.

At the same time, after a period of adjustment, other suburbs have responded in a more supportive manner. Under the New Americans Initiative, the village of Melrose Park lobbied the state government in 2007 to establish the first "welcoming center" to connect recently arrived immigrants to important human, educational, and employment services. Since 2005, the town of Cicero has set several programs in motion to create a hospitable environment for its immigrants, including a popular Department of Community Affairs and Special Projects initiative to assist Spanish-speaking business owners, many of them legal immigrants, with translation on procedures and regulations for becoming licensed. Stone Park responded to its growing Latino immigrant population with community events and festivals in local schools, cultural competency training for municipal employees who provide services for immigrants, conflict resolution, and training (a financial literacy course and ESL) for immigrant parents.

The Chicago Democratic machine's control over Cook County has thus dampened (but not eliminated) the negative response of natives to new immigrants in the suburbs. Chicago also seems to differ from New York and Los Angeles in being better able to coordinate certain civic actions across jurisdictions. Here lies the intersection with the new regionalism we highlighted in the Utah example that began this chapter: Chicago Metropolis 2020, a business-led group, has addressed regional issues of affordable housing, and former mayor Daley made a consistent effort to meet with his suburban counterparts on issues of concern. Despite some attention from the Regional Plan Association in New York, that region lacks a comparable corporate regionalism, while it is entirely absent from Greater Los Angeles. Although the topic of immigrant integration has not been the most prominent theme in these regional approaches, strong regional visioning activities may have some positive spillover for immigrants, a point driven home in the Silicon Valley case.

Los Angeles

Though Los Angeles also has a large and firmly established immigrant presence, we have noted that the foreign-born share of the city's population is now declining, with the second and third generations now driving the growth of the immigrant-origin population. This maturing of the immigrant population represents the melding of immigrants into the native-born population and provides a sufficiently large political base that elected officials are open to immigrant concerns. However, the Los Angeles region is, in some ways, an "underperformer." Given its long and large immigrant presence, one might expect stronger immigrant integration institutions, policies, and attitudes.

To explore both the general regional response and the variation within the region, Manuel Pastor, Juan De Lara, and Rachel Rosner focused on two iconic parts of metropolitan Los Angeles (from an immigrant integration point of view): the city of Los Angeles and the small, dense, heavily Hispanic municipality of Maywood in Los Angeles County, east of the city. They argue that "movements matter" in Los Angeles—that is, that grassroots immigrant organizations are not only shaped by but also actively reshape the political context, particularly through their participation in the region's progressive multiracial movements that have produced tangible changes in labor, education, policing, and other policy areas that directly concern the needs of immigrant communities.

The turnaround to being a more sympathetic region is striking: Los Angeles has a long history of tense and at times exclusionary immigrant politics targeting the region's Latin American and Asian immigrants and longtime residents— from serving as the epicenter of deportation of Mexican immigrants and residents in the 1930s to becoming a central focus of the proponents of the anti-immigrant Proposition 187 in 1994. But in 2005, Antonio Villaraigosa won office as the first Mexican American mayor of the modern era (Sonenshein and Pinkus 2005). The son of an immigrant father and a U.S.-born mother, former mayor Villaraigosa forged a broad coalition of Latino, African American, and white liberal supporters—and he often led on immigration issues, not only welcoming immigrant marchers at City Hall, but also pushing for federal reform of the immigration system.

Villaraigosa's successor, Mayor Eric Garcetti, had one grandfather born in Mexico (himself the child of an Italian immigrant to Mexico), and a grandmother born in Arizona of Mexican descent on one side of his family, while his maternal grandfather on the other side was a Jewish immigrant from Russia. Along with New York's Mayor de Blasio, Garcetti has organized a group of thirty mayors, including Chicago's Rahm Emanuel, to file an amicus brief defending President Obama's executive action on immigration reform. Los Angeles has also elected numerous other city-level—and more recently, county and state—representatives with social-movement backgrounds who consider immigrant integration part of their charge, whether they are from immigrant communities or not.

Because of its large immigrant-origin population, that population's importance in the electorate, and the political coalitions that have provided majorities for elected officials sympathetic to immigrants, the city of Los Angeles has shifted to incorporate the concerns of immigrant communities. For example, recent Los Angeles Police Department (LAPD) chiefs have adamantly defended Special Order 40—originally passed in 1979, directing officers not to determine immigration status in the course of routine stops—against recent attacks. In 2011, the LAPD reformed its towing policies to allow undocumented drivers stopped in the course of a routine checkpoint to have someone with a driver's license come to pick up the car rather than have it hauled to a storage yard.

We can attribute these political shifts partly to the region's demographic changes. Immigrants arrived all through the post–World War II period, but flows were especially significant in the 1970s and 1980s, transforming Los Angeles into a majority-minority city by 1987. But consistent pressure from social movement and immigrant rights organizations working in broader coalition and keeping an eye on curbing regional inequalities gave these changes a progressive character. Los Angeles hosts a broad range of nationally known, politically independent immigrant advocacy organizations, such as the Coalition for Humane Immigrant Rights in Los Angeles, the Koreatown Immigrant Workers Association, the National Association of Latino Elected Officials, the National Day Labor Organizing Network, and the Mexican American Legal Defense and Education Fund, all of which have access to local and national decision makers and influence their decisions. These immigrant advocacy organizations have engaged in grassroots organizing, base building and leadership development, and forming cross-cutting alliances with other progressive movement builders. This strategy has made the needs of immigrant communities inextricable from broader policy conversations. For example, the needs of immigrant workers were articulated and central in recent (and successful) organizing efforts to raise the city's minimum wage to fifteen dollars per hour. Some of this change is now scaling up to the state level, leading to the replication of Los Angeles's altered DUI checkpoint policies, driver's licenses for undocumented immigrants, and statewide pro-immigrant policies.

At the same time, advocates criticize the city administration for being less systematic in its efforts than other locales with far smaller immigrant populations. For example, previous mayor James Hahn originated an Office of Immigrant Affairs, but it foundered over the past few years of the Villaraigosa administration; it was eventually rebooted in 2013 by Mayor Garcetti. Why the institutional wane under Villaraigosa? Political concerns may have been part of the problem. While one of Villaraigosa's first acts was to welcome over half a million immigrants as they marched on City Hall in 2006 to protest anti-immigrant legislation in Congress, some of his advisers cautioned him to be more restrained in promoting immigrant causes, lest he be seen as simply defending the interests of his own ethnic group.[1] White mayors like Michael Bloomberg or Bill de Blasio in New York and Richard M. Daley and Rahm Emanuel in Chicago did not face such pressures. Villaraigosa, however, did take a leadership position in the campaign to boycott Arizona over its 2010 adoption of Senate Bill 1070. Less ethnically pigeonholed than Villaraigosa, Garcetti (boasting Mexican, Italian, and Jewish heritage) has had more latitude to act—and has led in numerous ways.

As in New York, conditions vary considerably outside the central city. One of the five members of the powerful Los Angeles County Board of Supervisors has expressed significant concerns about undocumented immigrants and what he contends is the overuse of welfare and health services by their children.

The Los Angeles County Sheriff's Department maintained a so-called 287(g) agreement with the federal Immigration and Customs Enforcement (ICE) agency that allowed local law enforcement officers, during their normal duties, to identify and detain undocumented residents for handoff to ICE—until a newly elected group of supervisors voted to end this in May 2015. The Council on Immigrant Integration, a private-sector effort, has been working for a more uniform, welcoming approach. Hosted by a local community foundation, it seeks to bring civic actors together who are not necessarily in the forefront of the immigration struggle. Still, this effort is mostly city-based, reflecting the geographic variance within the metropolitan area.

Politics at the region's geographic extremes, however, do not simply run toward restrictionism. Pastor, De Lara, and Rosner's chapter also reviews the case of Maywood, a small town of about forty-five thousand people within LA County to the southeast of the city. Almost entirely Latino, with many undocumented immigrants, Maywood declared itself a sanctuary city in 2006, and its elected leadership went as far as eliminating its police department's traffic division for allegedly targeting undocumented drivers. Maywood's political leadership has embraced a range of immigrant integration policies, and while municipal advocates wish to use their platform to develop an immigrant-based political movement in southeast Los Angeles County, anti-immigrant activists have in response made Maywood a target for their activities. Still, the situation of Maywood suggests a particular feature of the Los Angeles landscape that the authors of this chapter stress: the way in which social movements can craft zones of opportunity through a concerted, coalition-based grassroots effort that takes the needs of immigrant communities seriously.

In any case, the long-standing immigrant population in the urban core, led by mayors and local elected representatives, has provided a climate in which public-sector and private-sector leaders push pro-immigrant measures in the most visible part of the region. This may be as much effect as cause, however, because the remarkable flowering of social movement organizing in contemporary Los Angeles moves them to take such positions. However, Los Angeles may still be an "underperformer," because local governments have lagged somewhat in translating these dispositions into the kinds of durable institutional changes that have taken place in New York and Chicago.

Inland Empire

Directly to the east of Los Angeles lies the Inland Empire—the combination of Riverside and San Bernardino Counties. Given traffic congestion, it is practically a different world—but the difference goes beyond the length of the drive.

The Inland Empire saw a dramatic increase in the foreign-born only in relatively recent times, between 1970 and now. This was driven by the same forces that led to its housing bubble: the area was and is the cheapest housing market in Southern California and therefore a good place to gain a stake in the American dream. Two in five of the area's residents are immigrants or children of immigrants. But distance does matter: this exurban housing market was the first to see its prices falling during the Great Recession, stripping assets from owners with the most modest grasp of middle-class life, many from immigrant backgrounds.

It is perhaps not surprising that this region has historically given immigrants a lukewarm reception. Immigrants and their children make up a smaller proportion of the electorate here as compared to Los Angeles (less than 30 percent, compared to half). The Inland Empire has long leaned in a politically conservative direction, with the native white electoral majority perhaps increasingly worried that it might decline into minority status. Local politicians have supported the repeal of citizenship for the U.S.-born children of undocumented immigrants. Prominent leaders of the Minuteman Project and assorted white supremacist movements also live there. This climate makes it difficult for elected officials to show sympathy for pro-immigrant policies and puts immigrant advocacy organizations on the defensive.

As Juan De Lara points out in his chapter, conservative opponents of immigrants describe them in highly racialized terms, seeing virtually all immigrants as Latinos. Along with recency of arrival, this reaction reinforces a poorer reception—and the area is also politically fragmented and lacks a clear regional business class. However, the Inland Empire also illustrates another important dimension of the story: that a more receptive nearby metro area can influence an adjacent less-welcoming metro region.

As we have noted, the strong social justice and social movement infrastructure of Los Angeles has not generally extended to its suburbs and exurbs, and even less so in the case of the Inland Empire as compared with analogous situations in metropolitan New York and Chicago. Some LA-based organizations do work within the rest of Los Angeles County, but few have ventured as far eastward as the Inland Empire. Recently, however, churches, labor unions, and community organizations have begun to test an immigrant rights agenda there, but these efforts are only fledgling, so receptivity suffers. On the other hand, the political winds may be shifting within the area, with a rising Latino Democratic vote that may ultimately change the region's willingness to prepare itself for immigrant integration, particularly through shifts in law enforcement and enhanced investments in education.

Charlotte

Shifting our focus to the East Coast, we find that the Charlotte metropolitan region has been less receptive to immigrants than has San José, but much more so than Phoenix. As we will see in a moment for San José, Charlotte's regional business leadership thinks of itself as building a model regional metropolis (though in a more politically conservative mode). Their aspiration—mostly achieved—is to make Charlotte the financial and logistics capital of the South. This has led them to see themselves as—and to convince others that they are—a "New South" location that acknowledges tolerance and diversity as key values. But day-to-day politics has not always played out in this manner, perhaps in part because Charlotte is the newest immigrant destination for the regions we consider, and immigrants and their children make up the smallest part of the metro area's electorate (at only around 6 percent) of any of our cases.

This newness and political and social marginality have made it easy for some local conservative political entrepreneurs to flip the switch from being relatively welcoming to more hostile. A significant portion of the recent economic and demographic transformation occurred when Pat McCrory, a Republican, served as mayor from 1995 through 2009. During this period, key public agencies, such as the schools, worked to adjust to the influx of non-English-speaking immigrants, providing immigrants with a modicum of "bureaucratic incorporation." Then (and to a considerable extent today), local civic elites were concerned about an "institutional mismatch" between the needs of the immigrant community and the services provided by public and nonprofit organizations. Immigrant organizations were in their infancy, and immigrant political representation had yet to emerge. Indeed, local service providers have been trying to manage increased demands from new immigrant clients, while forestalling negative reactions from native-born white and black residents. A 2007 immigration report commissioned by the former mayor adopted a schizophrenic tone, veering from suspicion of the legitimacy of new arrivals to a bureaucratic accounting of the services that the city and county provided them.

The reception may have chilled since 2006, partly because of rapid growth of the immigrant population and early signs of its civic political mobilization (Deaton 2008; Furuseth and Smith 2010). Indeed, in 2006, the Mecklenburg County Sheriff's Department became one of the country's first to train deputies under the 287(g) program. And former mayor McCrory raised concerns about illegal immigration in his 2008 campaign for governor of North Carolina (which he lost). After his subsequent victory in 2012, he shifted even further to the right, pushing for state policies that triggered weekly protests that are now called

"Moral Mondays." Under his leadership, North Carolina joined a lawsuit to challenge President Obama's November 2014 executive action to defer deportation of many undocumented immigrants.

While North Carolina as a whole may be headed in a less immigrant-friendly direction, Charlotte remains relatively welcoming, particularly given the recency and rapidity of the growth of its immigrant population. Business leadership may well account for this, as Michael Jones-Correa explains in his chapter. Observers of the city's transformation into a banking center describe how a "tight-knit, private-sector, philanthropic, economic growth machine" oversaw the transformation from textile and furniture manufacturing to banking and logistics and drove downtown development. As Furuseth and Smith note, "The Charlotte-Mecklenburg corporate community displayed little interest in targeting undocumented immigrants or designing strategies to punish or remove them from the area" (2010, 186). Jones-Correa underlines how that leadership, even after being battered by the 2008 financial crisis, still sees a need for immigrant workers and wishes Charlotte to be a model of the tolerant New South. While some local politicians may still want to whip up anti-immigrant sentiment to advance their careers, at least they cannot enlist Charlotte's business leaders in their efforts.

Phoenix

Few such restraining forces have been operative in metropolitan Phoenix. Surprisingly, given the area's adjacency to Mexico, immigration to Phoenix has been relatively recent. Partly as a result, Phoenix stands near the top of the nation's large metro areas in terms of the demographic divergence between older native-born residents and younger immigrant (and noncitizen) residents. This gap has helped to fuel native-Anglo angst. Non-Hispanic white residents tend to equate "immigrant" with "Mexican" and specifically "illegal immigrant." Undocumented Mexicans do indeed dominate the recently arrived foreign-born population, stemming partly from successful federal efforts to fortify the California and Texas borders in the late 1990s. This pushed unauthorized entry routes toward Arizona and made Phoenix a flashpoint for frustrations about border control. Unauthorized immigrants tend to keep a low profile, but many Phoenix residents are aware of black-market activities related to human smuggling taking place in the city's neighborhoods, as well as the high levels of crime and violence across the Mexican border.

As it turns out, there is significant variation within the Phoenix metropolitan region, despite the fact that the metro area is far less fragmented than the other study regions. The City of Phoenix occupies 517 square miles and holds 40 percent of Maricopa County's population, and it shares the metropolitan area with only twenty-five other municipalities. While this political geography is less complex than that of the other regions, Phoenix coexists alongside, and can be at loggerheads with, the cities of Chandler, Gilbert, Glendale, Mesa, and Scottsdale, all of which have more than two hundred thousand residents. And while Phoenix leans Democratic, the rest of Maricopa County and the state of Arizona are Republican bastions. Phoenix thus cannot easily dominate Maricopa County, much less Arizona. Rather than leading the region as Chicago leads Cook County or even Los Angeles leads LA County, Phoenix tends to be more isolated.

This larger regional and state context has contained immigrant advocacy within Phoenix itself. The heavily Republican Arizona legislature's passage of SB 1070 sparked national controversy and a backlash against Arizona and Phoenix in many other parts of the country. While supporters of SB 1070 deny that it has fostered racial profiling, a federal district court ruling found that Maricopa County sheriff Joe Arpaio's implementation of the law "violated the constitutional rights of Latinos by targeting them during raids and traffic stops" (Santos 2013). Indeed, the state seems to have embraced a "policy of attrition" in which it seeks to reduce the unauthorized population by ratcheting up local enforcement (Krikorian 2005).

Few organizations have attempted to build bridges between natives and immigrants or form coalitions in support of immigrant integration in metropolitan Phoenix, and advocacy organizations, service providers, and Latino elected officials have often found themselves on the defensive in the face of overwhelming popular hostility to unauthorized immigration, even in the relatively friendly environs of the central city.

Phoenix has significant factors that we argue limit receptivity. Its new immigrants are highly negatively racialized, the immigrant community is new and rapidly growing, and many recent immigrants are undocumented. The immigrant share of the vote in the city and region remains small, less than 15 percent. As noted, the demographic distance between the new younger immigrants and the older native-born population in the region is among the highest in the country. As Doris Marie Provine and Paul Lewis note in their chapter, many local elected officials who operate outside the city, especially Sheriff Arpaio, have sought to build their careers by tapping into the anxieties that these conditions create among the voters. In contrast to the situation in San José and to a lesser degree Charlotte, business and civic leadership in Phoenix has been less well organized and less willing to condemn anti-immigrant sentiments as detrimental to the region's broader economic and social interests. However, when the pendulum swung a bit too far, sixty business leaders did sign a letter in March 2011 arguing that Arizona's anti-immigrant legislation was hurting the state economically; this provided cover for state lawmakers to table a new set of anti-immigrant laws.

This general political vacuum has created an environment in which the Phoenix police and the county sheriff have bickered over the enforcement of immigrant policy, and local politicians continue to capitalize on public anxieties. It remains to be seen what all this will mean if a program of legalization (or temporary status such as in the 2014 executive order) emerges; Phoenix would have a great deal to gain economically and socially by authorization of its large undocumented population, but it may not have the civic infrastructure to do this well or effectively. Taken together, these factors lead to Phoenix being the least receptive toward immigrant integration of the regions studied.

San José

Although large-scale immigration is also relatively new to the San José metropolitan region, it offers a case that is the polar opposite to Phoenix. Attention to its immigrants has become an established part of the region's civic fabric. The region stretches from Palo Alto on its northwestern corner down through the Silicon Valley nodes of Mountain View, Sunnyvale, and Cupertino, through the city of San José to the agricultural districts of Morgan Hill and Gilroy, known for its annual garlic festival. While the information technology (IT) industries dominate the area's economy, the city of San José has emerged as the nation's tenth largest, and many adjacent municipalities are important in their own right. Not only did immigrant Indian and Chinese entrepreneurs found major IT companies (Saxenian 1999), but the IT industry generally employs many professional staff from immigrant backgrounds and has been a prime mover in the national push to increase the number of H-1B visas for technical workers. The growth of immigrant-origin communities supplying employees for technology firms has in turn created important constituencies for local elected officials. In terms of receptivity—and in particular the positive reactions of its suburbs—the region therefore may exceed even the immigrant-friendly tenor of the urban cores of the three traditional receiving destinations.

One clear reason why the region has responded so positively is that naturalized citizens have become an important part of the urban and suburban electorate, with half the voters in the area's principal cities being immigrants or their children.[2] As the region's immigrant communities matured, they have become civically engaged, electing a growing number of immigrant-origin candidates. The city of San José is roughly one-third Latino, one-third Asian, and one-third white and has a history of progressive reform (Trounstine 2008), and its ten-member city council not only has three Latino and two Asian members, but also an immigrant from Lebanon and another whose parents migrated from Italy.

The nearby city of Cupertino, home of Apple, has three Asian members on its five-member city council.

Overall, the region trends Democratic, which also provides a supportive tone. But the voters also expect the region's politicians to pay positive attention to issues concerning immigration. As former chair (and now ranking member) of the U.S. House Immigration Subcommittee, Zoe Lofgren, one of the region's Democratic representatives in Congress, consistently took up the issue of temporary visas allowing high-tech immigrants to work in Silicon Valley, and, more generally, supports comprehensive immigration reform. Another regional politician, U.S. Representative Mike Honda, chairs the Congressional Asian Pacific American Caucus. He was interned (along with his family) during World War II and is considered a stalwart defender of immigrant rights.

Not only does the region elect politicians sympathetic to its immigrant constituencies, but it also has a public and nonprofit infrastructure of immigrant services that is much better developed than those of most other new receiving areas. Santa Clara County's Human Relations Council founded the Immigrant Relations and Integration Services (IRIS) in 1996. In 2000, IRIS hosted a conference, Bridging Borders in Silicon Valley: Summit on Immigrant Needs and Contributions, and released a report with hundreds of recommendations for improving immigrant lives. While the office has suffered declining resources in the context of the Great Recession, IRIS has coordinated an immigrant leadership course in collaboration with San José City College, helping to develop the civic infrastructure and activism that are missing in the Inland Empire, the far Chicago suburbs, or Suffolk County on Long Island.

This "warmth of welcome," apart from modest tensions around day labor sites, is quite remarkable given that the San José metropolitan area saw the biggest recent jump in the share of immigrants of any of our cases. The high share of foreign-born who are high-skilled Asians makes it harder for would-be opponents of immigration within the native white majority to negatively "racialize" immigrants as the "other." The positive framing of immigrant IT workers and entrepreneurs seems to spill over to other immigrant populations as well. Even communities with many undocumented Mexicans, such as the Mayfair neighborhood in San José, give positive attention and support to their immigrant residents, perhaps because the majority population understands that low-skilled workers make an important contribution from which the majority benefits directly.

San José also provides a "warm welcome" because regional leaders can—and do—credibly argue that attracting and retaining immigrants is vital to the region's economic success. For example, various issues of the *Index of Silicon Valley* published by Joint Venture Silicon Valley Network, a grouping of new economy business and civic leaders, described immigrants under the rubric of "Talent Flows and Diversity," and the *Index* writers expressed concern when the flow of foreign-born slowed. The labor movement's own think tank, Working Partnerships USA, also put out a celebratory analysis of immigrant contributions in 2004 (Auerhahn and Brownstein 2004). Both business and labor interests, therefore, have *consistently emphasized the importance of immigrants to the region's social and economic health.* This sets an important tone—and demonstrates the significance of metropolitan leadership.

What Is to Be Learned?

The case studies analyzed in this volume suggest several tentative conclusions about the factors associated with greater or lesser degrees of regional receptivity to immigrants. These are summarized in table 10.1. First, a history of immigration matters. Areas with long legacies of immigrant arrivals and past experiences with immigrant integration are more likely to welcome contemporary immigrant populations now. New York and Chicago illustrate this, with New York priding itself as a city of immigrants and beacon of hope for many arriving from around the world. Los Angeles has had a more conflicted history, including mass deportations of Mexican immigrants in the 1930s, serving as a main staging point for interning Japanese Americans during World War II, and the displacement of Mexican Americans by urban redevelopment projects in the 1950s and 1960s. However, it recently elected first the son and then a grandson of Mexican immigrants to the position of mayor. As a result of their immigrant histories, these cities have a legacy of institutions designed to foster immigrant integration in the labor force, neighborhoods, and politics. The new reception areas lack this capacity.

Conversely, the cities without an immigrant history have fewer institutional resources with which to address potential conflicts over the rapid growth of new immigrant communities. In Phoenix, for example, the sharp recent buildup of immigrants generated a heightened sense of dislocation and conflict within the native-born white majority; in the Inland Empire, the legacy of racist and conservative organizations has also not helped the region's attempts to accommodate its sharp recent demographic changes. At the same time, Charlotte and San José also received rapid recent increases of immigrants but responded far less coldly, and indeed quite warmly in the case of San José.

This same point applies to central city–suburban differences. Urban cores tend to have had a longer experience with immigration and provide a more

TABLE 10.1 Shaping factors and warmth of welcome by principal cities vs. suburbs in metro regions

REGION	PART	HISTORY OF IMMIGRATION	RACIALIZATION OF IMMIGRANTS	IMMIGRANT SHARE (%) (1 THROUGH 2.5 GENERATION)				POLITICAL DYNAMICS				WARMTH OF WELCOME
				PEOPLE	VOTERS	V/P	MEXICAN	BUSINESS	IMMIGRANT-SERVING NONPROFITS	IAO	AIPE	
New York	City	Long	Low	62.8	48	76.4	6.2	Strong pro	Strong	Strong	No	Warmest
	Suburbs	Mixed	Mod	42.8	31.4	73.4	5.1	Weak pro	Weak	Weak	Yes	Mixed
Chicago	City	Long	Low	32.8	18.6	56.7	47.5	Strong pro	Strong	Strong	No	Warm
	Suburbs	Short	Mod	31.4	20.3	64.6	28.7	Weak pro	Weak	Weak	Yes	Mixed
Los Angeles	City	Long	Low	66.8	47.4	71	39.2	Strong pro	Strong	Strong	No	Warm
	Suburbs	Long	Low	52.8	42.2	79.9	44.5	Weak pro	Weak	Strong	No	Warm
Inland Empire	City	Short	High	39.7	28.9	72.8	56.1	Weak neg	Absent	Absent	Yes	Cold
	Suburbs	Short	High	40	30.6	76.5	59.7	Weak neg	Absent	Absent	Yes	Cold
Charlotte	City	Short	High	26.7	9	33.7	40.9	Strong pro	Weak	Absent	No	Tepid
	Suburbs	Short	High	8.7	2.8	32.2	n.a.	Strong pro	Absent	Absent	Yes	Cold
Phoenix	City	Short	Mod	33.6	15.7	46.7	54.3	Weak pro	Moderate	Weak	No	Tepid
	Suburbs	Short	High	22.9	11.7	51.1	40.8	Weak pro	Absent	Absent	Yes	Coldest
San José	City	Short	Low	66.5	49.7	74.7	25.6	Strong pro	Strong	Weak	No	Warm
	Suburbs	Short	Low	45.8	30	65.5	19.2	Strong pro	Weak	Weak	No	Warm

Note: Under *History of immigration, long* refers to continuous arrivals, *short* means many recent arrivals, *short* numbers suggest recent arrivals (i.e., first generation, youth, noncitizenship). *Mexican* is share of immigrant origin (1 through 2.5 generation) of Mexican parentage. *IAO* is immigrant advocacy organizations that seek to mobilize support for pro-immigrant positions (as opposed to providing services). *AIPE* is anti-immigrant political entrepreneur. Source: Case studies for qualitative measures, November 2012 Current Population Survey for quantitative measure.

supportive context of reception (although less so in most of the new destinations) than their suburban peripheries, in part because immigrants initially settled in the urban cores. They are thus more likely to have immigrant service organizations, develop informal and formal ways of representing immigrant interests, and have native-born populations open to positive narratives about immigrants and their contributions. Though the movement of immigrants to the suburbs has picked up its pace in recent decades, the peripheral parts of all the regions have much less experience with immigration, and their residents have greater demographic distance from immigrants. These peripheries often have a cooler response to their newcomers. They are less equipped to cope with the change and lean toward what de Graauw, Gleeson, and Bloemraad call "free riding"—that is, relying on nearby central cities to provide needed immigrant services (2013). Some suburban jurisdictions, especially those with sizable immigrant populations, provide services quietly, hoping to avoid attention or political conflict. But low levels of immigrant political mobilization can provide at best a thin political base for supporting such services, and so leave them vulnerable to cutbacks. In any case, given the steady suburbanization of immigration, researchers need to develop a better understanding of suburban responses—both by agencies and by immigrants themselves. Table 10.1 shows that most regions have a substantial gap between the immigrant shares in the core cities and the suburbs, though the suburbs have more than is commonly understood, and that share is growing rapidly in many places.

Racialization matters as well. Metropolitan areas with more diverse immigrant flows—by class as well as national origin—seem less likely to negatively stereotype immigrants as alien "others." Places where a single immigrant group dominates—particularly when that group is poor, undocumented Mexicans— seem to prompt the native majority to view the whole phenomenon of immigration in a negative light.[3] New York and San José have more varied flows than other regions, with the Mexican-origin population being the smallest, but New York's diversity is greatest. Along with the fact that one of its main "immigrant" groups, Puerto Ricans, are citizens, this may enable New York to respond more positively to the challenges of immigrant integration. Immigration is also relatively deracialized in San José and Chicago, where higher-income Asian immigrants in the former case and Eastern Europeans in the latter have a prominent presence. Finally, Mexican-origin populations make up a smaller share of LA County's immigrants than might be thought, and immigrant-origin voters make up a substantial share of the electorate. Conversely, the fact that so many immigrants in Phoenix are undocumented Mexicans and recent arrivals has fostered a racialization that diminishes empathy among the native-born for the immigrant experience.

The regional case studies and table 10.1 also suggest that the naturalization and voting of new immigrant populations, along with their racial and class diversity, exert considerable force on the degree to which the native-born population can negatively stereotype immigrant populations. All the areas in which immigrant-origin individuals (including the children of immigrants as well as the first generation) made up 40 percent or more of the voters in the 2012 presidential election offer warm receptions to immigrants. So do areas where immigrant-origin voters make up a smaller share of the electorate but nonetheless play an important role in constructing majority political coalitions, such as in Chicago and Santa Clara County. More than any other single factor, the rise of immigrant-origin political constituencies that can put immigrant-origin elected officials into office and hold native-born elected officials accountable for their responsiveness to immigrant community needs has delivered more positive reactions.

Other aspects of political dynamics also mediate the ways in which regions translate underlying demographic circumstances into patterns of regional receptivity. Many of the case studies highlighted the important role of business and civic elites in shaping and constraining the broader public response to rapidly growing immigrant populations. The San José and Charlotte cases particularly suggest how regional business elites can constrain the expression of anti-immigrant sentiments. Indeed, this has a national dimension: former New York City mayor Michael Bloomberg organized a group of CEOs and big-city mayors into the Partnership for a New American Economy, to push for immigration reform. At the other end of the spectrum, the weak business organizations in Phoenix and the Inland Empire left quite a bit of space open for anti-immigrant advocates to stir up fears. And the reach of the business voice also has its limits *within* regions: the business elites of New York City and Los Angeles did not extend their influence to the Long Island suburbs or the Inland Empire. These insights suggest that further work would be useful on how to build common regional understanding around the issue of immigrant integration (and other regional imperatives; see Benner and Pastor 2012).

Similarly, the development of immigrant-serving nonprofit organizations and the presence of immigrant advocacy organizations, including labor unions, have also played central roles in defining the political spaces for pro- and anti-immigrant activities. The development of robust networks of nonprofit organizations (as well as public agencies) partly or wholly serving immigrants can both formally and informally integrate immigrant communities into the civic fabric. Immigrant advocacy organizations, such as the New York Immigration Coalition, the Illinois Coalition for Immigrant and Refugee Rights, and the Coalition for Humane Immigrant Rights of Los Angeles, help these networks speak for their constituencies. Though their nonprofit status prevents them from overtly supporting political candidates, they nonetheless have political impacts. The Illinois Coalition, for example, played a key role in getting the State of Illinois to adopt immigrant-friendly programming. Of course, such organizations tend to be most fully and robustly developed in the central cities that have received immigrants for longer periods, and less present in the new suburban destinations. As other observers of the new suburban immigrant communities have noted, more informal bodies, such as religious institutions or hometown associations, can sometimes play this role.

Where the demographic conditions are favorable to anti-immigrant mobilization (recent immigration dominated by undocumented individuals into areas dominated by natives lacking immigrant heritage) and where other political actors have left this space open, our cases suggest that anti-immigrant politicians can have a powerful effect. The sheriffs of Maricopa County, Arizona, and Mecklenburg County, North Carolina, and the former county executive of Suffolk County, New York, exemplify this dynamic.

Finally, while our analysis of these seven metropolitan cases has traced their individual trajectories over recent decades, national political debates have also influenced the degree of local receptivity. Areas that had already developed substantial immigrant communities by the mid-1980s benefited from a Republican president's support for integrating the undocumented (IRCA under Ronald Reagan). The tensions so apparent in Phoenix occurred in a subsequent, more politically polarized era. The negative tenor of the national debate in the wake of the 2006 immigrant protest marches sometimes influenced local politicians to undertake new anti-immigrant tactics, and national anti-immigrant groups promoted the adoption of Arizona-style "attrition through enforcement" in other jurisdictions. Today, national divisions over the president's executive actions may play out in ways that foster more negative as well as more positive local responses. As we enter the 2016 presidential election cycle, national partisan polarization over the issue of immigration seems to have reached a particularly high level (Kafura and McElmurry 2015).

What Is to Be Done?

It is a unique time for immigrant integration policies. The continuing national political polarization and gridlock around immigration reform during the first Obama administration shifted the geographic focus of debate to the states and metropolitan areas. For example, when Congress failed to pass the DREAM Act in December 2010, immigrant advocates began to move on parallel legislation at the state level—and succeeded in California. Meanwhile, restrictionist forces not only hoped that adoption of SB 1070 copycat legislation would lead to "self-deportation" in other states, but even began to argue against birthright citizenship for the children of undocumented immigrants.

Actions taken by President Obama both before and after his reelection in November 2012 have revealed more about the shifting tone (and geographic locus) of the national debate. In the summer of 2012, the president experienced virtually no political blowback from issuing an order staying deportations for young people who would have qualified for the DREAM Act. The sharp Democratic swing in Latino and Asian votes in the 2012 presidential elections—partly in reaction to attempts by the Republican Party's candidates to be "more restrictionist than thou"—once more put comprehensive immigration reform on the national agenda. The Senate passed a comprehensive reform bill in the summer of 2013 that included key elements that many felt were needed to rationalize the nation's immigration system: new enforcement activities at the workplace and the border, some process for undocumented residents to gain authorization, and some agreement on future flows of immigrant labor in order to meet economic needs.

This fell on deaf ears in the House. The Republican-controlled House of Representatives refused to consider the Senate bill, and when the House Republican leadership attempted to jump-start the conversation in early 2014 with the declaration of some basic reform principles, it stirred up a conservative backlash. The political cost-benefit ratio for reform became even more problematic when House Majority Leader Eric Cantor lost a primary to a challenger who said Cantor was too liberal on immigration. Politics got even more heated during summer of 2014 when a wave of unaccompanied children from Central American countries attempted to cross the border into the United States.

Some sort of national legislative reform is inevitable in the long run. Underneath the surface stalemate, contending parties have identified the outlines of a log-rolling compromise, giving each side much of what it wants. The growth and naturalization of Latino and Asian populations nationally will continue to shift the electoral center of gravity, and business interests have expressed a consistent desire to regularize the immigration system. In the meanwhile, immigrant success at the local level, including for those who are legal permanent residents (LPRs), will depend on whether localities develop the infrastructure that can help immigrants navigate existing or new systems toward citizenship and incorporate them and their children into our society for the long haul. As noted, such infrastructure matters for all immigrants, and we believe the experiences of the metropolitan areas reported here contain lessons about how the federal government can help, what metropolitan regions can learn from one another, and what new questions researchers need to investigate.

Federal Opportunities and Responsibilities

In what follows, we glean policy recommendations from the case study regions as well as from immigrant integration efforts around the country. Many of these recommendations were also taken up by the multiagency Task Force on New Americans, which was set up as part of President Obama's executive actions in November 2014 and emphasizes civic, economic, and linguistic integration. Chaired by the director of U.S. Citizenship and Immigrant Services (USCIS) and the White House director of domestic policy, the task force offered its strategic action plan in April 2015 on the integration of immigrant and refugee communities (White House Task Force on New Immigrants 2015).

In alignment with the task force, our broadest recommendation is simple: the federal government, in particular USCIS, should support and expand programs fostering the welcoming and forward-looking civic best practices profiled in our case study regions. It should not leave regional receptivity purely up to the preexisting combination of immigrant-friendly business leaders, opportunity-seeking politicians, or legacies of regional collaboration. Given that the share of immigrant-origin voters in the active electorate is a driving force in favor of programs to help integrated immigrants, USCIS and its partners need to make even greater efforts to naturalize, register, inform, and engage immigrants who are eligible to become citizens. The task force's proposals to raise public awareness and provide grant funding to promote naturalization services and immigrants' opportunities to give back are strides in this direction.

Another priority outlined by the White House task force involves supporting existing immigrant integration efforts and guiding local-level governments toward implementing programs that foster welcoming communities. There are certainly models on which to build. The Networks for Integrating New Americans (NINA) is one example of a national effort to welcome immigrants. NINA, a project of the U.S. Department of Education, works with institutions offering adult education to help them become centers for immigrant integration through offering English-language courses, naturalization, and career assistance. Other federal actions to consider include making citizenship more affordable, promoting naturalization (as through USCIS's online Citizenship Resource Center), putting greater emphasis on immigrant services in federal grants, taking the lead on translating documents into other languages and extending health care options to all immigrants. As our case studies demonstrate, moving immigrants from legal residence to citizenship to active electoral participation is a key to fostering welcoming environments.

The federal government should continue to establish standards around immigrant integration. While the task force delivered a well-developed plan of actions, it has not clearly defined what immigrant integration means and how to measure it (an issue we also take up in the research section below). As such, the federal government should not only partner with immigrant service and advocacy professionals to identify the most pressing needs of immigrant communities, but should construct a comprehensive immigrant integration agenda with indicators that will allow us to measure delay or progress. The federal government can also establish standards for what local agencies should achieve.

Newer receiving metro areas can especially benefit from federal attention because they have less institutional capacity but face increasing need for services. This also holds for new suburban destinations within the older receiving areas (for example, the Inland Empire, Suffolk County, and the Chicago suburbs). The recent and rapid arrival of a big new immigrant population seems to trigger more negative reactions than do more gradual additions to a large existing immigrant base. The immigrant integration component of any eventual national policy reform will need to make a priority of providing resources and training, such as the proposed naturalization and learning tool kits and outreach programs, to newer receiving areas.

While newer areas do need special attention, financial support should also flow to the localities with the largest concentrations of aspiring Americans. If reform (or even temporary relief) occurs, the federal government should take accrued fines from undocumented immigrants as they move toward regular status and be sure to allocate those resources to the localities that will have to provide more services to them. Balancing these two imperatives will be challenging but necessary: providing a supportive political, economic, and social fabric at the federal level will allow states and regions to implement the policies and practices that foster receptivity and resilience.

State, Metropolitan, and Local Strategies

Our case-study regions provide numerous positive examples for state and local policy—but the base from which to draw creative new strategies is certainly not limited to the metro regions we consider. For example, municipal and metropolitan leaders are already sharing best practices through the National League of Cities immigrant integration initiative. The J.M. Kaplan Fund and other supporters are seeking to expand Welcoming America, a grassroots effort to build positive understanding toward immigrants in the newer receiving communities. The Haas

Foundation in California has supported efforts to work with black communities with a significant immigrant influx. Grantmakers Concerned with Immigrants and Refugees has compiled an "Immigrant Integration Toolkit" (Petsod, Wang, and McGarvey 2006) with best practices from across the nation, as has the Migration Policy Institute across five unique metro areas (McHugh 2014). A consortium of foundations, under the initial leadership of the Carnegie Corporation, established a "Four Freedoms Fund," to promote civic engagement among immigrants.

State and local governments should provide further support for sharing the best practices emerging from such efforts and creating a broader consensus on what works. Working together, states, localities, and existing networks of immigrant service and advocacy organizations also need to add a new dimension to their work by spreading expertise *within* regions. As we have frequently noted, immigrants first concentrated in the urban cores and are now moving outward to suburbs. Today, more new immigrants are moving directly to the suburbs. Suburban jurisdictions have less experience and fewer support organizations for responding to these immigrants. Although regional coordination can help extend capacities that have already developed in central cities, suburban governments need to be encouraged to move beyond "free riding" and develop their own capacities for receiving and integrating immigrants.

Immigrants, of course, need not be constrained by the environments they enter. They can also devise political advancement strategies and develop policy ideas about how to make these environments more responsive (or in some cases develop political defenses to reduce or at least defang hostility). Individual and organizational activists can draw on a repertoire of possible political actions, resources, and strategies to reframe those political opportunities.[4] New York, Los Angeles, and Chicago all have vibrant immigrant rights communities—but the impact is not felt just there. The immigrant rights groups in San José are quite active—they fielded 150,000 marchers on May 1, 2006, proportionally far larger than the Los Angeles marches—and they also have the benefit of a welcoming corporate and civic structure. Newer destinations typically lack this type of mobilization, and to the extent their service infrastructure is welcoming, it tends to engage immigrants as clients, not civic actors.[5] Mobilized populations create a new voice in civic debate and deliberation that can set a different tone, create new opportunities for pro-immigrant political leaders, and help to hold systems accountable. The immigrant communities of Phoenix, Charlotte, and the Inland Empire all have low levels of political mobilization—and building their social movement infrastructure would improve the receptivity of these regions.

Local leadership also matters. Los Angeles, Chicago, and New York all host a Mayor's Office of Immigrant Affairs that can help to project the civic, economic, and cultural resources for immigrant integration more broadly in their regions, an institutional innovation being adopted by an increasing number of cities (including San José). McHugh's (2014) comparison of five city-led initiatives found that mayoral leadership can be critical in leveraging and integrating existing resources, coordinating community stakeholders, and building feedback loops. Local authorities can also make it possible for noncitizen immigrants to participate in local planning exercises, school councils, and other forms of active "citizenship," partly as preparation for eventual naturalization and voting. But ongoing pressure from community organizations on legislative and administrative officials is needed to implement municipal immigrant integration policies (de Graauw 2015).

Research shows that immigrants are less likely to engage in traditional democratic processes such as voting but do participate in organizations, rallies, petitioning, and other practices (Ramakrishnan 2005; J. Wong 2006). Terriquez (2011) shows that immigrant parents who belong to labor unions subsequently become more engaged in bettering their children's schools. Although this might provoke short-term anxieties among the native-born, it will facilitate long-run political incorporation and maximize current investments.[6] For example, increased parental involvement may in turn improve K–12 education or after-school programs for everyone's children. Immigrants can participate in "get out the vote" efforts even if they cannot cast a ballot.

California has recently produced a handful of creative best practices. Many immigrant advocates called 2013 the "Year of the Immigrants" because the state legislature passed a slew of immigrant integration bills allowing undocumented drivers to obtain licenses, creating a domestic worker's bill of rights, and protecting workers from retaliation (California Immigrant Policy Center 2013). LA Voice—a PICO affiliate—won a policy allowing unlicensed drivers to avoid having their cars towed, easing the financial and transportation burdens of immigrant families who require private transportation to go to work or school.[7] Such policies help create conditions in which immigrants can thrive.

Promoting naturalization is a particularly effective way to foster immigrant integration. Key barriers to naturalization include lack of English-language skills and a relatively expensive application process. The White House Task Force on New Immigrants recognizes this and recommends initiatives that promote linguistic and educational integration, including increasing access to ESL programs for adults and early learning tool kits for parents, and grant awards toward citizenship preparation programs (White House Task Force on New Immigrants 2015).

Regionally based responses are also possible (Pastor et al. 2013). For example, in 2011, an immigrant-serving organization called CASA de Maryland joined Citigroup Foundation, the Latino Economic Development Corp., the Ethiopian Community Development Council Enterprise Development Group, and other financial and nonprofit institutions to pilot a $400,000 program to boost the naturalization rates of green-card holders—an estimated 210,000 permanent residents who live in Maryland and more in the greater Washington, D.C., area. Together, they provided microloans, legal referrals, one-on-one guidance, and civic and financial education classes to immigrants seeking to start their citizenship application process (CASA de Maryland, n.d.; Lazo 2011; USA Citizenship Services, n.d.). The Bethlehem Project, part of the New Americans Campaign and rebranded in 2014 as the New American Workforce, supports employers who encourage their employees to naturalize (Taxin 2013). Employers of health clinics, hotels, and clothing factories in Los Angeles, Miami, Washington, D.C., and the Silicon Valley partner with immigrant rights advocates to provide naturalization support services. Employers hold on-site information sessions, organize English classes, or provide interest-free loans to help workers naturalize. As this volume has shown, the involvement of businesses is imperative for shifting the overall tone—but there are many specific actions, such as encouraging naturalization, that are more direct ways to impact immigrant integration.

Increasing the mainstream population's knowledge and understanding of how immigrants contribute to regional economic and social vitality can also improve the warmth of reception. With help from the Colorado Trust, a health equity foundation, immigrant-serving community-based organizations "got ahead of the curve" (Petsod, Wang, and McGarvey 2006). Our case studies suggest that highlighting diversity in an immigrant population may make it easier to promote integration policies; encouraging one-on-one contacts seems to promote new perceptions; and data, information, and reports can persuade high-level business actors to counter anti-immigrant political entrepreneurs who might seek to capitalize on the worries often induced by rapid demographic transition. Welcoming America has codified a range of such welcoming activities and is trying to replicate itself in multiple regions and states. This campaign makes use of interactive technology to promote inter- and intra-generational collaborations among old-timers and newcomers.[8] The Council on Immigrant Integration in Los Angeles brings together individuals from across multiple sectors, including business, labor, faith, and law enforcement.[9] Anchor universities can play a role by providing data, community foundations can play a role by convening, and metropolitan planning organizations can help by incorporating consideration of nativity into regional planning (such as the generally higher use of public transit by immigrants).[10]

One ultimate test of immigrant integration will be the extent to which immigrants make progress in regional labor markets (Bean and Stevens 2003b). Many immigrants are now relegated to low-skill and low-wage occupations with limited opportunities to move up the economic ladder. Even the most highly educated often find it hard to translate degrees earned in their home country into credentials accepted in the U.S. labor market (Batalova and Fix 2008). Increasing opportunities for the economic mobility of immigrants, their families, and their communities will not only help immigrants financially, but will maximize their ability to contribute to the overall economy. This will require supporting entrepreneurship, improving English-learning systems, and working to ensure that professional credentials can be transferred—strategies the White House Task Force on New Americans identifies and recommends. Here, financial institutions, community colleges, workforce investment boards, and professional associations could play an important role.

For any of this to take place, immigrant and community organizations need to deepen their civic engagement. One intriguing example comes from the Illinois Coalition for Immigrant and Refugee Rights (ICIRR). The group was an early innovator in integrated voter engagement, going beyond get-out-the-vote efforts to encourage more consistent involvement in civic life. In 2004, the ICIRR successfully registered twenty-seven thousand new immigrant voters by relying on outside organizers—virtually all of whom later left town, taking their expertise and their valuable relationships with them. This prompted the ICIRR to develop "integrated voter engagement" as a way to engage naturalized citizens, U.S.-born children of immigrants, legal residents, and undocumented immigrants through training sessions, leadership development, and volunteer recruitment. It worked: not only did the ICIRR raise voter turnout substantially in immigrant communities in 2006 and 2008; it organized communities to block anti-immigrant legislation and at the same time increased state funding for citizenship programs, provided health care for undocumented children, and passed a day labor protection act (Winkelman and Malachowsky 2009). Such long-term work is the backbone of integrating immigrants into life in the United States and should receive continual support from local and regional agencies partnering with the federal Task Force on New Americans.

Developing the Research

No academic study would be complete without a call for more and better research. This volume echoes that usual admonition, but we hope that we are distinctive in suggesting that the field of immigrant integration would benefit from a sharper focus on politics *and* on the metropolitan scale. Linking together these two—paying more attention to how the political jockeying around immigration policy plays out at this level—could benefit both academic thinking and policy making. Our study only scratches the surface of both what is needed and what is possible in this intersectional arena.

For example, even though we recruited deeply experienced analysts to examine seven important case studies, they only begin to tap the dimensions of variation in the national experience. We did not focus on subareas where new immigrants are interacting with African American communities, nor did we examine the many declining manufacturing areas or weak market cities of the United States, some of which are currently being revived by immigration. We focused on larger metro areas, but not the smaller regions that are also important sites of immigrant integration. Should consensus be reached on reforming national immigration policies, we will face an unusually interesting "natural experiment." Our analysis of the cases suggests the kinds of actors that would play important roles in regional responses. Following a larger and more varied sample of regions would allow us to better understand their relative contributions to shaping and shifting patterns of regional receptivity to new immigrant communities.

We think scholars also need to pay much more attention to the political dynamics of responses to immigration. We have been able to identify the major actors and sketch out when and how they have reacted (or failed to react) to the rise of new immigrant communities, and to some extent why they react the ways that they do. While partisan balance is clearly an important factor, with Republican elected officials leaning in an anti-immigrant direction, the challenge of integrating immigrants can often involve coalitions of odd bedfellows (Zolberg 2008; Hochschild and Mollenkopf 2009). We need to know more about why business and labor groups, for example, end up on the pro-immigrant side rather than the anti-immigrant side.

The metropolitan politics of immigrant integration offers scholars and researchers a rich vein of evidence for determining best practices for immigrant integration and identifying the circumstances under which they work better or worse. A broader examination of how practices that appear to work well in one setting fare across a larger variety of localities would be helpful. This might be accomplished by interviewing leaders in different types of national networks (such as civic organizations and immigrant rights groups) to get a full set of possible practices and better specifics about which policies work well in which metropolitan settings.

The larger intersection between immigrant integration and regional developmental trajectories is also worthy of further exploration. We believe that the clear correlation between a rising share of immigrants and stronger metropolitan growth trends does not result simply from immigrants being attracted to growing locations, but also from the ways that immigrants promote growth and innovation (Benner and Pastor 2012). However, a rising share of immigrant workers can also lead to disturbing impacts, such as the growth of low-wage labor, poorly regulated suburban development, and declining labor standards (Hill et al. 2012). Looking at how regional leaders manage this mix of costs and benefits will be instructive not just in the realm of immigrant integration but for other studies of regional governance and resilience (Benner and Pastor 2015; Foster 2012; Weir et al. 2012).

Finally, we need better benchmarks for defining successful immigrant integration. New York City and Chicago and Welcoming America claim to be at the forefront of understanding and measuring what "welcome" requires, but this is not the same as deriving an academically rigorous and defensible approach. How many generations do we need to analyze? What aspects of the integration process are critical? The 2012 California Immigrant Integration Scorecard tracked four categories—Economic Snapshot, Economic Mobility, Warmth of Welcome, and Civic Engagement—and measured a series of counties against one another (Pastor et al. 2012); as in the qualitative case studies here, San José did better than Los Angeles! Key metrics for tracking clearly include age- and race/ethnicity-adjusted rates of naturalization and voting, as well as educational and occupational attainment. But whatever the specific choices, better tracking integration will help us to understand what success looks like *and* make the case for further investments. This would provide critical guidance for the community activists, policy makers, local officials, and regional leaders who will lead this effort in years to come.

America is at a crossroads with regard to immigration. Demographers project that future immigrant flows into the country will decline, partly because sending countries will become more prosperous, but also because fertility rates are falling in key sending countries like Mexico. While the politics frequently seem to be in flux—the 2012 election suggested that immigration reform was inevitable, while the 2014 electoral season declared it dead—some sort of systemic fix seems likely in the long run. In the meanwhile, we have a patchwork of presidential executive actions and a set of localized responses that range from draconian enforcement in some places to permissive "city cards" in others.

While this might seem a bit chaotic—and indeed it is chaotic—localities will always play the largest role in achieving immigrant integration under any system. Each metropolitan destination for immigrants has its own character, immigration history, integration challenges, and institutional and political capacity to respond. Our study suggests that providing a warmer welcome to new immigrant communities will enhance their future trajectories and could well serve regional interests. Gracefully accommodating new populations not only maximizes their economic potential, but makes civic life less brittle and more vibrant (Benner and Pastor 2012). If jurisdictional fragmentation, racial division, and political competition diminish the capacity and willingness to absorb and enhance new immigrant communities, the result will be unfortunate for everyone in the region.

Notes

1. THE ETHNIC MOSAIC

1. See the Utah Compact: A Declaration of Five Principles to Guide Utah's Immigration Discussion, http://www.utahcompact.com/.

2. This may surprise some who think of San José as having long had a strong Mexican presence, but this was true mainly before the nineteenth century, and not during its rapid growth in the post–World War II period.

2. THE CASES IN CONTEXT

1. The 1965 law capped visas at no more than twenty thousand from any single nation in the Eastern Hemisphere but did not apply a country limit in the Western Hemisphere, although it applied an overall cap. Prior to the shift, visas from Western European countries were going unused, even as there were backlogs for Eastern and Southern European countries (*CQ Almanac* 1966).

2. The 1970 Census is an appropriate base because it provides much more specific race and origin information than did the 1960 Census. John Iceland (2009, 36) estimates that about 86 percent of legal immigrants between 1900 and 1920 were European, while 87 percent of legal immigrants in the 1980–2000 period were non-European. Including undocumented residents would tip the balance further in the direction of non-European immigrants.

3. Singer does not give much attention to immigrant movement into traditional black neighborhoods, which is also a singularly important phenomenon. See Pastor 2014; Pastor and Carter 2009; McClain et al. 2007.

4. San José had a higher percentage of foreign-born than Chicago in our base year of 1980 (13.6 versus 9.8). Singer and others see San José as an emerging gateway because it lacked the older European ethnic groups and because its foreign-born share was only 8.0 percent in 1960, while it was 9.7 percent in the Chicago metropolitan area. See www.census.gov/population/www/documentation/twps0029/twps0029.html and www.bayareacensus.ca.gov/.

5. The numbers all come from http://www.migrationpolicy.org/programs/us-immigration-policy-program-data-hub/unauthorized-immigrant-population-profiles. They are derived by applying a multiple-imputation strategy to fill in information in a five-year pool of the American Community Survey based on information from the Survey of Income and Program Participation; for more on the actual method see Capps et al. 2013, as well as Van Hook et al. 2015. These county-based estimates may differ from early estimates for 2012 because of an improvement in the way MPI assigned individual observations to the counties.

6. The 2010 Civic Engagement Supplement, for example, asks only whether respondents contacted a public official or boycotted a product, not whether they engaged in a protest.

3. TEEMING SHORES

1. Levy changed parties in 2010, anticipating a gubernatorial run as a Republican.

4. MACHINE MATTERS

1. This and all other direct quotations not otherwise cited come from interviews conducted by the author.

5. MOVEMENTS MATTER

1. The Los Angeles Core-Based Statistical Area (CBSA), as defined by the federal Office and Management and Budget, includes Los Angeles and Orange County, but many think of the area as including Riverside, San Bernardino, and Ventura Counties. This chapter focuses on LA County; another takes up Riverside and San Bernardino, known as the Inland Empire.

2. All data, unless otherwise specified, originate from the authors' calculations based on the American Community Survey 2008–2012 (Ruggles et al. 2011).

3. Author analysis of 1980, 1990, and 2000 Census and 2008–2012 American Community Survey data.

4. The Justice for Janitors campaign became a major force in 1990, when its attempt to organize janitors in Los Angeles's Westside business hub and Century City turned into a confrontation with police. Demonstrators were beaten and arrested (Milkman 2006).

5. Curricula were developed in Spanish and in English and cover a range of topics, including ESOL instruction (English for speakers of other languages), financial literacy, citizenship, advocacy, leadership, labor history, and computer training.

6. "PICO" formerly stood for "Pacific Institute for Community Organizations," but as the California-based organization gained a national presence, it simply went by the name PICO.

7. Calculated from 2010–2011 data using QuickQuest at http://dq.cde.ca.gov/dataquest/content.asp.

8. Data come from the Accountability Progress Reporting System, available at http://www.cde.ca.gov/ta/ac/ap/apireports.asp. To calculate the percentages, we first reduce each of the group scores by 200, since that is the base (or lowest possible) score.

9. These are adjusted four-year dropout rates that attempt to account for those who reenroll and for lost transfers; the raw numbers are slightly higher. Data taken from the DataQuest system at http://dq.cde.ca.gov/dataquest/. We should note that a sizable share of these students will eventually complete some missing classes or secure a GED; still, the racial/ethnic gaps are quite large.

10. All data are from a pooled 2010–2012 sample of the American Community Survey.

11. Data are from the California Basic Educational Data System; see http://dq.cde.ca.gov/dataquest/. Author updates to analysis found in Pastor and Ortiz 2009a, 20, based on California Department of Education data.

12. 1970 data taken from the National Historical Geographic Information System (NHGIS); see http://www.nhgis.org/.

13. Data are from the 2008–2012 American Community Survey.

14. For more on the scandal see Whitcomb 2010.

6. THE LAST SUBURB

1. See the March 2013 USC Dornsife / Los Angeles Times Poll, at http://dornsife.usc.edu/usc-dornsife-la-times-march-2013-poll-immigration/.

2. In 2010, according to the dissimilarity index, the Riverside–San Bernardino–Ontario metro area ranked thirty-fifth in Latino-white segregation among fifty metro

areas with the largest Latino populations; but, as noted, it ranked eleventh in terms of the change in that index (Logan and Stults 2011).

3. Singer and Wilson (2010) show a decline in the Inland Empire's foreign-born population from a total of 911,982 in 2007 to 883,150 in 2009; this represents a 3.2 percent decline.

4. Data are from the Field Poll (2009) and from author's analysis of voter registration statistics from the California secretary of state.

5. This contrasts with Riverside, the region's largest city, which is governed by an almost completely white and conservative political establishment. All but one of Riverside's eight city council members are white, a surprising situation in a city where non-Hispanic whites made up only 31 percent of the population in 2013 and where African Americans and Latinos both have a historical presence (2013 American Community Survey via American Fact Finder).

6. Both Riverside and San Bernardino Counties signed 287(g) agreements with the U.S. Immigration and Customs Enforcement agency.

7. Lewis has sponsored bills and amendments to expand border enforcement spending and the use of E-verify.

8. Members of the Justice for Immigrants Coalition filed a FOIA request demanding to see documents from the local Border Patrol office in response to what they claim was a growing connection between immigration control enforcement and local police enforcement. According to advocates, local police and the Border Patrol were conducting coordinated sweeps of day labor sites.

9. Local police agencies receive funding for checkpoints from the California Office of Traffic Safety. The state increased checkpoint grants from $5 million in 2009 to $8 million in 2010 (McKinnon 2010).

10. Data from the American Community Survey, 2008–2012, at www.NationalEquityAtlas. org.

11. Author analysis of data from the California Department of Education (www. cde. ca.gov).

12. A number of organizations, including the Catholic Diocese of San Bernardino, the Pomona Day Laborers Center, PICO, and CLUE, are involved in the Justice for Immigrants Coalition.

13. Foundations provided $27 per capita in the Inland Empire during 2005 (Martinez, Rogers, and Silverman 2009). Compare this to $139 per capita in Los Angeles and $119 per capita for California.

7. "THE KINDNESS OF STRANGERS"

1. In a 2008 report by the Tijeras Foundation, Charlotte ranked in the top ten most "giving cities" in the United States. The foundation's survey found that Charlotte tied for fourth place for percent of household income given to philanthropy; residents in the city gave an estimated 3.1 percent of their household income to charity (Chazwold 2008).

2. See *Plyler v. Doe*, 457 U.S. 202 (1982) and *Lau v. Nichols*, 414 U.S. 563 (1974).

3. "If it is has just expired and it is not revoked or anything like that and it has just simply been expired, the typical course of action is, as long as you have got an ID of who that person is, that they would be able to either be given a verbal warning and nothing or they could be issued a citation. More than likely they are going to be issued a citation as long as you have some confidence that that is who the person is. They maybe ask for a second form of ID or something else that has their name on it in the car insurance or registration paperwork or something. If all that stuff matches up and the officer has a reasonable belief that, yeah, this is John Smith and his license has just expired . . . they would probably just get a citation" (author's interview, April 18, 2009).

4. "El uso que se esta dando que es totalmente inapropiado. [Fue diseñada] para unas situaciones especificas para detener a personas que no estaban cumpliendo la ley o que estaban . . . delinquiendo, cometiendo delitos. Entonces . . . para eso fue el ley creada."

8. CHILL WINDS IN THE VALLEY OF THE SUN

1. Arizona accepts twice as many refugees per capita as California, for example. According to a vice president of the International Rescue Committee, "In the degree of welcome and receptivity we see, I would put Arizona at the top" (DeParle 2010). See also U.S. Departments of State, Homeland Security, and Health and Human Services, n.d., table 6, p. 55.

2. Cuban refugees were seen as more "worthy" than unauthorized immigrants from Mexico for a more pragmatic reason: their expenses were paid by the government (Horton 2004).

3. Pinal County, on the southeast border of Maricopa County, with a population of just over four hundred thousand in 2014, was added to the metropolitan area in 2000 because of significant in-commuting from formerly rural areas there.

4. By federal definitions, not only Phoenix but also Mesa, Scottsdale, and Tempe are considered central ("principal") cities.

5. Calculated from the U.S. Census Bureau's American Community Survey, 2010–2012 Three-Year Estimates.

6. The demographic data in this paragraph are from the Census Bureau's 2012 American Community Survey. Racial percentages include people identifying with that race alone or in combination with one or more other races.

7. 2013 ACS author tabulations.

8. In 1980, 15 percent of Phoenix's neighborhoods contained more than half the Hispanic population, while 32 percent of the city's neighborhoods had few or no Latino residents (Oberle and Li 2008).

9. Two-thirds of foreign-born Arizonans from Latin American countries had arrived since 1990, and more than one-third since 2000, according to McConnell and Skeen (2009).

10. And 63 percent of the foreign-born are from Latin America more generally, according to the 2013 American Community Survey. McConnell and Skeen report that in 2007, 89 percent of Latinos in Arizona identified their national origin as Mexican (2009, 24).

11. Phil Gordon, the mayor of Phoenix from 2004 to 2012, staked out a relatively supportive position regarding immigrants but was also quite vocal in complaining about the fiscal and human strains on public safety caused by unauthorized immigration.

12. See *Lopez-Valenzuela v. Arpaio*, No. 11–16487, slip op. (9th Cir. October 15, 2014) (en banc); cert. denied, June 1, 2015 (*County of Maricopa, Arizona, et al. v. Angel Lopez-Valenzuela et al.*), 575 US, June 1, 2015.

13. U.S. District Court Judge Susan Bolton declared that the law (later amended slightly in 2010 in the state's omnibus immigration enforcement law, SB1070) was "preempted by federal law," and so she permanently enjoined its enforcement (Stern 2014).

14. County Attorney Andrew Thomas, a frequent partner in anti-illegal-immigration efforts with Sheriff Joe Arpaio, resigned in 2010 to run (unsuccessfully) for state attorney general. In 2012 he was disbarred from the practice of law in Arizona for "defiled" public trust, accused by an ethics panel of misusing the powers of his office to bring questionable charges against political opponents.

15. Title VI of the 1964 Civil Rights Act has been interpreted to require administrative agencies at various levels of government to hire bilingual personnel and to translate forms, notices, and applications for people with limited English proficiency. This was supplemented in 2000 with Executive Order 13166 and reaffirmed by the Bush administration

in 2002. Section 203 of the 1975 Voting Rights Act also requires bilingual voting assistance in communities where a single-language minority makes up 5 percent of the voting-age population. In 2006 Congress renewed these provisions for the next twenty-five years. The federal government has done little, however, to provide programs to teach English. For a helpful discussion of these issues see Bloemraad and de Graauw (2012).

16. For more details on the conflict between Mesa police and the county sheriff's office see Varsanyi et al. 2012.

17. Other Republican candidates attempted to ride the coattails of SB 1070 as well in 2010. Barry Wong, a candidate for the state Corporation Commission (which regulates utilities), made a campaign promise to require utilities to check the immigration status of their customers. Wong was not elected.

18. The council-manager form of government in Phoenix gave Gordon limited prerogatives as an executive, and the city attorney issued an opinion that the mayor could not sue the state on behalf of Phoenix without council approval.

19. Interviewees told us that SB 1070 split the cities in the state politically, and so the statewide League of Cities and Towns did not articulate a unified response to the legislation. The organization tends to avoid immigration issues, focusing instead on fiscal concerns in the state-local relationship.

20. Phoenix Police Department, Operations Order 1.4 (2008), pp. 10–11, states that "federal immigration law may be utilized to further a criminal investigation, with the approval of a supervisor, but will not be utilized as the sole cause for a stop or contact." During an investigation, if an officer found an ICE (Immigration and Customs Enforcement) detention-and-removal order when checking a person for prior wants or warrants, the officer was instructed to call ICE to find out whether the hold was for a civil or a criminal violation, and to detain and transport to ICE only those with a criminal hold.

21. Former state senate president Pete Rios said of Latino legislators, "The other side pretty much disregards anything they have to say" (Wingett 2006).

22. The number of Latino legislators in the sixty-member house went from three to eight but stayed the same in the thirty-member senate, with five.

23. The city council size of nine includes the mayor, who under Phoenix's council-manager system sits as a member (and presiding officer) of the council. The mayor is elected at large, while the other eight members are elected from districts.

24. Arizona exported about $6.3 billion in goods to Mexico in 2012, compared with $26.4 billion from California and $94.5 billion from Texas.

25. Remarks of Danny Ortega, a longtime Latino leader and lawyer in Phoenix, quoted in "Latino Leadership Waning" (*Arizona Republic* 2006).

26. One of our more politically connected interviewees said that one reason Latino leaders are ineffective in influencing the state legislature is that they tend to approach legislators from a position of anger, rather than looking for ways to work with them. Another source, an activist, complained that "there are . . . people who've been around for a long time and are operating out of their anger or their hurt. . . . We have people saying things that just aren't that helpful. I don't think it's helpful to call the sheriff a racist."

27. Of the sixteen members of the Phoenix Human Relations Commission in January 2014, only three had Hispanic surnames. The group has not been very active on immigrant-related issues.

28. In 2010, Stand for Children cooperated with the Republican chair of the House Education Committee to get a bill creating a statewide system of teacher and principal evaluation introduced in the state legislature. Stand's then-organizer argued that although most of the struggling or deprived students in the state are probably Hispanic or black, "if we presented ourselves as a Hispanic parent group, we wouldn't get very far. We wouldn't win just based on [veteran Democratic state legislator] Ben Miranda voting yes or no. We

have to reach out to those legislators in other districts who are drafting the bills" (Avila 2010).

29. Another interviewee related how a local monsignor had fought attempts to hold a Spanish-language Sunday Mass at the lovely main parish, arguing that there were not enough Hispanics to justify it, even though Spanish speakers were the fastest-growing element of the congregation. (The Spanish Masses were held in smaller facilities off-site.)

30. Chicanos por la Causa is a community development corporation focused on employment and training programs and housing assistance. Valle del Sol concentrates on providing behavioral health services. Friendly House works on adult education, workforce development, home care for the elderly, and family counseling.

31. The neutrality among nonprofits seemingly ended jarringly in late 2009 when Sheriff Arpaio's deputies executed a search warrant for records at the offices of Chicanos por la Causa, as part of one of his investigations of Latino county supervisor Mary Rose Wilcox, who had ties to that nonprofit. See Chicanos por la Causa (n.d.) and Stern 2009. On the Friendly House lawsuit, in which the group was part of a coalition including the ACLU, MALDEF, the NAACP, the Asian Pacific American Legal Center, and others, see American Civil Liberties Union 2010.

32. Gordon noted that some nearby tribal governments that had worked with the city in the past on certain social services have, as a matter of tribal sovereignty, refused to sign documents that would require them not to help unauthorized immigrants.

33. Phoenix's nine-member city council, which for decades had been elected at-large and dominated by business-oriented Anglos, was converted to district elections in 1982, a change widely viewed as transforming city politics toward more of a neighborhood orientation and inclusivity; see Bridges 1997. Changes that made the council's membership more representative of the city's demographics came slowly, however, as there was never more than one Latino at a time on the council until 2013, when the number increased to three (partly at the expense of the one traditionally African American seat). Arguably, the Hispanic proportion of voters in Phoenix has reached the point where at-large voting, perhaps in combination with other reforms, such as ranked-choice voting or preference voting, might provide for more descriptive representation of Latinos than district-based plurality elections.

9. OUT OF MANY, ONE

1. As of September 2012, the Children's Health Initiative had served 214,315 children through Healthy Kids, Medi-Cal, and Healthy Families (Children's Health Initiative, Santa Clara County 2015).

2. Aside from data collection and a literature review, we conducted twenty-eight interviews with elected officials and individuals from education, local government, religious organizations, labor, media, philanthropy, and nonprofit community-based organizations.

3. The data for 1900 to 1990 come from data provided by the U.S. Census Bureau's Population Division (see Gibson and Lennon 2011). For 2000 and after, we draw on the 2000 Census and the subsequent American Community Survey data.

4. Data from the 2009 American Community Survey.

5. 2010–2012 American Community Survey. Calculations are restricted to those in the civilian labor force between the ages of twenty-five and sixty-four.

6. Data from the 2010–2012 American Community Survey.

7. Data from the 2010–2012 American Community Survey.

8. Current Population Survey, 2012.

9. The resolution is available for download at http://sccgov.iqm2.com/Citizens/FileOpen.aspx?Type=4&ID=54755, and the minutes of the meeting documenting its passage at http://sccgov.iqm2.com/Citizens/FileOpen.aspx?Type=12&ID=1512&Inline=True.

10. See https://www.sccgov.org/sites/opa/nr/Pages/County-of-Santa-Clara-Affirms-Commitment-to-Public-Health-and-Safety-for-its-Diverse-Community.aspx.

11. Since then the board has advocated for immigrants by supporting and opposing various measures, such as backing state funding for the state naturalization program.

12. According to a case study by the Bay Area Social Services Consortium Research Response Team (housed at UC Berkeley's Center for Social Services Research). See Ward 1999.

13. The Opportunity Fund provides immigrants with $450 of matching grant money if they are eligible for citizenship, save $225, and attend a free money-management course. More details and other eligibility requirements for this program can be found at http://www.immigrantinfo.org/events/SavingForCitizenship.pdf or www.opportunityfund.org/ida.

14. For the numbers see Galewitz 2005 and Howell and Trenholm 2007.

15. See http://www.siliconvalleycf.org/immigration-integration.

16. For the Border Protection, Antiterrorism, and Illegal Immigration Control Act of 2005, HR 4437, see http://thomas.loc.gov/cgi-bin/bdquery/z?d109:H.R.4437http://thomas.loc.gov/cgi-bin/bdquery/z?d109:H.R.4437.

17. Telemundo's Channel 48, Univision's Channel 14, Spanish-language radio, and local print weeklies (*El Observador*, *La Oferta*, *El Mensajero*, and *Alianza*) all have a strong presence in the region.

18. See also: http://sahesjsu.org/home/4580575180. The Development, Relief and Education of Alien Minors Act, also called the DREAM Act, would have helped those who meet certain requirements gain the opportunity to enlist in the military or go to college and have a path to citizenship.

19. The new acting vice-chief is the first woman in the position in the city's history.

20. Members are as diverse as the population of San José, including African American, Asian, and Latino service and advocacy groups.

21. See JV:SVN and Silicon Valley Community Foundation (2010).

22. See the American Leadership Forum Silicon Valley website: http://www.alfsv.org/index.php?submenu=Silicon_Valley_Collaborative&src=gendocs&ref=Silicon_Valley_Collaborative&category=Programs.

23. They belong to other statewide leadership bodies, including the California Immigrant Policy Center, the California Table of Reform Immigration for America, and the California Partnership.

24. Formerly available at http://somosmayfair.org/about/. Since the time of field research, Somos Mayfair revamped itself and its web page, and the language quoted is no longer available on the organization's website. However, the longer mission statement is available on their Facebook page: https://www.facebook.com/SomosMayfair/info/?tab=page_info.

10. SYNTHESIZING THE RESEARCH

1. Stepping into the gap, the California Community Foundation, headed by Antonia Hernandez, former executive director of the Mexican American Legal Defense and Educational Fund, launched an immigrant integration initiative, including the creation of a multi-sector Council for Immigrant Integration, a step recommended in Pastor and Ortiz (2009a).

2. The principal cities are San José, Sunnyvale, Santa Clara, Mountain View, Milpitas, Palo Alto, and Cupertino.

3. Also see Brown 2013 for more on social policy effects of the racial frame on the perception of immigrant groups.

4. Bada et al. (2010) review Latino civic engagement in nine U.S. cities, including four—Charlotte, Chicago, Los Angeles, and San José—that anchor the metropolitan areas we explore.

5. Given the potential for conflict in new receiving areas, some argue that a "depoliticized" strategy for providing immigrant services is the best way to achieve a minimum service level. This, however, can lead to a truncated form of immigrant integration with shallow political roots.

6. Space limits us from exploring how immigrant integration can affect more general public systems. See Fix's (2009) analysis of the 1996 welfare reform's failure to redesign systems with immigrants in mind. Capps and others (2009) explore how to adjust Workforce Investment Act funding to better respond to adult English learners, while Batalova and Fix (2008) describe ways to alter the "credentialing" and other challenges facing skilled immigrants in the United States.

7. For more on the fair towing policies see http://www.lavoicepico.org/LA_Voice_PICO/Towing_Policy.html.

8. See the Friends of Welcoming website at http://www.welcomingamerica.org/friends/.

9. For more on the Los Angeles Council on Immigrant Integration see http://dornsife.usc.edu/csii/council-on-ii/.

10. Experimentation with such local and state programs is especially critical since the Affordable Care Act explicitly forbade undocumented immigrants from Medicaid expansion, subsidies, or even the right to buy a policy in the newly established health exchanges. As such, the burden of care will be local—and the real question is whether it will be addressed through emergency room services or more preventive and consistent health care.

References

Aguilar, Alfonso. 2010. "On Latinos, Listen to the Gipper." *Politico*, March 14, 2014. http://www.politico.com/news/stories/0510/36754.html.

Aguirre, Felipe. 2010. Author interview.

Alagot, Calvin. 2014. "Students Camp on LAUSD Doorstep Demanding Funds for Poor Kids." *LA Weekly*, April 8. http://www.laweekly.com/informer/2014/04/08/students-camp-on-lausd-doorstep-demanding-funds-for-poor-kids.

Alamillo, Jose. 2006. *Making Lemonade out of Lemons: Mexican American Labor and Leisure in a California Town, 1880–1960*. Urbana: University of Illinois Press.

Alba, Richard, and Victor Nee. 1997. "Rethinking Assimilation Theory for a New Era of Immigration." *International Migration Review* 31(4): 826–74.

———. 2003. *Remaking the American Mainstream: Assimilation and Contemporary Immigration*. Cambridge, MA: Harvard University Press.

Altshuler, Daniel, and Theo Oshiro. 2012. "Suffolk County, a Bellwether on Immigration Politics." *Fox News Latino*, November 19. http://latino.foxnews.com/latino/opinion/2012/11/19/suffolk-county-bellwether-on-immigration-politics/.

Alvarado, Hector. 2010. Author interview.

Amaya, Emilio. 2010. Author interview.

American Civil Liberties Union. 2010. "ACLU and Civil Rights Groups Ask Court to Block Implementation of Arizona's Racial Profiling Law." https://www.aclu.org/immigrants-rights-racial-justice/aclu-and-civil-rights-groups-ask-court-block-implementation-arizon-0.

American Community Survey, U.S. Census Bureau. 2012a. "Table DP02: Selected Characteristics in the United States, 2012 American Community Survey 1-Year Estimates." *American FactFinder*. http://factfinder2.census.gov/faces/nav/jsf/pages/index.xhtml.

———. 2012b. "Table S0501: Selected Characteristics of the Native and Foreign-Born Populations, 2012 American Community Survey 1-Year Estimates." *American FactFinder*. http://factfinder2.census.gov/faces/nav/jsf/pages/index.xhtml.

———. 2012c. "Table S0501: Selected Characteristics of the Native and Foreign-Born Populations, 2012 American Community Survey 5-Year Estimates." *American FactFinder*. http://factfinder2.census.gov/faces/nav/jsf/pages/index.xhtml.

American Institutes for Research. 2005. *Findings and Recommendations of the Citizens' Task Force on Charlotte-Mecklenburg Schools*. Washington, DC: Citizens' Task Force on Charlotte-Mecklenburg Schools. http://www.fftc.org/NetCommunity/Document.Doc?id=100.

America's Voice and Latino Decisions. 2014. *Arizona Report*. http://www.latinodecisions.com/files/2413/9387/3160/Arizona_AV_Report.pdf.

Andrade, Juan. 2010. Author interview.

Anonymous. 2010. Author interview.

Aragon, Cynthia. 2010. "The Struggle for a Chicano Power in Los Angeles: The Contribution of a Grassroots Activist." *Perspectives: A Journal of Historical Inquiry* 37. http://web.calstatela.edu/centers/perspectives/vol37/37_Aragon.pdf.

Arango, Carlos. 2010. Author interview.

Arizona Republic. 2006. "The Issue: Hispanic Political Status; Latino Leadership Waning." Opinions, September 3.

Arizona Republic. 2015a. "Brnovich Wasting Money, Time on Misguided Appeal." Editorial, June 9.

———. 2015b. "Hold on Phoenix, Leave Immigration to the Feds." Editorial, April 25. http://www.azcentral.com/story/opinion/editorial/2015/04/25/phoenix-overreaches-direction/26330029/.

Ascher-Webber, Alison. 2010. Author interview.

Auerhahn, Louise, and Bob Brownstein. 2004. *The Economic Effect of Immigration in Santa Clara County and California.* San José, CA: Working Partnerships USA. http://www.wpusa.org/Publication/wpusa_immig.pdf.

Avila, Luis. 2010. Author interview.

Avitia, Cynthia. 2010. Author interview.

Aydemir, Abdurrahman, and George J. Borjas. 2010. "Attenuation Bias in Measuring the Wage Impact of Immigration." National Bureau of Economic Research.

Bada, Xóchitl, Jonathan A. Fox, Robert Donnelly, and Andrew Dan Selee. 2010. *Context Matters: Latino Immigrant Civic Engagement in Nine US Cities; Reports on Latino Immigrant Civic Engagement.* Washington, DC: Woodrow Wilson International Center for Scholars. http://www.escholarship.org/uc/item/47f308pd.

Baker, Bob. 1990. "Police Use Force to Block Strike March Labor: About Two Dozen Demonstrators Are Injured during Protest by Janitors in Century City." *Los Angeles Times,* June 16.

Barreto, Matt A., and José A. Muñoz. 2003. "Reexamining the 'Politics of In-Between': Political Participation among Mexican Immigrants in the United States." *Hispanic Journal of Behavioral Sciences* 25(4): 427–47.

Batalova, Jeanne, and Michael Fix. 2008. *Uneven Progress: The Employment Pathways of Skilled Immigrants in the United States.* Washington, DC: Migration Policy Institute. http://www.migrationpolicy.org/pubs/BrainWasteOct08.pdf.

Batista, Sarah. 2009. "Hundreds Attend Latino Issues Forum." *WBTV.com,* March 13. http://www.wbtv.com/story/10003532/hundreds-attend-latino-issues-forum.

Beal, Frank. 2007. "Preparing Metropolitan Chicago for the 21st Century." Chicago: Metropolis 2020.

Bean, Frank D., and Gillian Stevens. 2003a. *America's Newcomers and the Dynamics of Diversity.* New York: Russell Sage Foundation.

———. 2003b. "Linguistic Incorporation among Immigrants." In *America's Newcomers and the Dynamics of Diversity,* 143–71. New York: Russell Sage Foundation.

Benito, Lawrence. 2012. Author interview.

Benner, Chris. 2003. "Learning Communities in a Learning Region: The Soft Infrastructure of Cross-Firm Learning Networks in Silicon Valley." *Environment & Planning A* 35(10): 1809–30.

Benner, Chris, and Manuel Pastor. 2012. *Just Growth: Inclusion and Prosperity in America's Metropolitan Regions.* New York: Routledge.

———. 2015. "Whither Resilient Regions: Equity, Growth and Community." *Journal of Urban Affairs.*

Blackwell, Angela Glover, Stewart Kwoh, and Manuel Pastor. 2010. *Uncommon Common Ground: Race and America's Future.* New York: W. W. Norton & Co.

Blankstein, Andrew, and Richard Winton. 2008. "Ask and Deport, Family Urges." *Los Angeles Times,* April 9. http://www.latimes.com/local/la-me-specialorder9apr09-story.html#page=1.

Bloemraad, Irene, and Els de Graauw. 2012. "Immigrant Integration and Policy in the United States: A Loosely Stitched Patchwork." In *International Perspectives:*

Integration and Inclusion, edited by J. Frideres and J. Biles, 205–32. Montreal and Kingston, ON: McGill–Queens University Press.

Blume, Howard. 2012. "All L.A. Unified Students Must Pass College-Prep Courses." *Los Angeles Times*, May 9. http://articles.latimes.com/2012/may/09/local/la-me-0509-lausd-20120509.

Bohn, Sarah. 2009. *New Patterns of Immigrant Settlement in California*. San Francisco: Public Policy Institute of California. http://www.ppic.org/main/publication.asp?i=812.

Borjas, George J., Jeffrey Grogger, and Gordon H. Hanson. 2009. "Immigration and the Economic Status of African-American Men." *Economica* 77(306): 255–282.

——. 2012. "Comment: On Estimating Elasticies of Substitution." *Journal of the European Economic Association* 10(1): 198–210.

Brackman, Harold, and Stephen P. Erie. 1993. "The Once and Future Majority: Latino Politics in Los Angeles." In *The California-Mexico Connection*, edited by A. F. Lowenthal and K. Burgess, 196–220. Stanford, CA: Stanford University Press.

Brand, Rick. 2012. "Clearly, Bellone Is No Levy on Immigration." *Newsday*, July 14. http://www.newsday.com/long-island/columnists/rick-brand/clearly-bellone-is-no-levy-on-immigration-1.3838505.

——. 2013. "Monica Martinez Defeats Suffolk Legis. Rick Montano." *Newsday*, September 11. http://www.newsday.com/long-island/suffolk/monica-martinez-defeats-suffolk-legis-rick-montano-1.6050392.

Brettell, Caroline B. 2008. "Immigrants in a Sunbelt Metropolis: The Transformation of an Urban Place and the Construction of Community." In *Immigration and Integration in Urban Communities: Renegotiating the City*, edited by L. M. Hanley, B. A. Ruble, and A. M. Garland, 143–76. Washington, DC: Woodrow Wilson Center Press.

Bridges, Amy. 1997. *Morning Glories: Municipal Reform in the Southwest*. Princeton, NJ: Princeton University Press.

Brookings Institution. 2010. *State of Metropolitan America: On the Front Lines of Demographic Transformation*. Washington, DC: Brookings Institution. http://www.brookings.edu/metro/stateofmetroamerica.aspx.

Brown, Hanna E. 2013. "Race, Legality, and the Social Policy Consequences of Anti-Immigration Mobilization." *American Sociological Review* 78(2): 290–314.

Brown, Joyce. 2011. "A Historic, and Essential, LI Debate." *Newsday*, November 5. http://www.newsday.com/columnists/joye-brown/a-historic-and-essential-li-debate-1.3299377.

Brune, Tom. 2012. "With Redistricting Comes New Constituents." *Newsday*, March 20. http://www.newsday.com/long-island/politics/with-redistricting-comes-new-constituents-1.3614593.

Burger, Warren E. 1971. *Swann v. Board of Education*. http://caselaw.findlaw.com/us-supreme-court/402/1.html.

Bustamante, Salvador. 2010. Author interview.

Calavita, Kitty. 1996. "The New Politics of Immigration: 'Balanced-Budget Conservatism' and the Symbolism of Proposition 187." *Social Problems* 43(3): 284–305.

California Immigrant Policy Center. 2013. "Fall Legislative Update: Huge Victories for Immigrant Communities in Sacramento Make 2013 the 'Year of the Immigrant!'" https://org2.salsalabs.com/o/5009/images/CIPC%20Fall%202013%20Legislative%20Update%2010.11.13%20(website).pdf.

Capps, Randy, James D. Bachmeier, Michael Fix, and Jennifer Van Hook. 2013. *A Demographic, Socioeconomic, and Health Coverage Profile of Unauthorized Immigrants in the United States*. Washington, DC: Migration Policy Institute. http://www.migrationpolicy.org/research/demographic-socioeconomic-and-health-coverage-profile-unauthorized-immigrants-united-states.

Capps, Randy, Michael Fix, Margie McHugh, and Serena Yi-Ying Lin. 2009. *Taking Limited English Proficient Adults into Account in the Federal Adult Education Funding*

Formula. Washington, DC: Migration Policy Institute. http://www.migrationpolicy. org/pubs/wia-lep-june2009.pdf.

Card, David E. 2005. "Is the New Immigration Really So Bad?" *Economic Journal* 115(507): F300–323.

CARECEN-LA. 2014. "Education Reform." *CARECEN*. http://www.carecen-la.org/ advocacy/education-reform/.

CASA de Maryland. n.d. "Citizenship Maryland." http://casademaryland.org/what-we-do/ citizenship-maryland/.

Castaneda, Jesse. 2010. Author interview.

Castellanos, Teresa. 2010. Author interview.

CBS SF Bay Area. 2015. "San Jose Approves First-Ever Office of Immigrant Affairs Called Unnecessary by Some." June 12. http://sanfrancisco.cbslocal.com/2015/06/12/san-jose-approves-first-ever-office-of-immigrant-affairs-called-unnecessary-by-some/.

Charlotte-Mecklenburg Schools Task Force. 2013. *22 Task Force Recommendations for the Superintendent*. http://www.cms.k12.nc.us/mediaroom/taskforce/Documents/22_ Task_Force_Recommendations%20online%203.pdf.

Chazwold. 2008. "Grand Rapids in Top Ten for Giving Hours and Dollars." *Right Michigan*, June 10. http://rightmi.com/old/www.rightmichigan.com/story/2008/6/10/12915/7998. html.

Chicago (City of). 2012. "Mayor Emanuel Introduces Welcoming City Ordinance." http:// www.cityofchicago.org/city/en/depts/mayor/press_room/press_releases/2012/ july_2012/mayor_emanuel_introduceswelcomingcityordinance.html.

——. 2014a. "Mayor Emanuel Announces Internships and Job Opportunities for DREAMer Students." http://www.cityofchicago.org/city/en/depts/mayor/provdrs/ office_of_new_americans/news/2014/apr/mayor-emanuel-announces-internships-and-job-opportunities-for-dr.html.

——. 2014b. "Mayor Emanuel Makes Preparations to Welcome Unaccompanied Child Migrants." http://www.cityofchicago.org/city/en/depts/mayor/press_room/press_ releases/2014/jul/mayor-emanuel-makes-preparations-to-welcome-unaccompanied-child-.html.

Chicanos por la Causa. n.d. *Frequently Asked Questions regarding a Search Warrant Delivered to CPLC Recently by the Maricopa County Sheriff's Office*. http://www.cplc. org/Common/Files/FAQPrestamosLoans.pdf.

Children's Health Initiative, Santa Clara County. 2015. "Home—CHI Kids." *Children's Health Initiative*. https://www.chikids.org/Pages/default.aspx.

Chu, Kansen. 2010. Author interview.

Clark, William A. V., and Sarah A. Blue. 2004. "Race, Class, and Segregation Patterns in U.S. Immigrant Gateway Cities." *Urban Affairs Review* 39(6): 667–88.

Coalition for Humane Immigrant Rights of Los Angeles. 2008. *Local Law Enforcement and Immigration: The 287(g) Program in Southern California*. Los Angeles. http:// chirla.org/files/287g%20Factsheet%2011–24–08.pdf.

Coalition for Justice and Accountability. 2011. *Community Input Report for the Selection of San Jose Police Chief*. SJ Beez.

Cohen, Laurie, Jorge Luis Mota, and Andrew Martin. 2002. "Political Army Wields Clout, Jobs." *Chicago Tribune*, October 31. http://articles.chicagotribune.com/2002-10-31/ news/0210310296_1_city-hall-mayor-richard-j-daley-patronage.

Cortés, Zaira. 2011. "Children of Immigrants Hope for Change in Suffolk." *Voices of NY*, December 5. http://www.voicesofny.org/2011/12/children-of-immigrants-hope-for-change-in-suffolk/.

Cowman, Amy. 2010. "Latino Community Forms Committee to Work with Police." *WCNC*, June 9. http://www.wcnc.com/story/news/2014/06/20/11120419/.

CQ Almanac. 1966. "National Quotas for Immigration to End." In *CQ Almanac 1965*, 21st ed., 459–82. Washington, DC: Congressional Quarterly. http://library.cqpress.com/cqalmanac/cqal65-1259481.

Dahl, Robert Alan. 1961. *Who Governs? Democracy and Power in an American City*. New Haven, CT: Yale University Press.

Daily News Wire Services. 2011. "New LAPD Impound Policy in Effect at DUI Checkpoints." *Los Angeles Daily News*, March 12. http://www.dailynews.com/20110312/new-lapd-impound-policy-in-effect-at-dui-checkpoints.

Danley, Ian. 2010. Author interview.

Davis, Mike. 1990. *City of Quartz: Excavating the Future in Los Angeles*. New York: Verso.

Dean, Amy, and David B. Reynolds. 2009. *A New New Deal: How Regional Activism Will Reshape the American Labor Movement*. Ithaca, NY: ILR Press.

Deaton, Joyce. 2008. *Charlotte: A Welcome Denied*. Washington, DC: Woodrow Wilson International Center for Scholars. http://www.wilsoncenter.org/publication/charlotte-welcome-denied.

Decker, Scott H., Paul G. Lewis, Doris M. Provine, and Monica W. Varsanyi. 2009. "On the Frontier of Local Law Enforcement: Local Police and Federal Immigration Law." *Sociology of Crime Law and Deviance* 13:261–76.

de Graauw, Els. 2015. "Polyglot Bureaucracies: Nonprofit Advocacy to Create Inclusive City Governments." *Journal of Immigrant & Refugee Studies* 13(2): 156–78.

de Graauw, Els, Shannon Gleeson, and Irene Bloemraad. 2013. "Funding Immigrant Organizations: Suburban Free Riding and Local Civic Presence." *American Journal of Sociology* 119(1): 75–130.

Del Olmo, Frank. 2003. "Towing Policy Is Not off the Hook." *Los Angeles Times*, August 17. http://articles.latimes.com/2003/aug/17/opinion/oe-delolmo17.

DeParle, Jason. 2010. "Arizona Is a Haven for Refugees." *New York Times*, October 8. http://www.nytimes.com/2010/10/09/us/09refugees.html?pagewanted=all&_r=0.

DeSipio, Louis. 2011. "Immigrant Incorporation in an Era of Weak Civic Institutions: Immigrant Civic and Political Participation in the United States." *American Behavioral Scientist* 55(9): 1189–1213.

de Uriarte, Richard. 2005. "The Long, Passionate Journey of Alfredo Gutierrez." *Arizona Republic*, June 13.

DOJ-CRD (Department of Justice, Civil Rights Division). 2011. "Suffolk County Police Department Technical Assistance Letter." http://www.justice.gov/crt/about/spl/documents/suffolkPD_TA_9–13–11.pdf.

Dominguez, Jaime. 2007. "A Strategy towards Political Empowerment: Latinos in Chicago (1975–2003)." PhD diss., University of Illinois.

——. 2010. "Illinois Latinos in the 2004 Election: The Waiting Game Continues." In *Beyond the Barrio: Latinos in the 2004 Elections*, edited by R.O. de la Garza, L. DeSipio, and D.L. Leal, 271–92. Notre Dame, IN: University of Notre Dame Press.

Dreier, P., J. Mollenkopf, and T. Swanstrom. 2001. *Place Matters: Metropolitics for the Twenty-First Century; Studies in Government and Public Policy*. Lawrence: University Press of Kansas.

Duchon, Richard. 2009. "LAUSD School Construction Full Steam Ahead." *Annenberg Radio News*. http://www.annenbergradio.org/segments/lausd_school_construction_full_steam_ahead.

Dupont-Walker, Jackie. 2010. Author interview.

Epton, Abraham, and Alex Bordens. 2015. "Mayoral Runoff Results by Precinct." *Chicago Tribune*, April 8. http://apps.chicagotribune.com/elections/2015-mayoral-results/.

Faller, Mary Beth. 2013. "Maricopa Community Colleges Sued over In-State Tuition for Migrants." *Arizona Republic*, June 26. http://www.azcentral.com/community/scottsdale/articles/20130626maricopa-community-colleges-sued-in-state-tuition-migrants.html.

Federal Bureau of Investigation. 2004. *Crime in the United States: 2004.* http://www2.
fbi.gov/ucr/cius_04/.

Fermino, Jennifer. 2015. "Pope Francis Issued Municipal NYC ID Card by Mayor
de Blasio." *New York Daily News,* September 25. http://www.nydailynews.com/
news/politics/pope-francis-issued-municipal-nyc-id-card-mayor-de-blasio-
article-1.2374988.

Field Poll. 2009. *The Changing California Electorate.* San Francisco: Field Research Corp.
http://www.field.com/fieldpollonline/subscribers/COI-09-Aug-California-Elector-
ate.pdf.

Fieldhouse, E., and D. Cutts. 2010. "Does Diversity Damage Social Capital? A Comparative Study of Neighbourhood Diversity and Social Capital in the US and Britain."
Canadian Journal of Political Science / Revue Canadienne de Science Politique 43(2):
289–318.

Fiscal Policy Institute. 2009. *Immigrants and the Economy: Contribution of Immigrant
Workers to the Country's 25 Largest Metropolitan Areas with a Special Focus on
the Five Largest Metro Areas in the East.* New York: Fiscal Policy Institute. http://
www.immigrationresearch-info.org/report/fiscal-policy-institute/immigrants-
and-economy-contribution-immigrant-workers-countrys-25-lar.

——. 2011. *New Americans on Long Island: A Vital Sixth of the Economy.* http://www.
fiscalpolicy.org/FPI_NewAmericansOnLongIsland_20120119.pdf.

Fix, Michael, ed. 2009. *Immigrants and Welfare: The Impact of Welfare Reform on America's Newcomers.* New York: Russell Sage Foundation.

Flamming, Douglas. 2006. *Bound for Freedom: Black Los Angeles in Jim Crow America.*
Berkeley: University of California Press.

Flores, Cesar, and Charisse Domingo. 2013. "Infographic: Santa Clara Community
Supports Policy That Keeps ICE out of Jails." *Silicon Valley De-Bug,* November 2.
http://www.siliconvalleydebug.org/articles/2013/11/02/infographic-santa-clara-
community-supports-policy-keeps-ice-out-jails.

Foley, Elise. 2013. "Undocumented Driver's License Bill Passes Illinois House." *Huff-
ington Post,* January 8. http://www.huffingtonpost.com/2013/01/08/undocumented-
drivers-licenses-illinois_n_2434246.html.

Forrest, Ray, and Ade Kearns. 1999. *Social Cohesion and Urban Inclusion for Disadvantaged Neighborhoods.* York, UK: Joseph Rowntree Foundation. http://www.jrf.org.
uk/knowledge/findings/foundations/pdf/F04109.

Foster, Kate. 2012. "In Search of Regional Resilience." In *Urban and Regional Policy and
Its Effects: Building Resilient Regions,* edited by N. Pindus, H. Wial, H. Wolman, and
M. Weir, 24–59. Washington, DC: Brookings Institution Press.

Foster, Suzanne. 2010. Author interview.

Fox News Latino. 2014. "Illinois Issues 14,000 Drivers Licenses to Undocumented For-
eigners in 2 Mo." *Fox News Latino,* March 13. http://latino.foxnews.com/latino/
news/2014/03/13/illinois-issues-14000-drivers-licenses-to-undocumented-foreigners-
in-2-mo/.

Frank, Stephen. 2014. "Antonovich: The Economic and Human Toll of Illegal Immigration."
California Political Review, September 8. http://www.capoliticalreview.com/capolitical-
newsandviews/antonovich-the-economic-and-human-toll-of-illegal-immigration/.

Frey, William. 2010. "Age." In *State of Metropolitan America: On the Front Lines of Demographic Transformation,* 76–89. Washington, DC: Brookings Institution Metropolitan Policy Program.

Frontline. 2011. "Sheriff Mark Curran: Why He Changed His Mind about Secure Communities." October 18. http://www.pbs.org/wgbh/pages/frontline/race-multicultural/
lost-in-detention/sheriff-mark-curran-why-he-changed-his-mind-about-secure-
communities/.

Fulton, William B. 2001. *The Reluctant Metropolis: The Politics of Urban Growth in Los Angeles*. Baltimore: Johns Hopkins University Press.

Funes, Daisy. 2010. Author interview.

Furuseth, Owen J., and Heather A. Smith. 2010. "Localized Immigration Policy: The View from Charlotte, North Carolina, a New Immigrant Gateway." In *Taking Local Control: Immigration Policy Activism in U.S. Cities and States*, edited by M. Varsanyi, 173–92. Palo Alto, CA: Stanford University Press.

Galewitz, Phil. 2005. "Silicon Valley County Finds Health Coverage for Almost All Kids." *Palm Beach Post*, September 11. http://www.100percentcampaign.org/news/release.php?_c=10smdubtiqt91ny&1=1&id=xknqs4q6zz5yj7&done=.10smdubtiqta1ny.

Garcia, Eugene. 2015. "Opening Address: The State of Latino Education in Arizona." 2015 AHCF Symposium: A Latino Education Policy Agenda, Arizona Hispanic Community Forum, June 4. Gateway Community College, Phoenix.

Garcia, F. Chris. 1997. *Pursuing Power: Latinos and the Political System*. Notre Dame, IN: University of Notre Dame Press.

Garcia, Jesus "Chuy." 2009. Author interview.

Garcia, Mario. 1995. *Memories of Chicano History: The Life and Narrative of Bert Corona*. Berkeley: University of California Press.

Garcia, Matt. 2001. *A World of Its Own: Race, Labor, and Citrus in the Making of Greater Los Angeles, 1900–1970*. Chapel Hill: University of North Carolina Press.

García, Ofelia. 2002. "New York's Multilingualism: World Languages and Their Role in a U.S. City." In *The Multilingual Apple: Languages in New York City*, edited by O. García and J. A. Fishman, 3–51. New York: Walter de Gruyter.

Gardiner, Dustin. 2013a. "Phoenix Convention Slump Tied to SB 1070." *Arizona Republic*, January 2. http://www.azcentral.com/community/phoenix/articles/20121217phoenix-convention-slump-tied-sb-1070.html.

——. 2013b. "Phoenix to Open Trade Office in Mexico." *Arizona Republic*, December 3. http://www.azcentral.com/community/phoenix/articles/20131120phoenix-to-open-trade-office-in-mexico.html.

Gibson, Campbell, and Emily Lennon. 2011. "Table 22. Nativity of the Population for Urban Places Ever among the 50 Largest Urban Places since 1870: 1850 to 1990." http://www.census.gov/population/www/documentation/twps0029/tab22.html.

Gleeson, Shannon. 2012. *Conflicting Commitments: The Politics of Enforcing Immigrant Worker Rights in San Jose and Houston*. Ithaca, NY: Cornell University Press.

Gleeson, Shannon, and Irene Bloemraad. 2011. *Where Are All the Immigrant Organizations? Reassessing the Scope of Civil Society for Immigrant Communities*. Berkeley, CA: UC Berkeley Institute for Research on Labor and Employment.

Glover, Scott, and Matt Lait. 2007. "Corruption Probe Focuses on Maywood." *Los Angeles Times*, June 18. http://articles.latimes.com/2007/jun/18/local/me-tow18.

Glover, Scott, and James Wagner. 2009. "California Attorney General Seeks Reform of Maywood Police." *Los Angeles Times*, April 29. http://articles.latimes.com/2009/apr/29/local/me-maywood29.

Godwin, R. Kenneth, Suzanne M. Leland, Andrew D. Baxter, and Stephanie Southworth. 2006. "Sinking Swann: Public School Choice and the Resegregation of Charlotte's Public Schools." *Review of Policy Research* 23(5): 983–97.

Gonzales, Alfonso. 2013. *Reform without Justice: Latino Migrant Politics and the Homeland Security State*. New York: Oxford University Press.

Gonzalez, Daniel. 2008. "Radio Voice for Migrants in the Valley Is Going Silent." *Arizona Republic*, July 22. http://archive.azcentral.com/arizonarepublic/news/articles/2008/07/22/20080722overandout0722.html.

Gonzalez-Barrera, Ana, and Jens Manuel Krogstad. 2014. "U.S. Deportations of Immigrants Reach Record High in 2013." Factank: News in the Numbers, Pew Research Center, October 2.

http://www.pewresearch.org/fact-tank/2014/10/02/u-s-deportations-of-immigrants-reach-record-high-in-2013/.

Goodno, James. 2005. "S.F. May No Longer Be the State's Most Progressive City." *SFGate*, January 9. http://www.sfgate.com/books/article/S-F-may-no-longer-be-the-state-s-most-2740201.php.

Gordon, Phil. 2010a. Author interview.

———. 2010b. "The Localization of Immigration Law." Presentation to the Harvard Law School, February 5.

Gorman, Anna. 2008. "L.A. County Jails to Expand Immigration Screening." *Los Angeles Times*, June 22. http://www.latimes.com/local/la-me-immigjail22–2008jun22-story.html#page=1.

Gorman, Anna, and Rich Connell. 2009. "Latinos Who Flocked to the Once-Burgeoning Inland Empire Are Hard-Hit in Economic Downturn." *Los Angeles Times*, August 2. http://articles.latimes.com/2009/aug/02/local/me-immig2.

Gottlieb, Robert. 2007. *Reinventing Los Angeles: Nature and Community in the Global City*. Cambridge, MA: MIT Press.

Gottlieb, Robert, Regina Freer, and Mark Vallianatos. 2005. *The Next Los Angeles: The Struggle for a Livable City*. Berkeley: University of California Press. http://books.google.com/books?id=8punhYqrhYEC.

Guido, Michelle. 2001. "Kids' Insurance Program Proves Healthy Success." *San Jose Mercury News*, July 31.

Gulasekaram, Pratheepan, and S. Karthick Ramakrishnan. 2012. *Restrictive State and Local Immigration Laws: Solutions in Search of Problems*. Washington, DC: American Constitution Society. https://www.acslaw.org/publications/issue-briefs/restrictive-state-and-local-immigration-laws-solutions-in-search-of-proble.

———. 2015. *The New Immigration Federalism*. New York: Cambridge University Press.

Haines, David W., and Karen E. Rosenblum. 2010. "Perfectly American: Constructing the Refugee Experience." *Journal of Ethnic and Migration Studies* 36(3): 391–406.

Hanchett, Thomas W. 1998. *Sorting Out the New South City: Race, Class, and Urban Development in Charlotte, 1875–1975*. Chapel Hill: University of North Carolina Press.

Harstad Strategic Research. 2013. "Survey of Registered Voters on Long Island, May/June 2013." http://www.longislandwins.com/downloads/Harstad.LongIsland_.May2013_.RELEASE_.pdf.

Harwood, Stacy, and Dowell Myers. 2002. "The Dynamics of Immigration and Local Governance in Santa Ana: Neighborhood Activism, Overcrowding, and Land-Use Policy." *Policy Studies Journal* 30:70–91.

Hemphill, F. Cadelle, Alan Vanneman, and Taslima Rahman. 2011. *Achievement Gaps: How Hispanic and White Students in Public Schools Perform in Mathematics and Reading on the National Assessment of Education*. Washington, DC: National Center for Education Statistics, Institute of Education Sciences, U.S. Department of Education. https://nces.ed.gov/nationsreportcard/pdf/studies/2011459.pdf.

Henton, Douglas, John Melville, and Kimberly Walesh. 1997. *Grassroots Leaders for a New Economy: How Civic Entrepreneurs Are Building Prosperous Communities*. San Francisco: Jossey-Bass.

———. 2004. "The Rise of the New Civic Revolutionaries: Answering the Call to Stewardship in Our Times." *National Civic Review* 93(1): 43–49.

Hesson, Ted. 2013. "Los Angeles Bucks Federal Government on Secure Communities." *Fusion.net*, October 11. http://fusion.net/justice/story/los-angeles-bucks-federal-government-secure-communities-15437.

Hill, Edward, et al. 2012. "Economic Shocks and Regional Economic Resilience." In *Urban and Regional Policy and Its Effects: Building Resilient Regions*, edited by N.

Pindus, H. Wial, H. Wolman, and M. Weir, 24–59. Washington, DC: Brookings Institution Press.

Hobbs, Richard. 2010. Author interview.

Hochschild, Jennifer L., and John H. Mollenkopf, eds. 2009. *Bringing Outsiders In: Transatlantic Perspectives on Immigrant Political Incorporation.* Ithaca, NY: Cornell University Press.

Hoefer, Michael, and Nancy Rytina. 2012. *Estimates of the Unauthorized Immigrant Population Residing in the United States: January 2011.* Washington, DC: Office of Immigration Statistics, Department of Homeland Security. http://www.dhs.gov/xlibrary/assets/statistics/publications/ois_ill_pe_2011.pdf.

Hollyfield, Amy. 2011. "SJPD's New Chief Reviews Racial Profiling Tactics." *ABC News San Francisco, Oakland, San Jose,* February 22. http://abc7news.com/archive/7972725/.

Hopkins, Daniel J. 2010. "Politicized Places: Explaining Where and When Immigrants Provoke Local Opposition." *American Political Science Review* 104(1): 40.

Horton, Sarah. 2004. "Different Subjects: The Health Care System's Participation in the Differential Construction of the Cultural Citizenship of Cuban Refugees and Mexican Immigrants." *Medical Anthropology Quarterly* 18(4): 472–89.

Howell, Embry M., and Dana Hughs. 2006. "A Tale of Two Counties: Expanding Health Insurance Coverage for Children in California." *Milbank Quarterly* 84(3): 521–54.

Howell, Embry M., and Christopher Trenholm. 2007. "The Effect of New Insurance Coverage on the Health Status of Low-Income Children in Santa Clara County." *Health Services Research* 42(2): 867–89.

Husing, John. 2010. Author interview.

Iceland, John. 2009. *Where We Live Now: Immigration and Race in the United States.* Berkeley: University of California Press.

Iceland, John, and Melissa Scopilliti. 2008. "Immigrant Residential Segregation in U.S. Metropolitan Areas, 1990–2000." *Demography* 45(1): 79–94.

Illinois (State of). 2013. *Expanding Immigrant Integration Policy Priorities and Increasing Accountability: New Americans Phase 3 Report.* Governor's Office of New Americans. https://www2.illinois.gov/gov/newamericans/Documents/Final%20Report%20040113.pdf.

Im, Anne. 2010. Author interview.

Immigrant Integration Task Force. 2015. *Immigrant Integration Task Force Report Presented to Charlotte City Council.* Charlotte, NC. http://charmeck.org/city/charlotte/cic/Documents/IITF%20Report%20with%20Appendices.pdf.

Immigration and Customs Enforcement. 2005. "Fact Sheet: Section 287(g) Immigration Enforcement." http://www.ice.gov/pi/news/factsheets/section287(g).htm.

———. 2009. "Fact Sheet: Delegation of Immigration Authority Section 287(g) Immigration and Nationality Act." http://www.ice.gov/factsheets/287g.

———. 2013. *Activated Jurisdictions: ICE Secure Communities.* Washington, DC: U.S. Department of Homeland Security. http://www.ice.gov/doclib/secure-communities/pdf/sc-activated.pdf#97.

Immigration Policy Center. 2010. *Separating Fact from Fiction: The Truth about Kidnapping in Arizona.* New York: Immigration Policy Center.

InnerCity Struggle. 2014a. "A-G Life Prep!" Inner City Struggle: Building a Movement in the Eastside. http://innercitystruggle.org/section/view/ag_life_prep.

———. 2014b. "East L.A. for Pilots." Inner City Struggle: Building a Movement in the Eastside. http://innercitystruggle.org/section/view/east_la_for_pilots.

Irwin, Megan. 2007. "The Bermudez Triangle." *Phoenix New Times,* November 15. http://www.phoenixnewtimes.com/news/the-bermudez-triangle-6395197.

Jayadev, Raj. 2001. "Leadership Vacuum in Silicon Valley." *Pacific News Service*, November 23. http://www.modelminority.com/joomla/index.php?option=com_content&view=a rticle&id=91:leadership-vacuum-in-silicon-valley-&catid=43:leaders&Itemid=56.

———. 2009. "Vietnamese Man Killed by San Jose Police, City Policies Questioned." *San Francisco Bay Area Independent Media Center*, May 29. https://www.indybay.org/ newsitems/2009/05/29/18598965.php.

Jayadev, Raj, and Albert Cobarrubias. 2011. "Santa Clara County DA's Office to Now Consider 'Collateral Consequences.'" *Silicon Valley De-Bug*, September 23. http:// www.siliconvalleydebug.org/articles/2011/09/23/santa-clara-county-das-office-now-consider-collateral-consequences-policy-shift-bodes-well-immigrants.

Jensen, Lene Arnett. 2008. "Immigrants' Cultural Identities as Sources of Civic Engagement." *Applied Developmental Science* 12(2): 74–83.

Jiménez, Tomás. 2009. *Replenished Ethnicity: Mexican Americans Immigration and Identity*. Berkeley: University of California Press.

Johnson, Hans P., Deborah Reed, and Joseph M. Hayes. 2008. *The Inland Empire in 2015*. Public Policy Institute of California.

Johnson, James H., Jr., Walter C. Farrell Jr., and Chandra Guinn. 1997. "Immigration Reform and the Browning of America: Tensions, Conflicts and Community Instability in Metropolitan Los Angeles." *International Migration Review* 31(4): 1055–95.

Johnson-Webb, Karen D. 2002. "Employer Recruitment and Hispanic Labor Migration: North Carolina Urban Areas at the End of the Millennium." *Professional Geographer* 54(3): 406–21.

Jones-Correa, Michael. 1998. *Between Two Nations: The Political Predicament of Latinos in New York City*. Ithaca, NY: Cornell University Press.

———. 2005a. *The Bureaucratic Incorporation of Immigrants in Suburbia*. New York: Russell Sage Foundation.

———. 2005b. "Structural Shifts and Institutional Capacity: Possibilities for Ethnic Cooperation and Conflict in Urban Settings." In *Governing American Cities: Interethnic Coalitions, Competition, and Conflict*, edited by M. Jones-Correa, 183–209. New York: Russell Sage Foundation.

———. 2008a. "Immigrant Incorporation in the Suburbs: Differential Pathways, Arenas and Intermediaries." In *Immigration and Integration in Urban Communities: Renegotiating the City*, edited by L. M. Hanley, B. A. Ruble, and A. M. Garland, 19–47. Baltimore: Johns Hopkins University Press.

———. 2008b. "Race to the Top? The Politics of Immigrant Education in Suburbia." In *New Faces in New Places: The Changing Geography of American Immigration*, edited by D. S. Massey, 308–40. New York: Russell Sage Foundation.

Jones-Correa, Michael, and Katherine Fennelly. 2009. *Immigrant Enforcement and Its Effects on Latino Lives in Two Rural North Carolina Communities*. Connecticut College.

JV:SVN. 1995. *The Joint Venture Way: Lessons for Regional Rejuvenation*. Vol. 1. San José, CA: Joint Venture: Silicon Valley Network. http://www.jointventure.org/images/stories/ pdf/lessons1.pdf.

JV:SVN and Silicon Valley Community Foundation. 2010. *Index of Silicon Valley*. http:// www.jointventure.org/images/stories/pdf/2010%20Index-final.pdf.

Kabba, Alle. 2010. Author interview.

Kafura, Craig, and Sara McElmurry. 2015. "Growing Partisan Divides on Immigration." Research Report, Chicago Council on Global Affairs, September 18.

Kalra, Ash. 2010. Author interview.

Kasinitz, Philip, John Mollenkopf, and Mary C. Waters. 2004. *Becoming New Yorkers: Ethnographies of the New Second Generation*. New York: Russell Sage Foundation.

Kasinitz, Philip, John H. Mollenkopf, Mary C. Waters, and Jennifer Holdaway. 2008. *Inheriting the City: The Children of Immigrants Come of Age*. Cambridge, MA: Harvard University Press.

Katznelson, Ira. 2005. *When Affirmative Action Was White: An Untold History of Racial Inequality in Twentieth-Century America*. New York: W. W. Norton & Co.

Keely, Charles B. 1971. "Effects of the Immigration Act of 1965 on Selected Population Characteristics of Immigrants to the United States." *Demography* 8(2): 157–69.

Keilman, John. 2010. "Carpentersville Tries to Move on from '06 Immigration Battle." *Chicago Tribune*, May 25. http://articles.chicagotribune.com/2010-05-25/news/ct-met-carpentersville-0525-20100525_1_illegal-immigration-immigration-battle-village-trustee-judy-sigwalt.

Kennedy, Scott. 2015. *2015 Chicago Mayoral Runoff Election Analysis*. Illinois Campaign for Political Reform. http://www.ilcampaign.org/blog/2015-mayoral-election-analysis-a-tale-of-two-cities/.

Kersten, Ellen, Rachel Morello-Frosch, Manuel Pastor, and Marlene Ramos. 2012. *Facing the Climate Gap: How Environmental Justice Communities Are Leading the Way to a More Sustainable and Equitable California*. Los Angeles: USC Program for Environmental and Regional Equity.

Kesler, Christel, and Irene Bloemraad. 2010. "Does Immigration Erode Social Capital? The Conditional Effects of Immigration-Generated Diversity of Trust, Membership, and Participation across 19 Countries, 1981–2000." *Canadian Journal of Political Science / Revue Canadienne de Science Politique* 43(02): 319–47.

King, Kathleen. 2014. "Message from the Chief Executive Officer, Healthier Kids Foundation of Santa Clara County." http://www.hkidsf.org/content/message-chief-executive-officer.

Klampe, Michelle. 2011. "Districts, Schools Fail to Meet Federal Goals." *Press-Enterprise* (Riverside, CA), September 1. http://www.pe.com/articles/schools-597969-districts-percent.html.

Kneebone, Elizabeth, and Alan Berube. 2014. *Confronting Suburban Poverty in America*. Washington, DC: Brookings Institution Press.

Koch, James L., and Ross Miller. 2001. *Building Community Social Connections and Civic Involvement in Silicon Valley: Preliminary Findings Report*. Santa Clara, CA: Center for Science, Technology, and Society, Santa Clara University. http://www.cfsv.org/communitysurvey/ca5.html.

Kohout, Michal. 2009. "Immigration Politics in California's Inland Empire." *Yearbook of the Association of Pacific Coast Geographers* 71: 120–43.

Kotkin, Joel, and William H. Frey. 2007. *The Third California: The Golden State's New Frontier*. Washington, DC: Brookings Institution.

Krikorian, Mark. 2005. *Downsizing Illegal Immigration: A Strategy of Attrition through Enforcement*. Washington, DC: Center for Immigration Studies. http://www.cis.org/ReducingIllegalImmigration-Attrition-Enforcement.

Krysan, Maria, Matthew Hall, and Patrick Washington. 2010. "Immigration Ambivalence in Suburbia: Evidence from Lake County." Chicago Area Study Public Policy Brief. Chicago: University of Illinois–Chicago.

Kurhi, Eric. 2014. "Santa Clara County Budget Includes Restoration of Services, Health Care Expansion." *San Jose Mercury News*, June 20. http://www.mercurynews.com/bay-area-news/ci_26002523/santa-clara-county-budget-includes-restoration-services-health.

LA County Federation of Labor, AFL-CIO. 1990. "L.A. Fed's Setup Sets Pace." July. http://socialjusticehistory.org/projects/justiceforjanitors/items/show/199.

Lacour, Greg. 2014. "The Toxic Residue of 287(g)." *Charlotte Magazine*, June. http://www.charlottemagazine.com/Blogs/Poking-the-Hornets-Nest/June-2014/The-Toxic-Residue-of-287g/.

Lazo, Luz. 2011. "Microloan Program to Help Legal Immigrants Cover Naturalization Costs." *Washington Post,* October 31. http://www.washingtonpost.com/local/microloan-program-to-help-legal-immigrants-cover-naturalization-costs/.

Learmonth, Michael. 1997. "Hard Times Ahead for Immigrants." *Metroactive,* July 31. http://www.metroactive.com/papers/metro/07.31.97/cover/welfare4-9731.html.

Lewis, Paul G. 2004. "An Old Debate Confronts New Realities: Large Suburbs and Economic Development in the Metropolis." In *Metropolitan Governance: Conflict, Competition, and Cooperation,* edited by R. C. Feiock, 95–123. Washington, DC: Georgetown University Press.

Lewis, Paul G., Doris Marie Provine, Monica W. Varsanyi, and Scott H. Decker. 2012. "Why Do (Some) City Police Departments Enforce Federal Immigration Law? Political, Demographic, and Organizational Influences on Local Choices." *Journal of Public Administration Research and Theory* 23(1): 1–25.

Lewis, Paul G., and Karthick Ramakrishnan. 2007. "Police Practices in Immigrant-Destination Cities: Political Control or Bureaucratic Professionalism?" *Urban Affairs Review* 42(6): 874–900.

Li, Wei. 1998. "Anatomy of a New Ethnic Settlement: The Chinese Ethnoburb in Los Angeles." *Urban Studies* 35(3): 479–501.

——. 1999. "Building Ethnoburbia: The Emergence and Manifestation of the Chinese Ethnoburb in Los Angeles' San Gabriel Valley." *Journal of Asian American Studies* 2(1): 1–28.

Light, Ivan. 2006. *Deflecting Immigration: Networks, Markets, and Regulation in Los Angeles.* New York: Russell Sage Foundation.

Lin, Diane. 2009. Author interview.

Linthicum, Kate. 2013. "Groups Call for Halt to Impounding of Unlicensed Drivers' Cars." *Los Angeles Times,* August 7. http://www.latimes.com/local/lanow/la-me-ln-unlicensed-driver-car-impounds-20130807-story.html.

Liu, Laura. 2000. "The Place of Immigration in Studies of Geography and Race." *Social and Cultural Geography* 1(2): 169–82.

Lobo, Arun Peter, Ronald J. O. Flores, and Joseph J. Salvo. 2002. "The Impact of Hispanic Growth on the Racial/Ethnic Composition of New York City Neighborhoods." *Urban Affairs Review* 37(5): 703–27.

Logan, John R., and Brian J. Stults. 2011. *The Persistence of Segregation in the Metropolis: New Findings from the 2010 Census.* Providence, RI: Brown University. http://www.s4.brown.edu/us2010/Data/Report/report2.pdf.

López, David, and Vanessa Estrada. 2007. "Language." In *The New Americans: A Guide to Immigration since 1965,* edited by M. C. Waters, R. Ueda, and H. B. Marrow, 228–42. Cambridge, MA: Harvard University Press.

Lopez, Mark Hugo, and Brent A. Elrod. 2006. *College Attendance and Civic Engagement among 18–25 Year Olds.* College Park, MD: CIRCLE.

Lopez, Mark Hugo, Emily Kirby, and Jared Sagoff. 2005. *The Youth Vote 2004.* College Park, MD: CIRCLE. http://generation18.com/pdf/FS_Youth_Voting_72-04.pdf.

Lopez Rogers, Marie. 2010. Author interview.

Lovett, Ian. 2011. "Patch of California Cracks Down on Illegal Immigration." *New York Times,* January 4. http://www.nytimes.com/2011/01/05/us/05verify.html?module=Search&mabReward=relbias%3Ar%2C%7B%222%22%3A%22RI%3A16%22%7D.

Magee, Breandán. 2012. Author interview.

Marcelli, Enrico A. 2004. "From the Barrio to the Burbs? Immigration and the Dynamics of Suburbanization." In *Up against the Sprawl: Public Policy and the Making of Southern California,* edited by J. Wolch, M. Pastor Jr., and P. Dreier, 123–50. Minneapolis: University of Minnesota Press.

Marrow, Helen. 2005. "New Destinations and Immigration Incorporation." *Perspectives on Politics* 3(4): 781–99.

——. 2007. "Southern Becoming: Immigrant Incorporation and Race Relations in the Rural U.S. South." PhD diss., Harvard University.

——. 2009. "Immigrant Bureaucratic Incorporation: The Dual Roles of Professional Missions and Government Policies." *American Sociological Review* 74(5): 756–76.

Martinez, Arleda, Jamie Rogers, and Carol Silverman. 2009. *The Inland Empire Nonprofit Sector: A Growing Region Faces the Challenges of Capacity.* James Irvine Foundation. http://www.issuelab.org/resource/inland_empire_nonprofit_sector_a_growing_region_faces_the_challenges_of_capacity_the.

Massey, Douglas S. 1985. "Ethnic Residential Segregation: A Theoretical and Empirical Review." *Sociology and Social Research* 69:315–50.

——, ed. 2008. *New Faces in New Places: The Changing Geography of American Immigration.* New York: Russell Sage Foundation.

Massey, Douglas S., Jorge Durand, and Nolan J. Malone. 2003. *Beyond Smoke and Mirrors: Mexican Immigration in an Era of Economic Integration.* New York: Russell Sage Foundation.

Matthews, Channing. 2007. *The Heart of Our Difference: Assessing Racial Tensions in Mecklenburg County.* Charlotte: Charlotte HELP. http://www.wilsoncenter.org/sites/default/files/The%20Heart%20of%20Our%20Difference%20-%20FINAL%20copy%20%28Charlotte%29.pdf.

Mayor's Immigration Study Commission. 2007. *Immigration: Legal and Illegal. A Local Perspective: Charlotte, North Carolina.* Charlotte. http://charmeck.org/city/charlotte/cic/resources/documents/immigration%20legal%20and%20illegal%20-local%20perspective-jan%202007.pdf.

McClain, Paula D., Niambi M. Carter, Victoria M. DeFrancesco Soto, Monique L. Lyle, Jeffrey D. Gynaviski, Shayla C. Nunnally, Tomas J. Scotto, J. Alan Kendrick, Gerald F. Lackey, and Kendra Davenport Cotton. 2006. "Racial Distancing in a Southern City: Latino Immigrants' Views of Black Americans." *Journal of Politics* 68(3): 571–84.

McClain, Paula D., Monique L. Lyle, Niambi M. Carter, Victoria M. DeFrancesco Soto, Gerald F. Lackey, Kendra Davenport Cotton, Shayla C. Nunnally, Thomas J. Scotto, Jeffrey D. Grynaviski, and J. Alan Kendrick. 2007. "Black Americans and Latino Immigrants in a Southern City: Friendly Neighbors or Economic Competitors?" *Du Bois Review: Social Science Research on Race* 4(1): 97–117.

McConnell, Eileen Díaz, and Amanda Skeen. 2009. "Demographics: Contemporary Characteristics of a Dynamic Population." In *State of Latino Arizona*, 23–31. Tempe: Arizona State University and the Arizona Latino Research Enterprise. http://www.evanspubrelations.com/documents/StateofLatinoArizona_web_complete.pdf.

McHugh, Margie. 2014. *Immigrant Civic Integration and Service Access Initiatives: City-Sized Solutions for City-Sized Needs.* Washington, DC: Migration Policy Institute. http://www.migrationpolicy.org/research/immigrant-civic-integration-and-service-access-initiatives-city-sized-solutions-city-sized.

McKinnon, Julissa. 2010. "Whiners Complain about Crackdown on Unlicensed Drivers: Immigrant Advocates Say Crackdown on Unlicensed Drivers Is Unfair." *OC Connect: Orange County Forums*, May 15.

Mendoza, Susana. 2010. Author interview.

Michelson, M. R. 2000. "Political Efficacy and Electoral Participation of Chicago Latinos." *Social Science Quarterly* 81(1): 136–50.

Mihalopoulos, Dan. 2014. "SEC Charges UNO with Defrauding Investors, Warns Probe 'Not Done.'" *Chicago Sun Times*, June 3. http://chicago.suntimes.com/chicago-politics/7/71/165041/sec-charges-uno-with-defrauding-investors-warns-probe-not-done.

Milkman, Ruth. 2006. *L.A. Story: Immigrant Workers and the Future of the U.S. Labor Movement*. New York: Russell Sage Foundation.

Milld, Allison. 2012. *Immigrant Integration in Chicago's Suburbs: A Survey of Current Activities and Efforts*. Metropolitan Mayor's Caucus. http://www.cleanaircounts.org/documents/DTF%20GUIDEBOOK%20FINAL.pdf.

Mollenkopf, John. 2003. "New York: Still the Great Anomaly." In *Racial Politics in American Cities*, edited by R.P. Browning, D.R. Marshall, and D.H. Tabb, 115–40. New York: Longman.

——. 2013. "Dimensions of Immigrant Political Incorporation." In *Outsiders No More? Models of Immigrant Political Incorporation*, edited by J. Hochschild, J. Chattopadhyay, C. Gay, and M. Jones-Correa, 107–18. New York: Oxford University Press.

Moore, Joe. 2010. Author interview.

Munoz, Rick. 2009. Author interview.

Myers, Dowell. 2008. *Immigrants and Boomers: Forging a New Social Contract for the Future of America*. New York: Russell Sage Foundation.

Myers, Dowell, John Pitkin, and Ricardo Ramirez. 2009. *The New Homegrown Majority in California: Recognizing the New Reality of Growing Commitment to the Golden State*. Los Angeles: University of Southern California, School of Policy, Planning and Development. http://www.usc.edu/schools/price/private/documents/news/HomegrownMajority.pdf.

Navarro, Gil. 2010. Author interview.

NDLON (National Day Laborer Organizing Network). 2015. "Our History." http://www.ndlon.org/en/about-us/our-history.

Newsday. 2011. "Statement of Suffolk County District Attorney Thomas Spota." March 24. http://www.newsday.com/news/breaking/statement-of-suffolk-county-district-attorney-thomas-spota-1.2780693.

New York Times. 2010. "The Utah Compact." Editorial, December 4. http://www.nytimes.com/2010/12/05/opinion/05sun1.html.

Nicholls, Walter. 2013. *The DREAMers: How the Undocumented Youth Movement Transformed the Immigrant Rights Debate*. Palo Alto, CA: Stanford University Press.

Nicolaides, Becky M. 2002. *My Blue Heaven: Life and Politics in the Working-Class Suburbs of Los Angeles, 1920–1965*. Chicago: University of Chicago Press.

Nowakowski, Michael. 2010. Author interview.

Nunez, Abel. 2010. Author interview.

NYC Mayor's Office of International Affairs. 2015. http://www.nyc.gov/html/ia/html/home/home.shtml.

NYIC (New York Immigration Coalition). 2015. "About Us: Who We Are." http://www.thenyic.org/about-us.

NYU School of Law, Immigrant Defense Project, and Families for Freedom. 2012. *Insecure Communities, Devastated Families: New Data on Immigrant Detention and Deportation Practices in New York City*. http://immigrantdefenseproject.org/wp-content/uploads/2012/07/NYC-FOIA-Report-2012-FINAL.pdf.

Oberle, Alex, and Wei Li. 2008. "Diverging Trajectories: Asian and Latino Immigration in Metropolitan Phoenix." In *Twenty-First Century Gateways: Immigrant Incorporation in Suburban America*, edited by A. Singer, S.W. Hardwick, and C.B. Brettell, 87–104. Washington, DC: Brookings Institution Press.

O'Connor, Paul. 2007. "A Shared Future: The Economic Engagement of Greater Chicago and Its Mexican Community." Chicago Council on Global Affairs. http://www.idpl.org/images/publicationsPDFs/DeLeon_ChicagoCouncilFull_2006.pdf.

Olsen, David. 2008. "Minutemen Press On against Mexican ID Cards, Mobile Consulates." *Press-Enterprise* (Riverside, CA), May 9.

Olvera, Adel. 2010. Author interview.Orfield, Myron. 2002. *American Metropolitics: The New Suburban Reality*. Washington, DC: Brookings Institution Press.

Ottaviano, Gianmarco I. P., and Giovanni Peri. 2012. "Rethinking the Effect of Immigration on Wages." *Journal of the European Economic Association* 10(1): 152–97.

Pamuk, Ayse. 2004. "Geography of Immigrant Clusters in Global Cities: A Case Study of San Francisco." *International Journal of Urban and Regional Research* 28(2): 287–307.

Paral, Rob. 2011. *Key Facts on Illinois Immigrants*. Rob Paral and Associates. http://www.robparal.com/downloads/Key_Facts_Illinois_Immigrants.pdf.

——. 2014. "Illinois' Undocumented Immigrant Population: Summary of Recent Research." Illinois Coalition for Immigrant and Refugee Rights. Chicago.

Parks, Bernard. 2010. Author interview.

Passel, Jeffrey S., and D'Vera Cohn. 2011. "Unauthorized Immigrant Population: National and State Trends, 2010." http://www.pewhispanic.org/2011/02/01/unauthorized-immigrant-population-brnational-and-state-trends-2010/.

Pastor, Manuel. 1993. *Latinos and the Los Angeles Uprising: The Economic Context*. Claremont, CA: Tomas Rivera Center.

——. 2001. "Looking for Regionalism in All the Wrong Places: Demography, Geography, and Community in Los Angeles County." *Urban Affairs Review* 36(6): 74–82.

——. 2012. "Spatial Assimilation and Its Discontents: The Changing Geography of Immigrant Integration in Metropolitan America." In *The Oxford Handbook of Urban Economics and Planning*, edited by N. Brooks, K. Donaghy, and G.-J. Knaap, 340–70. New York: Oxford University Press.

——. 2013. "Maywood, Not Mayberry: Latinos and Suburbia in Los Angeles County." In *Social Justice in Diverse Suburbs: History, Politics, and Prospects*, edited by C. Niedt, 129–54. Philadelphia: Temple University Press.

——. 2014. "Keeping It Real: Demographic Change, Economic Conflict, and Inter-Ethnic Organizing for Social Justice in Los Angeles." In *Black and Brown in Los Angeles: Beyond Conflict and Coalition*, edited by L. Pulido and J. Kun, 33–66. Berkeley: University of California Press.

——. 2015. "Migrating toward Justice: How the Immigrant Rights Movement Catalyzed Progressive Politics in Los Angeles." *Dissent*, winter. http://www.dissentmagazine.org/article/how-immigrant-activists-changed-los-angeles.

Pastor, Manuel, Chris Benner, and Martha Matsuoka. 2009. *This Could Be the Start of Something Big: How Social Movements for Regional Equity Are Reshaping Metropolitan America*. Ithaca, NY: Cornell University Press.

Pastor, Manuel, and Vanessa Carter. 2009. "Conflict, Consensus, and Coalition: Economic and Workforce Development Strategies for African Americans and Latinos." *Race and Social Problems* 1(3): 143–56.

Pastor, Manuel, and Enrico A. Marcelli. 2013. *What's at Stake for the State: Undocumented Californians, Immigration Reform, and Our Future Together*. Los Angeles: USC Program for Environmental and Regional Equity. http://csii.usc.edu/undocumentedCA.html.

Pastor, Manuel, and Rhonda Ortiz. 2009a. *Immigrant Integration in Los Angeles: Strategic Directions for Funders*. Los Angeles: USC Center for the Study of Immigrant Integration. http://dornsife.usc.edu/pere/documents/immigrant_integration.pdf.

——. 2009b. *Making Change: How Social Movements Work—and How to Support Them*. Los Angeles: USC Program for Environmental and Regional Equity. http://dornsife.usc.edu/pere/publications/index.cfm.

Pastor, Manuel, Rhonda Ortiz, Vanessa Carter, Justin Scoggins, and Anthony Perez. 2012. *California Immigrant Integration Scorecard*. Los Angeles: USC Center for the Study of Immigrant Integration. http://csii.usc.edu/CAimmSCORECARD.html.

Pastor, Manuel, and Michele Prichard. 2012. *LA Rising: The 1992 Civil Unrest, the Arc of Social Justice Organizing, and the Lessons for Today's Movement Building.* Los Angeles: USC Program for Environmental and Regional Equity. http://dornsife.usc.edu/pere/larising/.

Pastor, Manuel, and Deborah Reed. 2005. *Understanding Equitable Infrastructure Investment for California.* San Francisco: Public Policy Institute of California. http://www.ppic.org/main/publication.asp?i=613.

Pastor, Manuel, Jared Sanchez, Rhonda Ortiz, and Justin Scoggins. 2013. *Nurturing Naturalization: Could Lowering the Fee Help?* Los Angeles: Center for the Study of Immigrant Integration, University of Southern California. http://csii.usc.edu/NurturingNaturalization.html.

Pastor, Manuel, and Justin Scoggins. 2012. *Citizen Gain: The Economic Benefits of Naturalization for Immigrants and the Economy.* Los Angeles: Center for the Study of Immigrant Integration, University of Southern California. http://dornsife.usc.edu/csii/citizen-gain/.

Pastor, Manuel, Justin Scoggins, Vanessa Carter, Jared Sanchez, and the Center for American Progress. 2014. *Citizenship Matters: How Children of Immigrants Will Sway the Future of Politics.* Washington, DC: Center for American Progress and the USC Center for the Study of Immigrant Immigration. http://dornsife.usc.edu/assets/sites/731/docs/Citizenship_Matters_CAP_CSII.pdf.

Payne, Stephanie. 2010. Author interview.

Pedigo, John. 2010. Author interview.

Pellow, David N., and Lisa Sun-Hee Park. 2002. *The Silicon Valley of Dreams: Environmental Injustice, Immigrant Workers, and the High-Tech Global Economy.* New York: NYU Press.

Perez, Fernando, and Raj Jayadev. 2011. "Santa Clara County Ends Collaboration with ICE, Creates Local Protections against Controversial 'Secure Communities' Program." *Silicon Valley De-Bug,* October 18. http://www.siliconvalleydebug.org/articles/2011/10/18/santa-clara-county-votes-end-collaboration-IC.

Perez, William, Roberta Espinoza, Heidi Coronado, and Richard Cortes. 2010. "Civic Engagement Patterns of Undocumented Mexican Students." *Journal of Hispanic Higher Education* 9(3): 245–65.

Peri, Giovanni. 2006. "Rethinking the Effects of Immigration on Wages: New Data and Analysis from 1990–2004." *Immigration Policy Center* 5(8). http://www.immigrationpolicy.org/special-reports/rethinking-effects-immigration-wages-new-data-and-analysis-1990-2004.

Petsod, Daranee, Ted Wang, and Craig McGarvey. 2006. *Investing in Our Communities: Strategies for Immigrant Integration (a Toolkit for Grantmakers).* Sebastopol, CA: Grantmakers Concerned with Immigrant and Refugee Rights. http://www.gcir.org/publications/toolkit.

Pew Research Center. 2014. "Neither Party Gets Good Marks from Its Base for Handling Illegal Immigration." Pew Research Center for the People and the Press. http://www.people-press.org/2014/09/23/neither-party-gets-good-marks-from-its-base-for-handling-illegal-immigration/.

Phoenix Police Department. 2008. Operations Order 1.4.

Pinderhughes, Dianne M. 1997. "An Examination of Chicago Politics for Evidence of Political Incorporation and Representation." In *Racial Politics in American Cities,* edited by R. P. Browning, D. R. Marshall, and D. H. Tabb, 117–36. New York: Longman.

Pitti, Steven. 2003. *The Devil in Silicon Valley: Northern California, Race, and Mexican Americans.* Princeton, NJ: Princeton University Press.

Plascencia, Luis F. B. 2013. "Attrition through Enforcement and the Elimination of a 'Dangerous Class.'" In *Latino Politics and Arizona's Immigration Law SB 1070*, edited by L. Magaña and E. Lee, 93–128. New York: Springer.

Portes, Alejandro, and Rubén G. Rumbaut. 2001. *Legacies: The Story of the Immigrant Second Generation*. Berkeley: University of California Press.

Postelle, Brian. 2009. "New Latino Paper Comes to WNC." *Mountain Xpress* (Asheville, NC), December 9. http://mountainx.com/news/120909buzz3/.

Puente, Sylvia. 2010. Author interview.

Putnam, Robert. 2007. "E Pluribus Unum: Diversity and Community in the Twenty-First Century—the 2006 Johan Skytte Prize Lecture." *Scandinavian Political Studies* 30(2): 137–74.

Quinn, Pat (governor of Illinois). 2011. Letter to Marc Rupp, Acting Assistant Director of Secure Communities, Immigration and Customs Enforcement, Department of Homeland Security, May 4. Chicago: Office of the Governor. http://personal.crocodoc.com/JedzqSN#redirect.

Qureshi, Naheed. 2010. Author interview.

Ramakrishnan, Karthick. 2004. *The Ties That Bind: Changing Demographics and Civic Engagement in California*. San Francisco: Public Policy Institute of California.

——. 2005. *Democracy in Immigrant America: Changing Demographics and Political Participation*. Stanford, CA: Stanford University Press.

——. 2007. *Survey of Political and Civic Engagement in the Inland Empire*. www.politicalscience.ucr.edu.

Ramakrishnan, Karthick, and Celia Viramontes. 2006. *Civic Inequalities: Immigrant Volunteerism and Community Organizations in California*. San Francisco: Public Policy Institute of California.

Ramakrishnan, Karthick, and Tom K. Wong. 2010. "Partisanship, Not Spanish: Explaining Local Ordinances Affecting Undocumented Immigrants." In *Taking Local Control: Immigration Policy Activism in U.S. Cities and States*, edited by M. Varsanyi, 73–93. Sanford, CA: Stanford University Press.

Ready, Timothy, and Allert Brown-Gort. 2005. *The State of Latino Chicago: This Is Home Now*. Notre Dame, IN: University of Notre Dame, Institute for Latino Studies.

Reason Foundation. 2009. *Belmont Pilot Schools Network, Los Angeles Unified School District: Weighted School Formula Yearbook 2009*. Los Angeles.

Reimers, David. 2005. *Other Immigrants: The Global Origins of the American People*. New York: NYU Press.

Rice, Connie. 2012. *Power Concedes Nothing: One Woman's Quest for Social Justice in America, from the Courtroom to the Kill Zones*. New York: Scribner.

Roberts, Laurie. 2015. "Contempt Hearing Unmasks Joe Arpaio." *Arizona Republic*, April 24. http://www.azcentral.com/story/laurieroberts/2015/04/24/joe-arpaio-contempt-hearing/26316123/.

Rocco, Raymond. 1999. "The Formation of Latino Citizenship in Southeast Los Angeles." *Citizenship Studies* 3(2): 253–66.

Rodríguez, Cristina. 2014. "Law and Borders." *Democracy Journal* (33): 52–65.

Romero, Rigoberto. 2010. Author interview.

Rosales, F. Arturo, and Christine Marin. 2009. "Histories of Mexican-Origin Populations in Arizona." In *State of Latino Arizona*, 15–21. Tempe: Arizona Latino Research Enterprise and Arizona State University.

Rosenberg, Mike. 2015. "San Jose Moves Forward on First Immigration Office." *San Jose Mercury News*, January 28. http://www.mercurynews.com/immigration/ci_27407294/san-jose-moves-forward-first-immigration-office.

Rubin, Joel. 2013. "LAPD Rescinds Vehicle Impound Policy." *Los Angeles Times*, September 28. http://articles.latimes.com/2013/sep/28/local/la-me-0929-lapd-impound-20130929.

Rubin, Joel, and Ari Bloomekatz. 2011. "LAPD Limits Impounding of Unlicensed Drivers' Cars." *Los Angeles Times*, March 12. http://articles.latimes.com/2011/mar/12/local/la-me-lapd-tow-20110312.

Ruggles, Steven J., et al. 2011. *Integrated Public Use Microdata Series: Version 5.0 [Machine-Readable Database]*. Minneapolis: University of Minnesota.

Ruiz, Albor. 2014. "A New Immigrants' Rights Campaign Calls on New York to End All Collaboration with Immigration and Customs Enforcement." *New York Daily News*, May 4. http://www.nydailynews.com/new-york/advocates-city-freeze-ice-article-1.1776442.

Saenz, Thomas. 2010. Author interview.

Salas, Angelica. 2010. Author interview.

Salonga, Robert. 2013. "San Jose: Breakthrough 'Curb Sitting' Policy to Roll Out following Delay." *San Jose Mercury News*, July 3. http://www.mercurynews.com/ci_23606015/san-jose-breakthrough-curb-sitting-policy-roll-out.

Sanchez, Evelyn. 2010. Author interview.

Sanchez, George J. 1993. *Becoming Mexican American: Ethnicity, Culture, and Identity in Chicano Los Angeles, 1900–1945*. New York: Oxford University Press.

Sanders, Todd. 2010. Author interview.

Santa Clara County Citizenship and Immigrant Services Program. 2000. *Bridging Borders in Silicon Valley: Summit on Immigrant Needs and Contributions*. San José, CA: Santa Clara County Office of Human Relations. http://www.immigrantinfo.org/borders/coverpage.pdf.

Santa Clara County Office of Education and the City of San Jose. 2011. *San Jose 2020 Annual Report, 2010–2011*. http://www.sccoe.org/sj2020/.

Santos, Fernando. 2013. "Judge Finds Violations of Rights by Sheriff." *New York Times*, May 24. http://www.nytimes.com/2013/05/25/us/federal-judge-finds-violations-of-rights-by-sheriff-joe-arpaio.html?_r=0.

Saxenian, AnnaLee. 1996. "Inside-Out: Regional Networks and Industrial Adaptation in Silicon Valley and Route 128." *Cityscape: A Journal of Policy and Development and Research* 2(2).

——. 1999. *Silicon Valley's New Immigrant Entrepreneurs*. San Francisco: Public Policy Institute of California.

——. 2002. "Silicon Valley's New Immigrant High Growth Entrepreneurs." *Economic Development Quarterly* 16(20).

Scheer, Brenda. 2012. *The Utah Model: Lessons for Regional Planning*. Las Vegas: Brookings Mountain West, University of Nevada, Las Vegas. http://www.unlv.edu/sites/default/files/TheUtahModel_0.pdf.

Shore, Elena. 2011. "SJ Expands Definition of Racial Profiling." *Ethnoblog*, March 3. http://ethnoblog.newamericamedia.org/2011/03/sj-expands-definition-of-racial-profiling.php.

Sides, Josh. 2006. *L.A. City Limits: African American Los Angeles from the Great Depression to the Present*. Berkeley: University of California Press.

Simpson, Dick. 2001. *Rogues, Rebels, and Rubber Stamps: The Politics of the Chicago City Council, 1863 to the Present*. Boulder, CO: Westview Press.

Simpson, Dick, and Tom Kelly. 2011. "The New Chicago School of Urbanism and the New Daley Machine." In *The City, Revisited: Urban Theory from Chicago, Los Angeles, and New York*, edited by Dennis R. Judd and Dick Simpson, 205–19. Minneapolis: University of Minnesota Press.

Singer, Audrey. 2004. *The Rise of New Immigrant Gateways*. Washington, DC: Brookings Institution Center on Urban and Metropolitan Policy.

———. 2008. "Twenty-First-Century Gateways: An Introduction." In *Twenty-First Century Gateways: Immigrant Incorporation in Suburban America*, edited by A. Singer, S. W. Hardwick, and C. B. Brettell, 3–20. Washington DC: Brookings Institution Press.

———. 2010. "Immigration." In *State of Metropolitan America: On the Front Lines of Demographic Transformation*, edited by the Metropolitan Policy Program at Brookings. Washington, DC: Brookings Institution. http://www.brookings.edu/~/media/research/files/reports/2010/5/09%20metro%20america/metro_america_report1.pdf.

Singer, Audrey, and Jill H. Wilson. 2010. *The Impact of the Great Recession on Metropolitan Immigration Trends*. Washington, DC: Brookings Institution.

Skolnick, Jerome H., and David H. Bayley. 1988. *The New Blue Line: Police Innovation in Six American Cities*. New York: Simon & Schuster.

Smith, Heather Anne, and Owen J. Furuseth. 2004. "Housing, Hispanics, and Transitioning Geographies in Charlotte, North Carolina." *Southeastern Geographer* 44(2): 216–35.

———. 2008. "The 'Nuevo South': Latino Place Making and Community Building in the Middle-Ring Suburbs of Charlotte." In *Twenty-First Century Gateways: Immigrant Incorporation in Suburban America*, edited by A. Singer, S. W. Hardwick, and C. Brettell, 281–307. Washington, DC: Brookings Institution Press.

Solis, Danny. 2012. Author interview.

Sonenshein, Raphael J., and Susan H. Pinkus. 2005. "Latino Incorporation Reaches the Urban Summit: How Antonio Villaraigosa Won the 2005 Los Angeles Mayor's Race." *PS: Political Science & Politics* 38(04). http://www.journals.cambridge.org/abstract_S1049096505050389.

Soto, Cynthia. 2010. Author interview.

Soto, Juan. 2010. Author interview.

Southern Poverty Law Center. 2009. *Climate of Fear: Latino Immigrants in Suffolk County, N.Y.* Montgomery, AL: Southern Poverty Law Center. http://www.splcenter.org/get-informed/publications/climate-of-fear-latino-immigrants-in-suffolk-county-ny.

Specht, Jim. 2010. Author interview.

Stepick, Alex, Carol Dutton Stepick, and Yves Labissiere. 2008. "South Florida's Immigrant Youth and Civic Engagement: Major Engagement: Minor Differences." *Applied Developmental Science* 12(2): 57–65.

Stern, Ray. 2009. "Deputies Raid Chicanos Por La Causa Building, Take Boxes of Papers Out; Protest Sought by Activists." *Phoenix New Times*, December 10. http://blogs.phoenixnewtimes.com/valleyfever/2009/12/deputies_raid_chicanos_por_la.php.

———. 2014. "Arizona's 2005 Human-Smuggling Law Struck Down in Federal Court: Read Ruling Here." *Phoenix New Times*, November 8. http://blogs.phoenixnewtimes.com/valleyfever/2014/11/arizonas_2005_human-smuggling_law_struck_down_in_federal_court_read_ruling.php.

Sterngold, James. 2006. "Immigration Rallies Force LA Mayor into Political Tight Spot." *San Francisco Chronicle*, May 14. http://www.sfgate.com/politics/article/LOS-ANGELES-Immigration-rallies-force-L-A-2497211.php.

Stone, Jeff. 2010. Author interview.

Suffolk County (NY). 2011. "Suffolk County Comprehensive Plan 2035." http://www.suffolkcountyny.gov/Departments/Planning/SpecialProjects/ComprehensivePlan/DownloadPlan.aspx.

Tam Cho, Wendy K. 1999. "Naturalization, Socialization, Participation: Immigrants and (Non-) Voting." *Journal of Politics* 61(04): 1140–55.

Tate, Arthur. 2010. Author interview.

Taxin, Amy. 2013. "Companies Help Immigrants Obtain U.S. Citizenship." Associated Press, August 3. http://news.yahoo.com/companies-help-immigrants-obtain-us-citizenship-133559073.html.

Telles, Edward E., and Vilma Ortiz. 2008. *Generations of Exclusion: Mexican Americans, Assimilation, and Race.* New York: Russell Sage Foundation.

Terdiman, Daniel. 2007. "How NASA Helped Invest Silicon Valley." *CNET News.* http://news.cnet.com/How-NASA-helped-invent-Silicon-Valley/2009-11397_3-6211034.html#ixzz1RRuFEvoe.

Terriquez, Veronica. 2011. "Schools for Democracy: Labor Union Participation and Latino Immigrant Parents' School-Based Civic Engagement." *American Sociological Review* 76:581–601.

Terriquez, Veronica, and Caitlin Patler. 2012. *Aspiring Americans: Undocumented Youth Leaders in California.* Los Angeles: USC Center for the Study of Immigrant Integration. http://csii.usc.edu/aspiring_americans.html.

Terriquez, Veronica, John Rogers, Gary Blasi, Janna Shadduck Hernandez, and Lauren D. Appelbaum. 2009. *Unions and Education Justice: The Case of SEIU Local 1877 Janitors and the "Parent University"; Los Angeles, CA: UCLA Institute for Research on Labor and Employment.* Los Angeles: UCLA Institute for Research and Labor Employment.

Thomas, Charles. 2012. "Emanuel Promotes 'Welcome City' Immigration Policy." *ABC 7 Eyewitness News.* http://abc7chicago.com/archive/8731605/.

Thoresen, Craig. 2010. Author interview.

Timpson, Corey, and Tom Dolan. 2010. Author interview.

Torres, Maria de Los Angeles, and Teresa Cordova. 2015. "The Chicago Mayoral Race: Why Jesus 'Chuy' Garcia Has a Shot at Becoming Mayor." http://www.thepraxisproject.org/chicago-mayoral-race-why-jesus-chuy-garcia-has-shot-becoming-mayor.

Trenholm, Christopher, and Sean Orzol. 2004. "The Impact of the Children's Health Initiative (CHI) of Santa Clara County on Medi-Cal and Healthy Family Enrollment." Mathematic Policy Research Inc.

———. 2007. "The Effect of New Insurance Coverage on the Health Status of Low-Income Children in Santa Clara County." *Health Services Research* 42(2): 867–89.

Trounstine, Jessica. 2008. *Political Monopolies in American Cities: The Rise and Fall of Bosses and Reformers.* Chicago: University of Chicago Press.

Tsering, Lhakpa. 2010. Author interview.

Twigg, Liz, Joanna Taylor, and John Mohan. 2010. "Diversity or Disadvantage? Putnam, Goodheart, Ethnic Heterogeneity, and Collective Efficacy." *Environment and Planning A* 42:1421–38.

UNC Charlotte Urban Institute. 2006. *Mecklenburg County Latino Community Needs Assessment.* http://ui.uncc.edu/sites/default/files/pdf/2006LatinoNeeds_Report_Final7-11-06.pdf.

USA Citizenship Services, Naturalization Eligibility and Applications. n.d. "U.S. Citizenship Application." http://www.usacitizenship.info/application.html.

U.S. Census Bureau, Educational Finance Branch. 2015. *Public Education Finances: 2013.* Washington, DC: Government Printing Office. http://www2.census.gov/govs/school/13f33pub.pdf.

U.S. Departments of State, Homeland Security, and Health and Human Services. n.d. *Proposed Refugee Admissions for Fiscal Year 2012: Report to the Congress.* Washington, DC: Committees on the Judiciary, United States Senate and the United States House of Representatives. http://www.state.gov/documents/organization/181378.pdf.

Valdez, Elsa. 2010. Author interview.

Vallejo, Jody Agius. 2013. "Leveling the Playing Field: Patterns of Ethnic Philanthropy among Los Angeles' Middle and Upper-Class Latino Entrepreneurs." *Ethnic and Racial Studies* 38(1): 125–140.

Valley News (Fallbrook, CA). 2011. "Early Story: Temecula City Council Votes 4–0 to Uphold Decision Approving Mosque." January 26. http://myvalleynews.com/local/early-story-temecula-city-council-votes-4-0-to-uphold-decision-approving-mosque/.

Van Hook, Jennifer, James D. Bachmeier, Donna L. Coffman, and Ofer Harel. 2015. "Can We Spin Straw into Gold? An Evaluation of Immigrant Legal Status Imputation Approaches." *Demography* 52(1): 329–54.

Varsanyi, Monica, ed. 2010. *Taking Local Control: Immigration Policy Activism in U.S. Cities and States*. Stanford, CA: Stanford University Press.

Varsanyi, Monica, Paul Lewis, Doris Provine, and Scott Decker. 2012. "A Multilayered Jurisdictional Patchwork: Immigration Federalism in the United States." *Law & Society* 34(2): 138–58.

Verba, Sidney, Kay Lehman Schlozman, and Henry E. Brady. 1995. *Voice and Equality: Civic Voluntarism in American Politics*. Cambridge, MA: Harvard University Press.

Vicino, Thomas J. 2013. *Suburban Crossroads: The Fight for Local Control of Immigration Policy*. Lanham, MD: Lexington Books.

Vital, Rosario. 2010. *Coming Out and Making History: Latino Immigrant Civic Participation in San Jose*. Washington, DC: Woodrow Wilson International Center for Scholars. http://www.wilsoncenter.org/news/docs/MEX_090307_SanJose.rpt_END_0507L.pdf.

Vives, Ruben, Jeff Gottlieb, and Hector Becerra. 2010. "Maywood to Hire Others to Run the City." *Los Angeles Times*, June 23. http://articles.latimes.com/2010/jun/23/local/la-me-0623-maywood-20100623.

Vuong, Quyen. 2010. Author interview.

Waldinger, Roger. 1999. *Still the Promised City? African-Americans and New Immigrants in Postindustrial New York*. Cambridge, MA: Harvard University Press.

Walton, Gloria. 2010. Author interview.

Ward, Paul. 1999. *Community-Based Safety Net Services in Santa Clara County*. Santa Clara, CA: Santa Clara County Social Service Agency. http://cssr.berkeley.edu/CaseStudiesDB/default.aspx?formID=basscCases&group=BASSC&titleKey=&year=&agency=SANTA+CLARA&subject=&B1=Browse.

Watterson, Yvonne. 2010. Author interview.

Webby, Sean. 2008. "Drunkenness Arrests in San Jose Outpace Other California Cities." *San Jose Mercury News*, October 18. http://www.mercurynews.com/san-Jos%C3%A9-police/ci_10755739?source=pkg.

——. 2010. "San Jose to Stop 30-Day Car Impounds for Unlicensed Drivers." *San Jose Mercury News*, December 8. http://www.mercurynews.com/ci_16810554.

Weir, Margaret, Nancy Pindus, Howard Wial, and Harold Wolman. 2012. *Urban and Regional Policy and Its Effects: Building Resilient Regions*. Washington, DC: Brookings Institution Press.

Whitcomb, Dan. 2010. "Mayor, Officials Arrested in California Pay Scandal." Reuters. http://www.reuters.com/article/2010/09/22/us-california-payscandal-arrests-idUSTRE68K40N20100922.

White, Brian. 2010. Author interview.

White House Task Force on New Immigrants. 2015. *Strengthening Communities by Welcoming All Residents: A Federal Strategic Action Plan on Immigrant and Refugee Integration*. Washington, DC: White House.

Wilson, Jill H., and Nicole Prchal Svajlenka. 2014. "Immigrants Continue to Disperse, with Fastest Growth in the Suburbs." *Brookings*, October 29. http://www.brookings.edu/research/papers/2014/10/29-immigrants-disperse-suburbs-wilson-svajlenka.

Winders, Jamie. 2013. *Nashville in the New Millennium: Immigrant Settlement, Urban Transformation, and Social Belonging*. New York: Russell Sage Foundation.

Wingett, Yvonne. 2006. "Ariz. Latinos Lack Impact on Legislature." *Arizona Republic*, August 28.

Winkelman, Lee, and Jeff Malachowsky. 2009. *Integrated Voter Engagement: A Proven Model to Increase Civic Engagement*. New York: Funders' Committee for Civic Participation. http://funderscommittee.org/files/FCCP_Integrative_Voter_Engagement_Case_Studies_2009_FINAL_0.pdf.

Winton, Richard, and Duke Helfand. 2007. "LAPD Takes Blame for Park Melee." *Los Angeles Times*, October 10. http://articles.latimes.com/2007/oct/10/local/me-melee10.

Wong, Esther. 2010. Author interview.

Wong, Janelle. 2006. *Democracy's Promise: Immigrants and American Civic Institutions*. Ann Arbor: University of Michigan Press. http://site.ebrary.com/lib/uscisd/docDetail.action.

Wood, Robert C. 1961. *1400 Governments: The Political Economy of the New York Metropolitan Region*. Cambridge, MA: Harvard University Press.

Wright, Richard, Mark Ellis, Steven R. Holloway, and Sandy Wong. 2014. "Patterns of Racial Diversity and Segregation in the United States: 1990–2010." *Professional Geographer* 66(2): 173–82.

Yaro, Robert, and Tony Hiss. 1996. *A Region at Risk: The Third Regional Plan for the New York–New Jersey–Connecticut Metropolitan Area*. Washington, DC: Island Press.

Yimer, Erku. 2010. Author interview.

Zhou, Min. 1999. "Segmented Assimilation: Issues, Controversies, and Recent Research on the New Second Generation." In *The Handbook of International Migration: The American Experience*, edited by C. Hirschman, P. Kasinitz, and J. DeWind, 196–211. New York: Russell Sage Foundation.

Zhou, Min, Yen-Fen Tseng, and Rebecca Y. Yim. 2008. "Rethinking Residential Assimilation: The Case of a Chinese Ethnoburb in the San Gabriel Valley, California." *Amerasia Journal* 34(3): 53–83.

Zierer, Clifford M. 1934. "The Citrus Fruit Industry of the Los Angeles Basin." *Economic Geography* 10(1): 53–73.

Zolberg, Aristide R. 2008. *How Many Exceptionalisms? Explorations in Comparative Macroanalysis*. Philadelphia: Temple University Press.

———. 2009. *A Nation by Design: Immigration Policy in the Fashioning of America*. Cambridge, MA: Harvard University Press.

Zúñiga, Víctor, and Rubén Hernández-León. 2006. *New Destinations: Mexican Immigration in the United States*. New York: Russell Sage Foundation.

Contributors

John Mollenkopf is Distinguished Professor of Political Science and Sociology and Director of the Center for Urban Research at the Graduate Center of the City University of New York. He has authored or edited eighteen books on the role of immigration, race, and ethnicity in urban America, including *Bringing Outsiders In: Transatlantic Perspectives on Immigrant Political Incorporation* (edited with Jennifer Hochschild, Cornell 2009). His current research focuses on the impact of immigration on racial and ethnic empowerment in New York and Los Angeles and the comparative politics of immigrant political incorporation in new and old metropolitan areas. He currently serves on the steering committee of the 8th Annual National Immigrant Integration Conference.

Manuel Pastor is Professor of Sociology and American Studies and Ethnicity at the University of Southern California where he holds the Turpanjian Chair in Civil Society and Social Change, serves as Director of the Program for Environmental and Regional Equity, and serves as co-Director of the Center for the Study of Immigrant Integration. His most recent book is *Equity, Growth, and Community: What the Nation Can Learn from America's Metro Areas* (University of California 2015) which was coauthored with Chris Benner. Previous volumes include *Just Growth: Inclusion and Prosperity in America's Metropolitan Regions* (Routledge 2012), also with Chris Benner, and *Uncommon Common Ground: Race and America's Future* (Norton 2010, coauthored with Angela Glover Blackwell and Stewart Kwoh).

Els de Graauw is Assistant Professor of Political Science at Baruch College, City University of New York, and was the Immigration Research Associate at the Institute for the Social Sciences at Cornell University (2011–2012). She specializes in American politics, immigration, civic and political participation, and (sub)urban politics and public policy. Her forthcoming book is *Making Immigrant Rights Real: Nonprofits and the Politics of Integration in San Francisco* (Cornell 2016). She cofounded and was the first co-president of the Section on Migration and Citizenship of the American Political Science Association.

Juan De Lara is Assistant Professor of American Studies and Ethnicity at the University of Southern California. He is working on a book project about the geographies of global commodity distribution, emerging scales of metropolitan and regional growth, the role that labor and community organizations play in the social production of space, with a specific focus on the politics of race and representation in California's rapidly expanding inland counties. He is coauthor of *All Together Now: African Americans, Immigrants, and the Future of California* (Center for the Study of Immigrant Integration 2011).

Jaime Dominguez is a Lecturer in the Department of Political Science at Northwestern University. He is one of the principal architects of the Chicago Democracy Project, a thirty-year (1975–2005) online political database that provides citizens, community groups, and religious organizations with information on campaign finance, electoral outcomes, government contracts, minority appointments, and levels of public employment for the City of Chicago. Dominguez conducts research on how Latino heterogeneity and population growth are redefining traditional political and race relations between blacks and whites. He is author of "Illinois Latinos and the 2004 Elections: The Waiting Game Continues," in de la Garza and DeSipio's *Latinos and the 2004 Elections* (Notre Dame 2007).

Diana Gordon is Professor *Emerita* of Political Science and Criminal Justice at the City University of New York. She is the author of many books on criminal justice policy in the United States and South Africa, including *Transformation and Trouble: Crime, Justice and Participation in Democratic South Africa* (University of Michigan 2006). She recently completed an ethnography of immigrants on the East End of Long Island, *Village of Immigrants: Latinos in an Emerging America* (Rutgers 2015).

Michael Jones-Correa is Professor of Government at Cornell University. He is the coauthor of *Latino Lives in America: Making It Home* (Temple 2010) and *Between Two Nations: The Political Predicament of Latinos in New York City* (Cornell 1998) and the editor of *Governing American Cities: Interethnic Coalitions, Competition, and Conflict* (Russell Sage 2001). He is currently continuing the analysis of the 2006 Latino National Survey, a national state-stratified survey of Latinos in the United States for which he was a principal investigator, and is the team leader for the 2010–2013 theme project, "Immigration: Settlement, Immigration and Membership," at the Institute for the Social Sciences at Cornell.

Paul Lewis is Associate Professor in the School of Politics and Global Studies at Arizona State University. His research has examined the determinants and effects of local public policies, with a particular focus on urban development, community change, and local policies toward immigrants. Lewis is the author of *Shaping Suburbia: How Political Institutions Organize Urban Development* (Pittsburgh 1996) and coauthor of *Custodians of Place: Governing the Growth and Development of Cities* (Georgetown 2009), and his forthcoming coauthored book is *Policing Immigrants: Local Law Enforcement on the Front Lines* (Chicago 2016). Lewis's research has received funding support from the National Science Foundation and the MacArthur Foundation, and he has begun a new project that considers the implications of recent findings from moral psychology and the psychology of intuitions and heuristics for theories of public policymaking.

Doris Marie Provine is Professor *Emerita* of the School of Justice and Social Inquiry at Arizona State University. She came to Arizona State in 2001 to direct the School of Justice Studies and served in that role for six years. She has served as Director of the Law and Social Sciences Program at the National Science Foundation, and earlier as a Judicial Fellow assigned to the Federal Judicial Center. Her areas of interest reflect her background in law (JD Cornell) and political science (Ph.D. Cornell). Some of her research has focused on courts and policies related to them, most recently the role racism has played in the war on drugs. She is the author of *Unequal under Law: Race and the War on Drugs* (Chicago 2007). Her current work revolves around policies concerning unauthorized immigration.

Rachel Rosner is an independent consultant based in Florida. Previously a research associate and project manager at the Center for Justice, Tolerance, and Community at University of California, Santa Cruz, she works regularly with USC's Center for the Study of Immigrant Integration and the Program for Environmental and Regional Equity on analyses of social movement building. She has coauthored a number of academic articles in journals such as *Youth and Society*, *Latino Studies*, and *Economic Development Quarterly*.

Jennifer Tran currently works for the Our Children, Our Families Council of the City of San Francisco. She holds an MA in Urban Planning and a BA in Sociology from the University of California Los Angeles and was most recently a senior associate at PolicyLink in Oakland, where she led work on the National Equity Atlas. Previously she worked as a data analyst at the Center for the Study of Immigrant Integration at the University of Southern California, where she coauthored a report on the economic benefits for California of a path to citizenship for undocumented residents.

Index

Page numbers in italics refer to figures and tables.